PUBLIC ADMINISTRATION EVOLVING

Public Administration Evolving: From Foundations to the Future demonstrates how the theory and practice of public administration has evolved since the early decades of the twentieth century. Each chapter approaches the field from a unique perspective and describes the seminal events that have been influential in shaping its evolution.

This book presents major trends in theory and practice in the field, provides an overview of its intellectual development, and demonstrates how it has professionalized. The range from modernism to metamodernism is reflected from the perspective of accomplished scholars in the field, each of whom captures the history, environment, and development of a particular dimension of public administration. Taken together, the chapters leave us with an understanding of where we are today and a grounding for forecasting the future.

Mary E. Guy is past President of the American Society for Public Administration (ASPA) and a fellow of the National Academy of Public Administration (NAPA). Her research focuses on the human processes involved in public service delivery as well as public administration in general. She has earned a number of awards for her work, including five Best Book Awards for *Emotional Labor: Putting the Service in Public Service* and *Emotional Labor and Crisis Response: Working on the Razor's Edge* (co-authored with Sharon Mastracci and Meredith Newman).

Marilyn M. Rubin is Professor of Public Administration and Economics at John Jay College of the City of New York, USA and is Director of the College's MPA program. She has authored several publications on fiscal policy and budget-related issues and has served as a consultant to municipal, state, federal, and international entities. She is a fellow in NAPA and the winner of a Distinguished Research Award from ASPA.

PUBLIC ADMINISTRATION EVOLVING

From Foundations to the Future

Edited by Mary E. Guy and Marilyn M. Rubin

Routledge
Taylor & Francis Group

NEW YORK AND LONDON

First published 2015
by Routledge
711 Third Avenue, New York, NY 10017

and by Routledge
2 Park Square, Milton Park, Abingdon, Oxon OX14 4RN

Routledge is an imprint of the Taylor & Francis Group, an Informa business

Library of Congress Cataloging-in-Publication Data
A catalog record for this book has been requested

ISBN 978-1-138-92261-7

Typeset in Bembo
by Swales & Willis, Exeter, Devon, UK

SFI Certified Sourcing
www.sfiprogram.org
SFI-00453

Printed and bound in the United States of America
by Edwards Brothers Malloy

CONTENTS

1   The Public Context   1
David H. Rosenbloom

Public administration differs substantially from private-sector work. It must balance executive, legislative, and judicial demands; embrace federalism; honor constitutional obligations; and advance policy arenas.

2   From Intergovernmental to Intersectoral   18
Donald F. Kettl

Since the American Society for Public Administration's founding, there has been greater interweaving of the public, private, and nonprofit sectors. This has led to a flatter public bureaucracy with greater challenges for ensuring effective administration and strong accountability.

3   From Trust to Doubt: The Federal Government's Tough Challenges   38
Chester A. Newland

At the federal level, the practice of public administration through the eras has been punctuated by wars, partisan political swings, changing public opinion, and growing budgetary constraints.

ILLUSTRATIONS

Figures

Tables

FOREWORD

Richard Stillman

> The fact of the matter is that most of the problems that we now face . . . are administrative problems.
>
> *(President John F. Kennedy)*

> As I've gotten older, I've come to realize that the emphasis on public policy is mistaken, and what we should be focusing on is teaching basic public administration.
>
> *(Francis Fukuyama)*

> Sustained inability to provide welfare, prosperity, equity, justice, domestic order, or external security could over time undermine the legitimacy of even democratic governments.
>
> *(Samuel P. Huntington)*

Welcome to a ringside seat surveying the state of the art of the greatest academic study on earth, twenty-first century Public Administration![1] Arguably none today is more important to constitutional democracy's survival, even humanity's and the planet's future!

Why so? As David Rosenbloom's opening chapter reminds us, Woodrow Wilson's landmark 1887 article, "The Study of Administration," dramatically announced that the age of constitution writing is over. From now on, the American challenge would be to learn how "to run a constitution" by developing a new field, the study and practice of public administration. More than a century later, Wilson's words appear even more urgent and prescient: how can we make constitutional democracy work in our ever vaster, more populous, technologically complex, globally interconnected society? As Don Kettl suggests in his chapter, if effective public administration had worked successfully during many of the tragic, headline-grabbing events since the dawn of the twenty-first century, would any have occurred?

Think for a moment: Would 9/11 have happened if there had been administrative communications between the CIA and FBI, or even between the FBI's field and headquarters offices in regard to their information about impending terrorist threats?

Did prisoners at Abu Ghraib suffer needless torture and cruelty because they were in the hands of ill-trained, part-time, military police reservists? If full-time, experienced professionals in management and law enforcement had been in charge of the prison, could such flagrant, well-publicized human rights abuses have been preventable?

During Hurricane Katrina would many more lives have been saved if the emergency evacuation of New Orleans had been professionally planned, coordinated, and directed?

Would the Great Recession of 2008–2009 have devastated the American economy if the inchoate, fragmented, politicized, jerry-built regulatory system had been better coordinated, controlled, and strictly supervised?

Was the faulty roll-out of the Affordable Care Act avoidable if the fifty-two contractors charged with creating its websites had been professionally managed and their technical activities integrated?

Did the nationally embarrassing and seriously damaging intelligence leaks from the National Security Agency, thanks to Edward Snowden, result from lax oversight of his security clearance process performed by a private contractor, instead of having been reviewed via an "in-house" professional public agency directly accountable to intelligence experts?

We will never know for certain the answers to these "what if" questions about such massive government breakdowns since 9/11, but my hunch is that all were avoidable through improved public administration. In a nutshell, that is why this book is a "must read" for new students planning to enter the field, old hands who long served in the trenches of its practice, as well as citizens everywhere who want better government.

So from the reader's ringside seat, what sorts of salient features stand out about contemporary Public Administration as a field of study and research when perusing this book?

First, scan its sheer size, scope, and complexity. Administrative sciences seem to encompass everything and address anything. Not long ago the accepted demarcation between "public" and "private" boundaries was fairly clear-cut, but again as Kettl underscores, Public Administration is no longer confined to the "intergovernmental" but is now "intersectoral," encompassing public, private, and nonprofit. Who would have imagined just a few years ago that the government would run the biggest automaker and insurance company, General Motors and AIG, due to their bankruptcy or near collapse? "Too big to fail" suddenly became the rationalization for nationalization. Even the most ardent free-enterprisers asked for government bailouts during the dark days of the Great Recession, fearful that the cascading economy would quickly suck the nation into a second Great Depression. Few would admit to the obvious implications: an instantaneous transformation from rock-ribbed, fiercely independent businessmen into accursed "welfare queens." Or is the more accurate terminology, "welfare kings?" As Barry Bozeman astutely observed long ago: "All organizations are public." In response, Public Administration research and teaching vastly expanded its analytical coverage and sophistication. America, indeed the world, is witnessing a golden age of Public Administration scholarship. Never before are so many talented academics producing so many first-class publications, with advanced methodologies, on such a wide variety of topics! This rapid expansion and astonishing richness of serious thought, as evident throughout the following pages, is certainly a product of the increased demand for better government, the growth of the Internet, greater access to data, information, travel, as well as many more university programs and scholarly journals dedicated to advancing the field. Undoubtedly the plethora of first-class research also stems from a synergy of intense interactions among so many gifted people responding to the pressing public issues of our times. Many of these intellectual leaders of the field are represented in this book.

Second, glimpse the new categories framed as seminal challenges within the fluid rapidity of change. Earlier major surveys of the field, such as Leonard White's *Trends in Public Administration* (1933) or Naomi Lynn and Aaron Wildavsky's *Public Administration: The State of the Discipline* (1990), organized chapter headings around the bread-and-butter functional categories of the field, such as budgeting and personnel. Instead, these authors view the field as being in flux, eschewing stable functional categories while posing new impressive challenges: "From Local to Global," "From Paper to Cloud," and so on. Indeed much of the language here would seem peculiar, if not incomprehensible to earlier generations—what's a "cloud" floating around inside public administration? A few titles would be recognizable to older administrative scholars, such as "From Administration to Management." Though even here, they would puzzle at the odd claim that "management" could become an organizing concept for the entire field of Public Administration and not the reverse. A prior generation would undoubtedly ask: Doesn't the Latin root of "administration" mean "to serve" and, hence, isn't it the more appropriate umbrella title for defining the field? "Management" denotes activities as "direction by the single hand," or what is commonly practiced in business to achieve self-serving ends. Not only are old categories missing and the field itself depicted in rapid transition, but each chapter invites readers to see its topic as problematic as well as problem-focused, possibly raising more questions than offering recommended answers in the form of principles, proverbs, or practical rules of thumb for administrators in the firing-line. The contents imply a heuristic, open-ended process or variety of processes, without defined boundaries, fixed substance, or apparent connectedness to each other, as if the field is a shifting form akin to classic postmodernism. Nonetheless, every chapter encourages readers to understand the critical challenges facing public administration in the future.

Third, note the accelerating drive to specialize. Perhaps the origins of the field can be seen as itself the result of division of labor between politics and administration, but what strikes even the casual observer of these chapters is the specialization into numerous, seemingly detached subfields with their own language, priorities for research, and methods of study. Not only are many of the topics newly minted, but also some language seems arcane, with citations more often than not self-referential to other recent academic writings confined within the specialized subfield. Turning from chapter to chapter almost reminds one of the famous anthropological studies of Margaret Mead and Franz Uri Boas in which tribal cultures are demonstratively unique, separate, and difficult to comprehend or generalize about. Specialization unquestionably advances administrative research, but it also separates, divides, and isolates.

In a field born of practical necessity, or again in Wilson's words, with its chief mission to learn how "to run a constitution," how can anyone grasp its present-day enormity, substance, and value, or ultimately define what "it" is? Here is the nagging question running throughout these pages: Modern-day intellectual expansion and richness come with a price tag—what is "it" if "it" races forward at breakneck speed into fissiparous bits with only tenuous connections? What is the central core of modern Public Administration that holds its many parts altogether? Kaifeng Yang's insightful yet cautionary tale concerning the separation of the Public Management Research Association from the American Society for Public Administration (ASPA) beginning in the 1990s over what in retrospect seems trivial if not nonsensical differences underscores how relentlessly specialization moves forward and inhibits research collegiality and collaboration. Of course, other professions such as law and medicine exhibit the same proclivities. However, for administrative sciences that are financially weak and often viewed as legitimately questionable endeavors compared to others more prestigious, here is a poignant lesson on the limits of dividing a field further, especially one that extols the virtues of collaboration and cooperation.

Fourth, notice the glaring, often unarticulated, normative questions. While much is novel throughout these pages, fundamental normative conundrums remain apparent. No matter what new categories, language, or methodologies spring forth, none escape the nagging BIG value dilemmas inherent within each chapter. All confront one way or another a series of questions: What is the purpose of government? Who should rule? What form should public organizations take in order to best serve the public, centralized or decentralized? What is a proper criterion for deciding administrative action? How should politics and administration be divided, or linked together? How is authority assigned and responsibility ensured? How is "efficiency" defined, "equity" valued, the meaning of "public" fathomed, and, most basic, what are the field's core values? To be sure, some chapters explicitly tackle head-on these knotty normative issues such as David Rosenbloom's discussion of "public," Norma Riccucci's on "diversity," Susan Gooden's on "social equity," and Jeremy Plant's on "professionalization," but the majority deals only implicitly with such profound theoretical dilemmas. At the extreme, again citing Kaifeng Yang's data, both Public Management Research Association meetings and articles in its *Journal of Public Administration Research and Theory* reflect little or no normative content.

Devotion to methodological purity assumes a new level of technological irrationality, or in the apt phrase Wallace Sayre used to describe personnel administration, "the triumph of technique over purpose." Nonetheless, values never disappear. Indeed, embedded throughout the arguments, normative assumptions abound even though they are implied rather than explicit. This, in turn, decidedly influences the perspectives taken, conclusions reached, and prescriptions proposed. Even among those aforementioned chapters that directly focus on normative issues, there is a tendency of reification or the unstated belief that one value should or must be better than others and therefore pursued as an end in itself. The preferred direction embraces one rather than advocates for a juggling act among competing values.

Reification sharply separates these authors from earlier scholars such as Dwight Waldo, Frederick Mosher, Herbert Kaufman, Don Price, and James Fesler, all of whom were keenly aware of the relativity of administrative ends. Much of the former generation's academic writings repeatedly stressed a deep respect for a clear-eyed realism about the complex diversity of ends as well as the ongoing competition among administrative values that never goes away, at least within a constitutional democracy such as ours. Hence, readers are encouraged to think critically as they peruse the following pages: Is the field devoting adequate attention to confronting its fundamental value questions? Are contemporary scholars adequately grounding their administrative analyses on humane ethics, cultural norms, and legal and constitutional understandings? Certainly one finds no challenging polemic among these articles, such as is found in the book by Alasdair Roberts, *Large Forces: What's Missing in Public Administration* (2013) nor pathbreaking reconceptualization as developed by Jos C.N. Raadschelders in *Public Administration: The Interdisciplinary Study of Government* (2011). Are we confronting the most pressing normative issues? If not, where and how should we begin?

Fifth, watch for the ghosts of Woodrow Wilson, John Dewey, and Louis Brownlow dance about in the ring. While differences from the past are obvious, striking continuities with earlier contributors to the field are evident. Despite the "bad press" Woodrow Wilson and founding scholars receive over their advocacy of a politics/administration dichotomy, efficiency goals, and classical orthodox models of administration, these twenty-first century scholars make no secret of their conviction that better administration means better government and their willingness to cheerlead for reforms in order to make that a reality. Like Wilson and his kin, these writers universally favor positive government that produces goods and services as effectively as possible for the public. Their means and methods may differ radically, but the rationale for the field's value and worth remain unquestioned.

No laissez faire, public choice, or small government enthusiasts can be found in the ranks of the authors in this book. Most would feel at home with late nineteenth- and early twentieth-century British political theorists who were intellectual progenitors of modern positive government, such as T.H. Greene and Beatrice and Sidney Webb, though without any taint of their professed Fabian socialism. Likewise, John Dewey's ghost, though unacknowledged, pops up again and again. Dewey's book, *The Public and Its Problems* (1926), decidedly influenced the intellectual development of the field, as Patricia Shields and David Hildebrand recently reminded us in the pages of *Public Administration Review*.

Pragmatism emphasized the applied, experimental process over arcane academic exercise; the scientific empirical method over a fixed conceptual order; purposeful instrumentalism over indirection; plus open-ended pursuit of democratic goals over closed-ended, pie-in-the-sky ideals. Certainly the contributors to this volume share the same enthusiasm for "that which works best is best to try," while aiming to promote the benefits of democracy for all. Rosemary O'Leary's "From Silos to Networks" and Kathy Newcomer's "From Outputs to Outcomes" especially reflect the pragmatic fruit of the applied, empirical, scientific, ever-changing research for promoting democratic ends, but so do most of the other chapters.

Finally, the omnipresent ghost of Louis Brownlow, the godfather of generalist public professionalism, hovers throughout, his knowledge gleaned firsthand from grassroots involvement as a city manager, and later chair of the Public Administration Clearing House and the Brownlow Commission, as well as an ASPA founder and president. All the following pages underline the critical importance of professionals and professionalism for enhancing government performance. The application of expertise to public affairs, a shared sense of corporate identity through ASPA and other professional associations, and above all, a deep commitment to ethical responsibility, were the core beliefs fostered by Brownlow and other ASPA forefathers, forming the fundamental gospel of modern public professionalism. None of these contributors dispute its significance for the field and its centrality is reflected in James Svara's chapter on ethics, though some, such as Chester Newland's chapter, "From Trust to Doubt," pointedly lament the recent decline in trust of government, especially at the federal level.

Jeremy Plant's "Seventy-Five Years of Professionalization" thoughtfully reviews the field's origins and development and astutely articulates the changing content of modern public professionalism. He traces an apparent decline in the shared commitment to generalist public professional ideals, the growing role of the academic over the practitioner, a focus upon ethical conduct through written codes of ethics as opposed to the Founders' early unspoken assumption that anyone dedicated to public administration *is* ethical, as well as the emphasis on democratization, equity, and diversity rather than respect for seniority, expertise, and hierarchical rank. As Plant sums up: "Taken together, these normative tectonic forces have redefined the field of public administration and the meaning of public professionalism." Readers ought to think carefully about the telling implications of Plant's message for the field as a whole.

Sixth, witness the globalist context but nation-state content of the field. Donald Klingner's overview in "From Local to Global," shows vividly the explosion of comparative and international administrative science knowledge in recent decades as well as the complicated reasons why this profound intellectual transformation occurred. The Internet, instantaneous communication, the ease of foreign travel, growth of new transnational organizations, demand for regional and international collaboration to discover joint policy and administrative solutions to pressing cross-border issues, suddenly shifted from the traditionally localist-oriented field into something far broader and more meaningful. Again, compared to the earlier cited White text or the Lynn and Wildavsky survey of the field, contributors to this book, virtually all of whom have significant international teaching and research experience, highlight the interconnectedness with, and interdependence upon, administrative sciences worldwide. Or, do they? It does not take much digging to see how few of the chapters in this book frame their studies from a comparative/international perspective. All the writers draw most references and perspectives from the United States. I must quickly emphasize that this is neither a criticism nor suggestion for doing otherwise. Indeed state-centeredness for administrative sciences is commonplace everywhere in the world. From its origins in seventeenth- and eighteenth-century "cameralism," the first university administrative studies were designed to improve and strengthen emerging nation-states throughout the European continent. Similarly, Wilson's 1887 essay appeared when America's administrative state began to develop. (The first federal civil service law had just been adopted in 1883 and the Interstate Commerce Commission, the first federal regulatory commission, was established in 1887.)

My point is that the theory and study of Public Administration from its inception to this day was—and is—intricately connected to the rise of the modern administrative state and that remains the focus of the field in any country. Yes, some scholars conclude that the "nation-state" is dead as a doornail and we are moving into an era of clashing civilizations, regional or sub-regional governing units, and/or a virtual state. However, as the chapters consistently illustrate, the nation-state is alive and well, at least for serving as the central focus and topic of analysis in Public Administration—for now. Thus a logical question arising from this book is how can the international/comparative context be better incorporated into the traditionally localized content of American teaching and research? Or should we simply dispense worrying about the relatively limited globalist penetration into American Public Administration studies?

And don't miss the grand finale on stage: Is the entire field shifting from an elephantine problem to an inverted, randomized POSDCORB? What do all the foregoing observations conclude about this book's survey of the state of art of contemporary Public Administration? In sum, what do these pages written by a representative cross-section of prominent academic leaders tell us about what "it" is, how the field defines itself in the twenty-first century, and what it hopes to become?

Since 1990, Public Administration scholars have been busy on many fronts striving to find an all-encompassing conceptualization of this immense yet seemingly indefinable field: from new public management (or reinventing government), to interpretative post-modernism, communitarianism, public choice, rational choice, evidence-based public management, decision theory, institutional theory, bureaucratic politics, gender as well as governance perspectives, and much more. Some actually labeled the past generation of scholarship as an era in search of a new paradigm for Public Administration, "the Re-founding Movement," or, as Dwight Waldo envisioned organization theory more than a half century ago, "an elephantine problem." Recall the fable of three blind men describing an elephant: one touches the tail characterizing the animal as a "rope" and so on. None agreed what the creature was even though they touched the same one. Indeed a reader could come away from this impressive intellectual survey with a similar conclusion. Each chapter approaches the subject from a new perspective, exhibiting little or no apparent connectedness with one another. Yet, clearly they talk about the same thing and share the certainty of its critical importance as a field of study and practice. Public Administration is ubiquitous, expanding, everywhere around us, profoundly influencing all our lives, essential to making modern society tick and government operate—or not operate. Yet, like giant abstractions, "God," "Beauty," "Truth," "Love," the term remains ambiguous, elusive, seemingly indescribable, although its presence and influence is pervasive—and growing!

Or does this text intend to offer a glimmer of insight into resolving the persistent definitional quandary of the field? Certainly on stage (or throughout this book), we witness its reality and significance today as defined by some of its best and brightest scholars. The topics they discuss demonstrate the priorities that define the field's substance, boundaries, and challenges in the twenty-first century. Thus by examining collectively these contributions, perhaps a distinct pattern emerges—one characterized by an inverted, randomized POSDCORB? Remember that POSDCORB was an acronym proposed by Luther Gulick in an essay in Gulick and Urwick's *Papers on the Science of Administration* (1937) as a general rule of thumb for doing "good" public administration by following a logical sequence of steps, that is, planning, organizing, staffing, and so on. Many in the field at that time optimistically believed that proverbs of administrative sciences would evolve into universal scientific principles that could be applied to making government more efficient and the lot of citizens vastly improved.

Hence, the era became tagged as "POSDCORB Orthodoxy." Certainly those days are long gone. It is absurd now to talk about "principles of administration," "the one best way," "a logical sequence of steps for doing good administration," or that "economy and efficiency" ought to be the sole twin goals of successful administrators. If anything, the common view shared by authors throughout this book appears precisely the reverse: an inverted, randomized POSDCORB. Yes, words have changed in that acronym, but not their basic meaning. "Collaboration" has replaced "coordination," "staffing" is now "human resource management," "direction" is "management," "planning" is "policy-making," and so on. As indicated earlier, each POSDCORB topic under a new label is addressed more or less as open-ended questions in the book, critical areas of inquiry, without expressing absolutes, such as principles or rules of thumb for doing "good" administration.

Indeed no prescribed best way is offered up here—only potential directions and possible tendencies that remain in flux, "From . . . To . . . " as many of the chapters are entitled. Nor is there an agreed upon set of objectives. Yes, differences, diversity, and ethics are encouraged but by no means are they the only purposes recommended for deciding upon administrative direction. And so where and in what direction should public administration head? Nor is there much commitment expressed throughout these pages that bold administrative action of any sort will make much difference in determining the fate of society. Yes, the field is important, but let's not go as far as suggesting "bold action!" Certainly there is no over-arching, generalist, integrative administrative framework offered up to do "good" public administration—only bits and pieces hinted at here and there. Rather than synthesize and integrate, writers prefer to analyze and disaggregate, or the reverse of much of what the day-to-day work of public administration is all about. As for a logical sequence of steps, administrators are left to their own devices for finding a fixed starting point among these seemingly independent topics. They can simply pick any one and next choose where to go from there. POSDCORB, born as a bold extrovert, now seems a timid introvert, reductionist, largely self-referential, cut off from practice, lacking any conviction, perhaps thereby acknowledging its own irrelevance as both a study and practice. No wonder passing, highly questionable fads such as "re-inventing government," promoted by well-paid contractors and consultants find support and application among practitioners when the academic field itself fails to present a united front or any common core thinking. Has contemporary Public Administration unwittingly embraced an inverted, randomized POSDCORB in which there is "no there there"?

As you read through these fascinating chapters about the most important field on the planet, judge for yourself as to how you describe what "it" is today and "it" should be all about in the future? Whether or not its early self-confident role and recognized public importance to "run a constitution" remains influential, or as influential as it might be? How can "it" achieve the potential in the twenty-first century that its early founders hoped for, namely promoting good government and the good society for all citizens as well as preventing future catastrophic government failures, such as occurred on 9/11, at Abu Ghraib, and during Hurricane Katrina?

Note

1 The author follows Dwight Waldo's method of using capital letters, Public Administration, to denote the study, research, and theory of the field and lower case letters when referring to its practice, institutions, and processes.

PREFACE

Mary E. Guy and Marilyn M. Rubin

The genesis of this book comes on the occasion of the seventy-fifth anniversary of the American Society for Public Administration (ASPA). The benchmark of a discipline is that it has a professional organization dedicated to advancing its work, a well-recognized journal that provides an outlet for research in the field, and a code of ethics that crystallizes predominant values and provides guidance for its members. These are the functions that ASPA has filled since its creation in 1939.

The year 1939, of course, was not the beginning of public administration. Rather, it is the date that marks the collaboration of a critical mass of scholars and practitioners in the United States who recognized that political science's boundaries were too constraining for the work that public administrators do. They came together in 1939 at the annual meeting of the American Political Science Association to form ASPA, thus giving a separate confidence and identity to a profession specifically focused on advancing excellence in public service.

Looking toward the future, it is worthwhile to take stock of the field and the intellectual path that it has traveled. To do that, we bring you this collection of chapters, each of which traces the evolution of thinking and practice in a particular dimension of public administration. The book is written for those seeking to understand the trends, forces, and events that shape the practice and theories of the field. For practitioners trying to make sense of why things are as they are, the chapters trace developments over the decades, explaining how today's practices are rooted in yesterday's innovations. Students in Master of Public Administration programs will learn how the intersections of policy-making, implementation, management, and technology continue to reshape the environment they strive to understand. Doctoral candidates will find that the volume provides a context for the important questions they are studying.

Taken individually or read in sequence, the chapters will boost understandings of publicness, intersectoral relations, constraints posed by budget shortfalls and shifting public opinion, globalization, networks, public administration versus public management, program evaluation, e-government, diversity, social equity, professionalization of the field, and public integrity. In other words, whether practitioner, student, or researcher, this volume provides an x-ray of the field, showing its foundations as well as its contemporary shape and form.

At the outset of this project, we debated whether to commission chapters on specializations in the field such as budgeting, human resource management, organization theory, leadership, and so on—the POSDCORB regulars. We decided, instead, to "slice" the field differently, capturing trends that have influenced how scholars and practitioners have altered these staples of administrative practice. The trends identified throughout the chapters will continue in motion and the field will continue to adapt and reshape itself. To provide a picture of this dynamic, each chapter is accompanied by a timeline showing events that have punctuated the subject matter over the decades.

Ours is a field that is both proactive and reactive, anticipating trends and responding to them. Muddled together are public opinion about every possible policy stance under the sun, citizen attitudes about government and its rightful place in their lives, partisan political theater, macro-and micro-economics, leadership, administrative and managerial acuity, and the interconnections that bind us together as a field, a nation, and a world. Within this complex environment, contributors were asked to focus on one dimension of the field and to trace its evolution from the formative years to the present time. First, Rosenbloom sets forth the context and discusses the legal forces that have shaped the field into what it is today. Kettl then shows the shift from intergovernmental to intersectoral relations and how this has produced a complicated patchwork of business, government, and nonprofits pursuing public ends. Newland's chapter focuses on the federal government and highlights both continuities and discontinuities. The global context of contemporary public administration is outlined by Klingner, while O'Leary traces the path from hierarchy to heterarchy. In the late twentieth century, divisions occurred within the public administration academy and Yang questions whether these have become a distinction without a difference. Newcomer's work traces the transition in public management from a focus on outputs to outcomes and discusses how this is integrated into current practice. From filing cabinet to Internet servers, Lee and Reed describe the ever-growing reliance on e-government and information technology and discuss its implications for the delivery of public services.

Looking at how demographic changes alter the administrative landscape, Riccucci contrasts the necessity for representative bureaucracy with the reality of how differentness is accommodated and Gooden writes about social equity and contrasts theory with practice. Amid all these cross-cutting trends, Plant describes the emergence of a growing number of organizations and associations dedicated to the study and practice of public administration and teases out the tensions that exist. And Svara describes the challenges that surrounded the development of a code of ethics for ASPA and the field. Finally, Guy and Rubin take a step back and look at the field as a whole, its progression from modernism to metamodernism, and the emerging global trends that will shape the work of public administrators long into the future.

We hope you enjoy this work and that it provides an understanding of where we are today and a grounding for forecasting the future. We also hope that once you have finished the book, you will ponder the path taken and think about the future and what similar chapters will say when ASPA is commemorating its one-hundredth anniversary.

ACKNOWLEDGMENTS

We would like to acknowledge the commitment to excellence in public service that ASPA has embraced and nurtured over the past seventy-five years. And we are grateful to ASPA's former Executive Director Antoinette Samuel for her foresight in appreciating the many reasons for celebrating the Society's seventy fifth anniversary. Thanks to ASPA's leaders and the 75th Anniversary Commission, the celebration culminates in this book. And thank you to doctoral candidate Sean McCandless for creating the index.

ABBREVIATIONS

ACSI   American Consumer Satisfaction Index
AICP   American Institute of Certified Planners
APA   American Psychological Association
APPAM   Association of Public Policy Analysis and Management
ASPA   American Society for Public Administration
BoB   Bureau of the Budget
CAG   Comparative Administration Group
CBO   Congressional Budget Office
CEA   Council of Economic Advisors
CHEA   Council for Higher Education Accreditation
CIO   Chief Information Officer
CSRA   Civil Service Reform Act of 1978
DoD   Department of Defense
EAS   electronic approval systems
EEOC   (U.S.) Equal Employment Opportunity Commission
EOP   Executive Office of the President
FASB   Financial Accounting Standards Board
FEI   Federal Executive Institute
FEPC   Fair Employment Practices Committee
FIPSE   Fund for the Improvement of Postsecondary Education
FOIA   Freedom of Information Act
FRD   family responsibilities discrimination
GAO   Government Accountability Office
GASB   Government Accounting Standards Board
GDP   gross domestic product
GIS   Geographic Information Systems

GPO	Government Printing Office
GPRA	Government Performance and Results Act of 1993
GTI	Global Transparency Initiative
GWU	George Washington University
HR	human resources
ICC	Interstate Commerce Commission
ICMA	International City/County Management Association
ICT	information and communication technology
IFI	international financial institution
IIAS	International Institute of Administrative Sciences
IMF	International Monetary Fund
IT	information technology
JPAE	*Journal of Public Affairs Education*
JPART	*Journal of Public Administration Research and Theory*
JTPA	Job Training Partnership Act
LGB	lesbian, gay, and bisexual
LGBT	lesbian, gay, bisexual, transgendered
LGBTQ	lesbian, gay, bisexual, transgendered and questioning
MPA	Master of Public Administration
NAPA	National Academy of Public Administration
NASA	National Aeronautics and Space Administration
NASPAA	Network of Schools of Public Policy, Affairs, and Administration (originally National Association of Schools of Public Affairs and Administration)
NGO	nongovernmental organization
NPM	New Public Management
NPR	National Performance Review
NSA	National Security Agency
OECD	Organisation for Economic Co-operation and Development
OMB	Office of Management and Budget
OPA	Office of Price Administration
OPM	Office of Personnel Management
PA	Public Administration
PACH	Public Administration Clearing House
PMA	President's Management Agenda
PMRA	Public Management Research Association
PPBS	Planning, Programming, and Budgeting System (also known as PPB)
PSEC	Professional Standards and Ethics Committee
RCT	random control trial
ROI	return on investment
RSJI	Race and Social Justice Initiative (Seattle)
RWJF	Robert Wood Johnson Foundation
SAGE	Semi-Automatic Ground Environment

SAS	Supervisor Assistant Systems
SES	Senior Executive Service
SICA	Section on International and Comparative Administration
TAM	technology acceptance model
UN	United Nations
UNO	University of Nebraska, Omaha
USAID	U.S. Agency for International Development

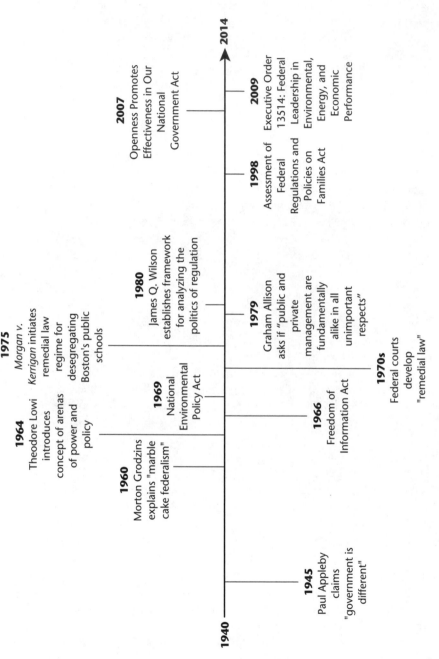

FIGURE 1.1 The Public Context: Benchmarks across Time

1

THE PUBLIC CONTEXT

David H. Rosenbloom

What is public about public administration? This question has been raised in the literature of public administration at least since 1945 when Paul Appleby claimed that "government is different" (Appleby 1945). In the late 1970s, taking Wallace Sayre's (1958) aphorism, "public and private management are fundamentally alike in all unimportant respects" as his lead, Graham Allison sought to provide a framework for "systematic investigation" of the "similarities and difference among public and private management" (Allison 1979). Since then a number of authors have compared public and private organizations with regard to red tape, research and demonstration, employee motivation, and other phenomena. Nevertheless, there is no consensus on how to answer what seems to be a simple question.

Perhaps this is because as a field of study, public administration has been without a dominant paradigm for almost all of the American Society for Public Administration's life, and certainly since the late 1940s. Lacking one, some researchers seek an answer to what makes public administration public by looking at the organizational level—how does the behavior of public and private organizations differ, if at all? (Bozeman 1987). Others focus on differences between public and private employees (Perry and Wise 1990). Still others examine the different environments in which both public and private organizations and employees operate. This body of research is ongoing, which suggests that it remains inconclusive and/or incomplete.

Yet there may be some consensus on what public administration is, regardless of whether it differs in important respects from private management, as Sayre implied. Since the 1980s, it has become commonplace that public administration combines management, politics, and law (Rosenbloom 1983; see also Meriam 1939). How it does so defines a great deal about the enterprise of public administration and the overall context in which it operates. This is not meant to suggest that the public and private sectors do not parallel each other in significant ways or that specific jobs in both sectors may be virtually identical. Note that Sayre did not explicitly state that public and private organizations are dissimilar in all important ways. The point is that by looking at management, politics, and law in the public sector we can observe a context that, as Appleby claimed, Sayre suggested, and others have researched, makes public administration different.

Management

What public managers do is another question without an immediate or straight-forward answer (Ban 1995; Kaufman 1981; Morgan et al. 1996). They manage people, budgets, organizations, programs, stakeholders, information, communication, and more. Much depends on their level, political jurisdictions, organizations, and environments. The usual answer to what makes them *public* managers is that they overwhelmingly work in organizations that do not compete in output markets for their revenues. Even where they require user fees, such as those for obtaining a U.S. passport, they may act as monopolies. Further, although public managers may earn bonuses and salary raises, organizational profits (that is, excess revenues) are not ordinarily shared by managers, other employees, and/or stakeholders (including taxpayers). Nonprofit management is often taught in public administration programs rather than in business administration partly because under U.S. law, as with public agencies, their profits cannot be distributed to directors, officers, and members.

Whether being nonprofit is a sufficient answer as to what makes public managers public is a moot point. Perhaps Woodrow Wilson (1887) and John Rohr (1986) provided a better answer: they "run" the federal and state constitutions. Wilson did not expound on what he meant by "running a constitution." Rohr was more concerned with the legitimacy of the administrative state than the likelihood that running a constitution will be problematic if the government working under it lacks the capacity effectively to implement policies, laws, international agreements, and judicial and other decisions. Implementation is what gives government the capacity to govern. Although legitimacy may contribute to capacity, history teaches that it is not a prerequisite except, possibly, in what may be a very long run.

Public managers at the federal and state levels run constitutions by coordinating the separation of powers. They are under the "joint custody" of, and subordinate to, three sets of "directors": legislatures, chief executives, and courts (Rosenbloom 2001; Rourke 1993). Mission, authority, organizational structure, staff, and funding depend very heavily on legislatures. If legislatures do nothing, there is no administration, which is why W.F. Willoughby referred to Congress as the source of federal administration and asserted that it is "the possessor of all administrative authority" (1927, 11; 1934, 115, 157). Gubernatorial powers vary across the states and governors may have authority such as the line item veto that the president lacks. Regardless of these differences, the president and governors are expected to coordinate and manage government administration on a day-to-day basis. As the U.S. Constitution puts it, the president is expected to "take care that the laws *be* faithfully executed" (Article 2, section 3; emphasis added).

When justiciable cases are before the courts, judges and justices apply the law to challenged administrative actions. If law is in the form of constitutional law, they not only apply it, but also, to put it uncomfortably, they *make* it. As Justice Lewis Powell once said, "constitutional law is what the courts say it is" (*Owen v. City of Independence* 1980, 669). Note that with the exception of the thirteenth amendment, banning slavery and involuntary servitude other than as punishment for crime, and what constitutional law regards as state action (that is, governmental action), the federal Constitution has no direct application to private relationships. Remedial law, as developed by the courts themselves in the last third of the twentieth century, enables federal and state judges to become deeply involved in the administrative operations of public schools, public housing, personnel, welfare, prisons, mental health systems, and other governmental activities (Chayes 1976; Cramton 1976; Rosenbloom, O'Leary, and Chanin 2010, chapter 7). It is more common for remedial law to involve state and local administration than federal activities. However, the way applicants for many federal positions are tested today reaches back to court decisions finding traditional merit system examinations legally defective for their lack of predictive validity and surfeit of negative disparate impact on the employment interests of minorities (see *Ricci v. DeStefano* 2009).

Public managers are legally required to act as instructed by chief executives and their appointees, legislatures, and courts. When all agree and are precise, the direction should be clear. When their directives are ambiguous, containing terms such as "feasible," "public interest," and "adequate," or at odds with one another, the public administration and political science literature tells us coordination comes through bureaucratic politics. Public managers find themselves in the "Web of Politics," as Aberbach and Rockman (2000) explain. The web has governments of strangers, issue networks, iron triangles, hollow cores, and its "lifeblood" may be political power (Long 1949). The rule of law should be followed, of course, but it is not always clear what it requires in terms of substance and pace. The choices Lipsky's street-level bureaucrats and O'Leary's guerrillas make and how upper-level managers, including political appointees, respond to them also affect coordination and implementation (Lipsky 1980; O'Leary 2006; Riccucci 1995; Maynard-Moody and Musheno 2003). So does agency "nonacquiescence," which is not unusual, as when a federal agency bound by a ruling in one judicial circuit does not change its practices in the others, even though in all likelihood those processes are illegal or unconstitutional.

Subordination of public management to tripartite direction and supervision under the separation of powers can accommodate congressional authorization for a court to appoint an independent counsel with authority to exercise all the investigatory and prosecutorial powers of the Department of Justice while shielding the counsel from removal by the president and allowing dismissal only by the direct action of the attorney general for specified causes (*Morrison v. Olson* 1988). Coordination of the separation of powers goes to the very center of what Kerwin says is the most important thing agencies do, rulemaking (Kerwin 2003, xi). Congress delegates its legislative authority for agencies to make substantive (legislative) rules having the power of law. The president, through the Office of Management and Budget, exercises a considerable amount of control over the agencies' rulemaking agendas and proposed and final rules. The latter are subject to congressional review and potential disapproval by joint resolution, subject to presidential veto and override. If litigation follows the enactment of substantive rules, which is common, the federal courts apply a "hard look" at their basis and purpose, and the connection between the two. Public managers have to manage rulemaking with the president's agenda, congressional committees and subcommittees, and judicial decisions in mind. Relying on the simplifying proposition that their primary obligation is to follow the president's direction is a copout. As Rohr emphasized, their oath is to support the Constitution (Article VI, section 3; Rohr 1978).

Public managers also coordinate federalism and intergovernmental relations. So many programs now involve two or three levels of government that coordinating them can be a full-time public management job. If coordination were not necessary, presumably there would be a much smaller literature on "cooperative federalism," "new federalism," and the Supreme Court and a return to "dual federalism." Grodzin's classic description of a health officer's job not only reminds us that collaborative governance is not new, but also may still best convey the intermixing of administrative programs across federal, state, and local governments.

The sanitarian is appointed by the state under merit standards established by the federal government. His base salary comes jointly from state and federal funds, the county provides him with an office and office amenities and pays a portion of his expenses, and the largest city in the county also contributes to his salary and office by virtue of his appointment as city plumbing inspector. It is impossible from moment to moment to tell under which governmental hat the sanitarian operates. His work of inspecting the purity of food is carried out under federal standards; but he is enforcing state laws when inspecting commodities that have not been in interstate commerce; and . . . he also acts under state authority when inspecting milk coming into the county from producing areas across the state border. He is a federal officer when impounding impure drugs shipped from a neighboring state; a federal-state officer when distributing typhoid immunization serum; a state officer when enforcing standards of industrial hygiene; a state-local officer when inspecting the city's water supply; and (to complete the circle) a local officer when insisting that the city butchers adopt more hygienic methods of handling their garbage.

(Grodzins 1960, 265–266 as quoted in Grant and Nixon 1975, 37–38)

Competent sanitarians are required to coordinate and integrate all these health-related activities among the multiple jurisdictions involved. As an individual, a sanitarian may be quite adroit at doing so. However, supporting the sanitarian's work involves federal–state–local and local–local administrative coordination of budgeting, personnel administration, and allocation of office space, as well as the legal and policy aspects of implementing health regulations. Thinking in terms of bottom-up implementation theory, one can appreciate the amount of multi-jurisdictional and multi-agency effort necessary to make it possible for sanitarians to do their jobs effectively or even just to put them on the street (Elmore 1979–1980). When one multiplies this effort by the hundreds or thousands of programs requiring federal, state, and local governmental coordination, the importance of public managers in coordinating policy implementation is self-evident. Even in the single area of law enforcement, it may be daunting.

Public management is also complicated by legal mandates to implement "mission extraneous public values" (Baehler, Liu, and Rosenbloom 2014). At least in theory, one could spend an entire career in a federal agency working hard and diligently on something, such as freedom of information requests, which has nothing to do with the organization's core mission. Such mandates often fall within the rubric of "administrative law."

Administrative Law

Administrative law is the regulatory law of public administration. It regulates agency rulemaking, adjudication, enforcement, handling of information and transparency, formal relationships with stakeholders, public participation, and some aspects of decision making. It also covers a wide variety of mandates, such as the production of environmental impact statements, assessments of policies and activities on the strength of families, and sustainability efforts (National Environmental Policy Act of 1969 1970; Assessment of Federal Regulations and Policies on Families Act of 1998; Executive Order 13514 2009). To a large extent, administrative law requires administrative action to comport with the nation's democratic-constitutional values, including representativeness, public participation, transparency, and procedural due process. It also establishes the scope of judicial review and may provide for legislative review of agency rules.

One of administrative law's chief qualities is that it requires agencies to devote considerable resources to activities that have little or nothing to do with their primary missions and specialized expertise and technologies. Such activities are intended to promote public values that are generally extrinsic to the purposes for which individual agencies exist. As suggested above, freedom of information under federal and state statutes is a familiar example. It is intended to promote the public value of transparency, which has long been considered necessary for government accountability and an informed citizenry.

The federal Freedom of Information Act (FOIA) of 1966, as amended, extends very broadly across the executive branch, including to all departments and agencies outside the Executive Office of the President, and those that are not purely advisory within it. Transparency in the sense of answering freedom of information requests from individuals in the United States and around the world—there is no "standing" requirement such as citizenship—is very clearly not part of the core missions of the FBI, CIA, Environmental Protection Agency, Department of Homeland Security, and probably all other executive branch departments and agencies other than the National Archives and Records Administration. Nevertheless, the agencies are required to respond to requests within established statutory time limits, appoint chief FOIA officers and FOIA liaisons, and report on FOIA performance. When courts award attorney's fees to plaintiffs suing agencies for illegally withholding information, the agencies are required to pay them out of their own budgets rather than from the Treasury Department's Claims and Judgment Fund. Responding to the more than 600,000 FOIA requests the federal government can expect annually takes a great deal of staff time and costs millions of dollars (FOIA.gov, n.d.).

A reasonable definition of mission-extrinsic public values in the context of administrative law is that the values: (1) do not support achieving the central purposes, core activities, and *raison d'être* of agencies and programs; (2) are unrelated to an agency's specialized competencies and technologies; (3) promote preferences that are extraneous to organizational missions and may even impede them; (4) are often imposed across all agencies in one-size-fits-all fashion that is not strategically tailored to individual missions; and (5) are not necessarily supported by agency leaders and personnel (Baehler, Liu, and Rosenbloom 2014). Leading examples include FOIA as just mentioned, the Privacy Act of 1974, Paperwork Reduction Acts of 1980 and 1995, executive orders for environmental justice and sustainability, statutory requirements for environmental impact statements and assessments of agency actions on the strength of families, and a host of court decisions associated with running a constitution constitutionally by protecting the rights of clients, customers, public employees, contractors, individuals involved in street-level regulatory encounters, prisoners, and individuals confined to public mental health facilities (Rosenbloom 2014a; Rosenbloom, O'Leary, and Chanin 2010).

Bright lines do not always exist between mission-extrinsic public values and mission-supportive activities, such as human resource management and budgeting, which are ancillary to the achievement of agency core missions. For example, energy conservation pursuant to President Barack Obama's Executive Order 13514 (2009) can lead to lower operating costs that may be devoted to core mission activities. Paperwork reduction, which is intended to reduce the paperwork burden thrust by the federal government on private entities, can lead to administrative efficiencies by streamlining the collection and processing of information. Affirmative action to promote representative bureaucracy may also improve agency performance. However, the links, if any, between FOIA, environmental justice, family impact assessments, and several other mission-extrinsic public values and the achievement of core mission values are often attenuated at best.

Prioritizing mission-extrinsic public values presents a public management puzzle. They are mandates that in theory must be fulfilled, yet strategic plans and performance reports may give them short shrift, or ignore them altogether (Piotrowski and Rosenbloom 2002). Legislative committees are apt to focus on the achievement of core mission objectives. Political appointees, career managers, and rank and file employees may have little or no interest in pursuing mission-extrinsic public values. As Foerstel (1999, 94) explains, they may be pushed aside: "We all struggle with insufficient funds, insufficient staff, and too many requests to handle in a timely fashion. The people who run the daily mission programs in the agencies find it hard to devote the time to FOIA."

The extent to which mission-extrinsic public values differentiate the public context from private enterprise is a qualitative matter. Certainly, private corporations face open reporting, equal employment opportunity, collective bargaining, fair labor standards, safety, environmental, and other legal requirements that many would find mission extrinsic. However, there are no federal legal requirements of general applicability to the private sector regarding freedom of information, environmental justice and sustainability, paperwork reduction, and family assessments. Federal contractors are hybrids, being subject to freedom of information under the Openness Promotes Effectiveness in Our National Government Act of 2007 and are required to protect their employees' personal privacy and whistle-blowing rights under the Federal Acquisition Regulation (Acquisition Central n.d.). Another difference between the public and private sectors is that because they are not constrained by constitutional law, private entities have much greater freedom in dealing with their employees, customers and clients.

Constitutional Law

The federal and state constitutions also play a major role in establishing what public managers may do, and how. There is no true employment "at will" in the public sector because public employees at all levels and positions have constitutional protections against adverse actions even when they lack civil service, contractual tenure, or property rights or interests in their positions. The Supreme Court made this crystal clear in *Rankin v. McPherson* (1987), in which a *probationary* employee in a constable's office was terminated for remarking, upon learning of an assassination attempt on President Ronald Reagan: "Shoot, if they go for him, I hope they get him." The Court explained:

> Even though McPherson was merely a probationary employee, and even
> if she could have been discharged for any reason or for no reason at all,
> she may nonetheless be entitled to reinstatement if she was discharged for
> exercising her constitutional right to freedom of expression.
>
> *(381, 383–384)*

The first amendment also protects the right to freedom of association. Public
employees have protection through the whole gamut of personnel actions against
being negatively treated based on their partisan affiliations (*Rutan v. Republican
Party of Illinois* 1990). Public employees may be members of hate groups insofar
as they are legal. These rights, like others guaranteed by the Constitution, are
not absolute and must be balanced by the courts against governmental interests
in efficiency, effectiveness, harmony among employees, other work related factors, the public interest, and jurisprudential considerations (Rosenbloom 2014b).
There are also exceptions for prohibited partisan campaign speech and speech
that is the product of a work assignment (*U.S. Civil Service Commission v. National
Association of Letter Carriers* 1973; *Garcetti v. Ceballos* 2006). Nevertheless, like
McPherson's right to utter her remark to another employee in a discussion about
the impact of Reagan's policies on minorities, a great deal of public employees'
speech enjoys constitutional protection.

Public employees' freedom of speech includes the right to whistleblow, which
may also be protected by statutes. On the constitutional level, the Supreme Court
noted the value of public employee whistleblowing with particular reference to
public school teachers in *Pickering v. Board of Education* (1968, 571–572):

> [F]ree and open debate is vital to informed decision-making by the elector-
> ate. Teachers are as a class, the members of a community most likely to have
> informed and definite opinions as to how funds allotted to the operation of
> the schools should be spent. Accordingly, it is essential that they be able to
> speak out freely on such questions without fear of retaliatory dismissal.

The Court's logic applies to public employees in other areas of specialization
as well. Some state laws protect whistleblowers in the private sector. However,
these are less comprehensive than the coverage afforded to public employees
under the Constitution (National Conference of State Legislatures 2010).

Public employees also have constitutional rights under fourth amendment privacy and fourteenth and fifth amendment equal protection of the laws. *City of
Ontario, California v. Quon* (2010) is illustrative of the Supreme Court's reluc-
tance to permit public employees to be treated by their governmental employers
identically to the way the justices perceive that private employers deal with their
workers. The Court explained that a previous case, *O'Connor v. Ortega* (1987),
set forth two different approaches for assessing public employees' fourth amendment rights. In *O'Connor*, the

Court did disagree on the proper analytical framework for Fourth Amendment claims against government employers. A four-Justice plurality concluded that . . . a court must consider "[t]he operational realities of the workplace" in order to determine whether an employee's Fourth Amendment rights are implicated. . . . On this view, "the question whether an employee has a reasonable expectation of privacy must be addressed on a case-by-case basis." . . . Next, where an employee has a legitimate privacy expectation, an employer's intrusion on that expectation "for noninvestigatory, work-related purposes, as well as for investigations of work-related misconduct, should be judged by the standard of reasonableness under all the circumstances."

Justice Scalia, concurring in the judgment, outlined a different approach. His opinion would have dispensed with an inquiry into "operational realities" and would conclude "that the offices of government employees . . . are covered by Fourth Amendment protections as a general matter." . . . But he would also have held "that government searches to retrieve work-related materials or to investigate violations of workplace rules—searches of the sort that are regarded as reasonable and normal in the private-employer context—do not violate the Fourth Amendment."

(City of Ontario, California v. Quon 2010, 756–757)

In *Quon* the Court held that because the search of Quon's government-issued pager was reasonable there was no need to decide which of the two *O'Connor* approaches is the correct interpretation. In short, the majority was not ready to make public employees' fourth amendment rights depend on what is "normal" in the private sector (*City of Ontario, California v. Quon* 2010, 757). The fourth amendment also controls drug testing in the public sector (*National Treasury Union Employees v. Von Raab* 1989).

Under federal law, neither public nor most private employers may discriminate against employees based on race, color, religion, ethnicity, sex, age, or disability. However, in some circumstances civil rights law affords private employers more leeway to engage in affirmative action in order to promote diversity. This is because hiring and promotion goals based on race or ethnicity in the public sector are regulated by the equal protection clause and "must be analyzed by a reviewing court under strict scrutiny. In other words, such classifications are constitutional only if they are narrowly tailored measures that further compelling governmental interests" (*Adarand Constructors v. Pena* 1995, 227). Public-sector affirmative action based on sex also faces a constitutional test: the government must be "exceedingly persuasive" in demonstrating that the means used are substantially related to the achievement of an important governmental purpose (*United States v. Virginia* 1996, 533, 546).

Public administration also faces constitutional restrictions when dealing with contractors. This is true regarding equal protection as outlined immediately above, and also extends to freedom of speech. *Board of County Commissioners, Wabaunsee County v. Umbehr* (1996) provides a good example of how the U.S. Constitution complicates public administrative relationships with contractors. Umbehr, a contractor for trash collection, publicly criticized Wabaunsee's three-member board of commissioners for the county's landfill rates and for violating Kansas' Open Meetings Act. He also ran for election to the board. The board members "allegedly took Umbehr's criticism badly." The board terminated his contract, which Umbehr claimed was in retaliation for his exercise of his first and fourteenth amendment rights to freedom of speech. The Supreme Court made it clear that "the First Amendment restricts the freedom of federal, state, or local governments to terminate their relationships with independent contractors because of the contractors' speech" (*Board of County Commissioners, Wabaunsee County v. Umbehr* 1996, 672).

In *O'Hare Truck Service, Inc. v. City of Northlake* (1996), decided the same day as *Umbehr*, the Supreme Court extended first and fourteenth amendment protection to firms having preexisting noncontractual commercial relationships with government. Specifically, the Court held that constitutional protection applies when "government retaliates against a contractor, or a regular provider of services, for the exercise of rights of political association or the expression of political allegiance" (*O'Hare Truck Service, Inc. v. City of Northlake* 1996, 715).

The Constitution is also relevant to governmental relationships with clients and customers. Again, constitutional equal protection and civil rights statutory requirements prohibit government from discriminating based on race, color, national origin, religion, sex, age, and disability. Constitutional provisions applying to government have parallels applying to the private sector in statutory law. However, public agencies face the potential of judicially imposed remedial law reforms for constitutional violations. Remedial law often relies on "the continuing judicial intervention in the direct management and reform of departments and agencies" as judges undertake "deliberate, comprehensive and often complex court efforts to change the organizational behavior of school systems, prisons, mental hospitals, and public housing authorities judged to violate individual rights" (Wood and Vose 1990, ix).

Public schools, which have clear counterparts in the private sector (including nonprofits), provide a good example of the application and scope of remedial law. In perhaps the archetypal case, *Morgan v. Kerrigan* (1975), a federal district court completely revamped the Boston public school system. The court's remedial plan included the creation of eight school districts within which busing would operate to ensure a high degree of school desegregation. "Examination" schools were established for students with exceptional intellectual ability *and* were required to have student bodies that were at least 35 percent African-American and Hispanic. Citywide magnet schools with particular specializations were also created while twenty schools were closed. The ultimate inefficacy of the court's remedial plan notwithstanding, no private school has been or could be subject to such a degree of judicial intervention into its internal management. The private sector faces a variety of judicially imposed remedies for illegal behavior. Remedial law as it operates in the public sector is not among them.

Politics

An obvious quality that makes the public sector public is its authority to make laws and policies that are binding on the population as a whole, specific segments of it, and "legal persons" such as corporations and formal organizations. The public sector can exercise coercive governmental power. This aspect of the public sector goes a long way toward explaining the lack of output markets, the treatment of excess revenues, and the application of constitutional and administrative law. Much of what public administrators do is not directed by markets or a "hidden hand," but by political interest and power.

To a large extent, public administrators operate in areas characterized by market failure, collective action problems having negative consequences, the production of public goods, and a scale of activity thought to be too great for the private sector to support. Many agencies operate where markets fail or function in ways government deems inappropriate. For example, the following federal agencies are associated with specific market failures or performance deficits, including the commodification of labor and limited ability to take future generations into account with respect to the use of nonrenewable natural resources:

- Federal Trade Commission—monopolization, information asymmetry;
- Anti-Trust Division of the Department of Justice—monopolization;
- Environmental Protection Agency—externalities;
- Departments of Agriculture, Interior, and Commerce (National Oceanic and Atmospheric Administration), Army Corps of Engineers, Environmental Protection Agency—conservation;
- Department of Labor Employment and Training Administration—labor immobility;
- Equal Employment Opportunity Commission—systematic discrimination based on socio-biological factors;
- Security and Exchange Commission; Federal Energy Regulatory Commission; Commodity Credit Corporation, Federal Communications Commission; National Labor Relations Board; Federal Maritime Commission—various market functioning problems;
- Food and Drug Administration; Federal Aviation Administration; Federal Railroad Administration; National Highway Traffic Safety Administration; National Transportation Safety Board; Defense Nuclear Facilities Safety Board; Occupational Safety and Health Administration; Consumer Product Safety Commission; Mine Safety and Health Review Commission; Nuclear Regulatory Administration—public and worker safety.

In one way or another, all the cabinet-level departments and many independent agencies and regulatory commissions are involved in the production of public goods or quasi-public goods such as national security, education, and infrastructure and/or efforts to resolve collective action problems involving rational individual behavior that yields dysfunctional aggregate results such as some forms of environmental degradation. The National Aeronautics and Space Administration is an example of an administrative unit that was created in part because the scale of its operations was considered too great for the private sector to support.

Lacking markets to generate revenues, public administration is funded through political rather than economic processes. The politics of public budgeting has been well-researched (Borcherding 1977; Wildavsky 1984). Budgeting priorities are normative, and as a polity, the United States has no comprehensive agreed-upon answer to V.O. Key's famous question: "On what basis shall it be decided to allocate x dollars to activity A instead of activity B?" (Key 1940). Budgets deal with Lasswell's quintessential question of "who gets what, when, and how?" (Lasswell 1958). The answers are inherently political.

Relatedly, political controls substitute for market discipline in regulating public administrative behavior. The decisions whether to regulate and provide services, at what levels, where, and how, are largely driven by politics rather than marginal costs and technical capacity alone. This reality necessarily infuses public administration with policy considerations, and with policymaking comes political interest, pressure, competition, and conflict.

The study of bureaucratic politics offers many models and frameworks for answering Lasswell's question. Two of these, one offered by James Q. Wilson and another by Theodore J. Lowi, have been particularly comprehensive and enduring. In "The Politics of Regulation," Wilson (1980, 367–372) explained how the distribution of costs and benefits defines four familiar types of politics:

1. *Interest Group Politics* take place when the costs and benefits are narrowly concentrated. Interest group will oppose interest group if a regulation will "benefit a small group at the expense of another comparable small group" giving "[e]ach side . . . a strong incentive to organize and exercise political influence" especially if "[t]he public does not believe it will be much affected one way or another." A contest between employees and employers over the levels of toxic substances in workplaces in specific industries is an example.
2. *Client Politics* occur "when the benefits of a prospective policy are concentrated but the costs are widely distributed." A small and easily organized group can benefit with little opposition from those who will bear the widely distributed costs. Client politics is exemplified by subsidies to specific industries and crops.
3. *Entrepreneurial Politics* arise where "a policy may be proposed that will confer general (though perhaps small) benefits at a cost borne chiefly by a small segment of society." Because it is easier for those who will bear the costs to

organize, the entrepreneur's role is to mobilize a broad segment of the public in favor of a policy, such as automobile safety.

4. *Majoritarian Politics* occur when both the costs and benefits of a policy are widely distributed so that "[a]ll or most of society expects to gain; all or most of society expects to pay." Social security and anti-trust policy are examples.

Lowi's (1964) framework is based on the observation that different types of policies are associated with distinctive types of politics and administrative implementation. In his original formulation, Lowi identified the following "arenas of power":

1. In the *distribution arena*, the primary units involved are individual firms and relationships among them are nonconflictual and characterized by log-rolling and mutual interference. The locus of decisions is in Congress or administrative agencies and implementation is apt to be by an administrative bureau. This arena is characterized by an elite power structure.

2. In the *regulatory arena*, the primary unit will be groups and relationships among them will involve bargaining. The power structure will be pluralistic and Congress will be the key decision maker, though implementation will be by agencies relying on delegated authority.

3. The *redistribution arena* is characterized by conflict among peak associations, class, and ideology in contests among conflicting elites or elites and non-elites. Decision making is in the executive branch and implementation is centralized within agencies.

After formulating the original framework, Lowi added the arena of *constituent politics*, which addresses matters of constitutional and political system design, formal rules, and related matters central to how a polity functions. The primary actors in this arena are political and administrative elites at the top of a political system.

A great deal has changed in U.S. politics and administration since Wilson and Lowi developed their frameworks. Nevertheless, politics drives agency missions, structure, budgets, human resource policies, and many other facets of public administration. Sufficient stability in bureaucratic politics with respect to the distribution of costs and benefits and the structure of policy arenas enables these two frameworks to retain considerable and continuing explanatory power.

Conclusion

So what is public about the public sector? Looking through the lenses of management, politics, and law one can observe a number of attributes that, *taken as a whole*, differentiate the public context from everything else in society. Public managers run constitutions. This requires them to coordinate the separation of powers and federalism. It subordinates and places them in the joint custody of legislatures, chief executives, and the judiciary. Administrative law also regulates how they run their constitutions by infusing public administration with democratic-constitutional values including accountability, representativeness, participation, transparency, and due process. These and other values such as environmental justice and sustainability are mission extrinsic for most agencies most of the time when mission is defined as achieving the core objectives for which agencies were created. If mission is conceptualized more broadly, such as running a constitution, then perhaps with some exceptions, they would be viewed as intrinsic to appropriate performance (Rosenbloom 2007).

The constitutional law of public employment, which guarantees those working in the public sector first amendment, due process, and fourth amendment rights that set them apart from private-sector employees, exemplifies how a broad vision of agency mission could incorporate a wide range of public values. The term "at will employment" is a misnomer in the public sector, as McPherson's case makes clear, because curtailing the rights of a large segment of the population, such as public employees, is troublesome in a regime that partly defines itself as an exemplar and guarantor of human rights.

Additionally, because the public sector largely operates where markets cannot or do not function well, its revenues predominantly come from public budgets rather than profits. Where there is a mandate for universal service, as in answering FOIA requests, neither can public agencies use marginal costs as a guide to expanding or contracting services. Such mandates are driven by politics, not markets, as James Q. Wilson's and Theodore Lowi's frameworks help make clear.

It is possible to find private-sector functional equivalents to some of these public-sector attributes in some private-sector organizations; it may even be possible to find equivalents to all of them in a few such organizations. However, to one degree or another they are inherent in all public-sector organizations. That does not mean that Sayre's inference is correct: public and private organizations can be similar in *some important* respects. Taking a cue from Appleby, however, it is sufficient to conclude that the public context is different.

References

Aberbach, Joel, and Bert Rockman. 2000. *The Web of Politics*. Washington, DC: Brookings Institution.

Acquisition Central. N.d. "Federal Acquisition Regulation (FAR)." https://acquisition.gov/far/ (accessed July 8, 2014).

Adarand Constructors v. Pena. 1995. 515 U.S. 200.

Allison, Graham. 1979/2012. "Public and Private Management: Are They Fundamentally Alike in All Unimportant Respects?" In *Classics of Public Administration*, ed. Jay Shafritz and Albert Hyde, 395–411. Boston: Wadsworth.

Appleby, Paul. 1945. *Big Democracy*. New York: A.A. Knopf.

Assessment of Federal Regulations and Policies on Families Act of 1998. 1998. PL 105–277. 112 Stat. 2681. 5 U.S.C. 601.

Baehler, Karen, Chengcheng (Aviva) Liu, and David H. Rosenbloom. 2014. "Mission-Extrinsic Public Values as an Extension of Regime Values: Examples from the United States and the People's Republic of China." *Administration & Society* 46(2): 199–219.

Ban, Carolyn. 1995. *How Do Public Managers Manage?* San Francisco: Jossey-Bass.

Board of County Commissioners, Wabaunsee County v. Umbehr. 1996. 518 U.S. 668.

Borcherding, Thomas. 1977. *Budgets and Bureaucrats*. Durham, NC: Duke University Press.

Bozeman, Barry. 1987. *All Organizations Are Public*. San Francisco: Jossey-Bass.

Chayes, Abram. 1976. "The Role of the Judge in Public Law Litigation." *Harvard Law Review* 89(7): 1281–1316.

City of Ontario, California v. Quon. 2010. 560 U.S. 746.

Cramton, Roger. 1976. "Judicial Lawmaking and Administration in the Leviathan State." *Public Administration Review* 36(September/October): 551–555.

Elmore, Richard. 1979–1980. "Backward Mapping." *Political Science Quarterly* 94(4): 601–616.

Executive Order 13514. 2009. 74 U.S. Federal Register 52117.

Foerstel, Herbert. 1999. *Freedom of Information and the Right to Know: The Origins and Application of the Freedom of Information Act*. Westport, CT: Greenwood Press.

FOIA.gov. N.d. www.foia.gov (accessed July 8, 2014).

Freedom of Information Act of 1966. 1966. PL 89–487. 80 Stat. 250. 5 U.S.C. 552.

Garcetti v. Ceballos. 2006. 547 U.S. 410.

Grant, Daniel, and H.C. Nixon. 1975. *State and Local Government in America*, 3rd ed. Boston: Allyn & Bacon.

Grodzins, Morton. 1960. "The Federal System." In *Goals for Americans*, ed. The American Assembly, 265–282. Englewood Cliffs, NJ: Prentice-Hall.

Kaufman, Herbert. 1981. *The Administrative Behavior of Federal Bureau Chiefs*. Washington, DC: Brookings Institution.

Kerwin, Corneilus. 2003. *Rulemaking*, 3rd ed. Washington, DC: CQ Press.

Key, V.O. Jr. 1940. "The Lack of a Budgetary Theory." *American Political Science Review* 34(December): 1137–1140.

Lasswell, Harold. 1958. *Politics: Who Gets What, When, How*. Cleveland: World Publishing.

Lipsky, Michael. 1980. *Street-Level Bureaucracy*. New York: Russell Sage Foundation.

Long, Norton. 1949. "Power and Administration." *Public Administration Review* 9(Autumn): 257–264.

Lowi, Theodore J. 1964. "Distribution, Regulation, Redistribution: The Functions of Government." In *Classic Readings in American Politics*, 3rd ed., ed. Pietro S. Nivola and David H. Rosenbloom, 571–581. New York: St. Martin's/Worth.

Maynard-Moody, Steven, and Michael Musheno. 2003. *Cops, Teachers, Counselors*. Ann Arbor: University of Michigan Press.

Meriam, Lewis. 1939. *Reorganization of the National Government: Part I: An Analysis of the Problem*. Washington, DC: Brookings Institution.

Morgan, Douglas, Kelly Bacon, Ron Bunch, Charles Cameron, and Robert Deis. 1996. "What Middle Managers Do in Local Government." *Public Administration Review* 56(July/August): 359–366.

Morgan v. Kerrigan. 1975. 401 F. Supp. 216.

Morrison v. Olson. 1988. 487 U.S. 654.

National Conference of State Legislatures. 2010. "State Whistleblower Laws." November. www.ncsl.org/research/labor-and-employment/state-whistleblower-laws.aspx (accessed July 8, 2014).

National Environmental Policy Act of 1969. 1970. PL 91–190. 83 Stat. 852. 42 U.S.C. 4321 et seq.

National Treasury Union Employees v. Von Raab. 1989. 489 U.S. 656.

O'Connor v. Ortega. 1987. 480 U.S. 709.

O'Hare Truck Service, Inc. v. City of Northlake. 1996. 518 U.S. 712.

O'Leary, Rosemary. 2006. *The Ethics of Dissent: Managing Guerilla Government.* Washington, DC: CQ Press.

Openness Promotes Effectiveness in Our National Government Act of 2007. 2007. PL 110–175. 121 Stat. 2524. 5 U.S. C. 552.

Owen v. City of Independence. 1980. 445 U.S. 622.

Perry, James L., and Lois Recascino Wise. 1990. "The Motivational Bases of Public Service." *Public Administration Review* 50(May/June): 367–373.

Pickering v. Board of Education. 1968. 391 U.S. 563.

Piotrowski, Suzanne J., and David H. Rosenbloom. 2002. "Nonmission-Based Values in Results-Oriented Public Management: The Case of Freedom of Information." *Public Administration Review* 62(November/December): 643–657.

Rankin v. McPherson. 1987. 483 U.S. 387.

Ricci v. DeStefano. 2009. 557 U.S. 557.

Riccucci, Norma. 1995. *Unsung Heroes.* Washington, DC: Georgetown University Press.

Rohr, John A. 1978. *Ethics for Bureaucrats.* New York: Marcel Dekker.

———. 1986. *To Run a Constitution.* Lawrence, KS: University Press of Kansas.

Rosenbloom, David H. 1983. "Public Administrative Theory and the Separation of Powers." *Public Administration Review* 43(May/June): 219–227.

———. 2001. "'Whose Bureaucracy Is This, Anyway?' Congress' 1946 Answer." *PS: Political Science and Politics* 34(December): 773–777.

———. 2007. "Reinventing Administrative Prescriptions: The Case for Democratic-Constitutional Impact Statements and Scorecards." *Public Administration Review* 67(January/February): 28–39.

———. 2014a. *Administrative Law for Public Managers*, 2nd ed. Boulder, CO: Westview.

———. 2014b. *Federal Service and the Constitution*, 2nd ed. Washington, DC: Georgetown University Press.

———, Rosemary O'Leary, and Joshua Chanin. 2010. *Public Administration and Law*, 3rd ed. Boca Raton, FL: CRC/Taylor & Francis.

Rourke, Francis. 1993. "Whose Bureaucracy Is This, Anyway? Congress, the President, and Public Administration." *PS: Political Science and Politics* 26(December): 687–692.

Rutan v. Republican Party of Illinois. 1990. 497 U.S. 62.

Sayre, Wallace S. 1958. "Premises of Public Administration: Past and Emerging." *Public Administration Review* 18(2): 102–105.

United States v. Virginia. 1996. 518 U.S. 515.

U.S. Civil Service Commission v. National Association of Letter Carriers. 1973. 413 U.S. 548.

Wildavsky, Aaron. 1984. *The Politics of the Budgetary Process*, 4th ed. Boston: Little, Brown.

Willoughby, W.F. 1927. *Principles of Public Administration.* Washington, DC: Brookings Institution.

——. 1934. *Principles of Legislative Organization and Administration*. Washington, DC: Brookings Institution.

Wilson, James Q. 1980. "The Politics of Regulation." In *The Politics of Regulation*, ed. James Q. Wilson, chapter 10. New York: Basic Books.

Wilson, Woodrow. 1887/2012. "The Study of Administration." In *Classics of Public Administration*, ed. Jay Shafritz and Albert Hyde, 16–28. Boston: Wadsworth.

Wood, Robert and Clement Vose. 1990. *Remedial Law*. Amherst, MA: University of Massachusetts Press.

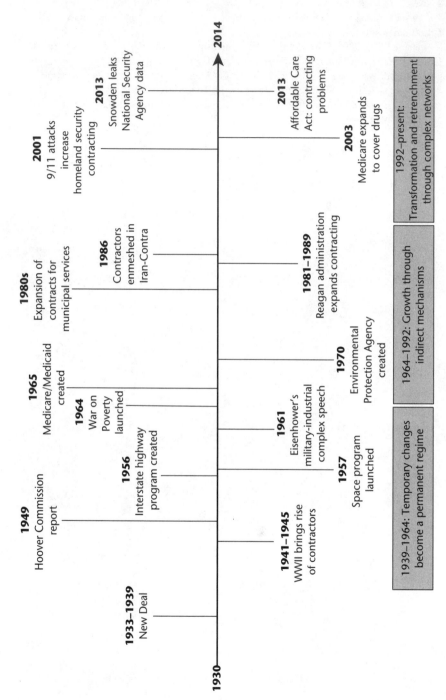

FIGURE 2.1 From Intergovernmental to Intersectoral: Benchmarks across Time

2

FROM INTERGOVERNMENTAL TO INTERSECTORAL

Donald F. Kettl

As the American Society for Public Administration (ASPA) was beginning to take shape in the 1930s, public administration had a sharp and clear focus. In 1933, one of the field's early giants, Leonard D. White (and its president from 1947–1948) set out to identify "trends in public administration." One chapter boldly titled "The New Management" quoted Maine Governor William T. Gardiner's view of "the contemporary philosophy of administrative organization," an approach that White said was "now broadly accepted and applied" at all levels of government. Gardiner's snapshot of the field in the mid-1930s captured the cutting edge of theory and practice:

> The principles that underlie any plan of administrative reorganization to meet these problems are: first, that there shall be consolidation and integration in a few orderly departments of similar functions of government; second, that there shall be fixed and definite responsibility for all governmental activities; third, that there should be proper coordination of terms of administrative officials in order that government may function harmoniously; fourth, that administrative responsibility can better be centered in a single individual than in a board . . . States have tried many elaborate schemes for improving their governments, but within the last decade have decided to try simple, direct, responsible government; and the verdict is that the more simple and direct, the more successful it has been.
>
> *(White 1933, 144)*

Simple, direct, and responsible: public administration at the time of ASPA's founding was about logical efficiency. Sort out government's functions and organize them in individual agencies; put one person in charge of each one;

ensure coordination among related functions. Structure was king, and getting it right was the key both to efficiency and accountability. Public administration had a sense of maturity about it. There was a strong sense that the big questions were on the table, and that the key was getting the answers right.

Big crises, however, soon intervened to undermine this sense of settled questions. The Great Depression brought the federal government into unprecedented intervention into what previously had been state and local government activities. Millions of dollars flowed into local communities to put people back to work and to build new public works. New streets and highways sprang up around the country. New York City got new bridges and tunnels. New highways and bridges connected the Florida Keys to the mainland. New city halls, libraries, and schools were constructed, often with remarkable works of art inside that remain a lasting legacy. Intergovernmental relations became *fiscal* relations. Federalism was transformed, with a growing sense that the federal government not only could but also should become involved in what previously had been state and local activities, and that state and local governments often could not rise to the challenges they faced without federal help.

Then, just a couple of years after ASPA's founding, the United States found itself in the midst of a two-front world war. The war not only marked a turning point for America's role in the world but it also fundamentally changed the role of public administration. The war-fighting effort brought an enormous expansion of federal spending, much of which flowed through private defense contractors who provided the planes, ships, equipment, and supplies to win the war.

The United States found itself with a far larger government, with growing ambitions, and an administrative state that was increasingly intertwined among levels of government and between government and the private sector. If it was hard to characterize what government had become, it was simple to describe what it was not. Public administration had drifted far from the "simple and direct" world of theory and practice that Gardiner had described. Gardiner's contention about government was that "the verdict is that the more simple and direct, the more successful it has been." Government became more complex and indirect, taking on more and bigger challenges and managing them across multiple governmental and sectoral boundaries. Structure was no longer king. That framed a big question: Has government's departure from public administration's roots made it less successful? And is it less responsible—both in terms of efficient use of scarce resources and accountability to the people? The bridge from ASPA's founding to its seventy-fifth anniversary charts some of the biggest puzzles facing American government.

Bigger Challenges, More Boundaries

In the immediate aftermath of World War II, public administration seemed destined to settle back to its pre-war puzzles. American government certainly had changed, but the basic questions seemed the same. President Harry Truman appointed former president Herbert Hoover to lead a top-to-bottom look at the federal government's operations, and he came back with sweeping recommendations. It was, Ferrel Heady (ASPA president from 1969–1970) wrote at the time, "the most extensive study ever made of the problem of executive reorganization in the federal government" (1949, 355). The Hoover Commission in 1949 made the case for performance budgeting, modernization of the civil service, reorganization of the executive departments, and strengthening the office of the president. Gardiner would have quickly recognized the main themes. That would scarcely be surprising, since White and many of the field's most distinguished figures helped shape the Commission's work. The first Hoover Commission proved remarkably successful—Congress and the administration implemented about three-fourths of its recommendations—and a second Hoover Commission followed a few years later.

Even as public administrationists celebrated the Commission's success, the governmental world was quickly eating away at its foundations. The basic questions of organization, structure, process, and responsibility remained just as important. But the standard approach to public administration relied heavily on drawing and maintaining boundaries: between functions, governmental organizations, levels of government, and the public and private sectors. It created processes to reinforce and manage those boundaries, and it imagined strong leaders who ensured efficiency. Those were the foundations of responsible government, but even as the Hoover Commissions marked the high-water line of that approach, its foundations were eroding. These changes grew out of a profound pragmatism: Americans wanted to grow public programs without growing their governmental apparatus. The nation's administrative strategies evolved through three stages, in roughly equal segments over the next seventy-five years, which transformed the American administrative state and posed huge challenges for the fundamental work of public administration.

1939–1964: Temporary Changes Become a Permanent Regime

The Roosevelt administration, of course, did not set out to transform public administration through its war-fighting strategy. Neither did the Truman and Eisenhower administrations plan on permanent changes to the administrative state by the new programs launched to manage the transition from the world war to peacetime expansion. But in a host of ways, the temporary tactics launched during World War II morphed into a long-term strategy that transformed American public administration.

Dwight Waldo's 1948 classic, *The Administrative State*, touched only briefly on the expansion of government into the private sector. State and local governments appeared principally as part of his broader exploration on centralization and decentralization. It was "scientific management" that preoccupied his look forward (p. 201). However, he did recognize that "these days of crisis and confusion" could lead to an erosion of the orthodoxy that had dominated the field for forty years. He concluded the book by wondering "if the demands of present world civilization on public administration are met, administrative thought must establish a working relationship with every major province in the realm of human learning" (p. 203).

And that is precisely what happened in the post-war years. The intense but secret effort to build a nuclear weapon continued in the race to ensure that the Soviet Union did not create more powerful weapons that would destabilize an uneasy peace. Then came the puzzle of how best to create delivery systems for the weapons that could not be taken out in a surprise attack. World War II's bombers evolved into jet-powered aircraft such as the B–52. Submarines became underwater launch vehicles. And the space race was not only a contest to see who could first put a man into space but also a battle for supremacy in quick-launch weapon-delivery systems. All of these efforts cemented the government's vast partnerships with private contractors, which had emerged during the war. So important and powerful had these partnerships become that Dwight Eisenhower, the general-then-president, warned: "In the councils of government, we must guard against the acquisition of unwarranted influence, whether sought or unsought, by the military-industrial complex" (Eisenhower 1961). Historians have parsed this speech in the decades since, but one point is clear: in the years since the start of World War II, government's relationship with the private sector had grown into a large and imposing force with implications for democracy that stretched far beyond the orthodoxy of public administration.

At a bit slower pace, the federal government's relationship with state and local governments changed just as fundamentally (Graves 1964). As the nation built the peacetime economy of the 1950s, the federal government provided substantial support to tear down large parts of many cities in the birth of urban renewal. It provided 90 percent of the funds for a new interstate highway system. State governments found it irresistible to buy new roads at ten cents on the dollar. The federal government justified the investment as a way to promote high-quality transportation and to help serve the nation's defense needs, including evacuating cities in case of attack, though the civilian case for the roads was vastly more important.

By the mid-1960s, the case for federal investment through intergovernmental grants, in what had previously been primarily state and local functions, was firmly established. There was an underlying sense of paternalism in these grants: the federal government would help and encourage state and local governments do what they could not or would not do on their own. These grants, coupled with the rise of government's contracting with the private sector, fundamentally changed the theory and practice of public administration. The movement was more tactical than strategic. These tools were pragmatic rather than ideological, and government relied on them to solve problems rather than change philosophy (Salamon 2002). In fact, much of the pre-war administrative orthodoxy remained uneasily in place, even as the practice of public administration grew further out of sync with its underlying theory. This mismatch strained the field's intellectual foundations, and it helped fuel the growth of new schools of public policy that tried to directly attack the big problems of poverty, the environment, and international affairs that were becoming ever more sharply defined. Wartime problem solving became the base for post-war government programs, especially through grants and contracts. The practice evolved much quicker than the theoretical foundations supporting it.

1964–1992: Growth through Indirect Mechanisms

That first post-war era set the stage for an even more expansive role for government. In the 1960s, the Johnson administration launched a War on Poverty, a new health care program for older Americans in Medicare, and another new health care program for poorer Americans in Medicaid. In the Nixon administration, the space program put a man on the moon and started a new shuttle program. A new era of environmental protection began, through grants, government regulations, and cleanup programs. Nixon transformed domestic programs by launching a general revenue sharing program and new block grants in functions such as health, community development, and job training to give state and local governments more flexibility in spending federal funds. Government grew, but most of its growth came through indirect tools relying heavily on state and local governments and the private sector.

But this era saw both the high water mark of government's growth as well as a fundamental shift in government's strategy. The founding of the federal Environmental Protection Agency in 1970 not only increased the government's regulatory reach but it also created a new network of contractors to clean up toxic waste sites around the country. In 1978, the growth in federal general-purpose grants to state and local governments ended. Even more important, in the late 1980s federal grants for payments to individuals—mostly for Medicaid—exceeded all other grants and continued its stratospheric growth (see Figure 2.2). This, in turn, is a two-part tale. First, federal aid became a two-track system, with flat expenditures for the traditional programs that began in the 1930s and rapidly rising spending for Medicaid. Second, Medicaid itself became embedded in a network of contracts with the private sector. The federal government gave grants to the states for the program. The states, in turn, contracted with private-sector fiscal intermediaries to manage the program by overseeing the payment systems to non-governmental hospitals, nursing homes, physicians, and other service providers. Medicare grew in the same pattern, without state governments serving in an additional intermediary role. For the most part, Medicaid grew into a privately provided, privately managed, and publicly funded health care system.

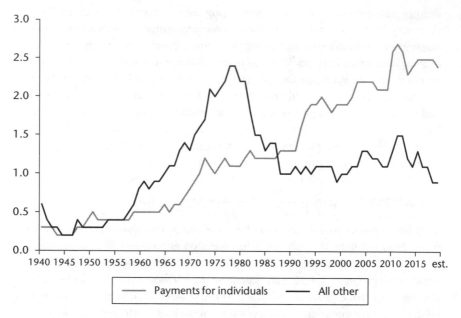

FIGURE 2.2 Trends in Federal Grants

Source: Table 12.1 from U.S. OMB 2013.

A pair of statistics, in fact, captures the transformation of this period. By fiscal year 2014, Medicare and Medicaid amounted to 18 percent of all federal outlays but the federal agency that managed the programs, the Centers for Medicare and Medicaid Services, accounted for just 0.22 percent of all federal civilian employees.[1] In no other part of the federal government do individual employees proportionately have that much leverage over that much money. It's little wonder that the famous citizen complaint to "keep your government hands off my Medicare" (Krugman 2009) has gotten such traction over the years. Most people didn't see government's hands on one of its biggest programs because private-sector providers worked the front lines and managed the flow of cash. Government's role is largely as funder, with private-sector and state-government partners responsible for making the two giant programs work.

The tactics were also, in part, ideological. The privatization movement began in earnest toward the end of the 1970s, and there was a growing belief in the power of privatization and contracting out (Savas 1982). In 1984, President Reagan launched his Private Sector Survey on Cost Control, more popularly known as the Grace Commission. Its report had 2,478 recommendations and concluded that the federal government could save more than $424 billion in just three years by using more businesslike practices, cutting programs, and contracting out more of government (Grace Commission 1984). Perhaps the most pointed attack on government itself came in a *Wall Street Journal* op-ed written by Terry W. Culler (1986), a former senior official in the federal government's own Office of Personnel Management—the agency charged with hiring employees to do the government's work. His article, entitled "Most Federal Workers Need Only Be Competent," argued that the government "should be content to lure competent people, not the best and most talented people. A good case can be made that those individuals are needed in the private sector where wealth is produced rather than consumed." But some of the expansion came for purely pragmatic reasons, including the use of private contractors during the Reagan administration to facilitate the trading of arms for hostages in Iran and arming rebels in Nicaragua.

The first era ended with a celebration of the government's role and a substantial expansion of its activities, but with grants and contracts the wheels on which that expansion rode. In the second era, government's role continued to grow. So did the importance of grants, especially for Medicaid, and contracts, to manage Medicare and Medicaid, to provide pragmatic flexibility, and to pursue the deep-seated belief in many quarters that government's role should be as small as possible and, where it did have a role, it should be pursued through private contracts. Much of government's blue-collar workforce, from janitors to cafeteria workers, was contracted out. So too were mechanics and security guards, to the point that private security guards protected some of the most dangerous material on earth—plutonium waste—behind high fences at the facilities—run by private contractors—that made nuclear bombs. Government's role might have grown, but support from many public officials for the job shrank. A cover of ideology grew over the pragmatism that drove the rising role of grants and contracts.

1992–Present: Transformation and Retrenchment through Complex Networks

In the third era, almost anything that could be contracted out *was* contracted out, at least some place at some time. State and local governments vastly expanded their contracting for social service programs, garbage collection, information technology (IT) and data processing, and public works, water, and sewer projects. Some communities contracted out their libraries and franchised fire protection, to the point that on occasion firefighters arrived on the scene of the fire but refused to put it out because the resident had not paid a fire protection fee. When he was mayor of Indianapolis, Steven Goldsmith (1999) created the "yellow pages test." He argued that if a service performed by the government could be found in the yellow pages, then it could be contracted out. From that base, many privatization advocates argued that if it *could* be contracted out, it *should* be. At the federal level, contracting out expanded significantly. In the post-September 11 world, the federal government vastly increased security, but most of the new security guards were private contractors.

All in all, it was hard to find an area of government untouched by grants and contracts. The government still engaged in a great deal of direct service provision, especially at the state and local level. Even at the federal level, forest rangers continued to patrol and analysts at the Centers for Disease Control continued to track the spread of flu. But especially with the spreading importance of IT to support the management of most parts of government, and with government's overwhelming reliance of private contractors for IT support, contracting affected every part of government—including intergovernmental grants. Management of complex networks increasingly became an essential part of managing government (Kettl 2009a).

The rise of these indirect tools, coupled with the rapid growth of spending for entitlement programs (which, themselves, required heavy reliance on grants and contracts), led to big changes in the nature of government's work. One measure is the index of just how much of the federal budget has been leveraged, on average, by each employee. Consider Figure 2.3, which charts federal government spending (in millions of constant 2005 dollars, which takes account of inflation) per employee. In the twenty-five years since 1980, each employee was responsible for twice as much money, even after allowing for inflation. How did this occur? More federal employees were responsible not for managing programs but for managing proxies who managed programs on the government's behalf (Kettl 1988). Some of this came through transfer payments such as Social Security, but much came through the rise of indirect mechanisms such as contracts in which federal employees were responsible for increasingly larger programs. The gulf between these two approaches grew—and so did the gap between traditional public administration theory and the strategies needed to manage these proxies well.

The United States was not the only nation to rely more on these indirect tools. Even in countries that had championed direct government in the welfare state, government outsourcing grew significantly in the 2000s (see Figure 2.4). Outsourcing grew by more than 40 percent in Finland, the Netherlands, and Great Britain. Denmark and Belgium joined the United States at about a 30 percent increase. Indeed, together with the emergence of enormous fiscal stress, this was one of the most important public administration movements of the era. These complex networks did not *replace* traditional administration. In all countries, direct service delivery remained extremely important, as did the administrative approaches that Governor Gardiner championed. Rather, the complex networks became layered atop and marbled throughout the administrative state. This movement not only wove government administration through all levels of government but also throughout a vast swath of the nongovernmental sector, as private and nonprofit organizations increasingly became part of the governmental apparatus. Even China is confronting the vast and surprising rise of partnerships with civil society (Florini, Lai, and Tan, 2012).

At least in the United States, this third era was less the culmination of an historical trend than an uneasy equilibrium among competing forces. On the

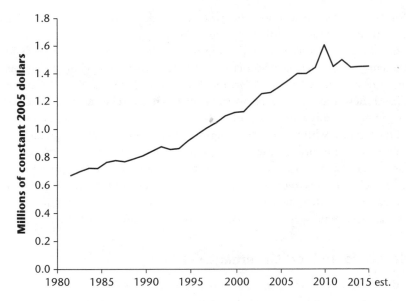

FIGURE 2.3 Leverage Index: Millions of Constant 2005 Dollars Per Federal
Employee

Source: Calculated from U.S. OMB 2013.

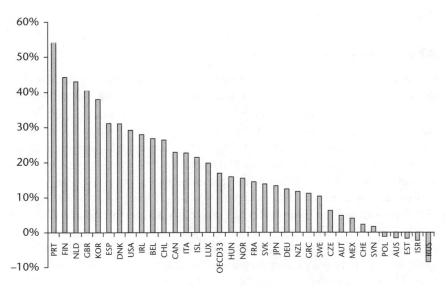

FIGURE 2.4 Change in Government Outsourcing: 2000–2009

Source: OECD 2011.

one hand, it was simultaneously the triumph of the movement to privatize government and restrain its growth through a heavy reliance on nongovernmental partners, especially through contracting out. It also was the maturing of the government's social safety net in a complex network of interlocking programs that relied heavily on federalism (Marmor, Mashaw, and Pakutka 2014). On the other hand, new arguments were bubbling up from the states to transform the system, yet again—this time by devolving programs back to the states in a new era of block grants, with the federal government providing funds and giving the states substantial authority to structure programs as they saw best. This movement struggled to get traction because the implications, both for state budgets and for the programs' recipients, were large and very uncertain. But the future of programs ranging from Medicaid and other health care initiatives to food stamps and other social welfare programs was anything but clear (Donahue 1997).

Challenges for Indirect Governance

Amid these ideological and pragmatic debates, one thing did seem certain: the future of American public administration would rest in an uneasy alliance of complex public–private–nonprofit/federal–state–local networks, layered atop the more traditional patterns of administrative orthodoxy that dominated the field through World War II. The orthodoxy had the unquestioned advantage of setting clear boundaries to focus administrative energy and to ensure administrative accountability. The strategies of indirect governance blurred both these boundaries. They required new administrative skills and created new challenges for securing accountability.

What Should Government Do?

In the years since World War II, American government has established that almost anything *can* be contracted out. If it could be, it should be, came the argument, from both ideologues and pragmatists. The "yellow pages test" reinforced the notion, especially since private-sector firms proved especially inventive in creating new products if government showed any interest in buying them. Over recent decades, we have seen the potential for turnkey government—government programs handed over to private contractors—with a skeleton staff of public officials to provide oversight. For example, Weston, Florida, has a population of 65,000 persons and just nine employees. The city's mayor, Eric Hersh, managed a budget of $121 million and relied on thirty-five different contracts to supply everything from code enforcement and public works to building permits and custodial services. Broward County supplies police and fire protection under a contract. The contract workforce was 285 full-time equivalent employees in 2012, who act like city workers but have no civil service protection. Weston's reliance on contracting has been going on for decades. In 2007, the city increased the number of employees from three to nine, but its public workforce remains thin: a city manager, two assistant city managers, the city treasurer, a communications director, the directors of three departments—parks and recreation, public works, and landscaping—and the city clerk. City manager John Flint acknowledges that the city has never done a systematic cost comparison, but he argued, "I'm not managing people." Rather, "I'm actually managing the city. How do you put a price on that?" (Holeywell 2012).

But that begs the question of what capacity government needs to manage its affairs properly. If virtually anything can be contracted out, what capacity does the government need to keep in-house? Consider the case of Edward Snowden, a former analyst for the National Security Agency (NSA) whose massive leaks of highly classified secrets caused enormous foreign policy problems in 2013. Snowden, in fact, had not been an employee of the NSA; he was an employee of the private firm Booz Allen Hamilton for fewer than three months, working in Hawaii thousands of miles from NSA headquarters in Ft. Meade, Maryland. He had a "top secret" security clearance. The background investigation for the clearance was conducted by USIS, itself a contractor to the federal government—that is, employees of one private company conducted a background investigation of the employee of another private company to determine whether he ought to have access to the most sensitive secrets in the government. The episode proved how exceptionally vulnerable the government is to the performance of its interlocking network of contractors.

Government needs the core capacity to make, enforce, and administer governmental decisions (Kettl 1993) But the federal government has also long recognized the value of contracting out. In 1954, the Eisenhower administration established a policy that "the federal government will not start or carry on any commercial activity to provide a service or product for its own use if such product or service can be procured from private enterprise through ordinary business channels" (U.S. Bureau of the Budget 1955). Over the succeeding decades, presidents of both parties have reinforced the policy.

But this process, enshrined in succeeding versions of the Office of Management and Budget (OMB) Circular A-76, leaves two big questions unanswered. First, the policy aims at turning over to private contractors any work they can do more cheaply. On what basis should cost comparisons be made? Comparisons have often been haphazard and have frequently struggled to balance short-term buy-in costs with long-term costs of providing goods and services. Moreover, they became engulfed in conflict over different levels of benefits provided to government and private-sector workers. Second, the policy prohibited contracting out "inherently governmental functions," but it has never precisely defined what is "inherently governmental." The Federal Acquisition Regulations (n.d.) state: "Contracts shall not be used for the performance of inherently governmental functions." Following the prohibition is a series of examples, including conducting criminal investigations, conducting foreign relations, determining agency policy, directing and controlling intelligence operations, and controlling federal employees.

Students of public administration will recognize in this puzzle the familiar policy–administration dichotomy with which the field has been wrestling for twice the length of ASPA's history. Woodrow Wilson tried to tackle the problem by arguing that accountable and effective administration relied on separating policy making from policy administration (1887). This same logic has carried forward to the "inherently governmental" problem: government should do those things that only government can properly do on behalf of its people, and the rest can be contracted out. It should be little surprise that such a deeply rooted puzzle continues to pose big problems in public administration—and that it frames one of the fundamental problems for contracting out of government services. What can and should be contracted out? Anything that the private sector can do more cost-effectively than government itself—except for those functions that cut to government's core role. And what is government's core role? We are no closer to defining it clearly than was Wilson. And the implications? As the U.S. Government Accountability Office (GAO) pointed out:

> While there are benefits to using contractors to perform services for the government, our prior work has shown that reliance on contractors to support core missions can place the government at risk of becoming overly reliant on contractors to perform [jobs] closely associated with inherently governmental functions or creating circumstances in which contractors perform functions deemed inherently governmental. Over the past decade, our work has also identified the need for DOD [Department of Defense] to obtain better data on its contracted services to enable it to make more strategic decisions. While DOD has begun a number of efforts to gain better insight into its acquisition of services, these efforts have had mixed success to date.
>
> *(US GAO 2013a, 1)*

Some questions from public administration's long history continue to endure, sometimes in surprising new shapes and forms.

Who Does Government Need to Do its Work?

Closely related is the problem of human capital—the skills that government employees need to do the work that only they can do. The complex indirect systems of grants and contracts have been layered atop more traditional administrative approaches. To manage this system, government workers need the traditional skill sets—but the indirect systems also need skills that allow them to manage boundaries. Moreover, because the indirect systems leverage so much money, failures to align the skill sets with the jobs to be done can have even more far-reaching consequences. Indeed, that was a central if subtle lesson of the

2013 rollout of the Affordable Care Act by the federal government and in many of the states. Websites failed and citizens found they could not enroll because the IT systems had not been well-managed. They were not well-managed because government leaders did not adequately steer the contractors responsible for actually doing the work. Sometimes there was no one at the wheel; at other times, the managers behind the wheel did not have the technical capacity to oversee the work being done.

The problem is so serious that the GAO has long identified human capital as one of its "high-risk" issues that threaten substantial performance problems in government. As the GAO (2013b, 99) pointed out: "Strategic human capital planning that is integrated with broader organizational strategic planning is essential for ensuring that agencies have the talent, skill, and experience mix they need to cost-effectively execute their mission and program goals." Compounding the problem is the coming retirement wave, as many governmental Baby Boomers retire. Governments at all levels not only must hire new workers to replace the retirees but also must pivot to recruit workers with mission-critical skills. The GAO's list includes IT managers, cybersecurity specialists, auditors, human resource specialists, contract specialists, economists, and science-technology-engineering-math specialists. Put differently, the GAO concludes that government needs experts who understand the high technical issues surrounding many governmental programs, who can create and oversee the indirect tools (especially contracting) on which the government increasingly depends, and who can check that the money is spent well. In short, it is an even more urgent statement of the smart-buyer problem: knowing what government wants to buy, buying it well, and ensuring that it gets what it pays for (Kettl 1993).

How Can We Track What Government Does?

This puts increased focus on IT. IT has become the central nervous system for much of what government does. For directly managed programs such as police, fire, and education, information systems are increasingly important for tracking performance. For indirect tools such as grants and contracts, such systems are essential. Indeed, the corollary of government through leveraged action is tracking and managing that leverage through information systems. As Jane Fountain (2001) pointed out at the dawn of the Internet age, not only is IT essential for understanding the modern function of the state but also that "[i]nstitutional theory has not accounted for information technology and its multifaceted role in changing the contours of the landscape within which rules and structure influence perception and action" (p. 193). Indeed, IT is both more important to public administration theory than the theory often recognizes, and it is more essential to the practice of public administration than its application comprehends.

The movement has spread into versions of performance-stat, with sophisticated tracking systems linking administrative activity with policy results

(Behn 2014). In government's indirect tools, it has become a two-headed issue. One is that IT is the only way of tracking the vast and interconnected networks responsible for so many of government's important programs, from defense and space to national security and transportation. The less government does directly, the more it needs a system to know what its proxies do. The other is that the management of IT systems has itself become a central problem for governments at all levels. Beyond the 2013 Affordable Care Act debacle, the federal government has suffered multi-billion dollar failures in modernizing systems in the Internal Revenue Service and the Federal Bureau of Investigation. In Los Angeles, a new $59 million computer billing system produced thousands of erroneous bills. California struggled for a decade, and spent more than a quarter of a billion dollars, but failed in its effort to update the state payroll system. Pennsylvania spent $45 million to update its computer system for processing workers' compensation, but problems delayed checks to hundreds of workers. In Massachusetts, a new online unemployment tracking system was two years late and $6 million over budget, and still produced problems for the benefits going to hundreds of workers. In addition to a bias toward large, custom-built systems,

> [w]e also do a poor job choosing contractors, as the Deloitte example makes clear. Our risk-averse purchasing rules favor large companies willing to navigate complex bidding processes, even if newer, more nimble firms can do the work more cheaply. And state government doesn't have enough managers with the technical expertise to craft and manage these contracts properly. We end up buying features we don't need, and we lack the flexibility to learn as we go.
>
> *(Threadgill 2013)*

Technology is a foremost manifestation of the modern state, and it weaves together triple issues. It provides the information without which leveraging grants and contracts would be impossible. It poses enormous human capital challenges, and without solving them the systems are prone to program failure and cost overruns. And it is among the foremost tools to advance accountability. If these elements fail to work in concert, the result can be policy failure, wasted funds, and lost accountability. Tackling each of these requires different strategies and tactics underlying the fundamental traditions of American public administration, and it is here that the need exists to layer new approaches atop the traditional ones for government to succeed.

Flattened Bureaucracy

Since the beginning of complex organizations, both theory and practice have always had both vertical and horizontal elements. The vertical pieces focus on control and accountability through the chain of command, while the horizontal ones concentrate on coordination. High-performing organizations require a seamless integration of both elements. In the first era explored in this chapter, the vertical elements were primary. Governor Gardiner, for example, focused on simple, direct government in the steady hand of a single, focused administrator. He talked a great deal about coordination, but his focus was on the coordinator who exercised authority because of the coordinator's place in the bureaucracy.

That vertical dimension remains just as important in the third—and subsequent—eras. If the practice of public administration teaches us anything, it is that some issues are eternal, and nothing is more fundamental to a bureaucracy than the essential role of a strong, effective leader. Indeed, when Max Weber explained his "ideal types"—that is, the fundamentals of complex organizations—he focused on the role of authority in the hands of a leader to separate bureaucracy from traditional and charismatic forms of organization (Weber 1958). Today, Governor Gardiner would certainly recognize many of the basic problems of public administration and their roots in the primarily vertical world he described. The puzzles, practices, and theories of the first era remain just as powerful in the twenty-first century.

What Governor Gardiner would not recognize, and what fundamentally distinguishes the third era from the first, is the enormous expansion of grants and contracts—and the rise of vastly complicated horizontal questions. Those questions, as we have seen, require robust vertical authority, with the strong capacity to exercise government's most fundamental responsibilities. Failing to do so risks serious consequences, ranging from the vast leakage of highly sensitive documents from private contractors such as Edward Snowden to the staggering launch of the Affordable Care Act. Government has become far more horizontally constructed. Indeed, one of the enduring themes of the second and third eras has been the growth of government, but its most explosive growth has come through more interweaving of government, its programs, its tools, and its funds into the private and nonprofit sectors. That, in turn, means that government's growth—and its growing administrative puzzles—has increasingly been horizontal. The rise of grants and contracts means that government's vertical functions need stronger horizontal leverage.

Public administration, in short, has gotten flatter. Without shrinking government's vertical dimensions, it requires more interconnection with its partners at other levels of government and in other sectors of society. That, in turn, poses a fundamental challenge for traditional administrative orthodoxy. These horizontal dimensions hinge on bargaining, financial oversight, acquisitions management, political leadership, and new variants in public law that Governor Gardiner could scarcely have foreseen. In some cases, as the GAO described, the steps needed are clear but sometimes hard to implement. In other cases, especially in framing new dimensions in public law, there is a growing gap between emerging administrative practice and underlying theory. We have drifted into a system of "blended power," as Jody Freeman (2003) describes it, a system that has neither a clear rule of law nor a straightforward alternative for accountability (Kettl 2009b).

The United States is certainly not alone in stumbling into this problem. Its system of federalism and long history of relying on state and local governments introduces intergovernmental complications not generally seen in other nations. But the growing interconnection of government with the private and nonprofit sectors is a movement spreading quickly around the world, even in nations with governmental systems very different from the United States (such as China) and nations with a vastly larger government apparatus (such as some of the Scandinavian and northern European nations). The United States is not alone in confronting the implications of a flattened, extended interconnection of government agencies with their partners. Moreover, as globalization inevitably spreads, these interconnections are sure to become even more important in policy making and complex in public administration.

Just as so many parts of the human body are inextricably interconnected, to the point that it is impossible to diagnose or treat problems in one system without treating those that are related, "government" itself is losing its traditional and unique meaning. So many governmental tools are now intergovernmental and intersectoral that it can be difficult to define where government begins and where it ends. At the same time, government's basic responsibility to govern—to make decisions and produce results—on behalf of its people is scarcely less important or central. When it exercises authority on behalf of its citizens, citizens rightly expect high performance and accountability, even if government itself is not producing the goods and services. So not only is this evolving system of flattened administration a fundamental challenge for existing theory and practice but also it's just as fundamental a challenge for the political philosophy of government itself.

Note

1 Calculated from the U.S. OMB 2013.

References

Behn, Robert D. 2014. *The PerformanceStat Potential: A Leadership Strategy for Producing Results*. Washington, DC: Brookings Institution Press.

Culler, Terry W. 1986. "Most Federal Workers Need Only Be Competent." *Wall Street Journal*, May 21: 32.

Donahue, John D. 1997. *Disunited States: What's At Stake as Washington Fades and the States Take the Lead?* New York: Basic Books.

Eisenhower, Dwight. 1961. "Farewell Address." *Dwight D. Eisenhower Presidential Library, Museum, and Boyhood Home*, January 17. www.eisenhower.archives.gov/research/online_documents/farewell_address/1961_01_17_Press_Release.pdf (accessed June 6, 2014).

Federal Acquisition Regulations. N.d. "Subpart 7.5—Inherently Governmental Functions." www.acquisition.gov/far/html/Subpart%207_5.html (accessed June 6, 2014).

Florini, Ann, Hairong Lai, and Yeling Tan. 2012. *China Experiments: From Local Innovations to National Reform*. Washington, DC: Brookings Institution Press.

Fountain, Jane. 2001. *Building the Virtual State: Information Technology and Institutional Change*. Washington, DC: Brookings Institution Press.

Freeman, Jody. 2003. "Extending Public Law Norms through Privatization." *Harvard Law Review* 116(March): 1285–1352.

Goldsmith, Steven. 1999. "The Yellow Pages Test." *Nevada Journal* (Nevada Policy Research Institute). http://nj.npri.org/nj99/05/govnt.htm (accessed June 6, 2014).

Grace Commission. 1984. *President's Private Sector Survey on Cost Control*. A Report to the President. Washington, DC: U.S. Government Printing Office.

Graves, W. Brooke. 1964. *American Intergovernmental Relations: Their Origins, Historical Development, and Current Status*. New York: Charles Scribner's Sons.

Heady, Ferrel. 1949. "The Reports of the Hoover Commission." *Review of Politics* 11(3): 355–378.

Holeywell, Ryan. 2012. "How Weston, Florida, A City of 65,000, Gets by on 9 Employees." *Governing*, May 14. www.governing.com/blogs/view/How-.html (accessed June 6, 2014).

Kettl, Donald F. 1988. *Government by Proxy: (Mis?)Managing Federal Programs*. Washington, DC: CQ Press.

———. 1993. *Sharing Power: Public Governance and Private Markets*. Washington, DC: Brookings Institution Press.

———. 2009a. *The Next Government of the United States: Why Our Institutions Fail Us and How to Fix Them*. New York: Norton.

———. 2009b. "Administrative Accountability and the Rule of Law." *PS: Political Science and Politics* 42(January): 11–17.

Krugman, Paul. 2009. "Why Americans Hate Single-Payer Insurance." *New York Times*, July 28. http://krugman.blogs.nytimes.com/2009/07/28/why-americans-hate-single-payer-insurance/?_r=0 (accessed June 6, 2014).

Marmor, Theodore R., Jerry L. Mashaw, and John Pakutka. 2014. *Social Insurance: America's Neglected Heritage and Contested Future*. Los Angeles: SAGE/CQ Press.

OECD (Organisation for Economic Co-operation and Development). 2011. "Indicator 48." In *Government at a Glance 2011*. Paris: OECD, June 24. www.oecd-ilibrary.org/governance/government-at-a-glance-2011_gov_glance-2011-en (accessed June 6, 2014).

Salamon, Lester M., ed. 2002. *The Tools of Government: A Guide to the New Governance*. New York: Oxford University Press.

Savas, E.S. 1982. *Privatizing the Public Sector: How to Shrink Government*. Chatham, NJ: Chatham House.

Threadgill, Melissa. 2013. "Why Public Sector Gets Technology Wrong." *Boston Globe*, November 11. www.bostonglobe.com/opinion/2013/11/11/why-government-can-get-information-technology-right/SA7f2rL6LxYZ1CCqXU4awJ/story.html (accessed June 6, 2014).

U.S. Bureau of the Budget. 1955. "Bulletin 55–4." Washington, DC: U.S. Government Printing Office.

U.S. GAO. 2013a. *Defense Acquisitions: Continued Management Attention Needed to Enhance Use and Review of DOD's Inventory of Contracted Services*. Report GAO-13-491. Washington, DC: U.S. GAO, May. www.gao.gov/assets/660/654814.pdf (accessed June 6, 2014).

———. 2013b. *High-Risk Series: An Update*. Report GAO-13–283. Washington, DC: U.S. GAO, February. www.gao.gov/assets/660/652133.pdf (accessed June 6, 2014).

U.S. OMB. 2013. "Historical Tables." *Fiscal Year 2014: Budget of the United States.* Washington, DC: U.S. Government Printing Office. www.whitehouse.gov/sites/default/files/omb/budget/fy2014/assets/hist.pdf (accessed June 6, 2014).

Waldo, Dwight. 1948. *The Administrative State.* New York: Holmes and Meier. (Second edition, 1984.)

Weber, Max. 1958. *From Max Weber: Essays in Sociology,* trans. and ed. H.H. Gerth and C. Wright Mills. New York: Oxford University Press.

White, Leonard D. 1933. *Trends in Public Administration.* New York: McGraw-Hill.

Wilson, Woodrow. 1887. "The Study of Administration." *Political Science Quarterly* 2. Reprinted in *Political Quarterly* 56(December 1941): 481–506.

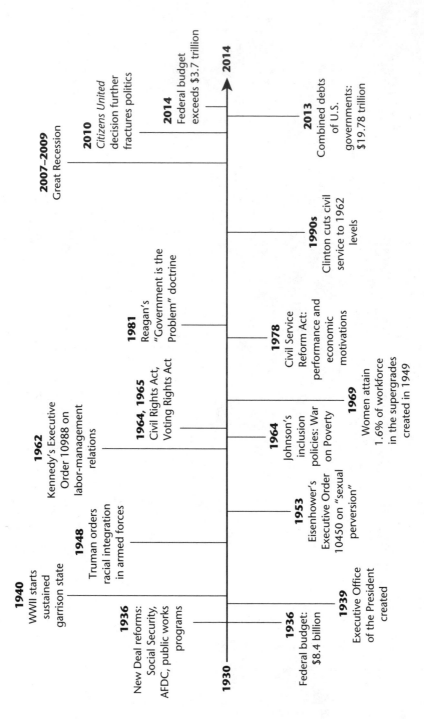

FIGURE 3.1 From Trust to Doubt: Benchmarks across Time

3

FROM TRUST TO DOUBT

The Federal Government's Tough Challenges

Chester A. Newland

In the seventy-five-year period since the founding of the American Society for Public Administration (ASPA), federal spending has ballooned, with outlays[1] growing from $9.5 billion in 1940 to an estimated $3.7 trillion in 2014 (U.S. OMB 2014). During this time span, wars, and more recently terrorist attacks, have propelled the United States into "garrison state" (war-ready) conditions, resulting in rapidly growing defense spending. In fact, federal government outlays on national defense grew from $13 billion in 1947 to an estimated $621 billion in 2014—an almost fifty-fold increase. Non-military spending has skyrocketed even more, from $3.5 billion in 1947 to an estimated $3,029 billion in 2014—an increase of more than 800 percent (U.S. CEA 2014b). In terms of the federal workforce, large-scale expansion occurred until the mid-1970s when the trend reversed and began a long-term contraction that has lasted until today with just a few interludes of modest growth, including that from 2004 to 2012.

The first section of this chapter focuses on budget growth and public work-force trends in the federal government. The second section describes the ideals of reform movements that emerged in the latter 1800s. It compares these ideals to those in the period in which ASPA was established—a period often referred to as the Golden Era of public administration in America. Then a section looks at impacts of sustained war and national security threats and discusses the impact of America's embrace of global leadership. This is followed by a section that focuses on federal expansion from 1960 to 1976 and the efforts to transform America and its public workforce from segregated exclusion to ideals of inclusion. The penultimate section describes challenges and opportunities for public administration over more recent decades. The chapter concludes with a reminder of the highest and best promises for the profession of public administration.

Federal Government Budget and Workforce Trends

Federal government budgetary expansion has been vast and sustained since the early 1930s. In 1932 when Herbert Hoover was president and Franklin D. Roosevelt was poised to take over the leadership of the nation, the government spent $4.7 billion and had a deficit of $2.7 billion, accounting for 4 percent of the nation's $68.5 billion gross domestic product (GDP), as shown in Table 3.1.

By 1936, when the Brownlow Committee (discussed later in this chapter) undertook its executive branch reorganization study, federal outlays had increased to $8.2 billion, with the $4.3 billion deficit accounting for 5.4 percent of GDP. In 1940, right before the U.S. entry in World War II, federal outlays totaled $9.5 billion and the deficit had fallen back to 3 percent of GDP. As the war ended in 1945, federal outlays had skyrocketed to $92.7 billion and the deficit to 21 percent of GDP. By 1950, in the aftermath of World War II and reflecting post-war recovery, federal outlays had dropped back to $42.6 billion and the budget deficit fell to 1.1 percent of GDP. By 1960, federal outlays had more than doubled to $92.2 billion. There was now, however, a small budget surplus representing 0.1 percent of GDP (U.S. OMB 2014).

Over the next forty years, federal spending continued to show dramatic decade-over-decade increases, reaching almost $1.8 trillion by 2000 and accounting for 18 percent of a $10.1 trillion economy (U.S. OMB 2014). As the budget was growing in the post-1960 era, the proportions allocated to defense and non-defense spending were flipping, partially reflecting changes in the proportion of military and non-military personnel within the total federal workforce (see Table 3.2). In 1960, the $48.1 billion allocated to defense spending accounted for 52 percent of federal outlays. By 2014, while outlays on national defense had grown to $621 billion, its proportion of federal outlays had dropped to 17 percent reflecting, in part, the decline in uniformed military personnel as a proportion of total federal employment.

TABLE 3.1 U.S. Federal Government Budget and GDP, Selected Fiscal Years, 1932–2014 ($ in billions)

Year	Outlays	GDP	Surplus/deficit	Deficit as % of GDP
1932	4.7	68.5	−2.7	4.0
1936	8.2	79.6	−4.3	5.4
1940	9.5	98.2	−2.9	3.0
1945	92.7	226.4	−47.5	21.0
1950	42.6	279.0	−3.1	1.1
1960	92.2	535.1	0.3	n.a.
1970	195.6	1,049.1	−2.8	0.3
1980	590.9	2,796.2	−73.8	2.6
1990	1,253.0	5,914.6	−221.0	3.7
2000	1,789.0	10,154.0	236.2	n.a.
2014 (estimate)	3,650.5	17,332.0	−648.8	3.7

Source: U.S. OMB 2014.

TABLE 3.2 Federal Outlays by Major Category of Spending, Selected Fiscal Years 1960–2014 ($ in billions)

Year	National defense		International affairs		Health, Medicare, income security, Social Security		Total outlays
	Outlay	% Total outlays	Outlay	% Total outlays	Outlay	% Total outlays	
1960	48.1	52	3.0	3	19.8	21	92.2
1970	81.7	42	4.3	2	58.1	30	195.6
1980	134.0	23	12.7	2	260.4	44	590.9
1990	299.3	24	13.8	1	553.1	44	1,253.0
2000	294.4	16	17.2	1	1,014.7	57	1,789.0
2014 (estimate)	620.6	17	48.5	1	2,369.3	65	3,650.5

Source: U.S. CEA 2014b.

The Federal Workforce

As shown in Figure 3.2, in 1962, the federal workforce stood at 5.3 million, climbing to 6.6 million by 1969 (U.S. OPM 2014), which reflected the military build-up in Vietnam. At the height of the U.S. troop build-up in Vietnam in 1969, there were 3.6 million uniformed military personnel, accounting for almost 55 percent of total federal employment. Since then, the federal workforce has been trending downward although there has been modest growth in civilian employment in some years, including the 2004–2012 period. In a report on the latest uptick in federal employment, the Government Accountability Office (GAO) noted: "While the federal civilian workforce grew in size from 2004 to 2012, most of the growth was concentrated in three federal agencies and was driven by the need to address some of the nation's pressing priorities" (U.S. GAO 2014, 2). These agencies were Departments of Defense, Homeland Security, and Veterans Affairs. Even with the post-2004 job growth in those three agencies, however, the 4.3 million federal personnel in 2012 was almost 20 percent below the 5.3 million mark reached in 1962 and 35 percent below the 6.6 million peak reached in 1969.

It is important to note that the federal government now spends more on contractors than it does on employees. While federal employment outside these three departments has been relatively flat, the number of workers paid as contractors and subcontractors has grown sharply, on a scale never before seen. In fiscal year 2011, for example, the Department of Defense spent $184 billion on contract employees and all other agencies spent $126 billion on contractors, for a total of $310 billion. In contrast, total payments to federal civilian employees (excluding the Postal Service), including salaries and benefits, was about $240 billion that same year (Schwellenbach 2014).

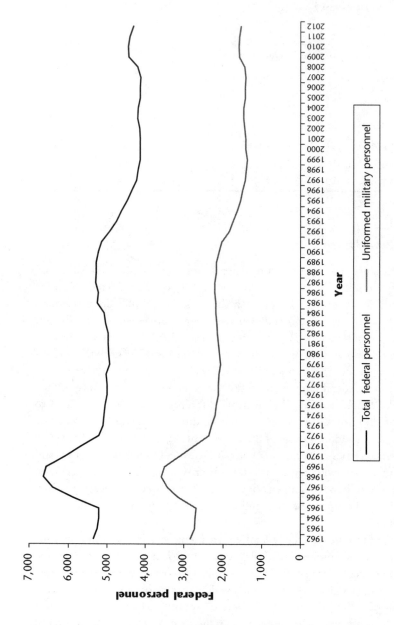

FIGURE 3.2 Federal Government Workforce, 1962–2012

Source: U.S. OPM 2014.

Note: Workforce data include both civilian and military personnel. As per OPM, civilian employment data come from agency monthly submissions and cover total end-of-year employment of full-time permanent, temporary, part-time, and intermittent employees. Uniformed military personnel data are from the Department of Defense.

The State/Local Workforce

It should be noted that, while federal employment has been declining, state/local government employment has been growing. In the thirty-five years from 1977 to 2012, the number of people working for subnational governments increased from 12.4 to 19.1 million (U.S. CEA 2014a), reflecting the downloading of many responsibilities from the federal government to subnational governments. As shown in Table 3.3, 19 percent of the public workforce worked for the federal government in 1977. By 2012, only 13 percent worked for the federal government. With these budgetary and workforce patterns setting the context, discussion now turns to the trends in federal goals and operations.

Reform-Period Ideals and Golden-Era Realities

Government reforms in the late 1800s and early years of the twentieth century focused nationally and locally on interconnected social, economic, and political issues. Concerns stretched across a broad range of governance in search of shared community ideals that had appeared lost in the prior era as the nation broke into civil war. By contrast to the reform years, by the 1930s—the era in which ASPA was created—concerns had narrowed to a focus on government and, within that, on an even more limited range of executive functions, separated from the legislative and political aspects of constitutional democracy.

Reform-Period Challenges and Ideals

In the latter nineteenth century and into the early decades of the twentieth century, reform-minded Americans were concerned that the nation was becoming increasingly divided between a few powerful "haves" who were in control of vast wealth and the levers of power and the growing numbers of "have-nots." Businesses such as railroads, slaughter houses, grain storage, and financial institutions were increasingly controlled by monopolistic trusts and other self-serving interests. Corruption of constitutional democracy, capitalist market failures, and fragile social institutions were impacting growing numbers of victims. Muckrakers

TABLE 3.3 State/Local and Federal Employment, Selected Years, 1977–2012 (in millions of persons)

Year	State/local	Percent of total	Federal	Percent of total	Total
1977	12.4	81	2.9	19	15.3
1987	14.1	82	3.1	18	17.2
1997	16.8	86	2.8	14	19.7
2007	19.5	88	2.7	12	22.2
2012	19.1	87	2.8	13	21.9

Source: U.S. CEA 2014a.

raised public awareness about these issues and took on corporate monopolies and crooked political machines. Tammany Hall, which controlled the Democratic Party in New York City from the 1850s into the 1930s, was emblematic of corrupt local government affairs that prevailed in many cities and counties. The Supreme Court and other parts of the judiciary generally took a laissez-faire approach, as did the U.S. Congress and many state and local legislative bodies. Government employment was rife with patronage jobs obtained under the "spoils system."

In 1883, in response to growing demands for government reform, the U.S. Civil Service Commission had been established by the Pendleton Act. Coverage under the Act stood at 10 percent in its early years but increased to 70 percent by 1919. In 1887, the year after the Supreme Court ruled that state governments could not regulate railroads, the U.S. Congress established the Interstate Commerce Commission (ICC). The purpose of the ICC was to create an independent legislative/executive/judicial commission to control "bigness" in general, and to sustain a workable capitalist market system under a reasonable rule of law.

In 1890, the Sherman Antitrust Act had become law. Creation of other independent commissions to regulate economic affairs followed, resulting in fragmentation into specialized turfs. Alongside the establishment of regulatory agencies, reforms were also going on at the community level via civic engagement and the establishment of nonprofit organizations. For example, the first settlement house, the Neighborhood Guild, was founded in New York in 1886. The National Municipal League was formed in 1894; the New York Bureau of Municipal Research began its influential work in 1906; the City Managers Association (now the International City/County Management Association) was organized in 1914; the Institute of Public Administration was organized in New York in 1921 by an early giant of the field, Luther Gulick; and the Public Administration Clearing House (PACH) was established in 1930 on the campus of the University of Chicago, dedicated to facilitation of government reform. (These developments are described in Chapter 11 but are noted here to highlight factors underpinning the professionalization of public service.) PACH was led by another public administration giant, Louis Brownlow. All of these developments were advanced outside of Washington, DC. Brownlow insisted that their shared objective of professionalization of public service could not be successfully promoted in the nation's capital. However, among ASPA's first leaders were officials who worked in Washington at the U.S. Bureau of Budget, situated in the newly created Executive Office of the President (EOP).

Complexities in the values and principles that troubled reformers remain today. For example, with respect to governmental personnel, reformers embraced two dominant public-service merit standards—education and career-service tenure—to limit patronage and to advance professional expertise. The almost exclusive hold of white males of all but the lower-level civil service jobs persisted until the 1960s, when Great Society actions began to transform America—including the public workforce—into a more inclusive culture, as will be discussed below.

Connectedness at the intersection of politics and administration became a most troublesome aspect of reform thinking and one of public administration's greatest Golden-Era concerns. It also became the centerpiece of creative local government reform, meaning the rejection of the disconnect between the executive and legislative functions and replacement with a parliamentary-like form of council-manager government. For some, the politics/administration dichotomy remained a framework that assured policy responsibility and expert professional implementation. By the late 1940s and 1950s, however, Dwight Waldo, America's most respected field-theory historian in public administration, re-focused thinking around the intersection of political and career public-service roles and responsibilities. Ironically, by then, professionals in city management and civic leaders with whom they served had already been demonstrating such connectedness for a third of a century.

The Golden Era's Accomplishments and Concerns

Like a medal for a race well run, public administration in the United States earned its Golden-Era reputation from 1930 into the 1960s. Civil and military services provided leadership in dealing with the Great Depression, World War II, domestic and international post-war imperatives, and rising social and political transitions. All required successful performance to tackle key domestic, defense, and international developments.

In the New-Deal struggle to rescue the nation from the Great Depression, President Roosevelt called upon public administration experts for leadership. For example, Louis Brownlow became chairman of the President's Committee on Administrative Management, which came to be known as the Brownlow Committee, with Charles Merriam and Luther Gulick as members. The Committee embraced two principles for reorganization of government: (1) enhanced presidential leadership rather than shared authority among branches; and (2) hierarchical bureaucratization of the executive branch under presidential control. In fact, one of the Committee's proposals was the replacement of the bipartisan Civil Service Commission by a federal personnel structure under presidential direction. By Roosevelt's order, the Brownlow Committee had done its work largely in secret. It was, after all, the President's Committee. Congressional leaders were suspect of it. The President had already replaced a large number of classified employees with political appointees, raising the specter of a return to spoils. Comparisons were drawn with dictatorships that were spreading elsewhere around the globe. Congress sought assistance of another early public administration luminary, William F. Willoughby, a foremost budget and government expert and first Director of the Brookings Institution. Ultimately, Congress rejected the Committee's recommendation to eliminate the Civil Service Commission but it did approve the creation of EOP referred to earlier, although it was not effectuated until two years later, in 1939.

Successes for public administration as a field were many but long-term impacts were a double-edged sword. The autonomy of public administration as a field and the authority of public service that had developed prior to the Brownlow Committee recommendations were based on assumptions of a politically neutral civil service assured under bipartisan legislative oversight. In short, shared authority under law underpinned the professional autonomy of the field. When public administration leaders lost sight of that (or were driven by Great-Depression realities to ignore it), foundations of civil service authority were undermined. Simultaneously, the need for such authoritative expertise expanded exponentially.

Facing these challenges, Congress and the Truman administration undertook governmental reorganization under the 1947 Lodge–Brown Act (sponsored in both the House and Senate by Republicans). Reflecting lessons of bipartisanship he had learned as a Senator, President Truman appointed former President Herbert Hoover as Chairman of the Commission on Organization of the Executive Branch of the Government. The Commission affirmed support for hierarchical bureaucratization under presidential leadership—but with articulated congressional authority through reorganized committee structures and processes. The Reorganization Act of 1949 instituted the Commission's proposals for extensive reorganization. Consequently, with underpinnings of shared congressional and presidential authority, public administration and public-service professionals recovered some measure of autonomy to serve in constitutive responsibilities, not merely in instrumental roles.

With respect to public-service professionalization, the Eisenhower administration was transitional. Following two decades with the Democrats in control of the presidency, Republicans sought change. President Eisenhower's Bureau of the Budget Director, Joseph M. Dodge, understood that many career professionals, including such later public administration giants as James Webb and Elmer Staats, were neutrally trustworthy. A second Hoover Commission was created by a Republican Congress but without the bipartisan requirement of the Truman years. Composed of seven Republicans and five Democrats, it focused as much on policy matters as government reorganization. While Commission votes were not fixed along party lines, Attorney General Brownell, a Commission member, advanced anti-antitrust and other Justice Department policies favored by Republicans. In keeping with the Republican perspective, the Commission's statement of policy "provides the foundation for a 'competition with private industry' theme" that established the tone for its Republican-driven recommendations (Devine 1955, 264).

Global Leadership and a Sustained Garrison State

Although most public administration scholarship attends to civilian matters, the military is a large, expensive, powerful, component of American government. Because of its importance, this section focuses on the impacts of sustained war, national security threats, and America's embrace of global leadership. Military personnel at high ranks have extensive autonomy as professional experts. Lessons associated with this reality are briefly highlighted here: (1) shared oversight and diverse force structures; (2) embrace of global leadership; and (3) conditions supporting a sustained garrison-state defense capacity.

Shared Oversight with Differentiated and Integrated Force Structures

The extensive authority entrusted to military leadership is derived historically from shared oversight and controls by Congress and the President, along with differentiation and integration of the armed forces structure. Military authorities are strengthened by separation not only among the three service branches and further divisions within them, but also by reliance on reserve units and on National Guard units under the political authority of state governments. This structure contrasts with the Brownlow Committee's advocacy of presidential predominance over civil service and, more recently, the adoption of a singularly concentrated presidential-control structure via the Civil Service Reform Act of 1978 (CSRA). A lesson learned from the military is that governance authority needs to be multi-faceted, deriving and thriving from varied sources and practices. When authority is narrowly concentrated as political power, trust withers and autonomy is lost.

Global Leadership Challenges and Imperatives

America's embrace of global leadership, which accompanied its involvement in World War I, was successful militarily but a failure diplomatically. President Wilson's insistence on redrawing national borders based on popular self-determination conflicted with European experience and interests. The latter prevailed. Wilson's conflicts with Senate Majority Leader Henry Cabot Lodge resulted in the United States not joining the League of Nations and, instead, returning to isolationism. Communist dictatorship, Fascist authoritarianism, Nazi totalitarianism, and Japanese imperialism spread along with the global Great Depression.

America had demobilized quickly following World War I—the war to end all wars, or so we thought. A boisterous decade later, the nation had become preoccupied with its own economic woes. At the time of ASPA's birth in 1939, with rumbles of war audible, American armed forces totaled only 370,000. With the recovery from the Great Depression barely underway, the country's workforce stood at 55.6 million, which included the military plus the 9.5 million unemployed. Following the attack on Pearl Harbor in 1941, military enlistments took a full four years to climb from 1.6 million in 1941 to 11.4 million by 1945.

World War II required full American mobilization and included a greatly expanded workforce. Older and younger workers who had not previously been in the labor force were recruited and a *Bracero* program was initiated that admitted workers to the United States from Mexico to work in agricultural establishments. Regarding gender, women became an important part of the nation's wartime workforce as depicted by "Rosie the Riveter." In 1940, 28 percent of women were in the workforce. At war's end in 1945, 34 percent of women were in the workforce (Bussing–Burks 2002). Six percentage points may not be a huge increase but it set a high water mark for women's labor force participation rate. Moreover, while some women left the workforce after the war's end, many remained and their range of accomplishments during the hostilities set the stage for further integration into the workforce in the decades to come.

Wartime also opened doors for members of minority groups. By Executive Order 8802, issued in June 1941, President Roosevelt created the Fair Employment Practices Committee (FEPC). It prohibited discrimination in the employment of workers in defense industries or government because of race, creed, color, or national origin. In 1943, Roosevelt strengthened inclusion provisions further with another Executive Order requiring a nondiscrimination clause in all government contracts. In 1948, as the Cold War with the USSR intensified, President Truman proposed legislation to create a permanent FEPC, abolish poll taxes, and act against lynching. Without waiting for congressional approval, he ordered racial integration of the armed forces. Ironically, war and Cold-War threats provided a lever for what would turn out to be a slow, gradual process of making the workforce more inclusive, but progress would be uneven. For example, as one of his earliest actions President Eisenhower issued Executive Order 10450 in April 1953 regarding federal employment that would become one of the most publicized of his administration's policies. It excluded "security risks" not only in political terms but also in behavioral terms with this description of banned behaviors: "Any criminal, infamous, dishonest, immoral, or notoriously disgraceful conduct, habitual use of intoxicants to excess, drug addiction, or sexual perversion." While Eisenhower's executive order did not refer to homosexuals, per se, the expression "sexual perversion" was used as a way to exclude them from government employment.

Conditions Supporting a Sustained Garrison-State Defense Capacity

The United States has been challenged by international conflicts since the early decades of the twentieth century and this became cemented in policy in the mid-twentieth century. First came the Lend Lease Act of 1941, which provided that the United States would make supplies available for its allies even before the nation had formally entered World War II. Then the Communist containment policy began in 1946 and marked the start of the "Cold War" with the USSR. In 1947, the United States launched a massive European Recovery plan, named by President Truman in honor of General George Marshall. In his 1949 inaugural address,

Truman announced his Point Four Program of global developmental assistance that intensified the Cold War. Throughout this entire period, universal conscription into the armed forces continued with strong political support. The Korean police action followed in 1950 and lasted until the July 1953 truce. Interestingly, this conflict has never formally ended. U.S. forces remain today in Korea with high-tech readiness.

American military involvement began in Vietnam in 1950 when the United States provided military assistance to the French colonial administration. Boots-on-the-ground warfare commenced in 1955 under President Eisenhower and American forces were tripled by President Kennedy in 1961 and 1962. After years of fighting, the United States finally retreated in defeat in April 1975. Two years earlier, Congress had abolished the draft, as conscription had lost popular political support. Volunteer military armed forces have been in place ever since.

Other than a brief war against Iraq in 1990–1991 (Operation Desert Storm in Kuwait), there was a halt in nation-state warfare for a decade and dissolution of the USSR in 1991 brought an end to the Cold War. Nation-state rivalries now pale in comparison to international terrorism, which has become a major national defense challenge as evidenced by the September 11, 2001 attacks on New York City's World Trade Center and the Pentagon. High-tech, undeclared wars costing billions in "black box" (meaning off-budget) funding followed for well over a decade in Iraq and Afghanistan (Gellman and Miller 2013). In sum, there is no end in sight to requirements for sustained American defense capacity. What we have is an enduring garrison state. The budget data cited in Table 3.2 bear stark evidence of this.

In his 1961 farewell address, President Eisenhower presciently summarized America's new reality stating:

> [W]e have been compelled to create a permanent armaments industry of vast proportions. . . . We annually spend on military security more than the net income of all United States corporations. . . . Akin to, and largely responsible for the sweeping changes in our industrial-military posture, has been the technological revolution during recent decades. . . . The prospect of domination of the nation's scholars by federal employment, project allocations, and the power of money is ever present.

Spinoffs from the garrison state beyond military uses account for a significant amount of public support. For example, digital technologies from garrison-state investments have accounted for transformation into a historic new era. This electronic/technologies age moved center stage in the 1960s, when the National Aeronautics and Space Administration (NASA) not only had men walk on the moon but also successfully returned them to earth. Jim Webb, NASA administrator behind that success (and ASPA president and a founder of the National Academy of Public Administration—NAPA), made creation of a steady stream of useful products into a vital means and ends of the space race and of garrison-state realities.

Suffice it to say that defense spending is an integral part of the U.S. economy and an industry that is embedded in the fabric of the nation, just as President Eisenhower had warned. America's role as police officer of the world has resulted in a Gordian knot of jobs, products, services, and budgets. The Internet would not have been developed, or would have developed much later, without the U.S. military's work. But neither would the mutually-assured-destruction policy of nuclear deterrence have developed. Whether boon or bane, America's garrison state is an integral part of federal operations. Discussion now turns to the role that the federal government played in leveling the playing field for its citizens at the same time that it endured a tumultuous social scene.

Civil Rights, Public Interest Groups, and Paradox

This section focuses on the growth of the federal government from 1960 to 1976 and efforts to transform America and its public workforce from segregated exclusion to ideals of inclusion. During the presidential election campaign in 1960, Democrats had blamed Republicans for the loss of Cuba to Soviet influence. Unknown to the Democrats, President Eisenhower had allocated $13.1 million to the Central Intelligence Agency to fund a "Democratic Revolutionary Front" to invade Cuba and overthrow Fidel Castro. When Kennedy became president and was informed of this clandestine plan, he sanctioned it. Less than three months after Kennedy assumed office in 1961, the invasion was attempted. Within three days, the amateurish "Bay of Pigs" effort became a widely publicized embarrassment to the United States. Some eighteen months later, in October 1962, after Russian nuclear-armed missiles were detected in Cuba, the Cuban missile crisis took center stage. The crisis ended when professionally expert military might and diplomacy supported a successful stare-down of the Soviets by President Kennedy. But the Cold War was in full swing and enhanced containment seemed vital. The number of American troops in Vietnam was tripled and young men were drafted in the face of mounting social protests against the war. The body count became the focus of news broadcasts and the war accentuated social and political divisions. Over the course of a decade, American military personnel became objects of derision among those opposed to the war, the numbers of whom increased each year.

Paradoxically, America was plagued more in those same years by enduring divisions over racial segregation, altered gender roles for a changing economy, and widespread poverty alongside enhanced wealth among the few. Although President Kennedy was reluctant to jeopardize southern support for his other initiatives by proposing civil rights legislation, he was under pressure to act in the face of massive demonstrations throughout the nation, most notably the August 1963 March on Washington for Jobs and Freedom. Key civil rights leaders led the more than 200,000-person march, including A. Philip Randolph, Roy Wilkins, Bayard Rustin, and Whitney Young. Its most dramatic and enduring moment came when Martin Luther King, Jr., delivered his "I Have a Dream" speech from the steps of the Lincoln Memorial. Finally, in response, Kennedy proposed a comprehensive civil rights bill but would not live to see it become law.

Following Kennedy's assassination, President Johnson vigorously promoted civil rights and alleviation of poverty. He sought inclusion as an historic path for shared prosperity and relied on experienced civic and political leaders and career government professionals to accomplish it. Johnson respected and worked with Senate and House members with whom he had closely collaborated during his twenty-five years in Congress. The Civil Rights Act of 1964, the Voting Rights Act of 1965 and many War on Poverty actions followed, moving America and the federal workforce toward a more inclusive society.

Social Security insurance provisions and welfare programs that originated in the New Deal were expanded in the 1960s. While many of these programs required large budget increases, they also created new opportunities for federal, state, and local government jobs. As the budget summary in the first section of this chapter showed, between 1960 and 1980 social services expenditures grew from 25 percent to 50 percent of federal expenditures. Some federal jobs growth followed, but the vastly expanding budget flowed, for the most part, into direct payments to beneficiaries, to states to fund intergovernmental obligations and to grant recipients and contractors. Heavy reliance on contracting to commercial for-profit businesses has continued to dominate federal government funding. For example, the design and implementation of the Obama administration's 2010 Affordable Care Act was heavily reliant on private insurance companies.

Johnson's Great Society's inclusiveness efforts encountered complex social, economic, and political crosswinds that slowed their impact. Even with doors of opportunity opening and fast-tracking encouraged, more than a generation would be required for transformation from centuries of exclusion to a reasonably inclusive society of widely shared human dignity. Transformation was particularly slow in the professional civil service. Affirmative action was thus needed to avoid "tokenism," with key provisions extending beyond government employment to private enterprises, especially contractors and grant recipients. Implementation of inclusionary processes was difficult, uneven, and triggered backlash and reverse-discrimination that continue today.

Johnson relied heavily on John Macy, who had been named Chairman of the Civil Service Commission by President Kennedy, to attract a greater share of the nation's most talented managers and thinkers to government jobs, especially members of minority groups. Macy, who was well-known for his speeches against gender and racial discrimination in the federal government, had been ASPA's president in 1958–1959 and had extensive public administration experience. He increased training and networking opportunities, understanding that today's professional expert is tomorrow's "failed has been" if a civil servant simply runs in place.

The Golden Era of public administration was advanced by federal civil servants, most of whom ascended into executive roles after having graduated from the nation's elite universities, many of which exclusively educated white males. Doors to public-service education and training opened wider in the 1960s. Johnson and Macy wanted to facilitate career service mobility to develop top generalists, somewhat paralleling military ideals. Creation of a Civil Service Academy for more-or-less compulsory training of generalists had been advocated for years in public administration circles. With the rapid changes and tumult of the 1960s, however, such centralized training had major downsides compared to diverse developmental programs at top external institutions. Given this reality, to facilitate connectedness and shared responsibility across government in what had become turbulent times, the Federal Executive Institute (FEI) was established in 1968 within the U.S. Civil Service Commission. It was authorized to function as a semi-autonomous professional unit in Charlottesville, Virginia, with only reimbursable funding—no appropriated funds. That compelled FEI programs to compete to attract agencies to pay for participation of their executives in development programs.

As agencies became increasingly politicized, civil servants found long absences from their agencies detrimental to their careers. Sessions were shortened to a maximum of four weeks. Numbers of upwardly mobile GS 15s (the top grade level) grew, including women and minorities. With respect to hopes to facilitate self-directed networking and shared responsibility, an independent FEI Alumni Association was organized during the FEI's first year of operations. It continues to function today, providing many short-term developmental activities, mostly in Washington, DC.

The Pinnacle of Professionalized Public Service: Alaska's 9.2 Earthquake

Public administration reached its pinnacle of relative autonomy early in the Johnson administration primarily as a result of the federal government's response to the level 9.2 Alaska Earthquake of 1964—the most powerful recorded earthquake in North American history. Public officials had two options. The first was to relocate two-thirds of Alaska's population out of the state and to spend three years designing and reconstructing the devastated areas. The second option was to have minimum relocation and to move rapidly so that the state would be up and running within a year. Upon career civil servant and congressional advice, President Johnson decided on the second option. He reconstituted his cabinet as the Federal Reconstruction and Development Planning Commission for Alaska and appointed the well-respected Senator Clinton Anderson of New Mexico as the Commission chairperson and Dwight Ink as its executive director. Ink, described by some as "The Remarkable Dwight Ink" held major leadership roles in the federal government for seven presidents from Eisenhower to

Reagan (Visions Across America 2013). Ink later recounted his efforts to achieve one-season recovery. He wrote that he told Senator Anderson and the President

> that unless we were free to abandon much of the usual governmental red tape, we would fail. Although I never received formal authority, neither Anderson nor Johnson objected to my pleading for a free hand. Therefore, I assumed I had tacit authority to modify or suspend any agency process that jeopardized our ability to get public facilities sufficiently rebuilt to avoid most Alaskans having to scramble to the lower 48, leaving them and their state bankrupt.
>
> *(Ink 2013, 2)*

In the wake of government's success, the *Anchorage Daily News* editorialized that it showed "government at its best," lauding "the 'remarkable performance' of the career leadership assigned to the task" (Ink 2013, 6). The success was a result of professionally expert civil servant autonomy coupled with collaborative presidential and congressional support. This stood in stark contrast with the then prevailing orthodoxy of separation of powers and aggrandizement of presidential control.

Transitions of Professional Associations and Unions into Public Interest Groups

During the 1960s, Chicago ceased to be the network center of professional public administration associations and related organizations. Most moved to Washington as federal funding grew for both intergovernmental programs and direct grants and contracts. These organizations are discussed in detail in Chapter 11, but are noted here to emphasize the changes that occurred in the public administration landscape during the 1960s and 1970s. The public interest groups not only identified themselves as looking out for the public interest but they also sought sustainability and advancement for themselves.

ASPA remained longer than most organizations in Chicago and finally moved to Washington in 1964, its twenty-fifth anniversary year. Like other associations, ASPA looked forward to opportunities to gain federal grants and contracts that were needed to help address its persistent financial challenges. However, when NAPA was organized in 1967 as an off-shoot of ASPA and became a contracts and grants recipient, it competed with ASPA's aspirations to receive federal dollars. In 1970, a second departure from ASPA occurred with the creation of the National Association of Schools of Public Affairs and Administration[2] (NASPAA), which established another funding competitor.

President Eisenhower's prescient reflections in his farewell address discussed earlier, in which he drew in part on his earlier experience as President of Columbia University, touched on his concerns with government money and its impact on organizations and institutions outside of government. He said:

[T]he free university, historically the fountainhead of free ideas and scientific discovery, has experienced a revolution in the conduct of research. Partly because of the huge costs involved, a government contract becomes virtually a substitute for intellectual curiosity. . . . The prospect of domination of the nation's scholars by federal employment, project allocations, and the power of money is ever present.

(Eisenhower 1961)

The movement from professionalized autonomy to income-seeking dependency, against which Eisenhower had warned, overtook not only professional associations but also many government employee organizations from the late 1950s through the 1970s. President Kennedy's Executive Order 10988 issued in 1962 recognized the right of federal employees to engage in collective bargaining. This executive order was a breakthrough for public sector workers who had not been protected under the 1935 Wagner Act, and it responded to Democratic Party politics as well. Collective bargaining under growing public union power morphed into partisan political bargaining, enforced by ballot-box politics and partisan appointments. For some federal, state, and local government employees, the culture of political neutrality and public-service values degenerated into attitudes of mere governmental employment—jobs to maximize self-serving interests. For many, however, unionization, like participation in professional associations, reflected (and still reflects) belief in responsible performance standards and reasonable working conditions that are often ignored or lost by contracting out the provision of public services to for-profit interests.

In state and local governments, Thom Reilly writes: "As the strength of public sector unionism rose, its formal role of collective bargaining expanded to encompass a much more powerful role as a political machine that enabled it to affect election outcomes and larger policy and spending issues" (Reilly 2012, 68). He further states: "Private sector bargaining operates within a market economy and public sector bargaining functions as a monopoly" (p. 71). Besides horizontal monopoly powers locally and regionally, vertically integrated powers result in state and federal laws that assure unilateral union power in key respects, limiting government authority to negotiate changes in employee benefits provisions in response to such crises as economic recessions, funding shortfalls, and municipal bankruptcies.

Despite the benefits that collective bargaining brings, these unionization developments have contributed to privatization and government out-sourcing. They have also generated support for removal of job protection and "work at will" provisions in civil service systems such as those in Florida, Georgia, and Texas. Of broader impact, the ending of political neutrality in public service has dealt a powerful blow to the autonomy of public administration as a field, already weakened by its embrace of presidential/executive aggrandizement.

Judicial, Political, and Academic Confirmation of Inclusiveness

The judiciary contributes to inclusion in government service through its rulings, such as that on homosexuals in public service. Exclusion had been vigorously enforced following Eisenhower's executive order referred to earlier. That policy was overturned in *Norton v. Macy* (1969) and in *Society for Individual Rights and Hickerson v. Hampton* (1973). The judicial holdings were that an adverse nexus must be demonstrated between personal sexual orientation and work performance to justify exclusion from public service. The Nixon administration quietly accepted the judicially ordered change. Exclusion of known homosexuals from military service would, however, continue for decades through shifting doctrines such as President Clinton's "don't ask; don't tell" until policy reversals in 2012.

Partisan politicization returned to federal executive staffing under Richard Nixon. He staffed the Domestic Council in EOP and politicized Office of Management and Budget (OMB) at least three levels down in job titles. He also politicized the Federal Regional Field Service. Nixon's aides, H.R. Haldeman and John Erlichman, who would later gain infamy in the Watergate scandal, kept Civil Service Chairman Bob Hampton tethered by delaying his reappointment. The FEI's autonomy remained largely protected through networks of its director and alumni. Upon Nixon's departure, President Ford's administration focused on efforts to restore measures of authority to professional civil service in order to regain the public's trust in government. Despite widespread admiration for Ford, the Watergate scandal had made it inevitable that the Democratic Party would regain the White House, which it did with the election of Jimmy Carter in 1976. While President Carter returned to partisan politicization, he embraced elimination of legally enforced racial segregation and supported racial and gender inclusiveness in public service.

Scholarship of the day demonstrates the values that infused public administration as a field of endeavor. As related to a professionalized civil service, Mosher's (1982) analysis of the democracy-and-bureaucracy paradox remains fundamental. The first Minnowbrook Conference, sponsored in 1968 by Dwight Waldo and the New Public Administration movement promoted by it, particularly George Frederickson's (1974) analyses highlighting social equity values, have had enduring impacts (see also Marini 1971). Waldo, himself, never lost sight of complexities and aspirations for connectedness (1948, 1972, 1980). The ground-breaking book by Pressman and Wildavsky on implementation, aptly titled *Implementation: How Great Expectations in Washington are Dashed in Oakland; or Why It's Amazing that Federal Programs Work at All* (1984; originally published in 1973), had impacts that more than matched the realistic title. It focused on a Great Society program in Oakland, California in which vast sums of money were thrown at a problem without disciplined policy analysis, intergovernmental administrative management, and community capacity to match political aspirations.

The commonalities among Mosher, Waldo, Frederickson, Pressman, and Wildavsky are in direct contrast to the views of William A. Niskanen (1994), an economist who was a contemporary of theirs. He advocated limits on the growth of the government workforce, restrictions of careerists to instrumental roles, and rejection of constitutive authority of professional public servants. His book, *Bureaucracy and Representative Government*, published just before his appointment as Assistant Director at Nixon's OMB, was emblematic of changes about to come. Although Niskanen's criticisms of the administration cut short his OMB service, his views have had enduring influence. President Reagan appointed him to the Council of Economic Advisors and his analysis that bureau personnel behaved in self-advancing ways and accounted for vast governmental growth complemented the libertarian views of Donald Devine, Reagan's appointee as Director of the Office of Personnel Management (OPM). Together, these two prominent libertarian believers were symbolic of Reagan's inaugural theme that government is not a solution but rather a problem. Niskanen later became Chairman of the influential Cato Institute, a libertarian think-tank headquartered in Washington, DC.

Structural Challenges, Ideological Fracturing, and Debt-Burdened Government

Public administration has faced significant challenges in recent decades. The tumult of the 1960s and the Vietnam War, followed by the Watergate scandal, resulted in a generation of voters who mistrusted government. Distrust at home, coupled with the growth of a global economy with interconnections where one strand could not be changed without unraveling others, shook the nation's confidence in the capacity of government to address big (and little) problems. The proliferation of extreme partisanship amidst a consumer culture, coupled with economic hardship and the continuing erosion of the middle class, gave rise to cavernous ideological differences. This scenario contributes to the current public-service environment in which problems seem almost insurmountable. A discussion of this dilemma is broken into three parts: the first focuses on changes brought about by advanced technology, workforce pressures, and globalization. The second looks at the social, economic, and political divisions, which are often ideologically intense, and the third at government burdened with debt and challenged by citizens who view government as a provider of consumer services, rather than as a civic responsibility.

Structural Challenges: Connectedness amidst Fracture

Structural changes constitute an ongoing transition into a new paradoxical era of global connectedness and fracture. Public expenditures mount by volcanic proportions while alternatives to the traditional governmental workforce accommodate the new age.

The service-driven economy is increasingly oriented to self-service convenience facilitated by the Internet. Self-governance, originally associated with civic responsibilities of constitutional democracy and manifested in face-to-face community meetings, has devolved into self-service kiosks where citizens can secure governmental services ranging from submissions for death certificates to income-tax calculations and securing a fishing license. Accessing public services online has become like shopping for any other product online. Who needs a large government workforce with this sort of technology? In a market-oriented economy where citizens confuse being a consumer with being a citizen, there is little appreciation for those who make the kiosks work.

Permeable borders are increasingly prevalent across governmental boundaries as well as sectors of the economy, as pointed out so well in Chapter 2. As Frederickson (1999) explained, local governmental functions and the resources to perform them stretch from municipality to county to large geographic regions. This requires not a delineation of actions, but rather a conjunction of actions. All the while, ballot-box politicians remain constrained by jurisdictional boundaries. Likewise, as Anne-Marie Slaughter (2004) has written, disaggregated sovereignty among nations is growing. Many forces of this electronic era are globally cosmopolitan, requiring paradoxical reconciliation with differentiated place-based values and capacities. Public administration has largely embraced these realities, bringing a redefinition to the field.

Ideological Divisions, Silos, and Fractured Institutions

The Reform Era of a century ago crystallized ideals about a shared community of human interests and capacities as the nation transitioned from an agrarian to an industrial economy. Siloed structures that had segregated people and institutions by economic and social status, ethnicity and race, and faith and ideology regained power following the Civil War and the flawed reconstruction that followed. By the 1920s, Progressive-era reforms reversed, or at least moderated, some of these challenges. Accomplishments, however, were achieved by reliance on increasingly specialized disciplines of positive science and on paradoxically fractured government: separated regulatory commissions as independent structures with conjoined legislative, executive, and judicial authority.

In short, the search for reasonable balance between differentiated and integrated ends and means of shared community was a challenge then and it has become more so through the years. The search has remained troublesome as the nation struggles to advance inclusiveness and deal with global economic forces (Rodgers 2011). Presently, the federal government as well as some state and local governments are fractured ideologically, inhibiting their performance. Even government shut-down is embraced by those who find compromise untenable.

Besides governments, other institutions seeking to reconcile new realities are also challenged. Universities, for example, have seen specializations proliferate as siloed fiefdoms while central administrations grow ever larger, funded by government, foundation and private-sector grants and contracts (Ginsberg 2011). The resulting divisive impact on society and its vital institutions—including professionalized civil service—are deep and broad. The underlying performance theory is that "every tub must float on its own bottom"—a design for narrow command-and-control from the top of hierarchies over divided instrumentalities at lower levels. This theory was applied by the Treaty of Versailles and in drawing post-colonial Middle Eastern and African boundaries. It was the means of control of the USSR by the Communist elite. It is a practical, utilitarian means for containing and controlling subordinate units within boundaries. But it is not broadly constitutive in terms of workable market economics and constitutional democracy.

Another example is the CSRA of 1978, the centerpiece of the Carter Presidency. It embedded in law the ideology of "economic man," which minimizes a culture of public service. Instead, it advances attitudes that government employment is merely a job without integral civic and professional responsibilities. President Carter and his OPM Director, Alan K. (Scotty) Campbell, embraced neo-liberal theory, which holds that individuals are most significantly self-seeking in terms of economic interests. Thus, CSRA performance incentives are basically monetary (performance-based pay and bonuses). Subsequent research, notably an article by Perry and Wise (1990), has demonstrated the role of public-service motivation, which is a complexity contrary to simplistic utility maximization.

Beyond that, CSRA resulted in partisan politicization of OPM. Carter's director sought to place the Bureau of Executive Manpower under direction of a former presidential election campaign leader. Similar partisanship continued from the outset of the Reagan administration under OPM's Director Devine's libertarianism. However, Deputy Director Loretta Cornelius moderated policies with the support of Edwin Meese, an advisor to the President. Devine's reappointment later failed.

Search for reasonableness among political differences over civil service roles and numbers is often complex. For example, President Reagan's agenda to encourage collapse of the USSR resulted in federal budgetary increases to 24.5 percent of gross national product. That vast expansion, resulting in high deficits, was contrary to Reagan's proclaimed opposition to governmental spending, but it earned him kudos in history books. In contrast, President Clinton's initial focus on post-partisanship, while successful in achieving a balanced-budget and civil service reductions, did not ward off his impeachment over personal faults. But he did escape Senate conviction. For President Obama, his initial post-partisan outreach efforts in search of collaboration were met with singular and sustained efforts by Congressional Republicans to defeat him above all else. The lesson to this is that passionate partisanship prevails and fracture worsens.

Debt-Burdened Government

Expansion of government is based to a large extent on borrowing. U.S. Census and Congressional Budget Office (CBO) reports at the end of federal fiscal year 2013 showed total indebtedness of U.S. governments to be $19.78 trillion. The federal debt was $16.8 trillion; state government debt $1.19 trillion; and local government debt $1.79 trillion (Barnett and Vidal 2013; U.S. CBO 2013). Beyond debt levels, unfunded state and local government retirement pensions and health benefits obligations were estimated at near $3 trillion (Ortiz 2013). In 2010, the National Research Council and NAPA jointly published a study, *Choosing the Nation's Fiscal Future*. It reported that the federal debt was more than $12 trillion and concluded

> that the debt that will result if the United States continues with current tax and spending policies will be at a level that poses too great a risk to the economic welfare of the current generation and would impose an unfair and crushing burden on future generations.
>
> *(National Research Council and NAPA 2010, 3)*

The study also reported that: "Over the long term, three major programs—Medicare, Medicaid, and Social Security—account for the projected faster growth on federal spending relative to revenues" (p. 1). Rapidly expanding federal debt reached over 70 percent of GDP by 2013 (U.S. CBO 2013). Growing costs of interest are unsustainable.

Powerful forces behind the massive expansion of spending, deficits, and indebtedness include widespread perceptions of government as a consumer service—not a civic responsibility. Dependency and entitlements—warranted for some but embraced more broadly—are damaging to social, economic, and political culture. Opposition to taxes increasingly defines America. Contractors, grant recipients, and other interests thrive—some without merit—on expansion of debt-burdened governments.

Conclusion

The mid- and later twentieth century brought economic recessions and "hot" and Cold War challenges. A century ago most reformers sought development of a broadly based field, not a narrow discipline. Multisector and shared civic engagement concerns shaped their goals (as now). Troubled by market failures and disregard for human values, along with appreciation for a constitutional democracy, they sought facilitative governance to help clean up business and government corruption. Bigness, whether in private business or government, was rarely trusted.

Public administration, while it did not abandon reform-era ideals, set them on the shelf for a while. Leonard White, writing in 1926, stated that "the study of public administration should start from the base of management rather than the foundation of law" (p. xvi). This narrowing in pursuit of status as a distinct discipline of empirical study supported years of successful development, particularly through the Great Depression and World War II, but it ultimately undermined its autonomy as a field broadly connected with redefining the nexus of law, political science, and management.

During crucial transition years, public administration cut itself off from the dynamics of law and other social sciences to enter a cul-de-sac of widespread orthodoxy: do-a-lot government emphasized professional experts "doing the doing" within executive-dominated bureaucracies. Despite sustained, broader understanding by the likes of Waldo (1980), Simon (1997), and Mosher (1980), the field became narrowed as a discipline, chiefly oriented to administrative management. In federal legal and political practice, nevertheless, a focus remained on the iron triangle of political science: policy relationships among powerful bureaus, congressional subcommittees, and special interests. Public administration became tethered for decades to institutions—many operating as silos—that the field had helped to create. For example, consider security agencies prior to the 9/11 attack. As Stillman points out in the Foreword, fixed disconnectedness of those silos was not simply an isolated, tragic example. Turf separation was a pattern throughout much of government and among its contractors and other special interests. Look again, for example, at today's plethora of separated welfare programs.

For over a third of a century, public administration has increasingly confronted bureaucratic and political complexities that challenge it as a broad field. Encouragingly, it is once again focusing on ideals and practices of shared community and engagement of all residents (although often only concerned with citizens, not human dignity and civic responsibilities generally—a questionable inheritance from New Public Management). The field is again working broadly across private businesses, not-for-profit organizations, civically engaged individuals and groups, and governments at all levels. Some like to look at this as a new public–private partnership "golden triangle." However, it needs to be less narrowly confined. Constructive connectedness, drawing widely on responsible self-governance among multi-dimensional and dynamic categories of participants, is needed, reminiscent of the ideals of a century ago. Promisingly, public administration now embraces broad expertise and perspectives, ranging across such fields as law, health care, and information technology to such disciplines as economics, sociology, psychology, and anthropology, all as means for varied and shared accomplishment.

Sadly, contrary to these constructive developments in public administration, American politics since the mid-1970s has increasingly inflamed divisions for partisan and personal gain instead of responsibly facilitating reasonable constitutional democracy. Consequently, historic challenges are unmet. Globally, nations are caught between worn-out frameworks of austerity versus Keynesian spending in ineffective efforts to cope with market economy failures. In the United States, that translates into vast expansion of governmental spending based on huge debt along with cutbacks in public-service workforces because of the absence of tax reforms that would provide enhanced revenues. Globally, concentrations of vast wealth and power among reduced percentages of "haves" are growing. Crucially, environmental challenges associated with climate and natural resources are rising.

These historic challenges and others—dangerously unmet—are among responsibilities that public administration is learning to embrace, along with facilitation of day-to-day governance. It is essential to understand that great civilizations and their people who account for achievements cannot succeed for long by cutbacks and indebtedness. Instead, it is necessary to multiply values and harmonize disciplined means of accomplishments. Among these talents, instead of stoking flames of creative but contrary views so as to produce irreconcilable ideologies, vital differences are embraced as wise paradoxes. This requires humility among leaders to understand they do not know it all, so that they reject dogma and seek wisdom. It also requires confidence in diverse people and their organizations and institutions to engage broadly in civic duty and public service, both as self-disciplined volunteers and in professionally expert workforces.

America's growing transformation into a broadly inclusive society demonstrates splendid capacities to accomplish further vital changes. American politics, however, fractured by ideologies and pursuit of self-interest, must be reformed. Further facilitation by Public Administration of such advancements of constitutional democracy remains basic for ASPA in its seventy-fifth year and beyond. The field's professionals are needed as catalysts in a disciplined search for human dignity and reasonableness.

Notes

1 Outlays are the measure of government spending. They occur when obligations are actually paid.
2 NASPAA has now expanded its name to Network of Schools of Public Policy, Affairs, and Administration.

References

Barnett, Jeffrey L., and Phillip M. Vidal. 2013. "State and Local Government Finances Summary: 2011." U.S. Census Bureau: Government Division Briefs (July). www2. census.gov/govs/local/summary_report.pdf (accessed July 10, 2014).

Bussing-Burks, Marie. 2002. "Women and Post-WWII Wages." *NBER Digest* (November). www.nber.org/digest/nov02/w9013.html (accessed June 20, 2014).

Devine, William E. 1955. "The Second Hoover Commission Reports: An Analysis." *Public Administration Review* 15(4): 263–269.

Eisenhower, Dwight D. 1961. "Military-Industrial Complex Speech." *Public Papers of the Presidents, Dwight D. Eisenhower,* 1035–1040. Washington, DC: U.S. Government Printing Office. http://coursesa.matrix.msu.edu/~hst306/documents/indust.html (accessed June 18, 2014).

Frederickson, H. George. 1974. "A Symposium: Social Equity and Public Administration." *Public Administration Review* 34(1): 1–2.

———. 1999. "The Repositioning of American Public Administration." *PS: Political Science and Politics* 32(4): 701–711.

Gellman, Barton, and Greg Miller. 2013. "'Black Budget' Summary Details U.S. Spy Network's Successes, Failures and Objectives." *The Washington Post*, August 29. www.washingtonpost.com/world/national-security/black-budget-summary-details-us-spy-networks-successes-failures-and-objectives/2013/08/29/7e57bb78-10ab-11e3-8cdd-bcdc09410972_story.html (accessed July 10, 2014).

Ginsberg, Benjamin. 2011. *The Fall of the Faculty*. New York: Oxford University Press.

Ink, Dwight. 2013. *Draft Memoirs*. Unpublished manuscript.

Marini, Frank E., ed. 1971. *Toward a New Public Administration: The Minnowbrook Perspective*. Chicago: Chandler Publishing.

Mosher, Frederick C. 1980. "The Changing Responsibilities and Tactics of the Federal Government." *Public Administration Review* 40(6): 541–548.

———. 1982. *Democracy and the Public Service*, 2nd ed. New York: Oxford University Press.

National Research Council and NAPA. 2010. *Choosing the Nation's Fiscal Future*. Washington, DC: The National Academies Press.

Niskanen, William A. Jr. 1994. *Bureaucracy and Representative Government*, reissued ed. Cheltenham: Edward Elgar.

Norton v. Macy. 1969. 100 U.S. App. D.C. 85.

Ortiz, Jon. 2013. "Pensions in Public Sector Rise Sharply." *The Sacramento Bee*, September 9: 1.

Perry, James L., and Lois Recascino Wise. 1990. "The Motivational Bases of Public Service." *Public Administration Review* 30(3): 367–371.

Pressman, Jeffrey, and Aaron Wildavsky. 1984. *Implementation: How Great Expectations in Washington Are Dashed in Oakland; Or, Why It's Amazing that Federal Programs Work at All, This Being a Saga of the Economic Development Administration as Told by Two Sympathetic Observers Who Seek to Build Morals on a Foundation of Ruined Hopes*, 3rd ed. Berkeley, CA: University of California Press.

Reilly, Thom. 2012. *The Public Interest?* Armonk, NY: M.E. Sharpe.

Rodgers, Daniel T. 2011. *Age of Fracture*. Cambridge, MA: Belknap Press of Harvard University.

Schwellenbach, Nick. 2014. "Is the Federal Civilian Workforce Really Growing? Some Important Context." *Center for Effective Government*, February 11. www.foreffectivegov.org/is-federal-civilian-workforce-really-growing-some-important-context (accessed June 23, 2014).

Simon, Herbert A. 1997. *Administrative Behavior*, 4th ed. New York: Free Press.

Slaughter, Anne-Marie. 2004. *A New World Order: Government Networks and the Disaggregated State*. Princeton, NJ: Princeton University Press.

Society for Individual Rights and Hickerson v. Hampton. 1973. 528 F.2d 925 (9th Cir.).

U.S. CBO. 2013. *Macroeconomic Effects of Alternative Budgetary Paths*. Washington, DC: U.S. CBO, February. www.cbo.gov/publication/43769 (accessed June 20, 2014).

U.S. CEA (Council of Economic Advisors). 2014a. "Table B–14." In *Economic Report of the President*, 391. Washington, DC: U.S. GPO, March. www.nber.org/erp/2014_economic_report_of_the_president.pdf (accessed June 20, 2014).

———. 2014b. "Table B–21." In *Economic Report of the President*, 391. Washington, DC: U.S. GPO, March. www.nber.org/erp/2014_economic_report_of_the_president.pdf (accessed June 20, 2014).

U.S. GAO. 2014. *Federal Workforce: Recent Trends in Federal Civilian Employment and Compensation.* Report GAO 14–215. Washington, DC: U.S. GAO, January. www. gao.gov/assets/670/660449.pdf (accessed June 23, 2014).

U.S. OMB (Office of Management and Budget). 2014. "Table 1.1: Summary of Receipts, Outlays, and Surpluses or Deficits (–): 1789–2019." www.whitehouse.gov/sites/ default/files/omb/budget/fy2015/assets/hist01z1.xls (accessed June 20, 2014).

U.S. OPM (Office of Personnel Management). 2014. "Data, Analysis & Documentation: Federal Employment Reports, Historical Workforce Tables." www.opm.gov/ policy-data-oversight/data-analysis-documentation/federal-employment-reports/his-torical-tables/total-government-employment-since-1962/ (accessed June 21, 2014).

Visions Across America. 2013. "Part I: The Remarkable Dwight Ink." April 15. http:// visionsacrossamerica.com/2013/04/15/part-i-the-remarkable-dwight—ink/ (accessed June 20, 2014).

Waldo, Dwight. 1948. *The Administrative State.* New York: Ronald Press Co.

———. 1972. "Developments in Public Administration." *The Annals of the American Academy of Political and Social Science* 404(November): 217–245.

———. 1980. *The Enterprise of Public Administration.* Novato, CA: Chandler/Sharp.

White, Leonard. 1926. *Introduction to the Study of Public Administration.* New York: Macmillan.

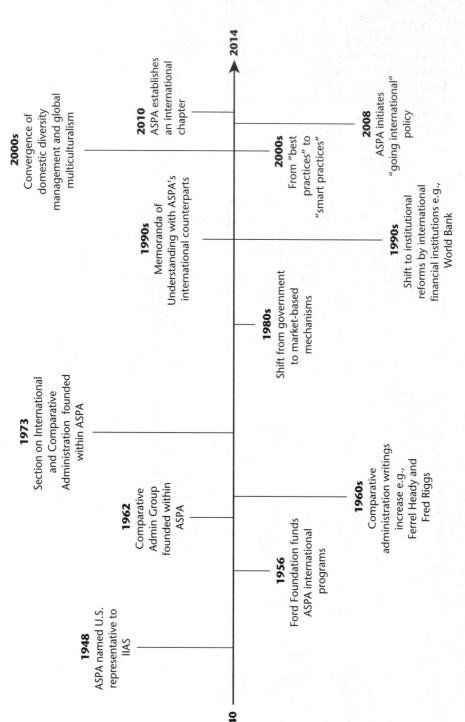

FIGURE 4.1 From Local to Global: Benchmarks across Time

4

FROM LOCAL TO GLOBAL

Donald E. Klingner

This chapter tracks the trajectory of public administration from a local to a global awareness. It begins by defining globalization and summarizing the relationship between that and governance. This is followed by a discussion of how the shift from a local to a global perspective has affected U.S. politics and public administration. Challenges in applying comparative public administration research to global development issues are then summarized. The last section of the chapter offers recommendations on how to prepare globally competent public administrators and organizations.

By way of background, it is instructive to study the early decades of the twentieth century as professionalization of the field was beginning. Donald Stone's (1975) landmark history of the genesis of the American Society for Public Administration (ASPA) reflects the domestic orientation of ASPA at its inception as well as the state of the field at the time. In it he never uses the terms "global" or "worldwide." In fact, he uses the term "international" only when specifically referencing the International City Manager's Association or the International Personnel Management Association. He tracked the origins of professionalization from the creation of the New York Bureau of Municipal Research in 1906 through the establishment of a national network of kindred associations in Chicago (the Public Administration Clearing House) in the 1930s (Stone 1975, 83). Stone's discussion of comparative study related to differences among state and local governments that "afforded a ready-made laboratory for comparative study of the application of new concepts" (p. 83).

Use of the term "comparative" has come a long way since then. While "comparative public administration" still measures the effect of contextual variables on outcomes, this comparison is more likely to be across nations or regions (Jreisat 2005;

Fitzpatrick et al. 2011). The aftermath of World War II had brought a new appreciation of the importance of international comparisons, conditions, and events. Several factors explain the expanding focus, including the "postwar occupation of nations by the United States and other allied powers; wartime and reconstruction experience of scholars and practitioners abroad; overseas technical assistance assignments; and the need for extended range and scope in public administration as a discipline" (Farazmand 1996, 343).

In 1948, ASPA became the U.S. representative to the International Institute of Administrative Sciences (IIAS). In 1956, ASPA received Ford Foundation funding for international training and development programs and in 1962 it established the Comparative Administration Group (CAG) under the sponsorship of the Foundation. CAG was "a loosely knit group of scholars interested in furthering the development of the field of comparative public administration in the U.S. and abroad" (SICA 2014). In 1973, CAG became ASPA's Section on International and Comparative Administration (SICA)—the organization's first section. Since the late 1990s, the growing emphasis on what has come to be called globalization has had a significant impact on the field and on ASPA, its premier membership organization.

In recognition of the movement from local to more global perspectives on the field, ASPA's executive directors and internationally minded presidents have moved the organization from its relatively parochial focus on "good government" in the United States to its current position as a supporter of professional public administration worldwide (Samuel 2008). Today, ASPA has over 20 affiliation agreements with its international counterparts, an international chapter for the increasing number of non-U.S. members, and dozens of attendees from around the world at its annual conferences.

The Relationship between Globalization and Governance

While it is well recognized that globalization is a rapidly increasing phenomenon, there is no universal agreement as to what it actually is. Kahler and Lake define globalization as "networks of interdependence that span intercontinental distances" (2003, 105). Others, however, define globalization more narrowly, generally from the perspective of economics. For example, according to the United Nations (UN): "The term 'globalization' is widely used to describe the increasing internationalization of financial markets and of markets for goods and services" (Carson 2006). Similarly, the International Monetary Fund (IMF) defines globalization as "an extension beyond national borders of the same market forces that have operated for centuries at all levels of human economic activity—village markets, urban industries, or financial centers" (IMF 2008, 45). The IMF, however, recognizes that globalization also involves cultural, political, and environmental dimensions.

Whether broadly defined or more narrowly characterized by one or a few dimensions, there is general agreement that globalization results from several factors that make the world more interconnected. These include the availability of faster and cheaper information and increasingly sophisticated communication and transportation technologies as well as evolving demographic, economic, political, social, and environmental conditions worldwide. Adverse circumstances and recurring events such as poverty, wars, terrorism, ethnic conflicts, natural disasters, and pandemics also affect the extent and pace of globalization.

Whatever the specific conditions that define and affect globalization, they generally increase demands for good governance. Kahler and Lake (2003, 1) succinctly link globalization and governance. They write:

> The state's monopoly of familiar governance functions is ending, as governance migrates up to supranational organizations; down to newly empowered regions, provinces, and municipalities; and laterally to such private actors as multinational firms and transnational non-governmental organizations (NGOs) that acquire previously "public" responsibilities. In this view, globalization not only transfers governance in conflicting directions, it also forces a convergence of state institutions and policies.

Good governance means enhanced government capacity to marshal resources and coordinate authoritative national and international responses (Farazmand 1999; Jreisat 2011; Pollitt and Bouchaert 2000). In developed countries, this typically means *maintaining* governments' abilities to coordinate policy, gather information, deliver services through multiple (often nongovernmental) partners, replace hierarchical bureaucracies with more flexible mechanisms for managing indirect government (Brudney, O'Toole, and Rainey 2000; DiIulio, Garvey, and Kettl 1993; Kettl 2002), and resolve issues of performance and accountability caused by interactions across sectors and levels of government (Klingner, Nalbandian, and Romzek 2002).

In developing countries and transitional regimes, good governance usually means that governments must *establish* the ability to deliver vital public services through core management functions such as budgeting, human resource management, and program evaluation while simultaneously focusing on more fundamental changes. These include citizen participation, decentralization, innovation, and entrepreneurial leadership (Kettl 1997) required for effective political systems.

Good governance is also the common denominator for addressing global threats such as Somali piracy, Taliban control of large portions of Afghanistan (Rubin 2007), Pakistan's inability to prevent the movement of al-Qaeda militants and supplies from Afghanistan (Traub 2009), sectarian conflict in Iraq (Brinkerhoff and Mayfield 2005), and flows of drugs, arms, and money across the Mexico–U.S. border (Astorga and Shirk 2010). Transnational criminal organizations thrive in areas where individual governments are unable to defend their borders or people. Demand for illegal goods or services creates economic opportunity and produces an endemic cycle of cynicism, corruption, and social violence.

It is also recognized that "good governance" in general—and institutional, political, and administrative reform in particular—is required for global development and to meet the UN Millennium Development Goals by 2015. These goals include building world partnerships; ending poverty and hunger; combating HIV/AIDS; achieving universal education and gender equality; and advancing child and maternal health, all with environmental sustainability (UN 2012). Yet, while the globalization of markets and institutions seems inevitable, people's deepest fears and aspirations often focus on issues defined by local ethnic and cultural identity (Friedman 2000). Riggs (2004) coined the term "glocalization" to describe the interactive effects of these two contradictory pressures.

The Transformation of U.S. Politics and Public Administration by Globalization

By increasing demands for effective and responsive governance, the shift from a local to a global perspective has helped transform U.S. politics and public administration. This shift, however, has not been a simple or unidirectional transition, but a more complex, contradictory, and evolutionary transformation of politics and administration. That is, global perspectives have been added to local ones rather than replacing them. The nature of this transformation can be illustrated by highlighting the U.S. ambivalence between globalism and parochialism, tension between public policy-making and market-driven solutions, and conflict between national sovereignty and networked governance.

Ambivalence between Globalism and Parochialism

The United States is one of the most diverse nations in the world. One in three U.S. residents is a member of an ethnic minority group. In 2014, the nation's population was 13 percent African American, 17 percent Hispanic, and 5 percent Asian American or Pacific Islander (U.S. Census Bureau 2014). Yet from its colonial beginnings to the present (Twain 1869/2013), Americans have had mixed feelings about the rest of the world. U.S. political culture was historically characterized by strong tendencies toward isolationism and parochialism. Warnings by the founding fathers about the dangers of "foreign entanglements" echoed long enough for Congress to reject President Wilson's efforts to bring the United States into the League of Nations in 1919. And despite the words of welcome by Emma Lazarus for immigrants arriving on Ellis Island, successive waves of migration to the United States have typically been followed by populist movements and exclusionary laws against "undesirable" immigrants. This tendency persists today as evidenced by controversies over immigration reform and the establishment of a pathway toward citizenship for millions of undocumented immigrants who currently reside in the United States.

However, the United States has been a major global power since the Spanish–American War (1898). This, combined with successful military interventions in what began as two "foreign" world wars in 1917 and 1941, led to a widespread U.S. presumption of "American exceptionalism." This term, which refers to the belief that because the United States has been favored by historical circumstances or God's blessing, it is responsible for bringing democracy and capitalism to developing countries, has often resulted in military interventions abroad (Zimmerman, 2002). In addition, while the attitudes of most Americans toward globalization are generally shaped by the perception that having U.S. citizenship is the genetic equivalent of winning the global lottery, they generally like to travel. Over one-third of the population now holds a valid passport (U.S. Department of State 2014).

The ambivalence in U.S. political culture between globalism and parochialism extends to public administration. While the field is indisputably comparative (Heady 1966; Riggs 1968, 1976, 1980; Stillman 1999), the fundamental tenets of public administration are firmly rooted in the United States and Western Europe. These include the constitutional separation of powers (Rosenbloom 1983), bureaucratic administrative theory (Weber 1922/1997), scientific management (Taylor 1912/1997), and the politics–administration dichotomy (Waldo 1948). Students from the United States generally focus on domestic public administration because it provides the competencies they need to get jobs in U.S. public agencies, nongovernmental organizations (NGOs), and U.S.-based businesses. Foreign students attend U.S. universities to improve their English and because they or their government sponsors consider Western policy and management skills to be essential career competencies.

Because the most prestigious schools, professional associations, and influential journals are based in the United States, Canada, and Western Europe, the historical bias toward Western-centric public administration tends to perpetuate itself in spite of globalization. As Heady wrote, "parochialism is a persistent dominant feature of American public administration, evidenced in the curricula of institutions of higher education and in the conduct of public administration by practicing professionals" (1987, 480). While this may be gradually changing due to increased comparative research in North America, Europe, and Asia, there is still relatively little research on Africa and Latin America published in English language journals (Fitzpatrick et al. 2011).

Furthermore, while the Network of Schools of Public Policy, Affairs, and Administration (NASPAA), the membership organization for schools of public service, requires that programs it accredits include comparative or international perspectives, its mission-driven approach allows wide latitude in how programs choose to operationalize this standard (NASPAA 2009). About 24 percent of its member schools have an international/global specialization.

This ambivalence between localism and globalism constrains Americans from seeing themselves as others see them and, thus, from understanding their own country in context. It limits their ability to learn from the rest of the world and thus from applying best practices from other places to their own advantage. By impeding U.S. politicians and public administrators from fully realizing the advantages of an international and comparative perspective (Klingner and Washington 2000), the ambivalence between localism and globalism inhibits them from becoming globally competent public administrators, both as individuals and as members of diverse multicultural organizations.

Tension between Public Policy-Making and Markets

The transition from local to global perspectives on politics and public administration also highlights a second ongoing conflict between market-driven solutions and traditional public policy-making as the most effective instrument for development, whether local or international. The ascendency of market solutions over government policy-making has arguably been the dominant global trend in public administration and development for more than thirty years (Yergin and Stanislaw 1998; Peters 2001). This trend began in the 1980s with a gradual transition in both domestic politics and the global development community from a post-World War II emphasis on the administrative state (Waldo 1948) to increased reliance on market mechanisms for achieving political, social, and economic objectives. As the role of government as a service deliverer at national and sub-national levels yielded to the concept of government as service "guarantor" (Osborne and Gaebler 1992), services were increasingly privatized or contracted out (Cooper 2003) and public jobs were increasingly filled by temporary workers or through contracts rather than by civil service employees (Klingner, Nalbandian, and Llorens 2010).

The main effect of the ascendency of market-based mechanisms has been the growth in the role played by international financial institutions (IFIs) such as the World Trade Organization, the World Bank, and the IMF, all of which were created to achieve prosperity, free trade, and economic growth. However, they have often fallen short of their objectives because of ideological insistence on the virtue of market-based solutions despite evidence to the contrary (North, Haber, and Weingast 2003; North et al. 2007; Reid 2007).

Conflict between National Sovereignty and Networked Governance

The transition between local and global perspectives in public administration and the ascendency of market mechanisms over government policy-making is also marked by conflict over whether effective politics and administration at either the local or the global level should emanate from traditional "government" or emergent "governance" (Nye and Donahue 2000; Kahler and Lake 2003; Klingner 2006a. 2009b). In this context, "government" refers to authoritative policy responses by public agencies, while "governance" includes government as well as broader collective interactions with significant public consequences by corporations and NGOs.

In the United States today, thousands of nonprofit organizations routinely provide local government social services funded by taxes, user fees, and charitable contributions. The distinctions between public and private sectors blurred during the surging economy in the 1990s, and continued to do so during the wars in Iraq and Afghanistan where private contractors not only provided support services but also fought alongside uniformed troops. Citizens expect that public services will be delivered conveniently and efficiently whether they are provided by a public agency, private contractor, or NGO. Public managers have had to adjust their thinking to include not only the management of people and services but also the management of contracts, knowing that they will be held politically accountable for the quality of services delivered (Cooper 2003) regardless of who delivers them.

As politics and public administration have transitioned from local to global, the emergent concept of "networked governance" has been less effective at replacing traditional government. In international relations generally, "national sovereignty" assumes that global development and stability can best be achieved through traditional government policies coordinated through international diplomacy and supplemented by programs sponsored by multinational corporations and NGOs. The emergent "networked governance" option presumes that these objectives can best be attained by combining traditional national government policies with market- and community-based initiatives sponsored by multinational corporations and NGOs.

As a result, the current structure supporting global development is a tenuous network of international aid programs run by sovereign nations, IFIs, and global NGOs. Given the heterogeneous and shifting international development environment, implementing coordinated development initiatives encounters the same kinds of issues that affect multinational military efforts. And the IFI leaders must be vigilant that their internal decision-making processes allow for dissent in order to counteract a tendency to put the interests of developed nations— primarily the United States and Western Europe—above those of poorer nations (Stiglitz 2001). Stiglitz recommends that IFIs cease operating behind closed doors and become more democratic and more transparent so that they may evolve into a system of global governance that can effectively counterbalance the more parochial interests of nation-states and corporate conglomerates (Berkman 2008; Berkman et al. 2008).

Concern for national sovereignty constrains IFIs in working with client governments and from interfering in countries' internal political affairs (Woods 2006), but these constraints are not as pronounced when working with international

NGOs (Mathiason 2008). The IFIs can influence government behavior through their expertise on governance and institutional reform, yet the conditional aid they favor is generally ineffective at ensuring institutional reform, particularly when other countries, such as China, use nonconditional aid to open markets and access raw materials (Foerstel 2008). Corruption is a major obstacle to aid effectiveness (Marquette 2003), yet IFIs' oversight and monitoring activities remain largely ineffective, particularly procurement and auditing (U.S. Government Accounting Office 2000; Thornburgh, Gainer, and Walker 2000).

Two examples illustrate this dilemma. First, while other countries generally opposed unilateral U.S. military initiatives in Iraq or Afghanistan, multinational NATO and UN peace-keeping efforts are hampered by communication, coordination, and control issues. Second, Europe's economic travails reflect tension between Europeans' shared commitment to end the nationalist, ethnic, and religious wars that have plagued them for the past millennium and the European Union's inability to reconcile national sovereignty with the need for uniform economic policies, monetary policies, and regulatory frameworks. While national sovereignty and networked governance can, in theory, be combined, whether this can be legitimized in law or effective in practice remains uncertain (O'Toole and Hanf 2002; Newland 2006; Nickel 2007).

Applying Public Administration Research to Global Development Issues

As public administration research becomes more global, applying it effectively to global development issues can be problematic (Riggs 1962, 1991; Jreisat 2005; Klingner 2009a). Since development is undeniably normative, the objective is not to eliminate bias, but to make it more explicit. Once we accept what goals we seek and which indicators we will use to measure them, we need to develop a focused and comprehensive action research agenda, select appropriate research methods (including participant observation as well as objective data collection and analysis) and disseminate research results effectively.

International development agencies, IFIs, and NGOs now collect and publish information that public administrators can use to benchmark performance on a range of descriptive indicators related to poverty (UN 2012), economic development (World Bank 2012), political liberty (Freedom House 2012), and perceived corruption (Transparency International 2012). While aggregated quantitative data do not give the complete picture, they help measure progress and pinpoint areas of concern.

However, collecting and organizing qualitative data so that they are useful to practicing administrators is challenging. Much of the information and "lessons learned" generated through existing case studies and expert workshops reflects the viewpoints of donors or outside scholars, and does not necessarily meet the needs of hard pressed institution builders (NAPA 2008). Researchers may overlook or discount the perspectives of practitioners not affiliated with development institutions, associations, and informal professional networks.

The most effective dissemination strategy is to relate stories of various experiences through a virtual, web-based network among individuals and organizations around the world who are grappling with similar institution- and capacity-building issues. To do this, we need to learn more about how administrative reforms work effectively in different cultural contexts. Fitzpatrick et al. (2011) conclude that comparative research involves building on theory and empirical research, making use of purposive samples, and using a mix of causal, descriptive, and exploratory methodologies.

Subject matter varies widely, but most research continues to focus on European, Asian, and North American countries. Comparative research is primarily qualitative, making extensive use of existing data. The authors recommend enhanced application of mixed methods, increased use of culture as a key concept, more interdisciplinary research, and integrated application strategies by policy-makers, students, practitioners, and scholars.

To be ultimately useful as a tool for global development, comparative public administration research must connect research results with policy outcomes and policy influences through performance measures (Julnes and Holzer 2001; Landry, Lamari, and Amara 2003). Implementation must be sustainable, grounded in what we know about successful knowledge management (Nonaka 1994), organizational learning (Klingner and Sabet 2005), innovation diffusion and adoption (Rogers 2003; Klingner 2006b), and the complex relationship between researcher results and policy adoption (Julnes and Holzer 2001). While the term "best practices" assumes that innovations may be transferred from one situation to another, the term "smart practices" is better. It more clearly explains how exogenous innovations are adapted and sustained, because it is based on the assumption that applying what we learn must take a number of contextual variables into account (Bardach 2000; Caiden and Sundaram 2004; Roberts 2000; Robinson 2007). We can take advantage of advances in information technology to supplement physical (traditional face-to-face) learning with parallel worldwide networks among individuals and organizations that are grappling with similar institution- and capacity-building issues around the world.

How to Prepare Globally Competent Public Administrators and Organizations

Responding effectively to the imperatives of globalization and governance means that public administrators need to become professionally competent and personally comfortable with diversity. This section will (1) describe the evolutionary convergence of domestic diversity and global multiculturalism; (2) explore what it means and what it feels like to be a global public administrator; and (3) discuss how to build these competencies in individuals and organizations.

The Convergence of Domestic Diversity and Global Multiculturalism

Globalization means more human migration in search of greater security and opportunity (Economist 2011; Friedman 2007). The United States is already one of the most diverse nations in the world; by 2060 it will be even more so (U.S. Census Bureau 2012). The population of non-Hispanic whites will peak at 200 million in 2024, then slowly decrease to 180 million. Hispanics will more than double, from 53 million in 2012 to 129 million. By 2060, nearly one in three U.S. residents will be Hispanic. Blacks will increase from 41 million to 62 million (from 13 percent to 15 percent of the population). Asians will increase from 16 million to 34 million, climbing from 5 percent to 8 percent of the population.

In an effort to keep out those who might take away American jobs or burden health, education, and criminal justice systems, many U.S. citizens—including some naturalized immigrants—resist the influx of illegal or unassimilated foreigners by supporting tight immigration controls or "English only" laws. But, as diversity increases, most Americans' perception of the desired societal goal has changed from a "melting pot" characterized by rapid cultural assimilation and linguistic homogeneity to a "salad bowl" characterized by immigrants learning at least enough English to communicate with monolingual U.S. citizens and becoming familiar with American values, customs, and society (Leonhardt 2013). At the same time, Americans' increased exposure to globalization and immigration is increasing their understanding and respect for other cultures and languages, and diminishing the effectiveness of nativist efforts to blame foreigners and cultural minorities for America's problems.

Economic considerations drive this cultural shift. Given the demographic challenges posed by an aging workforce and retiring baby boomers, the U.S. economy will not grow without an influx of younger immigrant workers at both ends of the skills spectrum. U.S. businesses recognize that they can best capture emerging minority markets by providing desired products and hiring minority representatives to sell them; governments have learned they can best meet the service demands of specialized constituencies by recruiting ethnic minorities who have the needed linguistic and cultural skill sets.

The political landscape is also changing. For the past five years, the net flow of migrants from Mexico to the United States has essentially stopped or even reversed because of Mexico's declining birth rate and booming economy (Economist 2012). Generally negative responses to the Republican Party's hardline stance on "illegal" immigrants contributed to its dismal showing among Hispanics in the 2012 elections. This combination of changing demographics and real-politik may lead to a policy window conducive to legislative and administrative immigration reforms that will offer foreigners now living in the United States a clear and understandable path to citizenship, thereby ending the need for them to choose between drawing attention to themselves and being deported, and living a marginalized existence marked by continued economic, social, and political discrimination (Sengupta 2013).

In the workplace, the emergent focus on international multicultural competence is converging with the traditional U.S. domestic focus on workforce diversity. Increasingly, it is recognized that the skills needed to contribute to or manage diverse, multi-disciplinary and multi-organizational work teams in the United States are congruent with the competencies required of globally competent public administrators (Rice 2004; Borrego and Johnson 2011; Gooden 2012). Therefore, workplace policies and programs that promote effective diversity management are indistinguishable from those promoting global multicultural competence (Mor Barak 2011).

What Does it Mean to Be "at Home in the World," and What Does it Feel Like?

A globally competent public administrator is one who has learned to be "at home in the world" by having the competencies needed to function in a diverse and multicultural context. This means learning to not only feel comfortable with diversity, but also to actively enjoy it. According to the theory of left-brain or right-brain dominance, each side of the brain controls different types of thinking and people are said to prefer one type of thinking over the other. A "left-brained" person is often said to be more logical, analytical, and objective, while a "right-brained" person is considered more intuitive, thoughtful, and subjective (Meindl 2012). Although dichotomous models are often more appealing for conceptual clarity than for accuracy, this one is useful because it emphasizes that "understanding" and "feeling" are both legitimate kinds of knowledge.

Becoming a globally competent public administrator requires both. Understanding diversity and multiculturalism means not only being able to categorize people based on their status as members of a protected class (for example, race, religion, age, gender, ethnicity, and national origin) under U.S. affirmative action laws, but also being able to recognize and respond to the whole spectrum of personal characteristics that define and differentiate each of us as a unique human being. It means not only being able to evaluate their credentials and competencies from an objective human resource management perspective, but also being able to appreciate and respect them for who they are and what they are becoming. By seeking, experiencing, and learning to be comfortable and confident through personal experiences with diversity at home and abroad, public administrators can intuit the sensibilities and understandings that allow them to meet a diverse spectrum of domestic and international colleagues as equals, to learn about them as individuals, to develop and nurture working relationships with them based on mutual respect and understanding, and to collaborate with them on long-term professional endeavors. This requires right-brain qualities such as empathy, courtesy, grace, and humor. It requires moving out of one's comfort zone, struggling to learn an unfamiliar culture and perhaps also an unfamiliar language.

Immersing oneself in another culture or language requires commitment and courage to take a risk. Even one as simple as buying unfamiliar food in an open-air market is to take a chance on not liking it. But the opposite may result. To risk something significant, like the time and commitment required to learn another language or live in another country, is to invite the possibility of growing and changing in unexpected ways.

Building Globally Competent Individuals and Organizations

The best public administrators see themselves as students and lifelong learners. Their peers consider them experts not only because of their experience and qualifications, but also because they continually learn and grow. Becoming a competent global public administrator is a continuous process rather than a discrete goal that, once achieved, is completed (Cleveland 1985; Argyriades and Pichardo Pagaza 2009).

This requires "left-brain" competencies in comparative administration, political science, economics, sociology, and information and communications technologies. It also requires the "right-brain" sensitivities needed to pay attention to, absorb, and intuit meaning from a universe of bewildering information. It means learning why colleagues in other cultures and countries think and behave as they do, viewing our assumptions and actions through colleagues' eyes, and adapting what we already know to the opportunities and constraints of a different context.

Public administrators need a range of disciplinary competencies to provide effective management consultancies and exchanges among countries and cultures. This challenge can be met by interdisciplinary professional training and education, interdisciplinary faculty exchanges, multidisciplinary team projects in Master of Public Administration (MPA) programs, and collaborative, multidisciplinary research for practicing public managers, MPA graduates, and public administration researchers (Posner 2009). Training programs should embrace concentrations or full integration of international issues within the regular curriculum in order to enrich students' diversity in their learning and to provide maximum exposure to different cultures and perspectives (Rice 2004). If an action research agenda is to drive public administration education so as to share what is known about program planning, active participation, and service delivery, most useful are interactive experiential modalities, simulations, decision situations, and technical problem-solving workshops (Cooley 2008; Thynne 1998).

Because they trace their roots back to that original taxonomy that separated science-based disciplines from the arts and humanities, academic public administration and policy programs traditionally focus on developing left-brain competencies. But many disciplines (for example, visual and performing arts, literature, and music) also emphasize right-brain functions such as creativity, intuition, and spontaneity.

Courses in diversity management or multicultural management must provide both kinds of learning. Left-brain learning involves facts about global demographic changes, their effects on the United States, awareness of how global cultural differences affect behavior, and the ability to develop diversity management programs that result in more culturally competent individuals and work teams (Mor Barak 2011). Right-brain learning involves making students more aware of what it feels like to be a foreigner or member of an excluded or marginalized minority group, by helping them recognize and appreciate a cultural kaleidoscope, and by teaching them how to grow by integrating left-brain analysis and right-brain experience (Bordas 2007).

Organizational learning reinforces individual learning. Multinational corporations promote international assignments not only as an explicit leadership development strategy, but also because their leaders share an implicit world view that "becoming global" is a necessary component for organizational survival in the global economy (Counihan 2009). As networked governance joins the more traditional concept of authority as the legal exercise of power in a defined geographic area, public agency heads may also come to view global public administrative competence—organizational and individual—as equally essential (Johnson and Thomas 2007).

Professional associations constitute an increasingly important part of the lifelong learning process (Klingner 2008). Long after formal education is completed, conferences, training, and professional certifications are the major ways administrators can maintain or increase their competencies. The professional associations that provide these member services must themselves be diverse, globally focused, learning organizations whose cultures are permeated by the same values and learning that are required for their individual and organizational clients. If so, they will increase competence through training and certification, technical assistance, publications, conferences, networking, and policy advocacy, as well as creating virtual spaces for global knowledge management and organizational learning.

Conclusion

Interacting global and local forces have increased demands for good governance globally. Responses to international trends and events have helped transform politics and public administration by highlighting tensions between globalism and parochialism, public policy-making and markets, and national sovereignty and networked governance.

Applying public administration research to global development issues is challenging. While "best practice" assumes that innovations may be readily transferred from one situation to another, "smart practice" more appropriately focuses on how culture and other contextual variables affect the feasibility and sustainability of administrative reforms. Implementation must be grounded in performance measurement, knowledge management, organizational learning, innovation diffusion and adoption, and the relationship between research results and policy adoption.

Because the same competencies are required of public administrators in multicultural work teams as in diverse ones, globalization has also contributed to the convergence of domestic diversity management and global multicultural policies and programs in the workplace. Public administrators are now called upon to become more professionally competent and personally comfortable with diversity. The context for public administration at all levels—local, regional, state, federal, and international—is a complex quilt made of many fabrics.

References

Argyriades, D., and I. Pichardo Pagaza, eds. 2009. *Winning the Needed Change: Saving our Planet Earth—A Global Public Service*. New York: IOS Press.

Astorga, L., and D. Shirk. 2010. *Drug Trafficking Organizations and Counter Drug Strategies in the U.S.–Mexican Context*. USMEX WP 10–01. San Diego, CA: Evolving Democracy, Center for U.S.–Mexican Studies, University of California at San Diego. www.escholarship.org/uc/item/8j647429 (accessed May 24, 2012).

Bardach, E. 2000. *Practical Guide for Policy Analysis: The Eightfold Path to More Effective Problem Solving*. New York: Chatham House.

Berkman, S. 2008. *The World Bank and the Gods of Lending*. Sterling, VA: Kumarian Press.

———, N. Boswell, F. Bruner, M. Gough, J. McCormick, P. Pedersen, J. Ugaz, and S. Zimmermann. 2008. "The Fight against Corruption: International Organizations at a Crossroads." *The Journal of Financial Crime* 15(2): 124–154.

Bordas, J. 2007. *Salsa, Soul, and Spirit*. San Francisco: Berrett-Koehler Publishers.

Borrego, E., and R. Johnson III. 2011. *Cultural Competence for Public Administrators: Managing Diversity in Today's World*. Boca Raton, FL: CRC Press.

Brinkerhoff, D., and J. Mayfield. 2005. "Democratic Governance in Iraq? Progress and Peril in Reforming State–Society Relations." *Public Administration & Development* 25(1): 59–73.

Brudney, J., L. O'Toole, Jr., and G. H. Rainey. 2000. *Advancing Public Management: New Developments in Theory, Methods, and Practice*. Washington, DC: Georgetown University Press.

Caiden, G., and P. Sundaram. 2004. "The Specificity of Public Service Reform." *Public Administration & Development* 24(5): 373–383.

Carson, Carol S. 2006. *Globalization: A Progress Report*. Fourth meeting of the Advisory Expert Group on National Accounts, January 30–February 8, Frankfurt. http://unstats.un.org/unsd/nationalaccount/AEG/papers/m4Globalization.pdf (accessed June 7, 2014).

Cleveland, H. 1985. "Educating for the Information Society." *Change: The Magazine of Higher Learning* 17(4): 13–21.

Cooley, L. 2008. "The State and International Development Management: Commentary from International Development Management Practitioners." *Public Administration Review* 68(s1): 1003–1004.

Cooper, P. 2003. *Governing by Contract*. Washington, DC: CQ Press.

Counihan, C. 2009. "Going Global: Why Do Multinational Corporations Participate in Highly Skilled Migration?" *Comparative Technology Transfer and Society* 7(1): 19–42.

DiIulio, J., G. Garvey, and D. Kettl. 1993. *Improving Government Performance: An Owner's Manual*. Washington, DC: Brookings Institution.

Economist. 2011. "The Magic of Diasporas." November 19. www.economist.com/node/21538742 (accessed April 9, 2013).

———. 2012. "Going up in the World: Special Report Mexico." November 24, 3–16.

Farazmand, Ali. 1996. "Development and Comparative Public Administration: Past, Present, and Future." *Public Administration Quarterly* 20(3): 343–364.

———. 1999. "Globalization and Public Administration." *Public Administration Review* 59(6): 509–522.

Fitzpatrick, J., M. Goggin, T. Heikkila, D. Klingner, J. Machado, and C. Martell. 2011. "A New Look at Comparative Public Administration: Trends in Research and an Agenda for the Future." *Public Administration Review* 71(6): 821–830.

Foerstel, Karen. 2008. *China in Africa: Is China Gaining Control of Africa's Resources?* Washington, DC: CQ Press.

Freedom House. 2012. *Freedom in the World: The Annual Survey of Civil Rights and Political Liberties*. New York: Rowman & Littlefield.

Friedman, T. 2000. *The Lexus and the Olive Tree: Understanding Globalization*. New York: Bantam.

———. 2007. *The World Is Flat: A Brief History of the Twenty-First Century*, Release 3.0. New York: Picador.

Gooden, S. 2012. *Cultural Competency for Public Administrators*. Armonk, NY: M.E. Sharpe.

Heady, Ferrell. 1966. *Public Administration: A Comparative Perspective*. Englewood Cliffs, NJ: Prentice Hall.

———. 1987. "American Constitutional and Administrative Systems in Comparative Perspective." *Public Administration Review* 47(1): 9–16.

IMF. 2008. "Globalization: A Brief Overview." May. www.imf.org/external/np/exr/ib/2008/053008.htm (accessed May 29, 2014).

Johnson, H., and A. Thomas. 2007. "Individual Learning and Building Organisational Capacity for Development." *Public Administration & Development* 27(1): 39–48.

Jreisat, J. 2005. "Comparative Public Administration Is Back in, Prudently." *Public Administration Review* 65(2): 231–242.

———. 2011. *Globalism and Comparative Public Administration*. Boca Raton, FL: CRC Press.

Julnes, P., and M. Holzer. 2001. "Promoting the Utilization of Performance Measures in Public Organizations: An Empirical Study of Factors Affecting Adoption and Implementation." *Public Administration Review* 61(6): 693–708.

Kahler, M., and D. Lake, eds. 2003. *Governance in a Global Economy*. Princeton, NJ: Princeton University Press.

Kettl, D. 1997. "The Global Revolution in Public Management: Driving Themes, Missing Links." *Journal of Policy Analysis and Management* 16(3): 446–462.

———. 2002. *The Transformation of Governance*. Baltimore: Johns Hopkins University Press.

Klingner, D. 2006a. "Building Global Public Management Governance Capacity: 'The Road Not Taken.'" *Public Administration Review* 66(5): 775–779.

———. 2006b. "Diffusion and Adoption of Innovations: A Development Perspective." In *Innovations in Governance and Public Administration: Replicating What Works*, ed. Guido Bertucci, 55–60. New York: UN/DESA/DPADM.

———. 2008. "Toward a New ASPA: Building Global Governance Capacity through Networked Professional Associations." *International Journal of Organization Theory and Behavior* 11(3): 355–372.

———. 2009a. "Reducing Poverty: Do We Have the Means to Reach this End?" *Public Administration Review* 69(6): 1180–1186.

———. 2009b. "Using U.S. Public Administration to Support Global Development." *Journal of Regional Studies and Development* 18(2): 1–30.

———, and G. Sabet. 2005. "Knowledge Management, Organizational Learning, Innovation Diffusion and Adoption, and Technology Transfer: What They Mean and Why They Matter." *Comparative Technology Transfer and Society* 3(3): 199–210.

———, and C. Washington. 2000. "Through the Looking Glass: Realizing the Advantages of an International and Comparative Approach for Teaching Public Administration." *Journal of Public Affairs Education* 6(1): 35–43.

———, J. Nalbandian, and J. Llorens. 2010. *Public Personnel Management: Contexts and Strategies*, 6th ed. Englewood Cliffs, NJ: Pearson/Simon & Schuster.

———, J. Nalbandian, and B. Romzek. 2002. "Politics, Administration and Markets: Competing Expectations and Accountability." *American Review of Public Administration* 32(2): 117–144.

Landry, R., M. Lamari, and N. Amara. 2003. "The Extent and Determinants of the Utilization of University Research in Government Agencies." *Public Administration Review* 63(2): 192–205.

Leonhardt, D. 2013. "Hispanics, the New Italians." *The New York Times*, April 21, SR5. www.nytimes.com/2013/04/21/sunday-review/hispanics-the-new-italians.html?hpw&_r=0 (accessed April 20, 2013).

Marquette, H. 2003. *Corruption, Politics and Development: The Role of the World Bank*. New York: Palgrave Macmillan.

Mathiason, J. 2008. *Invisible Governance: International Secretariats in Global Politics*. Sterling, VA: Kumarian Press.

Meindl, A. 2012. *At Left Brain, Turn Right: An Uncommon Path to Shutting Up Your Inner Critic, Giving Fear the Finger & Having an Amazing Life!* Los Angeles: Meta Creative.

Mor Barak, M. 2011. *Managing Diversity: Toward a Globally Inclusive Workplace*, 2nd ed. Thousand Oaks, CA: Sage.

NAPA (National Academy of Public Administration). 2008. *Building Public Administration in Fragile and Post-Conflict States: Why, What, How and Who?* Interim Report to the International Standing Panel, NAPA, on the Institutions for Fragile States Initiative of Princeton University and NAPA. Washington, DC: NAPA, May 8.

NASPAA. 2009. *NASPAA Standards 2009*. http://naspaaccreditation.files.wordpress.com/2014/09/naspaa-standards.pdf (accessed November 21, 2014).

Newland, C. 2006. "Facilitative Governance Organizations and Networks: Disaggregated and Offloaded Government and Aggregated Response to Onloaded Stress." *Public Administration Review* 66(3): 469–472.

Nickel, P. 2007. "Network Governance and the New Constitutionalism." *Administrative Theory & Praxis* 29(2): 198–224.

Nonaka, I. 1994. "A Dynamic Theory of Organizational Knowledge Creation." *Organization Science* 5(1): 14–37.

North, D., S. Haber, and B. Weingast. 2003. "If Economists Are So Smart, Why Is Africa So Poor?" *The Wall Street Journal*, July 30, A12.

——, J. Wallis, S. Webb, and B. Weingast. 2007. *Limited Access Orders in the Third World: A New Approach to the Problems of Development.* Policy Research Working Paper No. 4359. Washington, DC: The World Bank, April 4.

Nye Jr., J., and J. Donahue, eds. 2000. *Governance in a Globalizing World.* Washington, DC: Brookings.

Osborne, D., and T. Gaebler. 1992. *Reinventing Government: How the Entrepreneurial Spirit is Transforming the Public Sector.* New York: Perseus.

O'Toole Jr., L., and K. Hanf. 2002. "American Public Administration and Impacts of International Governance." *Public Administration Review* 62(4): 158–169.

Peters, B.G. 2001. *The Future of Governing.* Lawrence, KA: The University of Kansas Press.

Pollitt, C., and G. Bouchaert. 2000. *Public Management Reform: A Comparative Analysis.* Oxford: Oxford University Press.

Posner, P. 2009. "The Pracademic: An Agenda for Re-Engaging Practitioners and Academics." *Public Budgeting and Finance* 29(1): 12–26.

Reid, G. 2007. *A Proposal for Improving World Bank Support for Institutional Reform and Capacity Building (IRCB) in Client Countries.* Washington, DC: The World Bank, May.

Rice, M. 2004. *Diversity and Public Administration: Theory, Issues, and Perspectives.* Armonk, NY: M.E. Sharpe.

Riggs, F. 1962. "Trends in the Comparative Study of Public Administration." *International Review of Administrative Sciences* 27(1): 9–15.

——. 1968. "Administration and a Changing World Environment." *Public Administration Review* 28(4): 348–361.

——. 1976. "The Group and the Movement: Notes on Comparative and Development Administration." *Public Administration Review* 36(6): 648–654.

——. 1980. "The Ecology and Context of Public Administration: A Comparative Perspective." *Public Administration Review* 40(2): 107–115.

——. 1991. "Public Administration: A Comparativist Framework." *Public Administration Review* 51(6): 473–477.

——. 2004. "Global Studies Manifesto." *Globalizations* 1(2): 344–350.

Roberts, N. 2000. "Wicked Problems and Network Approaches to Resolution." *International Public Management Review* 1(1): 1–19.

Robinson, M. 2007. "The Politics of Successful Governance Reforms: Lessons of Design and Implementation." *Commonwealth & Comparative Politics* 45(4): 521–548.

Rogers, E. 2003. *Diffusion of Innovations,* 5th ed. New York: Simon & Schuster.

Rosenbloom, D. 1983. "Public Administrative Theory and the Separation of Powers." *Public Administration Review* 44(3): 219–227.

Rubin, B. 2007. "Saving Afghanistan." *Foreign Affairs* 86(1): 57–78.

Samuel, A. 2008. "Going International: A Mission-Driven Growth Strategy." *PA Times* (International Supplement) 31 (March): 9.

Sengupta, S. 2013. "Engineers See a Path Out of Green Card Limbo." *The New York Times,* May 22, A1. www.nytimes.com/2013/05/23/technology/long-wait-for-a-green-card-could-be-ending.html?nl=todaysheadlines&emc=edit_th_20130523&_r=0 (accessed May 23, 2013).

SICA. 2014. "Decades of SICA Leadership." American Society for Public Administration. http://aspasica.wordpress.com/four-decades-of-sica-leadership/ (accessed June 7, 2014).

Stiglitz, J. 2001. *Globalization and Its Discontents.* New York: W.W. Norton.

Stillman, R. 1999. *Preface to Public Administration*, 2nd ed. Burke, VA: Chatelaine.

Stone, Donald. 1975. "Birth of ASPA: A Collective Effort in Institution Building." *Public Administration Review* 35(1): 83–93.

Taylor, F. 1912/1997. "Scientific Management." In *Classics of Public Administration*, 4th ed., ed. Jay Shafritz and A. Hyde, 30–32. Fort Worth, TX: Harcourt Brace College Publishers.

Thornburgh, R., P. Gainer, and C. Walker. 2000. *Report to Shengman Zhang, Managing Director and Chairman of the Oversight Committee on Fraud and Corruption Concerning Mechanisms to Address Problems of Fraud and Corruption*. Washington, DC: World Bank, January 21.

Thynne, I. 1998. "IASIA Symposium on Education and Training for the Public Sector in a Changing World of Government." *International Review of Administrative Sciences* 64(3): 371–383.

Transparency International. 2012. *The 2012 Transparency International Corruption Perceptions Index*. http://cpi.transparency.org/cpi2012/ (accessed April 17, 2013).

Traub, J. 2009. "Can Pakistan Be Governed?" *The New York Times Magazine*, April 5, 28–33, 48, 51.

Twain, M. 1869/2013. *The Innocents Abroad*. Kindle ed. www.amazon.com/The-Innocents-Abroad-ebook/dp/B004SQTBKC/ref=sr_1_2_bnp_1_kin?s=books&ie=UTF8&qid=1366050780&sr=1–2&keywords=innocents+abroad+mark+twain (accessed April 14, 2013).

UN. 2012. *The Millennium Development Goals Report 2012*. New York: UN/DESA/DPADM.

U.S. Census Bureau. 2012. "U.S. Census Bureau Projections Show a Slower Growing, Older, and More Diverse Nation a Half Century from Now." News release, December 12. www.census.gov/newsroom/releases/archives/population/cb12-243.html (accessed April 15, 2013).

———. 2014. "State and County QuickFacts." July 8. http://quickfacts.census.gov/qfd/states/00000.html (accessed November 21, 2014).

U.S. Department of State. 2014. "Passport Statistics." http://travel.state.gov/content/passports/english/passports/statistics.html (accessed February 17, 2014).

U.S. Government Accounting Office. 2000. *World Bank: Management Controls Stronger, but Challenges in Fighting Corruption Remain*. Report to Congressional Committees, GAO/NSIAD-00-73. Washington, DC: U.S. Government Printing Office, April.

Waldo, D. 1948. *The Administrative State: A Study of the Political Theory of American Public Administration*. New York: Ronald Press.

Weber, M. 1922/1997. "Bureaucracy." In *Classics of Public Administration*, 4th ed., ed. J. Shafritz and A. Hyde, 37–43. Fort Worth, TX: Harcourt Brace College Publishers.

Woods, N. 2006. *The Globalizers: The IMF, the World Bank, and Their Borrowers*. Ithaca, NY: Cornell University Press.

World Bank. 2012. *World Bank Development Indicators 2012*. Washington, DC: The World Bank.

Yergin, D., and J. Stanislaw. 1998. *The Commanding Heights: The Battle between Government and the Marketplace that Is Remaking the Modern World*. New York: Simon & Schuster.

Zimmerman, W. 2002. *First Great Triumph*. New York: Farrar, Straus and Giroux.

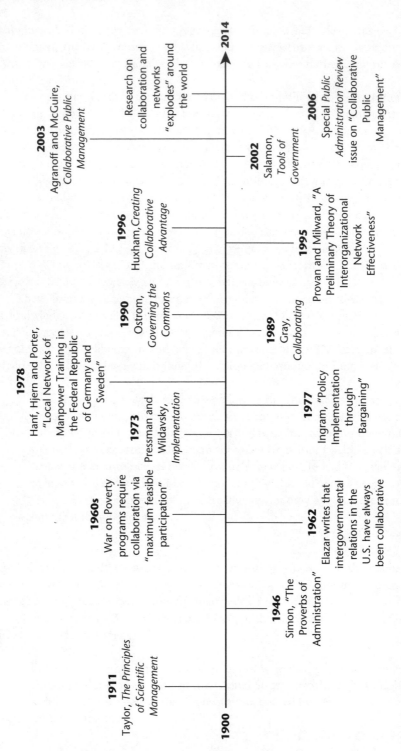

FIGURE 5.1 Silos to Networks: Benchmarks across Time

5

FROM SILOS TO NETWORKS

Hierarchy to Heterarchy[1]

Rosemary O'Leary

With the evolution from government to governance, public management scholars are giving increasing attention to collaboration across agencies, sectors, and levels of government. This phenomenon has been the subject of an explosion of research as public service morphs from the delivery of goods and services by centralized, hierarchical systems to delivery by a decentralized, heterarchical structure. This chapter describes the transition in public management from confidence in scientific management and hierarchical systems to an awareness of the multiplicity and interconnectedness of stakeholders in public service delivery and the growing reliance on collaborative efforts to deliver these services. The chapter begins with a description of Frederick Taylor's concept of scientific management followed by a discussion of how collaborative strategies have refocused management thinking. The subsequent sections of the chapter describe management skills required in the transition from silos to networks and from hierarchy to heterarchy.

Early Twentieth Century: The Scientific Management Approach

While collaboration has been a popular topic among public managers in recent decades, that was not the case in the early 1900s when scientific management was the vogue. Students of public administration are well versed in the scientific management movement that began with Frederick Taylor in the latter decades of the nineteenth century. Taylor, often referred to as the father of scientific management, articulated the philosophy of the movement in *The Principles of Scientific Management*, a monograph published in 1911. He and other scientific management proponents posited that optimizing the way in which people work would be more efficient than simply expecting people to work as hard as they could but without direction and guidance from their superiors. Proponents of the scientific management school used time-and-motion studies to identify and disaggregate work tasks. Structured to meet the needs of assembly-line production methods, work tasks were divided into tiny steps and workers were trained to follow each step exactly as prescribed. The rationale of scientific management is that by simplifying jobs and minimizing the energy required to perform them, productivity would increase. While not ruling out collaboration across organizational boundaries, scientific management's focus was on individual efficiency and productivity.

Beginning in the late 1800s and continuing into the 1930s, the scientific management movement in industrial manufacturing was paralleled by the development of principles of public administration that gained the credibility of proverbs. These prescribed unity of command, limited span of control and organizing by purpose, process, clientele, or place—as if each would work despite the policy or organizational setting. The principles eschewed ambiguity and gave the impression that there was one best way to accomplish a task, always with the goal of minimizing expenditures on people and resources (Simon 1946). As Stillman (2000) writes, it gave the field "both rational managerial methodology as well as solid scientific legitimacy to 'do good' public administration" (p. 19).

Mid-Twentieth Century: An Evolving Public Management Paradigm

Scientific management was a predominant theme in much of the public management literature for the first half of the twentieth century. Beginning in the 1960s, public management research began to expand its focus from individual to collaborative efforts. Pressman and Wildavsky (1973), for example, described policy implementation in terms of shared, collaborative management. In their description of the Economic Development Administration's attempts in the 1960s to address minority-group unemployment in Oakland, California, they coined the term the "complexity of joint action" to explain what happens when there are a multiplicity of participants and perspectives from all levels of government.

This finding was not surprising because intergovernmental relations in the United States have always been collaborative to some degree (Elazar 1962). The grants-in-aid system, certainly the most prominent context within which collaboration is essential, has often been characterized by the presence of bargaining and collaboration (Ingram 1977; Pressman 1975). American federalism may, in fact, be the most enduring model of collaborative problem resolution (Agranoff and McGuire 2003) in which "federal-state-local collaboration is the characteristic mode of action" (Grodzins 1960, 266).

Moreover, Hall and O'Toole's (2000, 2004) comparison of institutional arrangements in legislation enacted by Congress in 1965 and in 1993 found that most significant new legislation prescribed the involvement of collaborative structures for policy implementation. Their research showed that the implementation of new programs at the national level requires U.S. public administrators to be prepared to work with a variety of different kinds of actors both within and without government—actors drawn from different organizational cultures, influenced by different sets of incentives, and directed toward different goals.

(Hall and O'Toole 2004, 190)

Research on public management outside the United States also expanded its focus to look at collaboration. For instance, a study of manpower training programs in Germany and Sweden in the 1970s characterized them in terms of multiple power centers with reciprocal relationships, many suppliers of resources, overlapping and dynamic divisions of labor, diffused responsibility for actions, massive information exchanges among actors, and the need for information input from all actors (Hanf, Hjern, and Porter 1978). Findings from studies conducted in the 1980s reinforced the movement toward collaboration in public policy implementation (Hull and Hjern 1987; O'Toole 1985).

Latter Twentieth Century to Present: The Collaborative Model

Collaborative public management is an idea that resonates with many today but as a subject of inquiry it is young and researchers use a variety of terms to describe it. Some talk about the public manager's "toolkit" or "strategies" (O'Leary, Gerard, and Bingham 2006, 6). Some describe collaborative public management as an "option or a choice" (O'Leary, Gerard, and Bingham 2006, 6). Still others refer to collaborative networks as "models or structures" within which managers find themselves (Agranoff and McGuire 2003; O'Toole 1997; Provan and Milward 1995). The unit of analysis used by researchers also varies. While some focus on managers' (or their organization's) individual choice to collaborate, others look at intentional or fortuitous collaborative collective design. Overall, the concept lacks a common definition.

The work of three authors demonstrates the different perspectives on the subject. Gray (1989, 12–13) focuses on interorganizational collaboration and describes it as an emergent process between interdependent organizational actors who negotiate the responses to shared concerns. Huxham (1996, 1) defines collaboration as "working in association with others for some form of mutual benefit" and Bardach (1998, 8) views it as "any joint activity by two or more agencies working together that is intended to increase public value by their working together rather than separately."

Other definitions have emphasized preconditions, process, or outcomes of the relationship. For the purpose of this chapter, I use the following definition of collaborative public management, adapted from Agranoff and McGuire (2003, 1): "Collaborative public management is a concept that describes the process of facilitating and operating in multi-organizational arrangements to solve problems that cannot be solved or easily solved by single organizations. Collaboration can include the public."

While some scholars refer to collaboration as coordination or cooperation, Gray (1989), Gray and Wood (1991), and Selden, Sowa, and Sandfort (2002) observe that these terms are different because "cooperation" and "coordination" do not capture the dynamic, interdependent nature of true collaboration. The differences are illustrated in Figure 5.2 where the right side describes the highest level of service integration and the least autonomous relationships while the left side describes relationships where joint action is less central to organizational missions.

In contradiction to the notion of a continuum, however, Feiock (2009) and Feiock and Scholz (2010), examine these concepts through the lens of decision-making and game theory. They argue that these are not points on a single scale and that problems of coordination and cooperation are fundamentally different forms of collaboration in terms of the risks faced by potential collaborators. One seemingly simple yet powerfully important challenge for practitioners and researchers alike is to define collaboration and to make sure that there is a shared and generally accepted definition.

The Transition from Hierarchy to Heterarchy

There are several practical and theoretical explanations for the increase in public and nonprofit collaboration both in research and in practice. On the practical side, the first is that most public challenges are larger than one organization, requiring new approaches to addressing public issues (Ostrom 1990). Think of any major public policy challenge: housing, poverty, economic inequality, education, pollution, transportation, healthcare, energy, or any other. To address any one of these effectively, a "full court press" is needed including collaboration across agency boundaries (O'Leary, Gerard, and Bingham 2006).

The phrase "lateral thinking" is used to describe creativity that stems from taking knowledge from one substantive context or discipline and applying it to an entirely different one. One well-known example of a lateral thinker was Leonardo DaVinci whose genius stemmed from moving fluidly from art to science, engineering, mathematics, medicine, and architecture. Finding universal rules of nature in widely varying contexts, he dissected the human arm and a bird's wing and tried to use this information to engineer a machine that would enable people

Cooperation   Coordination   Collaboration   Service
                                                                  integration

FIGURE 5.2 Differences among Cooperation, Coordination, and Collaboration

to fly. In this way, DaVinci applied what he learned from human physiology and ornithology to engineering. "Think DaVinci" has become a common saying among collaborators because the primary reason to collaborate is to create something better than if it were done by only one stakeholder.

Huxham (1993, 603) writes that

> collaborative advantage will be achieved when something unusually creative is produced—perhaps an objective is met—that no organization could have produced on its own and when each organization, through the collaboration, is able to achieve its own objectives better than it could alone. In some cases, it should also be possible to achieve some higher-level . . . objectives for society as a whole rather than just for the participating organizations.

A second practical justification for the increase in collaboration is the desire to improve the effectiveness and performance of programs by encouraging public and nonprofit leaders to identify new ways of providing services. Collaboration can result in innovative approaches to service delivery, including multi-sector partnerships (Agranoff and McGuire 2001; Bingham and O'Leary 2008; Goldsmith and Kettl 2009; O'Leary and Bingham 2009).

A third explanation is that technology is helping public and nonprofit organizations and their employees to share information in a way that is integrative and interoperable, with the outcome being a greater emphasis on collaboration (O'Leary, Choi, and Gerard 2012; Pardo, Gil-Garcia, and Luna-Reyes 2010).

A fourth and final practical explanation for collaboration is that citizens are seeking additional avenues for engaging in governance resulting in new and different forms of collaborative problem-solving and decision-making (Bingham, Nabatchi, and O'Leary 2005; Nabatchi et al. 2012; O'Leary, Gerard, and Bingham 2006).

On the theoretical side, there are also several explanations as to why public and nonprofit organizations collaborate, despite the fact that most scholars of interorganizational collaboration agree that organizations prefer autonomy to cooperation and dependence (Bryson, Crosby, and Stone, 2006; Hudson et al., 1999; Rogers and Whetten, 1982). "Resource dependency" is the most well-developed theory of interorganizational partnership. The basic assumption of resource dependency theory is that individual organizations do not have all the resources they need to achieve their goals, and thus must acquire resources, such as money, people, support services, and/or technological knowledge, to survive (Pfeffer and Salancik 1978). That is, organizations must rely on a variety of inputs from the collection of interacting organizations, groups, and persons in the external environment (Gazley and Brudney 2007; Mitchell 2014; Sowa 2009; Van de Ven, Emmett, and Koening 1975).

As a consequence of resource-dependent activities, exchange relationships develop. Levine and White (1961, 588) define organizational exchange as "any voluntary activity between two or more organizations which has consequences, actual or anticipated, for the realization of their respective goals or objectives." More than just a way to acquire needed resources, interactions based on exchange are "a stabilizing force in the life space of organizations" (Alter and Hage 1993, 45). Exchange relationships stabilize interorganizational linkages by reducing uncertainty about the future provision of resources (see, for example, Galaskiewicz 1985) and by maintaining consistent interaction patterns (Kickert, Klijn, and Koppenjan 1997).

Although resource exchange theory is based on the notion of dependency, even relatively independent organizations may collaborate to take advantage of scarce resources (Ansell and Gash 2007; Berry et al. 2008; Emerson, Nabatchi, and Balogh 2012; Foster and Meinhard 2002; Gazley and Brudney 2007; Graddy and Chen 2006, 2009; Gray 1989; Gray and Wood 1991; Mitchell 2014; Pfeffer and Salancik 1978; Sowa 2009; Wood and Gray 1991). Organizations may actively look for funds within existing network structures or initiate collaboration to tap into funding sources (Agranoff and McGuire 2003; Alter and Hage 1993).

A second theoretical explanation as to why organizations collaborate is *common purpose*. Organizations form network linkages to achieve similar, compatible, or congruent goals (Gray 1989; Rogers and Whetten 1982). Issues that were previously thought of as the responsibility of a single agency are increasingly understood to have broad linkages and to be interconnected with other issues (Bryson, Crosby, and Stone 2006; O'Leary, Gerard, and Bingham 2006). Accordingly, many groups or organizations that are responsible for addressing public challenges (Crosby and Bryson 2005) are using collaboration to do so.

Related to common purpose is the notion of *shared beliefs*. A similarity in values and attitudes make the formation of interorganizational linkages more probable (Aldrich 1979; Alter and Hage 1993) and make these linkages more stable over time (Van de Ven, Emmett, and Koening 1975). A common "belief system," including norms, values, perceptions, and worldviews, provides "the principal 'glue' to hold together networks of actors" (Fleishman 2009; Sabatier and Jenkins-Smith 1993, 27).

A third theoretical rationale for collaboration is its use by stakeholders to advance their own political interests (Gazley and Brudney 2007; Heclo 1978; Kickert, Klijn, and Koppenjan 1997; Mitchell 2014; Sabatier and Jenkins-Smith 1993; Sowa 2009). Through participation in a policy network, for example, organizations may promote the views or desires of their members or constituencies; gain access to political officials or decision processes and cultivate political alliances; gain political legitimacy or authority; and promote organizational policies or programs.

Catalytic actors, or leadership both within the organization and by network leaders or coordinators, provide still another theoretical explanation for the formation of collaborative linkages (Agranoff and McGuire 2001; Bardach 1998; Kickert, Klijn, and Koppenjan 1997; O'Leary, Choi, and Gerard 2012). In this instance, individuals acting as leaders or catalysts may provide incentives for organizations to collaborate (Emerson, Nabatchi, and Balogh 2012). Sometimes this takes the form of an individual whose sense of what it means to be a highly professional actor includes the imperative to collaborate (McGuire 2009). Other times, catalytic actors may be individuals who naturally engage in networking throughout their careers (Hicklin et al. 2009).

Challenges Facing Collaborative Networks

There are many challenges in collaborative endeavors. While collaboration can and often does occur outside of networks (Agranoff 2006), this chapter focuses on collaborative networks defined by Isett et al. (2011, i158) as

> collections of government agencies, nonprofits, and for-profits that work together to provide a public good, service, or "value" when a single public agency is unable to create the good or service on its own and/or when the private sector is unable or unwilling to provide the good or services in the desired quantities.

Some networks are sophisticated and well run; others are simplistic and poorly run; most are somewhere in-between. Motivation to collaborate varies. Some leaders choose to collaborate to increase performance, to better serve the public, or to "think DaVinci." Others collaborate to be free-riders and obtain benefits without commensurate effort. For these and other reasons, collaboration is not always wise. In fact, it could negatively impact the primary mission of an organization. To complicate matters, there is the possibility that collaboration may lead to conflict among stakeholders and management issues that can present a formidable challenge.

By definition, networks are complex conglomerations of diverse organizations and individuals. The characteristics that add to the complexity of disputes among network members are numerous (O'Leary and Bingham 2007). They include, among other characteristics, a multiplicity of members and missions as well as variation across organizational structures, methods of operation, and stakeholder perspectives. Other sources of conflict arise from multiple issues and differences in degrees of power among members of the collaborating group as well as variation in governing structures. These characteristics are discussed below:

- *Multiple members and mission:* Network disputes involve many individuals and organizations. All bring their own interests that must be addressed or else members may leave the network. Network members bring both different and common goals. Although there must be some commonality of purpose to provide incentive for becoming a member of a network, each also has its own unique goals that inform their decisions. At times, these can clash with the network goals.

- *Organization culture:* Culture is to the organization what character is to the individual. Just as each individual is unique, so too is each organization's culture. Diversity among cultures in a network may present challenges to the network itself.
- *Methods of operation:* Member organizations will differ in their degree of hierarchy as well as forms of management control. These and other differences may affect what a network can accomplish and the speed at which it can be accomplished.
- *Stakeholder groups and funders:* To satisfy their diverse constituencies, network members embrace different perspectives on appropriate direction and activities. Some of these perspectives will overlap; some will not.
- *Degrees of power:* Not all network members have equal standing. Despite network rules that may give an equal vote to each member, some are more powerful than others. For example, in emergency management networks, federal organizations often are the beneficiaries of legislation that allows them to preempt local and state actors. Differences in power can pose significant challenges to collaborative entities.
- *Multiple issues:* Networks are formed to address complex problems that are not easily solved by one organization. Complex problems bring with them multiple issues and subissues. Multiple issues and subissues produce multiple challenges.
- *Multiple forums for decision-making:* Public decision-making may involve networks. At the same time, the same public issue may be debated and dealt with in the legislature, in the courts, or in the executive branch offices of career public servants. The role of the network can be a challenge.
- *Interorganizational and interpersonal networks:* Networks are spider webs of organizations with each represented by one or more agents of that organization. Just as networked organizations may clash, so too may networked individuals.
- *Governance structures:* How the network chooses to govern itself, lead members, develop consensus, and create conventions for dialogue and deliberative processes are exceedingly important and demanding for networks. Just the design of governance rules for the network can be a complex procedure.
- *Conflict with the public:* Increasingly, collaborative public management networks are engaging citizens through a variety of means. Because networks often address issues of concern to a diverse public with multiple interests, conflict may emerge.

The Management Paradox: Balancing Autonomy and Interdependence

Working within their own organizations as well as within networks, managers are challenged in ways that demand different skill sets from those of the traditional manager. Connelly, Zhang, and Faerman (2008) identify several challenges facing collaborative managers. Building on their work, this section presents additional challenges that face members of collaborations in and outside of networks:

- *Autonomy and interdependence:* As a leader of a single unit, managers often work autonomously, setting the rules and making decisions independently. As a member of a collaborative network, a manager is now one of many decision-makers with numerous intertwining interests.
- *Networks have common and diverse goals:* Each member of a network has goals that are unique to that member's organization or program. At the same time, as members of a network, managers share common goals.
- *Fewer players but greater diversity in networks:* When organizations combine to form a network, they become one body—hence the fewer number. Yet within this one body is a variety of organizations with different cultures, missions, and ways of operating—hence the greater diversity.
- *Need to be both participative and authoritative:* Behavior within a network is participative as members make decisions concerning the direction of the group. Yet as a manager of a single program or organization, a manager is expected to take command and make decisions singly. Connelly, Zhang, and Faerman (2008) emphasize that authoritative is the key word here, not authoritarian, which connotes a more dictatorial style.
- *Details and the whole picture:* Managers of a single program or organization must master the details and fine points of what they do on a daily basis. As a member of a network, these same managers must think holistically and laterally.
- *Balancing advocacy and inquiry:* All managers have an obligation to promote, support, and act in favor of their own organization. Yet because of intertwining interests, managers need to gather the information for decisions necessary to act in the best interests of the network.

What is a manager to do? Connelly, Zhang, and Faerman (2008) emphasize that these paradoxes should be accepted, embraced, and transcended, not resolved. These paradoxes are fundamental challenges of working collaboratively within and outside of networks.

Returning to the Importance of the Individual

The role of the individual in collaborations has largely been given short shrift in the public management literature. Much of the focus is on networks of organizations with scant attention given to the fact that, while organizations and jurisdictions collaborate, the individual is always the unit of analysis. For example, several decades ago Huxham (1993) researched the "collaborative capability" of organizations but emphasized that she was focusing "not on collaboration . . . between individuals, but on collaboration . . . between organizations" (1996, 1).

Four years later, Huxham shifted her attention to include, in part, the people who represent their organizations in collaborations, writing that the relationships between individual participants in collaborations are often fundamental to getting things done (Huxham 2000, 341). In still later work, Huxham explained:

> Collaborations are, of course, enacted by individuals. . . . [T]hese individuals are generally linked to the various organizations that form the collaboration. Commonly, they are acting in a representative function. In the course of collaborative activities, such individuals tend implicitly (and often unwittingly) to converse about their aims, and those of their partners at three levels: the level of the collaboration; the level of the participating organizations; and the level of the participating individuals.
>
> *(Huxham and Vangen 2005, 84)*

In all of Huxham's work on collaboration, references are made to the difficulties and challenges facing the individuals who represent their organizations. Her perceptions are echoed by Frederickson (2007). Clearly, collaboration is dependent on the skills of officials and managers who must have the skills to be effective collaborators. Who is representing an organization, agency, or jurisdiction at the table and whether they have the necessary skills to be an effective collaborator is an essential consideration. O'Leary, Choi, and Gerard (2012) surveyed members of the U.S. Senior Executive Service (SES) and asked the question, "What is the skill set of the successful collaborator?"

Based on the literature on collaboration and networks and given the fact that SES members are standard-setting senior executives who have significant authority as well as knowledge and long tenure in national governance issues, three findings were anticipated:

1. that respondents would say that the most important skills of the collaborative manager are thinking and acting strategically, including visioning (Goldsmith and Eggers 2004; McGuire and Silvia 2009; Milward and Provan 2006);
2. that the desired skills, after acting strategically, would be facilitation, collaborative problem-solving, and conflict management (Crosby and Bryson 2005; Emerson and Smutco 2011; Getha–Taylor 2008; Huxham 1993, 1996, 2000; Huxham and Hibbert 2004; Huxham and Vangen 2005; McGuire and Silvia 2009; Silvia and McGuire 2010; Williams 2002);
3. that interpersonal skills would be highly ranked (Emerson and Smutco 2011; Getha–Taylor 2008; Silvia and McGuire 2010).

Survey responses were surprising. The most frequent responses to the question of what constitutes the skill set of the collaborative manager were personal attributes and interpersonal skills, followed by group process skills, strategic leadership skills, and substantive/technical expertise, respectively. Responses citing personal attributes outnumbered those citing strategy and expertise two-to-one (O'Leary, Choi, and Gerard 2012). The most frequently mentioned personal attributes were, in order: open mindedness, patience, change orientation, flexibility, unselfishness, persistence, diplomacy, honesty, trustworthiness, respectfulness, empathy, goal orientation, decisiveness, being friendly, and having a sense of humor.

The most frequently mentioned interpersonal attributes were good communication and listening skills and the ability to work well with others. Tied with this were group process skills, which were ranked third in importance as part of the skill set for the successful collaborator. Specific among the group process skills were facilitation; interest-based negotiation; collaborative problem-solving; skill in understanding group dynamics, culture, and personalities; compromise; conflict resolution; and mediation. The common thread here is the emphasis on the human element and interpersonal skills. O'Leary and Gerard (2013) replicated their study with 1,417 city and county managers to see if the responses would be the same, and for the most part, they were—with a minor shift in order: individual attributes (74 percent) were mentioned first, followed by interpersonal skills (21 percent), strategic leadership (13 percent), group process skills (12 percent), and substantive/technical knowledge (4 percent). In fact, the emphasis on individual attributes was even more pronounced than with the SES respondents.

Previous studies have discussed collaborative competencies, including specific skills for collaborators, but, as previously mentioned, the individual attributes that leaders possess have not been emphasized in the literature and have been mentioned by only a few authors (Crosby and Bryson 2005, Linden 2002; Morse 2008). In analyzing this part of their survey, O'Leary and Gerard (2013) found themselves in a debate about whether effective collaborators are born or made and, more importantly, whether the individual attributes needed by collaborative leaders can be acquired.

Oftentimes, working in a collaborative capacity means that the individual is not in charge and is leading in a way that is nontraditional. In the early 1900s "great man" theories of leadership were popular. These theories focused on "identifying the innate qualities and attributes possessed by great social, political, and military leaders" (Northouse 2001, 15). Scholars at that time believed that leaders were born, not made, and numerous studies of "great" leaders were carried out to determine the specific traits that separated leaders from followers (Bass 1990; Jago 1982). The focus was solely on the talented individual who could single-handedly enter the picture and save the day.

Yet, in a world where collaboration is common place and where most complex public policy problems are larger than one organization can handle, very different leadership skills—the skills of being a leader when one is working in a network, for example—have become of utmost important. Salamon (2002) observed that collaboration and collaborative governance shift the emphasis from the control of large bureaucratic organizations and the bureaucratic way of managing public programs to enablement skills. These skills are used to bring people together, to engage partners horizontally, and to bring multiple collaborators together for a common goal in a situation of interdependence. Examples include negotiation, facilitation, collaborative problem-solving, and conflict management.

Conclusion

In the seventy-five years since ASPA was founded, views of management and administration have moved from a focus heavily weighted toward "silos" or individual entities (people, programs, and organizations) to a focus on collaboration both within and outside of networks. In 2014, despite the fact that the majority of the work of governments around the world still is carried out in hierarchies, we realize that a collaborative approach that reaches across boundaries of all kinds is essential to address society's most pressing public policy problems. At the same time, there is a realization that a specific collaboration is only as good as the people at the table—or on the ground—who have vision and drive, and consciously use their collaborative competencies to make it work. The future of the field will depend on the ability of stakeholders to accept the need for superior individual skills and superior collaborative efforts to address society's most pressing problems.

Note

1 Parts of this chapter have been previously published as Blomgren, Sandfort, and O'Leary (2008), O'Leary et al. (2009), and O'Leary and Vij (2012).

References

Agranoff, Robert. 2006. "Inside Collaborative Networks: Ten Lessons for Public Managers." *Public Administration Review* 66: 56–65.

——, and Michael McGuire. 2001. "Big Questions in Public Network Management Research." *Journal of Public Administration Research and Theory* 11(3): 295–326.

——, and ——. 2003. *Collaborative Public Management*. Washington, DC: Georgetown University Press.

Aldrich, Howard E. 1979. *Organizations and Environments*. Englewood Cliffs, NJ: Prentice-Hall.

Alter, Catherine, and Jerald Hage. 1993. *Organizations Working Together*. Newbury Park, CA: Sage.

Ansell, Chris, and Alison Gash. 2007. "Collaborative Governance in Theory and Practice." *Journal of Public Administration Research and Theory* 18(4): 543–571.

Bardach, Eugene. 1998. *Getting Agencies to Work Together: The Practice and Theory of Managerial Craftsmanship*. Washington, DC: Brookings Institution Press.

Bass, Bernard M. 1990. *Handbook of Leadership: A Survey of Theory and Research*. New York: Free Press.

Berry, Carolyn, Glen S. Krutz, Barbara Langer, and Peter Budetti. 2008. "Jump-Starting Collaboration: The ABCD Initiative and the Provision of Child Development Services through Medicaid and Collaborators." *Public Administration Review* 68(3): 480–490.

Bingham, Lisa Blomgren, and Rosemary O'Leary, eds. 2008. *Big Ideas in Collaborative Public Management*. Armonk, NY: M.E. Sharpe.

Bingham, Lisa Blomgren, Tina Nabatchi, and Rosemary O'Leary. 2005. "The New Governance: Practices and Processes for Stakeholder and Citizen Participation in the Work of Government." *Public Administration Review* 65(5): 547–558.

Bingham, Lisa Blomgren, Jodi Sandfort, and Rosemary O'Leary. 2008. "Learning to Do and Doing to Learn: Teaching Managers to Collaborate in Networks." In *Big Ideas in Collaborative Public Management*, ed. Lisa Blomgren Bingham and Rosemary O'Leary, 270–295. Armonk, NY: M.E. Sharpe.

Bryson, John M., Barbara C. Crosby, and Melissa M. Stone. 2006. "The Design and Implementation of Cross-Sector Collaborations: Propositions from the Literature." *Public Administration Review* 66(1): 44–55.

Connelly, David R., Jing Zhang, and Sue Faerman. 2008. "The Paradoxical Nature of Collaboration." In *Big Ideas in Collaborative Public Management*, ed. Lisa Blomgren Bingham and Rosemary O'Leary, 17–35. Armonk, NY: M.E. Sharpe.

Crosby, Barbara, and John M. Bryson. 2005. *Leadership for the Common Good*, 2nd ed. San Francisco: Jossey-Bass.

Elazar, Daniel J. 1962. *The American Partnership: Intergovernmental Cooperation in the Nineteenth Century United States*. Chicago: University of Chicago Press.

Emerson, Kirk, and Steven Smutco. 2011. *UNCG Guide to Collaborative Competency*. Portland, OR: Policy Consensus Initiative and University Network for Collaborative Governance.

———, Tina Nabatchi, and Stephen Balogh. 2012. "An Integrative Framework for Collaborative Governance." *Journal of Public Administration Research and Theory* 22(1): 1–29.

Feiock, Richard C. 2009. "Metropolitan Governance and Institutional Collective Action." *Urban Affairs Review* 44(3): 357–377.

———, and John Scholz. 2010. *Self-Organizing Federalism: Collaborative Mechanisms to Mitigate Institutional Collective Action Dilemmas*. Cambridge, MA: Cambridge University Press.

Fleishman, Rachel. 2009. "To Participate or Not to Participate? Incentives and Obstacles for Collaboration." In *The Collaborative Public Manager*, ed. Rosemary O'Leary and Lisa Blomgren Bingham, 31–52. Washington, DC: Georgetown University Press.

Foster, Mary K., and Agnes G. Meinhard. 2002. "A Regression Model Explaining Predisposition to Collaborate." *Nonprofit and Voluntary Sector Quarterly* 31(4): 549–564.

Frederickson, George. 2007. "Bureaucrats without Borders: Public Management and the End of Geography." Unpublished manuscript. Donald Stone Lecture presented at the American Society for Public Administration Conference, Washington, DC, March 26.

Galaskiewicz, Joseph. 1985. "Interorganizational Relations." *Annual Review of Sociology* 11: 281–304.

Gazley, Beth, and Jeffrey L. Brudney. 2007. "The Purpose (and Perils) of Government-Nonprofit Partnership." *Nonprofit and Voluntary Sector Quarterly* 36(3): 389–415.

Getha-Taylor, Heather. 2008. "Identifying Collaborative Competencies." *Review of Public Personnel Administration* 28(2): 103–119.

Goldsmith, Stephen, and William D. Eggers. 2004. *Governing by Network: The New Shape of the Public Sector*. Washington, DC: Brookings Institution Press.

———, and Donald Kettl. 2009. *Unlocking the Power of Networks: Keys to High-Performance Government*. Washington, DC: Brookings Institution Press.

Graddy, Elizabeth A., and Bin Chen 2006. "Influences on the Size and Scope of Networks for Social Service Delivery." *Journal of Public Administration Research and Theory* 16(4): 533–522.

———, and ———. 2009. "Partner Selection and the Effectiveness of Interorganizational Collaboration." In *The Collaborative Public Manager*, ed. Rosemary O'Leary and Lisa Blomgren Bingham, 53–70. Washington, DC: Georgetown University Press.

Gray, Barbara. 1989. *Collaborating: Finding Common Ground for Multiparty Problems*. San Francisco: Jossey-Bass.

———, and Daniel J. Wood. 1991. "Collaborative Alliances: Moving From Practice to Theory." *The Journal of Applied Behavioral Science* 23(3): 3–22.

Grodzins, Malcolm. 1960. "The Federal System." In *Goals for America: The Report of the President's Commission on National Goals*, ed. The American Assembly, 265–282. Englewood Cliffs, NJ: Prentice-Hall.

Hall, Thad E., and Laurence J. O'Toole. 2000. "Structures for Policy Implementation: An Analysis of National Legislation, 1965–66 and 1993–94." *Administration and Society* 31(6): 667–686.

———, and ———. 2004. "Shaping Formal Networks through the Regulatory Process." *Administration and Society* 36(2): 186–207.

Hanf, Kenneth, Benny Hjern, and David O. Porter. 1978. "Local Networks of Manpower Training in the Federal Republic of Germany and Sweden." In *Interorganizational Policy Making: Limits to Coordination and Central Control*, ed. Kenneth Hanf and Fritz Scharpf, 303–341. London: Sage Publications.

Heclo, Hugh. 1978. "Issue Networks and the Executive Establishment." In *The New American Political System*, ed. Anthony King, 87–124. Washington, DC: American Enterprise Institute.

Hicklin, Alisa, Laurence J. O'Toole Jr., Kenneth J. Meier, and Scott E. Robinson. 2009. "Calming the Storms: Collaborative Public Management, Hurricanes Katrina and Rita, and Disaster Response." In *The Collaborative Public Manager: New Ideas for the Twenty-First Century*, ed. Rosemary O'Leary and Lisa Blomgren Bingham, 95–114. Washington, DC: Georgetown University Press.

Hudson, Bob, Brian Hardy, Melanie Henwood, and Gerald Winstow. 1999. "In Pursuit of Inter-Agency Collaboration in the Public Sector: What is the Contribution of Theory and Research?" *Public Management* 1(2): 235–260.

Hull, Christopher J., and Benny Hjern. 1987. *Helping Small Firms Grow: An Implementation Approach*. London: Croom Helm.

Huxham, Chris. 1993. "Pursuing Collaborative Advantage." *Journal of the Operational Research Society* 44(6): 599–611.

———, ed. 1996. *Creating Collaborative Advantage*. London: Sage.

———. 2000. "The Challenge of Collaborative Governance." *Public Management* 2(3): 337–357.

———, and Paul Hibbert. 2004. *Collaborating to Know? Interorganizational Engagement and Learning*. Glasgow: AIM Working Paper Series.

———, and Siv Vangen. 2005. *Managing to Collaborate: The Theory and Practice of Collaborative Advantage*. London: Routledge.

Ingram, Helen. 1977. "Policy Implementation through Bargaining: The Case of Federal Grants-in-Aid." *Public Policy* 25(4): 499–526.

Isett, Kimberley R., Ines A. Mergel, Kelly LeRoux, Pamela A. Mischen, and R. Karl Rethemeyer. 2011. "Networks in Public Administration Scholarship: Understanding Where We Are and Where We Need to Go." *Journal of Public Administration and Theory* 21: i157–i173.

Jago, Arthur G. 1982. "Leadership: Perspectives in Theory and Research." *Management Science* 28(3): 315–336.

Kickert, Walter J.M., Erik-Hans Klijn, and Joop F.M. Koppenjan. 1997. "Public Management and Network Management: An Overview." In *Managing Complex Networks: Strategies for the Public Sector*, ed. Walter J.M. Kickert, Erik-Hans Klijn, and Joop F.M. Koppenjan, 35–61. London: Sage.

Levine, Sol, and Paul E. White. 1961. "Exchange as a Conceptual Framework for the Study of Interorganizational Relationships." *Administrative Science Quarterly* 5: 583–610.

Linden, Russell. 2002. *Working across Boundaries: Making Collaboration Work in Government and Nonprofit Organizations.* San Francisco: Jossey-Bass.

McGuire, Michael. 2009. "The New Professionalism and Collaborative Activity in Local Emergency Management." In *The Collaborative Public Manager: New Ideas for the Twenty-First Century*, ed. Rosemary O'Leary and Lisa Blomgren Bingham, 71–94. Washington, DC: Georgetown University Press.

——, and Christopher Silvia. 2009. "Does Leadership in Networks Matter? Examining the Effect of Leadership Behaviors on Managers' Perceptions of Network Effectiveness." *Public Performance and Management Review* 33(2): 179–206.

Milward, H. Brinton, and Keith G. Provan. 2006. *A Manager's Guide to Choosing and Using Collaborative Networks.* Washington, DC: IBM Center for the Business of Government.

Mitchell, George E. 2014. "Collaborative Propensities among Transnational NGOs Registered in the United States." *American Review of Public Administration* 44(5): 575–599.

Morse, Ricardo. 2008. "Developing Public Leaders in an Age of Collaborative Governance." In *Innovations in Public Leadership Development*, ed. Ricardo S. Morse and Terry F. Buss, 79–100. Armonk, NY: M.E. Sharpe.

Nabatchi, Tina, John Gastil, Michael Weiksner, and Matt Leighninger, eds. 2012. *Democracy in Motion: Evaluating the Practice and Impact of Deliberative Civic Engagement.* New York: Oxford University Press.

Northouse, Peter G. 2001. *Leadership Theory and Practice*, 2nd ed. Thousand Oaks, CA: Sage.

O'Leary, Rosemary, and Lisa Blomgren Bingham. 2007. *A Manager's Guide to Resolving Conflicts in Collaborative Networks.* Washington, DC: IBM Center for the Business of Government.

——, and ——, eds. 2009. *The Collaborative Public Manager: New Ideas for the Twenty-First Century.* Washington, DC: Georgetown University Press.

——, and Catherine Gerard. 2013. "Collaborative Governance and Leadership: A 2012 Survey of Local Government Collaboration." In *The Municipal Yearbook*, ed. The International City/County Management Association, 43–56. Washington, DC: ICMA.

——, and Nidhi Vij. 2012. "Collaborative Public Management: Where Have We Been and Where Are We Going?" *American Review of Public Administration* 42: 507–522.

——, Yujin Choi, and Catherine Gerard. 2012. "The Skill Set of the Successful Collaborator." *Public Administration Review* 72(s1): 70–83.

——, Beth Gazley, Michael McGuire, and Lisa Blomgren Bingham. 2009. "Public Managers in Collaboration." In *The Collaborative Public Manager*, ed. Rosemary O'Leary and Lisa Blomgren Bingham, 1–25. Washington, DC: Georgetown University Press.

——, Catherine Gerard, and Lisa Blomgren Bingham. 2006. "Introduction to Special Issue on Collaborative Public Management." *Public Administration Review* 66(6): 6–16. Washington, DC: ICMA.

Ostrom, Elinor. 1990. *Governing the Commons: The Evolution of Institutions for Collective Action.* Cambridge: Cambridge University Press.

O'Toole, Laurence J. 1985. "Diffusion of Responsibility: An Interorganizational Analysis." In *Policy Implementation in Federal and Unitary Systems*, ed. Kennth Hanf and Theo A.J. Toonen, 210–225. Dordrecht: Martinus Nijhoff Press.

———. 1997. "Treating Networks Seriously: Practical and Research-Based Agendas in Public Administration." *Public Administration Review* 57(1): 45–52.

Pardo, Teresa A., J. Ramon Gil-Garcia, and Luis F. Luna-Reyes. 2010. "Collaborative Governance and Cross-Boundary Information Sharing: Envisioning a Networked and IT-Enabled Public Administration." In *The Future of Public Administration around the World: The Minnowbrook Perspective*, ed. Rosemary O'Leary, David. M. Van Slyke, and Soonhee Kim, 129–140. Washington, DC: Georgetown University Press.

Pfeffer, Jeffrey, and Gerald R. Salancik. 1978. *The External Control of Organizations: A Resource Dependence Perspective*. Stanford, CA: Stanford University Press.

Pressman, Jeffrey L. 1975. *Federal Programs and City Politics: The Dynamics of the Aid Process in Oakland*. Berkeley, CA: University of California Press.

———, and Aaron Wildavsky. 1973. *Implementation*. Berkeley, CA: University of California Press.

Provan, Keith G., and H. Brinton Milward. 1995. "A Preliminary Theory of Interorganizational Network Effectiveness: A Comparative Study of Four Community Mental Health Systems." *Administrative Science Quarterly* 40: 1–33.

Rogers, David L., and David A. Whetten. 1982. *Interorganizational Coordination: Theory, Research, and Implementation*. Ames, IA: Iowa State University Press.

Sabatier, Paul, and Hank Jenkins-Smith. 1993. *Policy Change and Learning: An Advocacy Coalition Approach*. Boulder, CO: Westview Press

Salamon, Lester. 2002. *The Tools of Government: A Guide to the New Governance*. London: Oxford University Press.

Selden, Sally, Jessica Sowa, and Jodi Sandfort. 2002. "The Impact of Nonprofit Collaboration in Early Child Care and Education on Management and Program Outcomes." *Public Administration Review* 66(3): 412–425.

Silvia, Christopher and Michael McGuire. 2010. "Leading Public Sector Networks: An Empirical Examination of Integrative Leadership Behaviors." *The Leadership Quarterly* 21: 264–277.

Simon, Herbert A. 1946. "The Proverbs of Administration." *Public Administration Review* 6(1): 53–67.

Sowa, Jessica E. 2009. "The Collaboration Decision in Nonprofit Organizations: Views from the Front Line." *Nonprofit and Voluntary Sector Quarterly* 38(6): 1003–1025.

Stillman, Richard. 2000. "The Study of Public Administration in the United States: The Eminently Practical Science." In *Public Administration: Concepts and Cases*, ed. Richard Stillman, 17–30. Boston: Houghton Mifflin Company.

Taylor, Frederick Winslow. 1911. *The Principles of Scientific Management*. New York: Harper & Brothers Publishers.

Van de Ven, Andrew H., Dennis C. Emmett, and Richard Koening Jr. 1975. "Frameworks for Inter-Organizational Analysis." *Organization and Administrative Sciences* 6(1): 32–64.

Williams, Paul. 2002. "The Competent Boundary Spanner." *Public Administration* 80(1): 103–124.

Wood, Donna J., and Barbara Gray. 1991. "Toward a Comprehensive Theory of Collaboration." *Journal of Applied Behavioral Science* 27(2): 139–162.

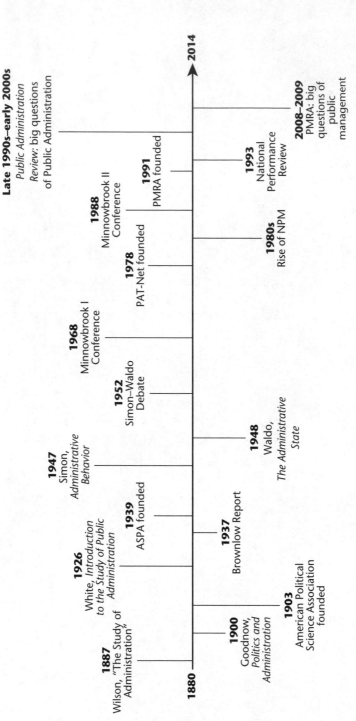

FIGURE 6.1 From Administration to Management: Benchmarks across Time

6

FROM ADMINISTRATION TO MANAGEMENT

Kaifeng Yang

Public management has become a trendy term for public sector practitioners and academicians alike. Many people assert the supremacy of public management over public administration. They believe the change in terminology from public administration to public management reflects a paradigm shift in practice (Aucoin 1990; Hood 1991; Lane 1994) or more theoretical and methodological rigor in research (Bozeman 1993a; Kelman et al. 2003). Others disagree and suggest public management in practice is less democratic and reflects an ideological preference for private sector values, managerialism, and instrumental rationality (Lynn 1996; Terry 1998). There is also suspicion that the pursuit of methodological rigor and empiricism pays the price of less practical relevance (Luton 2007). Still others believe that public management and public administration are synonymous (Lynn 2005; Pollitt and Bouckaert 2011), demonstrating "a distinction without a difference" (Hill and Lynn 2009, 10).

This considerable confusion is difficult to dismantle because the terms and their relationships are socially constructed by individuals possessing different values and assumptions. Thus, the confusion cannot be defined away by any single government or academic authority, nor can it be clarified by tracing the etymology of the terms. This chapter adopts an institutional perspective and examines whether the rise of public management as a practice and a field of study has led to an institutional field that is separated from and superior to the institutional field of public administration. It is possible that words can make a difference in practice. For example, the word *management*, on the negative side, may encourage undemocratic entrepreneurship and undermine the sense of citizenship in favor of customer satisfaction. For such a possibility to materialize, however, the words must become scripts of institutional forces that can lead to material change. Thus seen, the institutionalization of public administration as a field has always involved the delicate relationship between approaches that emphasize law, management, and political science, respectively. The different emphases are reflected in professional associations, education programs, journals, conferences, and perhaps standards. An institutional perspective is particularly appropriate because institutions are embedded in historical and cultural contexts and this chapter is primarily about public administration and public management in the United States. Part of the motivation for this essay is to celebrate the seventy-fifth anniversary of the American Society for Public Administration (ASPA). Before we can develop a generalized understanding of public administration and public management, if it is at all possible, we should have a nuanced and contextualized understanding for a particular setting.

The chapter has three sections. The first section briefly reviews the institutional history of public administration and public management as academic disciplines in the United States. It aims to show how public management has emerged as an independent institutional field and to show the extent to which the emergence is rooted in changing government practice. The second section analyzes whether there are substantive differences between the two fields in terms of their institutional home, research topics, methodology, theoretical orientation, and practical relevance. The third section makes a short conclusion.

The History: The Emergence of Public Management

The term public management did not gain general currency in its modern sense until the 1980s. But management has always been part of the intellectual history of public administration (Frederickson et al. 2012; Hood 2005; Lynn 2005). Tracing the historical development of public administration and the emergence of public management, however, shows a gradually increasing movement toward management and toward scientific studies of management.

Early Years: American Political Science Association as the Primary Home

In the early years, before ASPA—the primary professional home for public administration in the United States—was founded in 1939, public administration researchers and activists largely participated in meetings of the American Political Science Association. This organization had been founded a generation earlier (in 1903). Early on, public administration was dominated by political philosophy and a focus on law. As the growing democracy tried to develop its administrative apparatus, it had to answer big questions regarding the purpose of the state and its government. Is public administration legitimate within the context of the constitution? What are the legislative sources of authority for public administration? What objectives should government serve? Should the government directly provide public goods? The choices were inherently political (Rosenbloom and Kravchuk 2005). This was also the time when the emergence of the administrative state had much to do with designing and implementing new laws and regulations necessary for the society (Wilson 1975). Wilson (1975) observed that regulatory agencies in the United States were mainly created during four periods: from 1887 to 1890, from 1906 to 1915, during the 1930s, and during the 1960s. It was not surprising that Frank Goodnow, one of the most significant voices for early public administration, was a professor of administrative law. He authored two of the first public administration books: *Comparative Administrative Law* in 1893 and *Politics and Administration* in 1900.

But when political scientists and legal scholars acknowledged that the execution of the state's will could be separated from the expression of that will (Goodnow 1900; Wilson 1887), the door opened for the emergence of public administration as a field of study. Simultaneously, the door opened for management and its "scientific" or systematic study. Wilson (1887) referred to "a science of administration" and his belief in the separation between means and ends, facts and values, and administration and politics, all of which preceded more recent advocates of management such as Herbert Simon. Wilson used the metaphor of learning from a murderous fellow how to sharpen a knife to emphasize that studying administration is a means of putting our own politics into convenient practice (p. 27).

The increasing size and complexity of government required more scientific studies on management of both structures and processes. When Woodrow Wilson and his prominent colleagues at Johns Hopkins University started the first curriculum for educating public servants, they offered courses in politics, economics, history, and law. But the program was soon overshadowed by administrative management programs that focused on practical, applied, and efficiency-minded frameworks (Hoffman 2002).

Around twenty-six years after Goodnow's (1900) seminal textbook, Leonard White published *Introduction to the Study of Public Administration*. Moving beyond Goodnow and Wilson, White (1926) envisioned public administration as a "value-free" science and argued that management, not politics, should guide public administration because the former lends itself to scientific study. Asserting the premise that public administration is the execution of the public will, he stated: "The book . . . assumes that the study of administration should start from the foundation of law, and is therefore more absorbed in the affairs of the American Management Association than in the decisions of courts" (Preface). Similarly, Willoughby's 1927 textbook, *Principles of Public Administration*, emphasized the shift from legal rules and cases to an efficient bureaucracy—the formal framework and procedures of the administrative machine.

Since then, management studies became an inherent part of public administration. Scientific management, as pioneered by Frederick Taylor and his 1911 *The Principles of Scientific Management*, originated in business organizations, particularly factories, but its concepts soon became a central part of the Progressive movement to reform government. Indeed, many scientific management acolytes studied government agencies and were public administrationists such as Luther Gulick, Henri Fayol, and Lyndall Urwick. For example, in Gulick and Urwick's *Papers on the Science of Administration* (1937), they identified a set of management processes common to any organization, summarized them into the acronym POSDCORB (planning, organizing, staffing, directing, coordinating, reporting, and budgeting), and developed rules of conduct for each of the processes.

What had brought political scientists and management experts together was the desire to improve government practice and help government run better. The final report of the American Political Science Association's Political Science Committee in 1913 advocated for involving faculty members in government affairs and training students for government careers. The first school of public administration, the Training School for Public Service, was established not by universities but by the New York Bureau of Municipal Research in 1911. Because of the new field's practice orientation, public administration scholars "got the research grants" and "got the students" (Henry 1990). The healthy relationship between political science and management related to the healthy relationship between academic studies and administrative practices.

The healthy relationship was also reflected in the fact that management studies were strongly integrated with a concern for democratic control. Although the increasing attention to management was instrumental to the emergence of public administration as an independent field, it was not yet a self-contained world with its own separated values and rules as Sayre (1958) recommended. Woodrow Wilson (1887, 27) stated, "the principles on which to base a science of administration . . . must be principles which have democratic policy very much at heart." And Leonard White (1939, 578) said that "[a] responsible administration, cherished and strengthened by those to whom it is responsible, is one of the principal foundations of the modern democratic state." Similar points were made by V.O. Key, John Gaus, Charles Merriam, and Charles Hyneman, among others.

Public administrationists addressed significant management challenges faced by government and they gained considerable influence. In 1937, the President's Committee on Administrative Management (the Brownlow Committee) published a report that represents the high point of the pursuit of scientific management in government. Interestingly, the composition of the committee resembled the overall field of public administration at the time: it was a successful partnership between political scientists and management experts. Louis Brownlow and Charles Merriam were political scientists, while Luther Gulick was a management expert.

Developmental Years: ASPA as the Primary Home

The practice orientation of public administration and its growing influence led to its breaking away from the American Political Science Association in the late 1930s when political science began the positivist turn and strove to be more theoretical, empirical, and scientific in the behavioralist sense (Finifter 1983). In order to keep and improve the interaction between academics and practitioners, leading public administrationists sought to establish a new national organization. As a result, ASPA was created in 1939 and has become the primary associational home for public administration. The founding of ASPA was to build an identity for public administration academically and professionally that emphasizes practical relevance. As Caldwell (1965, 57) writes, ASPA "institutionalized and perpetuated the larger and more generalized concept of public administration as a potential field of study directed toward action."

While the term "administration" dominated, the increasing attention to management continued, although "original" management studies were now more associated with schools outside public administration, such as the work of Elton Mayo and his associates at the Harvard Business School. From the 1930s to the 1950s, management scholars made important modifications and adaptations to the principles of scientific management, such as Chester Barnard's (1938) classic organization theory and the human relations writings generated since the Hawthorne studies (for example, McGregor's theory X and theory Y, and Maslow's hierarchy of needs).

During this time, some management scholars started to follow the behavioralist approach that had gained momentum in political science in particular and the social sciences in general. Examples included Herbert Simon's *Administrative Behavior* (1947), V.O. Key's *Southern Politics in State and Nation* (1949), and Simon, Smithburg, and Thompson's *Public Administration* (1950). In the last one, for example, the authors' goal was to present a behavioral description of how administrative processes occur. Simon (1946) considered the principles of administration nothing more than proverbs that could not offer a scientific basis for public administration. To develop a scientific basis, he argued, it is necessary to separate facts from values and adopt logical positivism.

Simon's proposal seemed attractive to many scholars, but at the time the influence of political philosophy and law in public administration was still dominant. One year after Simon published *Administrative Behavior*, Waldo published *The Administrative State: A Study of the Political Theory of American Public Administration* (1948). Although Waldo also rejected the principles of administration, he did so for different reasons. Unlike Simon, who believed that the principles were not scientific, Waldo feared that the principles could lead to a primacy of administration over the democratic political process. Accordingly, Waldo did not envision a positivist science of administration but rather a professional inquiry rooted in political philosophy. The 1952 Simon–Waldo debate in the *American Political Science Review* captured two different visions of public administration that still echo today (see Harmon 1989; Simon 1952; Waldo 1952a, 1952b).

As hinted above, Mayo, Barnard, McGregor, Maslow, Simon, and many others who advanced management studies were not public administration scholars. The public administration community benefited from their research, however, because the core of its academic agenda in the 1950s and 1960s was philosophical, such as to reconnect political values and the administrative process. Although the textbooks written during the period (for example, Pfiffner and Presthus 1953; Simon, Smithburg, and Thompson 1950) included materials that reflected behavioral influences, public administration shunned mainstream political science where behavioralism had become the orthodoxy. This was reflected in the Minnowbrook I Conference, which was sponsored by Dwight Waldo in 1968 and deeply shaped the public administration agenda for the 1970s and 1980s. The conference called for a public administration based on relevance, participation, change, values, and social equity. The resulting New Public Administration was clearly policy-oriented, normative, and "anti-behavioral" (Frederickson 1974).

The importance of public administration continued to grow. The National Academy of Public Administration (NAPA) was founded in 1967 and the National Association of Schools of Public Affairs and Administration (NASPAA)[1] was founded in 1970, initially as affiliates of ASPA. However, for many people the field lacked an intellectual substance and a central theme that could meet the challenge of addressing the government's real problems. The field had rejected the principles of administration and shunned a science of administration. Left were a plea for political philosophy and management knowledge borrowed from other disciplines. The identity of public administration was in crisis.

In pursuing a separate identity for public administration, Minnowbrook I, influential as it was, fell short, as did Minnowbrook II, which was held twenty years later. In the 1980s, dissatisfaction with the theoretical and methodological rigor of the field was considerable. While Waldo (1990) noted that the field had made significant progress methodologically and theoretically, McCurdy and Cleary (1984, 49) lamented that "research methodology in public administration remains weak and fragmented." After examining *Public Administration Review* articles from 1975–1984, Perry and Kraemer (1986, 215) concluded that they were "predominately applied" and "not cumulative." Change was imperative. Despite the focus of Minnowbrook II on theoretical concerns about ethics, democracy, and philosophy, it included economics and was "receptive to contributions of behavioral science to public administration" (Frederickson 1989, 99).

In summary, the first historical period witnessed public administration scholars participating in creating management knowledge common to all organizations, with the goal of helping to address government problems. For its first half century, however, public administration scholars largely relied on the management knowledge created by other disciplines without generating its own original work. The political and philosophical inquiries did not help in solving many of government's problems, but they drew attention to government's environment, problems, and dynamics. This work made the compelling case that government is different from business and that the field of public administration needs management models that take into account the political nature of administration and its democratic purposes.

Public Management Research Association as an Alternative

In the 1980s there was understandable dissatisfaction with traditional public administration. As to "management," many researchers considered the norma- tive discourse of traditional public administration valuable but insufficient in addressing the strategic and operational changes faced by government. They were disappointed that traditional public administration's coverage of manage- ment topics—leadership, strategic management, organizational design, and moti- vation—was not as sophisticated as in business administration. But many felt the business literature they often had to rely on did not address the distinctive aspects of management in government.

The group of public administration researchers within ASPA and the American Political Science Association who wanted to have more management coverage and more scientific studies pushed for the creation of a new institutional home. In 1991 the Public Management Research Association (PMRA) was founded and adopted the *Journal of Public Administration Research and Theory (JPART)* as its official journal. As Harmon (1989) recounts, many people in this category, such as those who studied bureaucratic politics, disagreed with Simon on the separa- tion of facts/administration from values/politics, but they did not favor Waldo either as they wanted to build a scientific knowledge base. George Frederickson, a leading authority of public administration and also the founder of *JPART* and PMRA, in an interview with the newsletter of the University of Kansas's School of Public Affairs and Administration, recounted why he initiated *JPART:* "For as long as I have been in public administration it has been my opinion that the field needed its own first class, unapologetically theoretical and empirical scholarly journal"(Kansas University, School of Public Affairs and Administration 2014). The statement suggests that even a public administration leader such as Frederickson was dissatisfied with the field.

Two other groups of scholars joined the push (Bozeman 1993a; Brudney, O'Toole, and Rainey 2000). One group was comprised of business professors who were interested in the public and nonprofit sectors and had worked with public administration scholars in venues such as the Public and Nonprofit Divi- sion of the Academy of Management. They wanted to develop empirical theory and were impatient with case study as the predominant mode of inquiry.

The other group was comprised of some faculty members in public policy schools such as Harvard's Kennedy School of Government, who called for a "political and activist orientation" that distinguishes public management from traditional public administration (Roberts 1995). In fact, the policy schools began to use the term public management in the mid-1970s as they tried to have some- thing to strengthen their mission of training high-level government executives. They concluded that they needed something beyond applied economics and formal policy to help executive decision making and strategic leadership. They preferred this in contrast to the traditional craft-oriented public administration that concentrated on civil service employees and routine bureaucratic functions (Brudney, O'Toole, and Rainey 2000). This group was also behind the formation of the Association for Public Policy Analysis and Management. Mark Moore, a renowned Kennedy School faculty, stated:

> In the traditional conception of "public administration," the fundamental responsibility of public managers was to develop efficient programmatic means for accomplishing well-defined goals . . . In contrast, our conception of "public management" adds responsibility for goal setting and political management to the traditional responsibilities of public administration . . . [W]e think it inevitable and desirable that public managers should assume responsibility for defining the purposes they seek to achieve, and therefore to participate in the political dialogue about their purposes and methods.
>
> *(Moore 1983, 2–3)*

While scholars across the groups, or sometimes even within the same group, may have had different visions for what public management should be (Bozeman 1993a; Kelman et al. 2003), they shared the sentiment that traditional public administration was not sufficient. They all wanted something different—different from traditional public administration, general business management, and political science. Many of them went to the first PMRA conference in 1991, after which it was decided to become a regular biennial event. PMRA thus became an association independent from ASPA, the Academy of Management, and the American Political Science Association. Since then, the core circle of public management researchers has decreased or even stopped participating in ASPA meetings. They enthusiastically worked to improve their biennial conferences and to push the term "public management" into the names of schools, programs, courses, journals, and books.

With the insurgence and the growing influence of PMRA and *JPART*, the tension between public administration and public management increased. Normative inquiries continued to grow in public administration, such as the constitutional school at the Center for Public Administration and Policy at Virginia Tech, the work of David Rosenbloom, and the New Public Service model (Denhardt and Denhardt 2000). Outside ASPA, the Public Administration Theory Network (PAT-Net), an international network founded in 1978 and devoted to the development of public administration theory, continued to have a strong presence. The growing animosity between the public management circle and the traditional public administration circle became something like Lord Voldemort in the Harry Potter books: we know something very bad exists out there, but we do not talk about it in public. (One exception, however, may be the debate ignited by Larry Luton in 2007 that appeared in *Administration & Society*.)

The account above focuses on academic disciplines and research in the United States, but the increasing popularity of public management also has its roots in the shift of government policies and practices under the banner of New Public Management (NPM) in and outside the United States even before the 1990s (Hood 2005). Since the 1980s, most Western democracies have faced increasing welfare state burdens, size of government, mounting fiscal pressures, and challenges of globalization, as well as declining trust in government, and unresponsive and inefficient service operations. Desperate to increase economy, efficiency, and effectiveness of government, a wide array of programs and initiatives were taken in the general direction of liberalization, deregulation, decentralization, privatization, and marketization (Barzelay 1992; Kettl 2005). Unlike the traditional administrative practice that focused on rules, due process, legality, and formalism, the term *management* was used to advocate outcomes, efficiency, entrepreneurship, and customer satisfaction (Hood 1991; Lane 1994). The term "public management" became institutionalized in government documents, organizations, and policies, such as the New Zealand Treasury's 1984 report *Government Management*, the OECD's Public Management (PUMA) reports, the policies of Ronald Reagan and Margaret Thatcher, and the National Performance Review under the Clinton administration.

While NPM was claimed by some as a revolution (Barzelay 1992), many scholars find that it reflects incremental changes and a renewal of historical trends in public administration. For example, Page (2005) believes that human services innovations reflecting the NPM doctrine have built gradually on past reforms in the field. Williams (2003) finds that many features of the current performance measurement practice can be found in the first decade of the twentieth century at the New York Bureau of Municipal Research.

Perhaps American public management scholars share important management questions with NPM advocates. By and large, both attend to the policy or strategic choices government executives confront. Both are interested in improving the efficiency and effectiveness of public service delivery. Both would like to see public managers as entrepreneurs. Both emphasize the role of performance measurement.

However, the differences between them are significant. Most public management scholars do not share the NPM belief in the supremacy of market, public choice, and neoinstitutional economics (see, for example, Bozeman 2007). Instead, they study and emphasize topics such as public service motivation, publicness, public values, collaboration, and public accountability. Many of them are well aware of the limitations and problems of NPM, which has never really been worshiped by the majority of American scholars—regardless of whether they consider themselves in the camp of public administration or public management (Riccucci 2001; Terry 1998). NPM's belief in the separation of politics from management contradicts the public management scholars' premise that politics must be brought back into the management models. In addition, NPM writings are not the type of positivist theory public management scholars relish; they are best understood as the logic of rhetoric—an administrative argument based on its values and assumptions (Hood and Jackson 1991). Moreover, both public administration and public management scholars need to study and are studying the paradoxes and side effects created by the middle-aged NPM (Hood and Peters 2004). In summary, NPM may be part of the reason for the popularity of the term public management, but it does not help explain the distinction between public management and public administration as separate communities in the United States.

How Different Are They Today?

The different groups behind American public management scholarship and NPM might have big differences regarding what public management is or should be, but they had one thing in common: disappointment with the old-fashioned public administration. They joined forces in institutionalizing public management in practice and research. But to what extent are the two institutional communities different after more than twenty years have passed since the founding of PMRA? The theoretical and methodological development of both public administration and public management has evolved and improved since the 1990s.

In Bozeman's (1993a, 1993b) initial formulation, public management can be best understood as a distinctive *approach to knowledge* rather than a distinctive *body of theory*. It is a unique approach of inquiry that has the following characteristics:

> (1) a concern with prescription and, often, prescriptive theory; (2) a focus on the distinctive nature of *public* management and *public* organizations and, particularly, the effects of politics; (3) a problem focus more than a process focus; (4) a strong emphasis on contextual and experiential knowledge (as compared to empirically based theoretical knowledge); and (5) a focus on strategy and multiorganizational problems.
>
> *(Bozeman 1993b, 362)*

By now, it is not clear whether these five characteristics can differentiate between public administration and public management. Public management research seemed to have been more oriented toward explanatory theory instead of prescriptive theory. Public administration scholarship actually is more concerned with prescription. Public management research does focus on the effects of publicness and politics. Guy (2000, 162) once commented, "at the least, the term 'public management' merely reflects the transition in popularity from the word 'administration' to the word 'management.' At most, it reflects the appreciation that public managers must juggle both policy and administration to be effective." But this focus is even more true in public administration. Rosenbloom and Kravchuk's (2005) public administration textbook, for example, has a section "emphasizing the *public* in public administration" in Chapter 1, a whole chapter on political environment, and a whole chapter on "public administration and the public." Stillman's (2010) public administration textbook has a chapter on "the political environment," a chapter on "the relationship between politics and administration," and a chapter on "the relationship between bureaucracy and the public interest."

Similarly, as to the problem orientation, public administration scholars in general seemed to be more engaged in practical problem solving than public management scholars. Regarding the emphasis on contextual and evidence-based knowledge, it is actually more characteristic of public administration, with public management having largely gone to its opposite: empirically based theoretical knowledge. On strategy and multiorganizational problems, they have become big topics for both fields.

However, the two communities do have substantive differences. First, ASPA and PMRA represent two different institutional homes, with the former embracing practitioners in the membership while the latter includes only academic researchers. This is because the two associations have different missions and goals. ASPA membership includes approximately 8,000 practitioners, academics, and students. Its mission has five components. It

- advances the art, science, teaching, and practice of public and nonprofit administration;
- promotes the value of joining and elevating the public service profession;
- builds bridges among all who pursue public purposes at home and internationally;
- provides networking and professional development opportunities to those committed to public service values; and
- achieves innovative solutions to the challenges of governance.

In contrast, the PMRA website (2014) states it "*supports the development of empirical and normative inquiry, theory building and systematic testing of theory* consistent with the canons of social science, using the full range of quantitative and qualitative methodologies." The Association has four goals:

- organizing and sponsoring the biannual conferences and other conferences and symposia;
- supporting electronic and print publications;
- furthering professional and academic opportunities;
- serving as a voice for the public management research community.

In a nutshell, while ASPA aims to link theory to practice, PMRA promotes theory building and testing. ASPA meetings have practitioner panels or practitioner participation in panels, but PMRA meetings do not. ASPA gives annual awards to practitioners and organizations such as the Public Integrity Award, the John W. Gaston, Jr. Award for Excellence in Public Service Management, the

Harry Hatry Distinguished Performance Measurement Practice Award, the CAP Organizational Leadership Awards, and the National Public Service Awards. In addition to *Public Administration Review*, ASPA also publishes *PA Times*, a monthly newspaper that "focuses on issues in public management and the best practices in the field of public administration," and *The Bridge*, a biweekly newsletter that "details the organization's latest news as well as current news in the public service field." Even for *Public Administration Review*, an academic journal, it has or had sections such as Theory to Practice, Administrative Profile, and Cases. The current editorial team regularly invites practitioners to comment on the articles published there.

Second, while ASPA and PMRA meetings share many topics, they differ considerably. From 2009 to 2013, the five ASPA annual meetings had a total of 549 panel sessions, excluding poster sessions, discussion circles, and preconference workshops, as they are not easily comparable to PMRA sessions. During the same time period, the three PMRA conferences had a total of 173 panel sessions, excluding student posters. A comparison shows some notable differences. One is that forty-two ASPA panels (7.65 percent) were based on normative inquiries such as the role of constitutions, the implications of fear, freedom, and knowing, and the postmodern critique of public administration. Only one PMRA panel (0.58 percent) could be labeled as normative. In a sense, PMRA focuses on developing theories, but its view of theory is positivistic or behavioralistic. ASPA's view of theory is much broader.

Another notable topic difference is on ethics. About 6.74 percent of ASPA panels (thirty-seven) focused on issues such as corruption, administrative evil, transparency, and ethical practice, while only 0.58 percent of PMRA panels ($n = 1$) did so. In comparing the percentages, there was an eleven times difference. Relatedly, 7.47 percent of ASPA panels (forty-one) focused on social equity and diversity issues, while only 1.73 percent of PMRA panels (three) did, which is a four times difference. This is perhaps because ASPA has an ethics section, a section on democracy and social justice, and a conference of minority public administrators. According to the ASPA website (2014), it "promotes dialogue on social equity issues in all areas of public service." In its national conference, ASPA also hosts the Gloria Hobson Nordin Social Equity Award Luncheon to honor "a public administrator who has distinguished him or herself in achieving fairness, justice and equity in government." ASPA also had more panels on citizen participation (5.1 percent versus 2.31 percent), emergency management and disaster response (7.65 percent versus 1.16 percent), public affairs education (3.10 percent versus 0.00 percent), environment and sustainability (5.46 percent versus 2.31 percent), and heath care (2.73 percent versus 1.16 percent).

The PMRA conferences had more organizational behavior panels (17.34 percent versus 3.46 percent), which covered topics such as job satisfaction, public service motivation, goal ambiguity, turnover intention, and leadership. The PMRA conferences also had more organizational theory panels (13.29 percent versus 0.73 percent), which focused on topics such as organizational learning, innovation, publicness, and bureaucratic representation. Interestingly, the PMRA conferences also had higher percentages of panels on three topics that relate to NPM and governance: alternative service delivery—contracting, public–private partnerships, co-production—at 7.51 percent versus 3.10 percent, performance management (10.40 percent versus 6.56 percent), and governance/network/complexity (12.72 percent versus 5.83 percent). Furthermore, PMRA had more panels dealing with quantitative methodology such as advanced techniques and measurement issues (2.89 percent versus 0.00 percent).

The third comparison is on theoretical and methodological sophistication. To the extent that the citation impact can be used to gauge quality, *JPART* seemed to have won the battle. More *JPART* articles have formal hypothesis development and testing with more advanced statistics. However, most, if not all public management scholars do not confine themselves to *JPART*; they frequently publish in and review for *Public Administration Review* as well. Moreover, the best *Public Administration Review* articles have similar citation impact as do the best *JPART* ones. As far as quantitative papers go, the two journals have similar standards.

The quality difference is noted in comparing ASPA and PMRA conferences. PMRA screens the proposals more tightly, requires full paper submission before the actual conference, and posts or circulates the papers in advance. ASPA only asks for a short proposal. It is not a secret that most ASPA presenters do not have a full paper ready when they make their presentation and many of the presentations are not based on original or rigorous research. But this problem cannot be solved easily. If all the presentations contained statistical models that cannot really inform practice, ASPA conferences would lose most of its practitioner participants. Many scholars who have remained loyal to ASPA recognize this problem and some experiments have been designed to help address it. For example, Founders' Forum has become a regular conference track that features panels and presentations that are academically oriented, theoretically robust, methodologically vibrant, and/or historically grounded.

To a large extent, the quality concern about ASPA conferences is not an issue of standards, but an issue of purpose and vision. ASPA conferences are envisioned as a venue for scholars, students, and practitioners to meet and dialogue. In recent years they have introduced many new formats, such as discussion circles, "ask an expert," poster sessions, and super panels, in order to better achieve the purpose. But finding a balance between practical relevance and scientific rigor is not easy; regrettably, the quality concern has led many young scholars to not be interested in participating.

Fourth, neither public administration nor public management has an overarching paradigm. Neither approaches the status of a normal science in the Kuhnian sense (Kuhn 1961). If they were different paradigms, then a clear comparison between the two would be much easier. Absent a paradigm, both communities have resorted to the "big questions" methodology, which requires identifying a set of core questions that draw attention and efforts from a majority of the people in the field. It does not prevent people from studying other issues; rather, it aims to make breakthroughs by coordinating a collective effort. Despite the concerns with the utility of this methodology, it has been adopted by some influential scholars.

In public administration, big questions have been proposed for public affairs education, nonprofit management, administrative ethics, intergovernmental relations, and public administration in general. All these were published in *Public Administration Review*. Notably, Kirlin (1996, 417) identified seven big questions for a significant public administration:

1. What are the instruments of collective action that remain responsible both to democratically elected officials and to core societal values?
2. What are the roles of nongovernmental forms of collective action in society, and how can desired roles be protected and nurtured?
3. What are the appropriate tradeoffs between governmental structures based on function (which commonly eases organizational tasks) and geography (which eases citizenship, political leadership, and societal learning)?
4. How shall tensions between national and local political arenas be resolved?
5. What decisions shall be "isolated" from the normal processes of politics so that some other rationale can be applied?
6. What balance shall be struck among neutral competence, representativeness, and leadership?
7. How can processes of societal learning be improved, including knowledge of choices available, of consequences of alternatives, and of how to achieve desired goals, most importantly, the nurturing and development of a democratic polity?

In contrast, Behn (1995, 315) outlines three big questions for public management:

1. Micromanagement: How can public managers break the micromanagement cycle—an excess of procedural rules, which prevents public agencies from producing results, which leads to more procedural rules, which leads to . . . ?
2. Motivation: How can public managers motivate people (public employees as well as those outside the formal authority of government) to work energetically and intelligently toward achieving public purposes?
3. Measurement: How can public managers measure the achievements of their agencies in ways that help to increase those achievements?

If Behn's questions are at the micro-level and focus on individual and organizational behavior, Kirlin's questions are at the macro-level and are centered around democracy, society, and institutional design. But the public management community has also identified some macro-level questions as well. From 2008 to 2009, PMRA requested leading public management scholars to identify "big, unanswered questions," which were published in PMRA's newsletter, *Management Matters*. They include:

- Laurence E. Lynn: If there is no politics–administration dichotomy, what is there?
- Beryl Radin: How do administrators actually deal with the politics–administration interactions?
- Brinton Milward: Beyond the hollow state—the substitute state?
- Keith Provan: Network effectiveness and evolution?
- Laurence J. O'Toole Jr.: How does management matter in networks?
- Rosemary O'Leary: How do public managers become lateral thinkers to address policy problems?
- Richard Feiock: Who governs and how?
- Robert Durant: Explain the extent to which, why, and how government agencies comply with federal, state, local, and international laws?
- Jocelyn Johnston: How can public administrators balance democratic values and market strengths?
- Charles Wise: How should we measure and assess the capacity of public institutions to execute public policy?
- Donald Moynihan: Performance information use as a dependent variable?
- George Boyne: How does organizational change affect public service performance?
- Barry Bozeman: What is the effect of public managers' religious views and practices on their work-related attitudes and behaviors?
- David M. Van Slyke: How does investing shape public management capacity?

While some questions differ between public administration and public management, some overlap. More importantly, for all public management big questions, it is difficult to find any that are not big for public administration as well. Motivation, performance, the politics–administration dichotomy, the hollow state, networks, collaboration, and organizational change, are essential public administration topics. Another observation is that if the early PMRA conferences generated a fragmented array of studies that lacked systematic connectedness (Bozeman 1993b; Newland 1994), the situation has not become better since then.

Conclusion

Before we conclude, it is important to point out that the discussion in this chapter reflects the American experience. The evolution and meaning of public administration and public management may be very different in other countries.

This chapter traces the role of management in the evolution of public administration and the emergence of public management in the United States.

The following observations can be made: management has always been part of public administration. It was instrumental for public administration to become an independent field of study in the early twentieth century. The linguistic transition from public administration to public management was stimulated by dissatisfaction with traditional public administration research and practice. Today, much of the vision has been achieved: administrative practice is now very different from the past due to both intended and unintended effects, and public management research is more sophisticated theoretically and methodologically. However, as public administration has evolved to respond, the initially intended difference between administration and management is less relevant, both for practice and for theory. Nevertheless, the institutionalization of public management has led to two overlapping but discernible communities. Public management has a narrower scope and largely excludes normative discourse, ethics, and law from its domain. It is more isolated from the practitioner world and it strives to be scientific in the positivist sense.

Where should we go from here? Perhaps it does not really matter whether we use administration, management, or governance to label our work, as ultimately we share the same subject—the public sector. And we share the same purpose—to make the public sector stronger, better, and more democratic. For an applied field like ours, it is important to maintain close connections to practice and practitioners, methodological diversity, issue diversity, and theory diversity. Whether this should be achieved within one or more professional associations is a matter of debate. Newland (1994) argues that "actions to create the field by separatism and exclusion" would have damaging outcomes for the field. He concludes that "separatism in pursuit of a discipline detracts from the much-needed effort to enhance research and theory in public management" (p. 488). One could argue that if the public management advocates stayed within ASPA, public management research would not have grown so rapidly. One could also argue that without competition and pressure from a separated PMRA, ASPA would have been too slow to make changes and improve its conferences and activities. However, since both ASPA and PMRA are viable professional organizations now, it is essential to follow Newland's advice to increase the connectedness between the two communities.

The shift from public administration to public management reflected two visions: a more entrepreneurial market-based government and more scientific study of government. After decades, we have learned that the visions must be qualified. In terms of practice, the entrepreneurial government and its managers must be accountable and responsible. In terms of research, a scientific agenda on management should not be used as an excuse to exclude normative theories, value-laden topics, alternative research methods, or interaction with practitioners. In commenting on old and new public management, Riccucci (2001, 174) calls upon reasonable-minded scholars in public administration and public management to engage in "a dialogue on the importance of accepting diversity in research methods." I would go further and argue that we need to accept diversity not only in research methods, but also in research questions, ontology, epistemology, theory, and style. It is okay, and arguably beneficial, to have multiple camps or communities of practice, but effective collaboration between them will certainly enhance our capacity to solve public problems.

Note

1 NASPAA has now changed its name to Network of Schools of Public Policy, Affairs, and Administration.

References

ASPA. 2014. "About ASPA." www.aspanet.org/public/ASPA/About_ASPA/ASPA/About_ASPA/About_ASPA.aspx?hkey=98af1db8-67b2-4ac6-9731-953b52f982db (accessed July 15, 2014).

Aucoin, Peter. 1990. "Administrative Reform in Public Management: Paradigms, Principles, Paradoxes and Pendulums." *Governance* 3(2): 115–137.

Barnard, Chester. 1938. *The Functions of the Executive*. Cambridge, MA: Harvard University Press.

Barzelay, Michael. 1992. *Breaking through Bureaucracy*. Berkeley, CA: University of California Press.

Behn, Robert. 1995. "The Big Questions of Public Management." *Public Administration Review* 55(4): 313–324.

Bozeman, Barry. 1993a. "Introduction: Two Concepts of Public Management." In *Public Management*, ed. B. Bozeman, 1–5. San Francisco: Jossey-Bass.

———. 1993b. "Conclusion: Search for the Core of Public Management." In *Public Management*, ed. B. Bozeman, 361–363. San Francisco: Jossey-Bass.

———. 2007. *Public Values and Public Interest: Counterbalancing Economic Individualism*. Washington, DC: Georgetown University Press.

Brudney, Jeffrey, Laurence J. O'Toole, and Hal Rainey. 2000. "Introduction: Public Management in an Era of Complexity and Challenge." In *Advancing Public Management*, ed. J. Brudney, L. O'Toole, and H. Rainey, 1–14. Washington, DC: Georgetown University Press.

Caldwell, Lynton K. 1965. "Public Administration and the Universities: A Half-Century of Development." *Public Administration Review* 25(1): 52–60.

Denhardt, Robert, and Janet Denhardt. 2000. "The New Public Service: Serving Rather than Steering." *Public Administration Review* 60(6): 549–559.

Finifter, Ada, ed. 1983. *Political Science: The State of the Discipline*. Washington, DC: American Political Science Association.

Frederickson, George H. 1974. "A Symposium: Social Equity and Public Administration." *Public Administration Review* 34(1): 1–2.

———. 1989. "Minnowbrook II: Changing Epochs of Public Administration." *Public Administration Review* 49(2): 95–100.

———, Kevin Smith, Christopher Larimer, and Michael Licari. 2012. *The Public Administration Theory Primer*. Boulder, CO: Westview Press.

Goodnow, Frank J. 1893. *Comparative Administrative Law: An Analysis of the Administrative Systems, National and Local, of the United States, England, France and Germany.* New York: G.P. Putnam's Sons.

———. 1900. *Politics and Administration.* New York: Macmillan.

Gulick, Luther, and Lyndall Urwick, eds. 1937. *Papers on the Science of Administration.* New York: Institute of Public Administration.

Guy, Mary E. 2000. "Public Management." In *Defining Public Administration,* ed. J.M. Shafritz, 161–168. Boulder, CO: Westview Press.

Harmon, Michael. 1989. "The Simon/Waldo Debate: A Review and Update." *Public Administration Quarterly* 12(4): 437–451.

Henry, Nicholas. 1990. "Root and Branch: Public Administration Travel toward the Future." In *Public Administration: The State of the Discipline,* ed. N. Lynn and A. Wildavsky, 3–26. Chatham, NJ: Chatham House of Publishers.

Hill, Carolyn, and Laurence Lynn. 2009. *Public Management: A Three-Dimensional Approach.* Washington, DC: CQ Press.

Hoffman, Mark. 2002. "Paradigm Lost: Public Administration at Johns Hopkins University 1884–1896." *Public Administration Review* 62(1): 6–16.

Hood, Christopher. 1991. "A New Public Management for All Seasons." *Public Administration* 69: 3–19.

———. 2005. "Public Management: The Word, the Movement, the Science." In *The Oxford Handbook of Public Management,* ed. E. Ferlie, L. Lynn, and C. Pollitt, 7–26. New York: Oxford University Press.

———, and Michael Jackson. 1991. *Administrative Argument.* Brookfield, VT: Dartmouth Publishing.

———, and Guy Peters. 2004. "The Middle Aging of New Public Management: Into the Age of Paradox?" *Journal of Public Administration Research & Theory* 14(3): 267–282.

Kansas University, School of Public Affairs and Administration. 2014. Interview with H. George Frederickson, Distinguished Professor Emeritus. *School of Public Affairs & Administration Newsletter* (Winter): 2–4. www.kupa.ku.edu/sites/kupa.ku.edu/files/images/galleries/PublicAdminNewsletterWinter2014.pdf (accessed July 15, 2014).

Kelman, Steven, Fred Thompson, L.R. Jones, and Kuno Schedler. 2003. "Dialogue on Definition and Evolution of the Field of Public Management." *International Public Management Review* 4(2): 1–19.

Kettl, Donald. 2005. *The Global Public Management Revolution,* 2nd ed. Washington, DC: Brookings Institution Press.

Key, V.O., with the assistance of Alexander Heard. 1949. *Southern Politics in State and Nation.* New York: Alfred A. Knopf.

Kirlin, John. 1996. "The Big Questions of Public Administration in a Democracy." *Public Administration Review* 56(5): 416–423.

Kuhn, Thomas. 1961. *The Structure of Scientific Revolutions.* Chicago: Chicago University Press.

Lane, Jan-Erik. 1994. "Will Public Management Drive out Public Administration?" *Asian Journal of Public Administration* 16(2): 139–151.

Luton, Larry. 2007. "Deconstructing Public Administration Empiricism." *Administration & Society* 39(4): 527–544.

Lynn, Laurence Jr. 1996. *Public Management as Art, Science, and Profession.* Chatham, NJ: Chatham House.

———. 2005. "Public Management: A Concise History of the Field." In *The Oxford Handbook of Public Management,* ed. E. Ferlie, L. Lynn, and C. Pollitt, 27–50. New York: Oxford University Press.

McCurdy, Howard E., and Robert E. Cleary. 1984. "Why Can't We Resolve the Research Issue in Public Administration?" *Public Administration Review* 44(1): 49–55.

Moore, Mark. 1983. *A Conception of Public Management.* Cambridge, MA: Kennedy School of Government.

Newland, Chester. 1994. "A Field of Strangers in Search of a Discipline: Separatism of Public Management Research from Public Administration." *Public Administration Review* 54(5): 486–488.

New Zealand Treasury. 1984. *Economic Management.* Wellington: Government Print.

Page, Stephen. 2005. "What's New about the New Public Management?" *Public Administration Review* 65(6): 713–727.

Perry, James L., and Kenneth L. Kraemer. 1986. "Research Methodology in the *Public Administration Review*, 1975–1984." *Public Administration Review* 46(3): 215–226.

Pfiffner, John, and Vance Presthus. 1953. *Public Administration*, 3rd ed. New York: Ronald Press Company.

PMRA. 2014. "What Is PRMA?" www.pmranet.org/aboutpmra.htm (accessed July 15, 2014).

Pollitt, Christopher, and Geert Bouckaert. 2011. *Public Management Reform: A Comparative Analysis.* Oxford: Oxford University Press.

Riccucci, Norma. 2001. "The 'Old' Public Management versus the 'New' Public Management: Where Does Public Administration Fit in?" *Public Administration Review* 61(2): 172–175.

Roberts, Alasdair. 1995. "'Civic Discovery' as a Rhetorical Strategy." *Journal of Policy Analysis and Management* 14(2): 291–307.

Rosenbloom, David, and Robert Kravchuk. 2005. *Public Administration: Understanding Management, Politics, and Law in the Public Sector.* New York: McGraw Hill.

Sayre, Wallace S. 1958. "Premises of Public Administration: Past and Emerging." *Public Administration Review* 18(2): 102–105.

Simon, Herbert. 1946. "The Proverbs of Administration." *Public Administration Review* 6(1): 53–67.

———. 1947. *Administrative Behavior.* New York: Free Press.

———. 1952. "'Development of Theory of Democratic Administration': Replies and Comments." *American Political Science Review* 46(June): 494–496.

———, Donald Smithburg, and Victor Thompson. 1950. *Public Administration.* New York: Alfred A. Knopf.

Stillman, Richard. 2010. *Public Administration: Concepts and Cases.* Boston: Wadsworth.

Taylor, Frederick. 1911. *The Principles of Scientific Management.* New York: Harper and Row.

Terry, Larry. 1998. "Administrative Leadership, Neo-Managerialism, and the Public Management Movement." *Public Administration Review* 58(3): 194–200.

Waldo, Dwight. 1948. *The Administrative State.* New York: The Ronald Press Company.

———. 1952a. "Development of Theory of Democratic Administration." *American Political Science Review* 46(March): 81–103.

———. 1952b. "'Development of Theory of Democratic Administration': Replies and Comments." *American Political Science Review* 46(July): 501–503.

———. 1990. "A Theory of Public Administration Means in Our Time a Theory of Politics also." In *Public Administration: The State of the Discipline*, ed. Naomi Lynn and Aaron Wildavsky, 73–83. Chatham, NJ: Chatham House.

White, Leonard. 1926. *Introduction to the Study of Public Administration.* New York: Macmillan.

———. 1939. *Introduction to the Study of Public Administration.* New York: Macmillan.

Williams, Daniel. 2003. "Measuring Government in the Early Twentieth Century." *Public Administration Review* 63(6): 643–659.

Willoughby, William. 1927. *Principles of Public Administration.* Baltimore: Johns Hopkins Press.

Wilson, James. 1975. "The Rise of the Bureaucratic State." *The Public Interest* 41(Fall): 77–103.

Wilson, Woodrow. 1887. "The Study of Administration." In *Classics of Public Administration,* ed. Jay M. Shafritz, Albert C. Hyde, and Sandra J. Parkes, 22–34. Belmont, CA: Wadsworth/Thomson Learning.

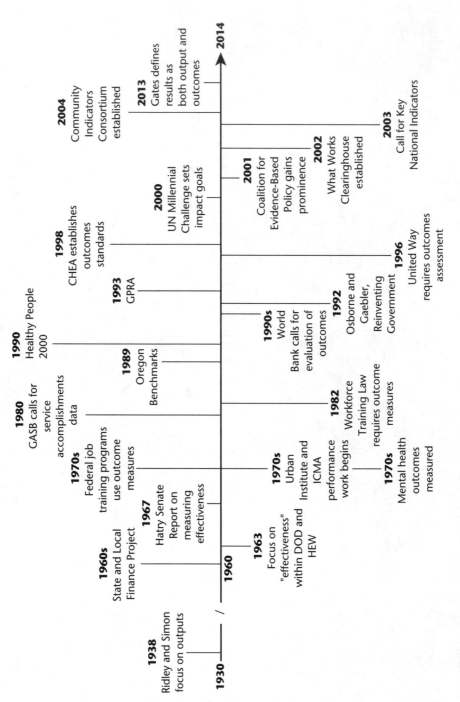

FIGURE 7.1 From Outputs to Outcomes: Benchmarks across Time

7

FROM OUTPUTS TO OUTCOMES

Kathryn E. Newcomer

Over the last seven decades the demand for systematic data about the efforts and results of public and nonprofit programs has increased due to the noncoincidental convergence of interests by institutions with stakes in the delivery of public services. These are both domestic and international: governments, foundations, the United Way of America, funders of international development endeavors such as the World Bank and the U.S. Agency for International Development (USAID), think tanks, and academics interested in improving the delivery of services. They have all contributed to an increasing focus on "results" as part of the exercise of accountability (Dubnick and Frederickson 2011a, 2011b; Hatry 2008; Imas and Rist 2009; Kettl 2005; Moynihan 2008; Moynihan and Pandey 2010; Newcomer 1997, 2008; Pollitt and Bouckaert 2000).

Both the level and sophistication of the dialogue about measuring and reporting operations and results of public programs and services have notably increased in OECD countries over the last few decades (Baruch and Ramalho 2006; Martin and Kettner 2010; Packard 2010; Schalock and Bonham 2003; Sowa, Selden, and Sandfort 2004; Stone and Cutcher-Gershefeld 2001). Many resources have been put into measurement, even while critics question whether or not performance data are used to improve services, inform budgeting, or to facilitate learning (Alexander, Brudney, and Yang 2010; Dahler-Larsen 2012; Ebrahim 2002, 2005, 2010; Metzenbaum 2006; Pollitt and Bouckaert 2000; Radin 2006, 2009).

While measuring programmatic performance is ubiquitous in public agencies and nongovernmental organizations around the world, decisions regarding what to measure have been affected by a number of societal trends as well as by seminal events that have shaped deliberations to privilege some types of measures over others. Program performance is itself an amorphous concept open to a multitude of operational definitions and may be measured and interpreted in a variety of ways by different stakeholders (Moynihan 2008; Newcomer 1997). In addition, selection of measures tends to occur in a politically charged arena and selection decisions typically are made by stakeholders who are invested in the programs and/or policies. The risks of generating performance data that could be used to embarrass governments, criticize programs or policies, reduce funding, and/or force change are likely to weigh heavily on those charged with making the measurement decisions (Moynihan 2008; Newcomer 1997).

Over the decades there have been increasing calls from many stakeholders for agencies not merely to measure workloads and accomplishments, referred to as "outputs," but also to measure the results, or "outcomes," of government and nonprofit efforts. Proponents of New Public Management, with their focus on adopting performance measurement as one of their market-oriented tools (Bromberg 2009; Kettl 2005; Pollitt and Bouckaert 2000) and of evidence-based policy and management, increasingly have called for the use of outcome data to assess the effectiveness of programs and policies (Nutley, Walter, and Davies 2007; Olsson 2007; Perrin 2006).

This chapter describes the evolution of preferences for how services and products provided by government and nonprofit organizations should be measured. After the journey from outputs to outcomes is outlined, challenges that these elevated demands for measurement and reporting impose for government and nonprofit providers are discussed.

The Evolution of Preferences for Measuring the Worth of Government

The story begins with a consideration of how government has been viewed post-World War II because preferences regarding how programs should be measured reflect how government is regarded. To this end, Peter Dahler-Larsen (2012) broadly characterizes public opinion of institutions in general, including governments, in Western democracies as having evolved through three somewhat overlapping socio-historical stages, or epochs. These three epochs correspond to different social conditions over time, and he labels them as modernity, reflexive modernity, and the audit society. During each epoch, there are social imaginaries that are configurations of meanings that define a particular society. The evaluation imaginaries define the purpose, meaning, and character of, and value added to, particular forms of evaluation in the light of the society in which they unfold. As Dahler-Larsen (2012, 100) writes:

> Modern society is characterized by an attempt to replace the tradition, prejudice, and religion with rationality and autonomy. Rationality entails that human beings should not subordinate themselves to illegitimate authorities who function on the basis of prejudice. Autonomy entails people's responsibility to govern themselves.

A modernity perspective implies that nothing is inevitable and all can be fixed. Thus a technological mode of thinking is an essential trait of the modernity mentality and has much in common with the principles of scientific management. Dahler-Larsen suggests that reflexive modernity followed the modernity epoch due to some disenchantment with the former's rational, technical approaches. Like modernity itself, it is a set of ideas and social structural forms that make their impact at a certain point of time and is more of a process. He states (2012, 121):

> As such, "reflexive modernization" includes both a kind of working through of the modern, a turning of the modern against the modern itself, and a process that, once it starts, has its own logic. . . . a great deal of the energy in the reflexively modern society is allocated to counterbalancing, managing, and allocating the risks and disadvantages of modernity's own products. . . . We discover that our actions constantly create problems for us, problems that often come back to us in changing and surprising forms.

The current adoption of complexity and systems theory as appropriate lenses for both the nature of the problems that programs address and the evaluation strategies they should use reflects this view (Patton 2011; Williams and Hummelbrunner 2011).

The third epoch Dahler-Larsen delineates is the *audit society* and it pertains to the calls for measurement of program outcomes during the last four decades. Michael Power coined the term the "audit society" when he labeled Western democracies engaged in constant checking and verification as audit societies in which a particular style of formalized accountability is the ruling principle (Dahler-Larsen 2012; Power 1997). Dahler-Larsen elaborates on how evaluation imaginaries operate when the audit society's values permeate public discourse about government efforts. He notes: "The audit society has lost the courage characteristic of progress–oriented modernity and the flexibility and curiosity of reflexive modernity. In the audit society, rationality strikes back, with all its connotations of predictability, antisubjectivism, and a focus on procedure" (2012, 169).

Under the privileging of the audit society's ideals, a number of values and principles are largely viewed as nonnegotiable, in stark contrast to reflexive modernization, where the ideal was that everything could be debated. For example, Dahler-Larsen observes that in the post-September 11, 2001 era in Western democracies the military and intelligence services have been deferred to and treated as out of bounds when it comes to being subject to evaluation. Another example of a nonnegotiable principle is the random control trial as the "gold standard" to measure the impact of any public program.

Paul Light offers another observation of relevance to our understanding of trends in preferences as to how government in the United States should be assessed. He suggests that there have been four competing philosophies of government reform that have ebbed and flowed over time (Light 1997). He delineates them as scientific management, war on waste, watchful eye, and liberation management. He suggests that trust in government—or lack of it—is a key influence on which reforms are favored. He notes:

> At the core of the confusion [on how to assess and improve government] is trust. No one is sure when and where to trust government to do its job, not ordinary Americans, not Congress, not presidents and vice-presidents, not public administration and management scholars.
>
> *(1997, 46)*

He concludes his critique by calling for more systematic experimentation to gauge which reforms work under which conditions. Light might be one of the earliest of what has become a seemingly large, or at least loud, number of advocates for "evidence-based policy" and "evidence-based management."

When trust in government declines, interest in obtaining information on what government produces rises. In contrast to many other Western democracies, citizen trust in government in the United States has tended to be low across time, with dips to low points correlating with government scandals and unpopular wars (Light 1997). A deep-seated preference for private sector rather than governmental approaches to production of goods and services is embedded in the U.S. culture, as well. The metaphor of government as an assembly line that converts inputs into outputs with the desired impact of a return on investment (ROI) has been the predominant model of government in the United States, as it has in other Western democracies. Reflecting the predominance of this metaphor, evaluators have struggled with how to provide a measure of public performance that is viewed as legitimate as is a private sector ROI. Relatedly, the term "Value for Money Audits" is used in the Commonwealth countries to refer to assessments of the results of public programs.

With the backdrop in the United States of a citizenry and politicians who are disposed to distrust government in general and demand information on what value they get for their taxes, and with the assumption that government does not operate as efficiently or effectively as the private sector, why have there been systematic changes in the nature of the information that is demanded from government? Several trends in Western democracies account for this. First is discomfort with generalized uncertainty, in part reflecting increased complexity in the problems government addresses accompanied with increased complexity in government structures, from hierarchies to networks and heterarchies (Agranoff 2007; Light 2005). Second is enhanced information technology that collects and provides data about both government and social conditions. Third is the fact that there are rising expectations about what constitutes "evidence" induced by social scientists' calls for more rigorous data about social programs. Fourth are changes in perspectives on accountability from procedural and legal concerns to performance accountability concerns (Behn 2001; Dubnick and Frederickson 2011a, 2011b; Light 1997). And fifth are recent fiscal stresses that have pushed public agencies to innovate and use both people and technology to forge synergies, in other words, to do more with less (Bromberg 2009; Newcomer and Caudle 2011).

In addition to, and perhaps reflecting the general trends across OECD countries, there have been some hallmark changes in thinking about the way the performance of public and nonprofit agencies should be viewed. In the United States, there have been some critical events that have signaled changes in preferences for what information should be collected. See Figure 7.1 at the beginning of this chapter for a timeline that identifies some of the more impactful events. To understand why the events were consequential, we need to recognize some influential and yet somewhat disconnected conversations that have occurred over the last seven decades.

Embracing Outcomes: Somewhat Independent Streams of Conversations

As shown in the following list, there have been consequential deliberations in the United States about what and how to measure government efforts, and their results, in at least seven somewhat distinct arenas:

1. local government measurement efforts connected with budgeting and management;
2. Government Accounting Standards Board (GASB) on "service accomplishments";
3. federal efforts to connect effectiveness/results/outcomes with budgeting;
4. program evaluation of social programs;
5. outcomes assessment requirements for nonprofit agencies and in accreditation processes;
6. social, national, state, and community indicators; and
7. evaluation and monitoring of international development efforts.

In some cases, the conversations have taken place among a fairly narrow set of professionals, such as labor economists, deliberating on how to assess the value of job training programs, and among accreditation entities as they determine which outcomes to require from colleges and universities. In other cases, the conversations have involved a more diverse set of professionals and politicians, such as when determinations are made about how to assess linkage between governmental efforts and social and community indicators, and how to evaluate the impact of international development investments.

In other cases, the discussions have taken place among a fairly compartmentalized set of professional staff, such as budget and finance staff in local governments, but have spread as the acceptability and inevitability of measuring government performance reached frontline program offices. In some cases, there have been heated disagreements about the most appropriate data to collect, and the most appropriate methods by which to collect it. International development efforts provide a case in point. In other cases, naive decisions to require collection of performance data have been made with little deliberation and without realistic expectations as to the consequences of the new measurement requirements. The Government Performance and Results Act (GPRA) is an example of this.

What is striking about the evolution of preferences regarding measurement of government efforts and results in the seven arenas is that there was little diffusion of learning across the separate streams of thought. For example, education measurement professionals were not consulted by labor economists as they deliberated on how to measure outcomes of job training programs, and social program evaluation experts were not consulted by local government budgeters. In some cases, there were condescending attitudes held by various groups toward others, such as the attitudes among professional evaluation experts about what local government budgeting staff were trying to accomplish (Bernstein 1999; Blalock 1999; Greene 1999). A brief discussion of the movement toward preference for measurement of outcomes in each of the seven arenas follows.

Arena 1: Local Government Measurement Efforts

In the United States, local governments have taken the lead in measuring program outcomes. The origin, however, of the outcomes push at the local level dates back to the federal effort in 1961 to link the "effectiveness" of programs to budget categories in the U.S. Department of Defense (DoD) using a system called the Planning, Programming, and Budgeting System (PPBS). When Robert McNamara became Secretary of Defense in 1961 he sought to locate control of the evaluation of military needs, and decisions on how to best meet those needs, within the Office of the Secretary, and to establish information systems to inform those decisions (Enthoven and Smith 1971). In an impactful move, McNamara hired Charles Hitch as his Comptroller (Enthoven and Smith 1971, 33). At the time, Hitch had been the leader of a group of analysts at the RAND Corporation and was viewed as one of the leading authorities on program budgeting and the applications of economic analysis to defense problems (Enthoven and Smith 1971, 33). Hitch set up a unit at the DoD that focused on measuring "effectiveness" of policies and programs and his staff included both Elmer Staats (later the head of what is now known as the Government Accountability Office—GAO) and Harry Hatry—two pioneers in assessment of government performance.

When Lyndon Baines Johnson took office following the death of President John Kennedy, he was supportive of the PPBS efforts, and wanted to spread the system into other federal agencies. Under Johnson, the Bureau of the Budget (BoB—precursor to the Office of Management and Budget) urged other agencies to do so. At the time, leadership in the Department of Health, Education, and Welfare (precursor to the Department of Health and Human Services and the Department of Education) showed interest in the idea. There were some efforts made in concert with program evaluation professionals at the Department of Health, Education, and Welfare to measure program effectiveness, but perhaps the most interesting legacy resulted from BoB efforts to spread the goal of measuring program effectiveness at the state and local levels (Harry Hatry, personal communication, January 17, 2014).

Instigated with support from the BoB and funded by a Ford Foundation grant, what is called the "5–5–5 Study" was undertaken by a state and local finance research institute at the George Washington University (GWU) to test the feasibility of implementing PPB in five states, five counties and five cities. The grant money was used primarily to train personnel in the fifteen jurisdictions on the principles of PPB and especially on how to develop criteria for assessing program effectiveness. In June 1969, the project's findings were published by GWU in the report *Implementing PPB in State, City and County: A Report on the 5–5–5 Project* that was produced by Selma Muskin and her group of researchers including Harry Hatry (Muskin et al. 1969). The quest to measure program effectiveness (the term used then, not outcomes) at the local level was pursued by both Selma Muskin and Harry Hatry when they joined the newly established Urban Institute in the late 1960s. Hatry's work at the Urban Institute has set the pace for local governmental performance measurement ever since then.

While still working on the 5–5–5 project in the mid-1960s, Hatry and his colleagues wrestled with the term "effectiveness" that they had inherited from PPB because it implied causation. They sought to move away from claims of causal impact of local government services. On July 21, 1967, Hatry presented a report to the Senate Subcommittee on Intergovernmental Relations of the Committee on Government Operations (Ninetieth Congress) entitled "Criteria for Evaluation in Planning State and Local Programs" that expressed the notion that attributing effectiveness was difficult.

The term effectiveness, not outcomes, was the operative term as local governments, especially their budget offices, moved to measure their efforts and accomplishments with guidance from the Urban Institute in the 1970s. Hatry acknowledges the inspiration for the work at the Urban Institute that was provided in an early report written by Clarence Ridley and Herbert Simon in 1938 on the need to move from a focus on inputs to measuring outputs for local government. The Institute's team, working on the mechanics of performance measurement for local governments, acknowledged the difficulty of measuring more than outputs, but turned to customer satisfaction with services as a measurable outcome (Ridley and Simon 1938).

In 1971, the Urban Institute received a grant from the National Science Foundation to collaborate with the International City/County Management Association (ICMA) to research local governments that were taking the lead in performance measurement (such as St. Petersburg, Florida, and Nashville, Tennessee).

The term "effectiveness" was still being used and appeared, rather than the term "outcomes," in the Urban Institute's first comprehensive examination of performance in local government: *How Effective Are Your Community Services? Procedures for Monitoring the Effectiveness of Municipal Services* published in 1977 (Hatry et al. 1977). One of the eight criteria suggested for measures of effectiveness was controllability: "Is the condition measured at least partially the government's responsibility? and Does the government have some control over it?" (Hatry et al. 1977, 5).

Interestingly, while the publication did not use the term "outcomes," another Urban Institute publication published in the same year did: *Monitoring the Outcomes of State Mental Health Treatment Programs: Some Initial Suggestions* (Schainblatt 1977). Apparently, there was not much overlap between the two research groups who were offering guidance on how to measure effectiveness vis-à-vis outcomes. During the 1980s, performance measurement efforts housed in local and state budget offices were more likely to be embraced among certain groups, such as mental health professionals, who already had been collecting data from clients.

In the 1990s, the Alfred Sloan Foundation and others funded the Urban Institute to work with ICMA. The ICMA Performance Project facilitated the use of performance measurement in local governments across the country. The project recruited cities, counties, and special districts to pay a fee for access to comparable measures from peer jurisdictions. This facilitated benchmarking on common measures, mostly output measures, with a few outcomes. During the time that the ICMA Project was gaining ground, and the book *Reinventing Government* by David Osborne and Ted Gaebler with its focus on outcomes and results was attracting attention across the country, the Urban Institute adopted the term "results," rather than effectiveness (Osborne and Gaebler 1992). By the time Hatry and his team at the Institute published their book on measuring outcomes, *Performance Measurement: Getting Results* in 1999, the term "outcomes" was ubiquitous at all levels of government (Hatry 1999).

Another local government phenomenon that started in the 1990s also had ripple effects first across local governments, then to some states and, finally, to the federal level. In 1994, New York City Police Commissioner William Bratton introduced a data-driven management model in the Police Department called CompStat. It involved the Chief holding weekly meetings with district commanders to review crime rates across the districts and to discuss changes and tactics to address rate increases. The use of the managerial tool was subsequently credited by its supporters with decreasing crime and increasing quality of life in New York City over the last two decades (Bratton 1997; Kelling and Bratton 1998; Shane 2007). The CompStat model was adopted by other cities across the United States, and Bratton became a consultant in much demand across the world. By 2000, over a third of police departments in the United States with 100 or more officers reported that they had implemented a "CompStat-like" program (Weisburd et al. 2003). Maryland's Governor Martin O'Malley used the model to create CitiStat when he had been Mayor of Baltimore and he implemented a state-level version (StateStat) when he became Governor of Maryland in 2006. As Governor, he expanded his CitiStat model to review data on outputs (and some outcomes) to manage multiple government agencies (Fenton 2007; Fillichio 2005). The basic frameworks underlying CompStat, then CitiStat, and then StateStat were adopted across the United States, especially by local governments. In 2010 the model was adopted by the Obama Administration for quarterly data reviews for federal agencies.

Arena 2: GASB

In the 1970s, while staff in budget offices and chief executive officers in local governments were considering how to demonstrate their programmatic effectiveness, an interesting development was taking place somewhat independently, though not in a totally disconnected manner, in the government accounting arena. Government accountants had traditionally examined the operations of government agencies through following their financial transactions. In December 1980, the Financial Accounting Standards Board (FASB) published a *Statement of Financial Accounting Standards Concept No. 4 on Objectives of Financial Reporting by Nonbusiness Organizations* (FASB 1980). The concept paper introduced the idea of measuring program accomplishments, meaning results.

In the statement FASB noted: "Periodic measurement of the changes in the amount and nature of the net resources of a nonbusiness organization and information about the service efforts and accomplishments of an organization together represent the information most useful in assessing its performance" (1980, xiv). The statement went on to say:

> Ideally, financial reporting also should provide information about the service accomplishments of a nonbusiness organization. Information about service accomplishments in terms of goods or services produced (outputs) and of program results may enhance significantly the value of information provided about service efforts. However, the ability to measure service accomplishments, particularly program results, is generally underdeveloped.
>
> *(1980, 25–26)*

FASB based its opinion of the challenges to measurement of outcomes on a study they had commissioned with Peat, Marwick, Mitchell and Company that studied how and to what extent nonbusiness organizations were measuring service accomplishments. The Peat, Marwick report was published by FASB in November 1980. Their research had looked at reporting practices in six types of nonbusiness organizations including colleges and universities, hospitals, human service organizations, state and local government units, trade and professional organizations, and philanthropic foundations.

The study found that most of the organizations reported output measures, but not data on results or impact on service recipients, and that few measures captured effectiveness. The study also noted that the vast majority of the measures reported were inputs, processes or outputs, and that most of the measures were found in budget documents provided by the organizations. Since 1980, governmental accounting professionals have continued to stress the need for more reporting of nonfinancial accomplishments. Virtually every annual conference of the Association of Government Accountants has featured guidance on how to address the challenges of measuring accomplishments (outcomes).

Arena 3: Federal Efforts to Connect Effectiveness/Results/Outcomes with Budgeting

Efforts to connect performance data with budgeting decisions have been made through both executive action and legislation at the federal level of the U.S. government. As noted earlier, the lead federal budget agency, now the Office of Management and Budget (OMB), started to promote measurement of effectiveness during the Johnson Administration as a result of the perceived positive effects of implementing PPBS in the DoD. The Nixon and Ford Administrations, however, turned more toward promoting internal process improvements, such as Managing by Objectives, and the Carter Administration initiated conversations about zero-based budgeting, but did not tackle the performance data collection challenge.

While some OMB budget examiners had been routinely asking for evidence about how well programs were working as part of their examination of agency budget requests for some time, it was not until 1992, under the leadership of President Clinton's OMB Director Alice Rivlin, that agencies would officially be required to include performance measures in their budget requests. A focus on measurement of results also accompanied President Clinton's 1993 initiative that was coordinated by Vice-President Gore. Commonly known as the National Performance Review (NPR), it emphasized results-oriented management as well as reforms such as cutting red tape and outsourcing (Breul and Kamensky 2008; Fox 1996; Moynihan 2008).

The NPR effort was organized from the Clinton White House. Its leaders recruited about 250 temporary staff on assignment from other executive agencies and placed them in teams to review the agencies and systems to which they had been assigned. In addition, Vice-President Gore reached out to the broader federal career workforce and the public for stories of what was wrong and what needed to be fixed. Gore received more than 50,000 letters and he attended listening sessions in several dozen federal agencies and around the country. The NPR teams developed recommendations and David Osborne was brought in to help craft the final report. The final report, *From Red Tape to Results: Creating a Government that Works Better and Costs Less* (Gore 1993) contained more than 1,200 recommendations (Breul and Kamensky 2008).

Some NPR recommendations focused on improvements to the way in which the government worked, such as streamlining procurement and setting customer service standards. Other recommendations, touting more than $100 billion in cost reductions, called for decreasing the number of federal employees by more than 250,000 and eliminating a range of programs such as the wool and mohair subsidy (Breul and Kamensky 2008). Some recommendations appealed to employees; others appealed to the general public. Critics have been quick to note that the most consequential result of the NPR was the reduction of the federal workforce. This, however, led to an increase in the number of federal contractors in subsequent years that brought a whole new set of governance problems (Fox 1996; Light 2008).

Directives of the George W. Bush Administration stepped up the pressure for agencies to align programmatic performance goals and performance data with budget categories. New initiatives were included in the President's Management Agenda (PMA). The PMA was similar to the NPR in intent, but streamlined its efforts to focus on a limited number of areas—strategic management of human capital, competitive sourcing, financial performance, electronic government, and budget and performance integration. To insert performance data into the President's budget, OMB employed the Program Assessment Rating Tool that assessed program performance and issued scores to programs that showed how well they were doing. President Bush also established agency performance improvement officers and OMB led meetings of these officers in a new Performance Improvement Council.

The legislative call for the provision of nonfinancial program performance and results data in agency financial statements was first made in the Chief Financial Officers Act of 1990. These reporting requirements were expanded in the Government Management Reform Act of 1994. Perhaps the most important legislative initiative was, however, the GPRA of 1993, which required all federal agencies to have strategic plans, performance goals, and performance reporting. The inclusion of the term "results" in the title of the law reflected the public dialogue inspired by the Osborne and Gaebler bestseller, as well as many other advocates of New Public Management reforms that included calls for managing by results, that is, outcomes. Since the enactment of the GPRA, dozens of federal laws have been passed that require performance measures in specific policy arenas. GPRA reporting requirements have been strengthened with the GPRA Modernization Act of 2010 (U.S. GAO 2008a, 2008b, 2012, 2013).

Several factors worked against managers as they strived to design and implement useful performance measurement systems during the Clinton and Bush Administrations. The GPRA, not NPR, was the prime mover in requiring federal managers to develop performance measures, but OMB played a critical role in working with agencies to meet the law's requirements. When OMB did not provide clear guidance or significant technical assistance to agencies, managers expressed uncertainty about what measures would be perceived as appropriate.

Federal managers were not convinced they would be granted sufficient authority or flexibility to change their way of doing business.

Securing agreement among diverse stakeholders and service delivery partners on program measures was difficult. Understandably, outcomes often were viewed as beyond the control of agency staff. More importantly, there was uncertainty about how performance data would be used in budgeting, and only spotty evidence existed that showed performance measures having much effect on budget allocation decisions.

A key component of the Obama Administration's approach to collection of performance data, or what it refers to as its performance management framework, has been to require all major federal agencies to identify a limited number of high-priority performance goals reflecting the near-term implementation priorities of their senior managers. The mandate from the Obama performance team, as seen on its website (performance.gov), is to use goals to improve performance and accountability, measure and analyze performance to find what works, and deliver better results using frequent, data-driven reviews.

Many, but not all, of the Obama Administration's high-priority performance goals were expressed as desired outcomes, such as one of their first and most publicized, which dealt with veterans' homelessness: "The Department of Housing and Urban Development and the Department of Veterans Affairs will jointly reduce homelessness among veterans. Together, the two agencies will reduce the number of homeless veterans to 59,000 in June, 2012" (U.S. Executive Office of the President n.d., 11). Most of the high-priority goals, however, were outputs; some were not supported with new funding. An example for the Education Department (U.S. Executive Office of the President n.d., 7) provides an illustration:

> Evidence Based Policy: Measuring Effectiveness and Investing in What Works: Implementation of a comprehensive approach to using evidence to inform the Department's policies and major initiatives, including:
>
> - Increase by 2/3 the number of Department discretionary programs that use evaluation, performance measures and other program data for continuous improvement;
> - Implement rigorous evaluations for all of the Department's highest priority programs and initiatives; and
> - Ensure all newly authorized Department discretionary programs include a rigorous evaluation component.

During the Obama Administration the terms "results" and "evidence" have been used when referring to the ongoing performance data being collected and reviewed in quarterly reviews that mimic the CompStat model described earlier (Brass 2011, 24, Table 1; Brass 2012; U.S. GAO 2013; Hatry and Davies

2011). Obama's OMB also has promoted the use of data analytics, which means sophisticated analyses of administrative and performance data to inform decision-making. This reflects the widespread popularity of the use of metrics as can be seen in Michael Lewis' bestselling book *Moneyball* (2003). Both the use of high-priority goals and quarterly reviews were originally Obama OMB initiatives, and were incorporated in the GPRA Modernization Act of 2010.

As noted with the administration's high-priority goals, the OMB also has been advocating more rigorous evaluation work to supply evidence on the extent to which specific programs produce results. Obama's OMB has presented a tiers-of-evidence framework that communicates which evaluation research designs are more likely to produce valid data from evaluation studies. The three tiers are entitled "Preliminary/Exploratory, Moderate/Suggestive, and Strong Causal."

The Obama OMB has also publicly voiced support (moral if not financial) for rigorous program evaluation more prominently than previous administrations. A series of memoranda from OMB between 2009 and 2013 signaled that performance measurement and evaluation were to be used to produce "evidence on what works" (OMB 2010, 2011, 2012a, 2012b, 2013; Metzenbaum 2011). Among the actions taken by OMB to give evaluation a facelift were:

- establishing a cross-agency federal work group to develop common evidence standards;
- signaling agencies that they are more likely to fund evidence-based programs;
- establishing Chief Evaluation Officers at the U.S. Department of Labor and the Centers for Disease Control;
- focusing on improving access to data and linking of data across program and agencies;
- calling for more collaborative evaluations both across agencies and across service providers in different sectors; and
- offering training on evaluation expectations to agency staff starting in Fall 2013 (Newcomer and Brass 2013).

Arena 4: Program Evaluation of Social Programs

A few accounts of the evolution of performance measurement practice have addressed the complex relationship between performance measurement and evaluation, as well as between the professionals who conduct the work. Some have characterized performance measurement and evaluation as "adjacent fields" or "complementary" (Van Dooren, Bouckaert, and Halligan 2010, 10; see also Nielsen and Ejler 2008; Nielsen and Hunter 2013). Still others have viewed performance measurement as a subfield of evaluation (Hatry 2006), but note that measurement and evaluation have traveled on "separate, but somewhat parallel paths" (Hatry 2013, 22), or note how "[c]onsiderable differences of opinion exist among evaluators as to how performance monitoring and evaluation studies are related, in particular the extent to which they are at odds with or complement each other" (Hatry, Wholey, and Newcomer 2010, 273; Talbot 2010, 183). In the field of international development, the two terms often are joined to form a single term of art, as "monitoring and evaluation" (Kusek and Rist 2001).

Heated debates occasionally have arisen in the evaluation community about how to view the value and role of ongoing performance measurement (Bernstein 1999; Feller 2002; Perrin 1998, 1999; Winston 1999). Others have cited dissatisfaction with evaluation practice, since some kinds of evaluation studies are viewed as taking too long to be useful (Nielsen and Ejler 2008). In 1999, one U.S. federal government evaluator, Ann Blalock, noted that the

> burgeoning performance management movement, with its emphasis on . . . a limited set of quantitative indicators, has developed a life of its own largely apart from the evaluation research movement. Reflecting the differences in the professional history, interests, and training underlying the two movements, the relationship between these disparate approaches to establishing public accountability has lacked coordination and defied integration.
>
> *(Blalock 1999, 119; see also Blalock and Barnow 2001)*

Blalock called for integration. However, that integration largely has not occurred. Both theory and experience at the federal level suggest that viewing performance measurement as something different and distinct from evaluation, or as something either inferior or superior, has contributed toward:

- reduced benefits from application of professional evaluation skills and standards in performance measurement practice;
- a proliferation of different offices in public agencies undertaking evaluation *or* performance measurement but not both;
- reduced capacity for a strategic or holistic evaluation approach within agencies; and
- obstacles to the generation of organizational learning and improved programmatic and policy performance stemming from synergies from a more unified approach to performance measurement and evaluation.

The movement toward collecting data on outcomes rather than outputs raises the implied assumption that the measured outcomes are the result, at least to some extent, of the government's actions undertaken to produce them. Such claims raise issues viewed by evaluators as firmly within the evaluation profession's turf. Some critics of performance outcome measurement have distanced its methodology from what they characterize as more "rigorous" evaluation of program impact.

During the period in which preferences for measuring outcomes rather than outputs has been increasing, there have been some rather dramatic and pertinent changes in evaluation practice. Many view the 1960s as the high point of support for federal funding of evaluation in the United States, with legislation starting to include requirements that evaluations be undertaken as early as 1962 for employment and training programs as mandated in the Manpower Development and Training Act of 1962.

Allocations were set aside for evaluation in many of the federal antipoverty programs starting with the Economic Opportunity Act of 1964. Senator Robert Kennedy's 1965 evaluation rider to the Title I section of the Elementary and Secondary Education Act provided major funding for evaluation. And in 1968 money was first set aside for evaluation of the Head Start program—a practice that continues to this day (Shadish, Cook, and Leviton 1991). Federal funds were earmarked for evaluation of many intergovernmental programs and there were spillover effects in that state and local funds were also directed toward evaluation. Millions of dollars were allocated for evaluation work in the 1960s into the 1970s. Estimates are that while perhaps $17 million was spent in 1969 by the major social service agency—Health, Education, Welfare, and Labor—that figure increased to roughly $100 million by 1972. The total federal investment in evaluation between 1975–1977 exceeded $3 billion.

During the 1980s, evaluation funding declined, in large part due to the budget cuts of the Reagan Administration. The number of evaluation studies and of evaluation staff in federal agencies declined. Professional evaluation staff decreased 52 percent between 1980 and 1988 in fifteen major evaluation units (Shadish, Cook, and Leviton 1991) but some legislation started including performance measurement requirements such as that included in the Job Training Partnership Act (JTPA) in 1982. While ongoing performance measurement was undertaken in job training programs during the Comprehensive Employment and Training Act period in the 1970s, its formal inclusion in the JTPA was notable. Unlike many of the performance measurement systems established a decade later in response to requirements of the GPRA of 1993, the JTPA system was designed primarily by economists who wanted to maximize outcomes in terms of employment and earnings gains of participants (Barnow and Smith 2004).

The JTPA was the first large federal program to require outcomes measurement as well as evaluation studies. The statute contained both equity (serving the hard-to-serve) and efficiency (maximizing the net gain) goals for the program. The federal government funded the program and set its broad outlines, but administration of the job training programs was devolved to the state level and operations were primarily the responsibility of local entities, thus introducing much intergovernmental complexity (Barnow and Smith 2004). As one evaluator noted: "The key problem with such an arrangement is that the state and local governments, and their contractors, may have goals different from those of the federal government" (Barnow and Smith 2004, 22).

Experience with the JTPA provided data to test how outcome data collection affected program performance and how findings from evaluation studies compared with those from analyses of outcomes data. The findings were not promising. For example, studies showed that training centers sometimes attempted to change their measured performance without changing their actual performance, in other words "gaming" the performance system occurred (Barnow and Smith 2004).

Subsequent studies of the use of performance measurement systems in federal agencies have offered similar criticisms (Frederickson and Frederickson 2006). Beryl Radin argues that a focus on performance measurement and reporting at the federal level has created tensions and misfits between expectations and practices that have produced pernicious consequences (Radin 2006, 2009). A number of empirical studies of performance measurement and reporting have documented some unintended or harmful consequences and little evidence of improved programmatic performance (Barnow 2000; Barnow and Smith 2004; Heinrich 1999, 2004a, 2004b, 2007, 2012; Heinrich and Marschke 2010; Heinrich, Lynn, and Milward 2010; Jacobs and Goddard 2007; Moynihan and Lavertu 2012; Moynihan and Pandey 2010).

Despite some skepticism about the cost effectiveness of performance measurement, during the 1990s many laws included requirements for outcomes measurement to enhance accountability. For example, in education, the Improving America's Schools Act of 1994 was the first legislation to put in place standards and accountability elements for states and local school districts that receive funding under the law. These accountability provisions were further developed in the most recent reauthorization of the No Child Left Behind Act (20 U.S.C. 6311 et seq.). The subsequent use of standardized test scores in public schools as the key outcomes used to rank schools has been controversial, to say the least.

The use of outcomes data in the public health sector has not been so controversial. Using disease prevalence rates has been routine for many years. A hallmark in the health arena was establishing national health goals. In 1990, the U.S. Department of Health and Human Services published an ambitious set of targets in *Healthy People 2000*. The comprehensiveness of the list of the health conditions covered, and the inclusive and transparent nature of the process used to set targets for the nation in the Healthy People initiative were unprecedented. The targets were subsequently reset and work is being undertaken on Healthy People 2020.

In the early 2000s, evaluation and measurement practice was affected by demands for evidence-based policy. It is hard to trace the origins of the adjective "evidence-based," but a confluence of influential events at the turn of the century heralded an increased public enchantment with the term. The establishment of the Campbell Collaboration in 2000, the Coalition for Evidence Based-Policy in 2001, and the What Works Clearinghouse at the U.S. Department of Education in 2002 were some of the more publicized commitments made to advance the use of systematic collection and analysis of research to inform decision-making in the public sector (U.S. GAO 2010).

The assumptions underlying the promotion of evidence-based decision-making in government and in the nonprofit sector are twofold: first, the more rigorous the social science research design, the more credible are the findings; and second, systematic reviews of rigorous studies of the same intervention can produce especially credible findings. There are widely accepted criteria by which the rigor of evaluation studies can be rated, although not all criteria are viewed to be of equal importance by evaluation professionals. Most advocates of systematic reviews tend to believe that true experiments are better than any other design for any purpose. The term for experimental designs that has become fashionable post-2000 is random control trials (RCTs) since that is the term used in medical research with tests of the efficacy of new drugs. Many of those who support evidence-based policy view RCTs as the "gold standard" for designing any research or evaluation study.

While there is disagreement within the evaluation profession regarding the sanctity of RCTs, and the relative weight to be given to different evaluation designs, the acceptance of the value of the "evidence-based" label is widespread. There are significant implications of the prevalence of this evaluation gold standard for both measurement of outcomes and evaluation practice:

- There are higher demands placed upon those reporting outcomes or evaluation findings to demonstrate the quality of the evidence they produce.
- There is a lack of a clear, shared understanding about when evidence is good enough.
- There is more uncertainty among both evaluators and audiences about how to produce high-level evidence in fieldwork where random assignment is simply not an option.

In short, it is simply harder to produce compelling "evidence" about public sector performance than it has ever been before.

Arena 5: Outcomes Assessment Requirements for Nonprofit Agencies and in Accreditation Processes

Foundations and other funders of nonprofit agencies started calling for measurement of the results produced by the services their grantees provided as early as the 1970s, although the heat turned up on this requirement in the 1990s. Three key influential events have had ripple effects across the nonprofit sector. First, when the Johnson family founded the Robert Wood Johnson Foundation (RWJF) in 1972 they issued a public call for measurement of the results of its investments.[1] Along with other large foundations, such as the Kellogg Foundation and the Gates Foundation, the funders of health, education, and social service nonprofits have set the pace for requirements for more outcomes reporting, rather than simply outputs, and for more evaluations to be undertaken to produce rigorous evidence of impact over the last two decades (Newcomer 2008).

The second seminal event was the requirement imposed by the United Way, a huge funder of social service providers in the United States, in which grantees must report on the outcomes of their work. This move was highlighted by the publication of the United Way manual *Measuring Program Outcomes: A Practical Approach* in 1996. Leading up to the publication of the very public commitment to outcomes reporting, a thirty-one-member Task Force on Impact had been working with the United Way to develop a new approach to identify benefits to clients, to measure the extent to which clients achieved the desired results and to report the results (Hendricks, Plantz, and Pritchard 2008). Many prominent members of the evaluation profession served on the Task Force, such as Carol Weiss and Joseph Wholey, as well as the key figure involved in promoting outcomes measurement among local governments, Harry Hatry. The nonprofit service providers heard the call to measure outcomes. However, capacity and the vulnerability of client outcomes to factors outside the control of the service providers has continued to make meeting the goals of the United Way's bold commitment challenging (Hendricks, Plantz, and Pritchard 2008).

Third, in 2011 an influential intermediary that individual and institutional donors use to inform their decisions on where to invest, Charity Navigator, made a public commitment to begin using outcomes assessment as one of the criteria it uses to rate service providers and charities with revenues exceeding $1 million. Since 2001, Charity Navigator has been rating charities by essentially the percentage that each spends on administrative overhead rather than direct services as taken from 990 income tax forms. Over the last three years Charity Navigator has deliberated on how to implement its plan to use more than simply financial information to rate the organizations. It alerted the nonprofit sector that it is moving beyond financial data to look more broadly at both accountability and transparency in assessing charities. As it states on its website:

> *Accountability* is an obligation or willingness by a charity to explain its actions to its stakeholders. For now, Charity Navigator is specifically evaluating the fiduciary actions of charities. In the future, we intend to evaluate other aspects of accountability such as results reporting and other indicators of the way organizations use the resources they raise to accomplish their mission. *Transparency* is an obligation or willingness by a charity to publish and make available critical data about the organization.
>
> *(Charity Navigator n.d.a)*

Charity Navigator has made a commitment to move toward incorporating assessment of charities by how well they do with outcomes reporting by 2016. The Charity Navigator leadership acknowledges that this will be a stretch for smaller nonprofits. Again, as noted on its website:

> We recognize that the majority of charities are in the early stages of measuring and reporting results, and do not yet have the necessary systems in place to meet the Results Reporting rating criteria. We will engage with

charities with the intention of encouraging and incentivizing progressive improvement in results measurement and reporting practices over the coming years. As charities demonstrate improved results reporting practices, the rating criteria will evolve to keep raising the bar of reporting requirements as more and more charities aspire to and become higher performing.

(Charity Navigator n.d.b)

As still another sign of the popular, yet intimidating nature of outcomes reporting in the nonprofit sector, Bill Gates devoted his open letter about his Foundation's work in January 2013 to highlighting the role of, and challenges to, measurement of outcomes for individuals and communities. Interestingly, for the Gates Foundation results now include both outputs and outcomes. Gates writes:

In previous annual letters, I've focused a lot on the power of innovation to reduce hunger, poverty, and disease. But any innovation—whether it's a new vaccine or an improved seed—can't have an impact unless it reaches the people who will benefit from it. That's why in this year's letter I discuss how innovations in measurement are critical to finding new, effective ways to deliver these tools and services to the clinics, family farms, and classrooms that need them.

(Gates 2013)

Higher education is another area where outcomes assessment is receiving heightened attention. It is one of the requirements for accreditation of universities and colleges and has been progressing along a somewhat parallel track with government accountability over the last four decades. Starting in the 1970s, the notion of measuring and tracking competencies in various professions was being discussed and critiqued (Grant 1979). Now it is a reality. Movement toward acceptance of measurement and reporting of outcomes in higher education was affected by work undertaken in projects funded by the Fund for the Improvement of Postsecondary Education (FIPSE), a grant-making office established within the U.S. Department of Health, Education, and Welfare to improve the quality of and access to higher education in 1973 by then President Nixon. Many projects were funded to test how student performance and outcomes might be measured in higher education, and many conferences were held to address student outcomes assessment.

One pioneer in outcomes assessment was Dr. E. Grady Bogue,[2] a Fellow in Academic Administration at the American Council of Education in 1974–1975 where he started focusing on outcomes measurement. For the following five years he directed the Tennessee Performance Funding Project, which designed and implemented the first state-level performance incentive policy in U.S. higher education. Bogue's work, along with that produced by other researchers, was initially funded by FIPSE-inspired accreditation bodies during the 1980s and 1990s to incorporate student outcomes assessment in their assessment criteria.

For example, the Association to Advance Collegiate Schools of Business adopted outcomes-based assessment in the 1980s. The Council for Higher Education Accreditation (CHEA), the accreditor of the accrediting bodies in the higher education field, was established in 1996, and issued its Standards for "Recognition of Accrediting Organizations Policy and Procedures" in 1998. CHEA revised the accreditation standards in 2006 and 2010, but requirements for monitoring outcomes have been included since 1998. Accordingly, the Network of Schools of Public Policy, Affairs, and Administration, the accrediting body for Master of Public Administration programs, requires performance outcome measurement.

Arena 6: Social, National, State, and Community Indicators

Back in 1969 an interesting but now largely forgotten report was published by the U.S. Department of Health, Education, and Welfare entitled *Toward a Social Report*. Preparation of the report was overseen by a Panel on Social Indicators chaired by Daniel Bell and co-chaired by Alice Rivlin. The Panel advocated that the United States adopt a set of national indictors on social progress to complement the economic indicators that were already being monitored.

The report lamented: "There is no Government procedure for periodic stocktaking of the social health of the Nation" (U.S. Department of Health, Education, and Welfare 1969, xi). The titles of the chapters were especially noteworthy as they raised important outcome questions. For example, for the chapter on Public Order and Safety the question was "What is the impact of crime on our lives?"; for the chapter on Learning, Science and Art, the question was "How much are they enriching society?"; and for the chapter on Participation and Alienation, "What do we need to learn?"

The call for collecting national-level indicators to monitor social progress was taken up again more than forty years later when David Walker, then Comptroller General of the United States (and head of the U.S. GAO) and others convened groups to deliberate on how to develop a set of "Key National Indicators." The GAO conducted one study in 2004 and another more extensive one in 2011 to investigate how other national and subnational governments have developed key indicator systems (U.S. GAO 2004, 2011). The Office also provided some suggestions on how to proceed with such a daunting effort.

"Key National Indicators" have been advocated, such as the social indicators were in 1969, to help track the social health of the nation, and, by implication, to test some interesting causal inferences on how effective governmental programs are in addressing persistent social problems. Understanding the relationship between what governments do and the changes that occur in social conditions—that is, the presumed outcomes of the government action—constitutes the challenge.

The state of Oregon took on this challenge, and drew quite positive publicity when it published "Benchmarks" in 1989. The state government established goals for changes in social indicators. The Oregon Progress Board published data and drew accolades for its work, until the legislature decided it was not that valuable and defunded the Board in 2012.

Starting in the early 2000s, a number of government agencies and nonprofit organizations in some U.S. cities and counties established what are called "Community Indicators" projects. In 2001, the Community Indicators Consortium was set up for representatives of the various Community Indicators projects across the country to share promising practices. As with the advocates of the social indicators in 1969, a goal for the local Community Indicators projects has been to draw the attention and resources of both citizens and governments to addressing social conditions. The Alfred P. Sloan Foundation funded research on these projects to examine the potential for facilitating synergies and learning across the Community Indicators advocates and local government measurement practitioners. As noted in the Sloan-funded report:

> A key assumption surrounding the dialogue was that if citizen-driven community indicators and government performance measurement were better linked, community indicators would have more influence on what government does to improve the community, and government performance measures would become more relevant to the community conditions of greatest concern to citizens.
>
> *(Lomax 2007, 4)*

The results of greatest concern to citizens who are involved in the Community Indicators movement are clearly the outcomes of government efforts rather than their outputs.

Arena 7: Evaluation and Monitoring of International Development Efforts

Public and nonprofit service providers in developing countries operate with the same expectations and challenges to measure the results of their efforts as their counterparts in developed countries. However, the capacity to collect, analyze, and learn from data on their performance is usually lower than in the more developed countries (Edwards and Hulme 1996; Imas and Rist 2009). Funder expectations about the data that can be collected by the social service providers they support, as well as the specific reporting requirements they impose, are especially critical in affecting the validity and reliability of the data collected (Edwards and Hulme 1996; Newcomer, El Baradei, and Garcia 2013).

International funders have been looking for "evidence" of what strategies work for several decades and have hired external evaluators to conduct impact studies to collect data on solutions for complex social problems (Armecin et al. 2006; Das Gupta et al. 2005; García-Moreno and Tines 2007; Hossain, Duffield, and

Taylor 2005; Khagram et al. 2009; Paxson and Schady 2007; Schady, Rüdiger, and Araujo 2006; Schneider, Luelmo, and Roses 2008; Soeung et al. 2008; Vio 2005; Waiswa et al. 2008). There is a dual-pronged movement toward: (1) an increase in transparency of where/how funds are allocated with a push to make contracts public and to track funds from the funder to the community, and (2) a push for evidence of how much "bang for your buck" that results. This emphasis requires impact evaluation and systematic reviews using experimental design. The two movements are somewhat distinct and antithetical in that the trends are not really moving in a linear fashion from "output" to "outcome," but are requiring "input" monitoring, "output" auditing and "impact" assessment. The funders have also been asking providers to collect data on a routine basis to track the use of funds and the progress made by the people and communities served (Edwards and Hulme 1996; Knutsen and Brower 2010; Manning 2007; Mumssen, Johannes, and Kumar 2010).

There have been several popular and well-publicized critiques of the effectiveness of international aid (Easterly 2002, 2006; Moyo 2010; Savedoff, Levine, and Birdsall 2005). Evaluation has been touted by funders as a necessary, if not sufficient, requirement to test the effectiveness of development interventions as well as to provide results data to inform efforts to make international development policies and programs more effective. Given the skepticism about the impact of international investments uncovered by earlier studies, aid agencies and donors have made an even stronger push toward improving the reporting and measurement of results (DFID 2009; USAID 2011).

A seminal event that has affected the way that results are viewed and evaluated in the international development arena was the setting of the Millennium Development Goals in 2000 (United Nations n.d.). Eight international development goals were established following the Millennium Summit of the United Nations in 2000, following the adoption of the United Nations Millennium Declaration. All 189 United Nations member states at the time (there are currently 193 members) and at least 23 international organizations committed to help achieve the Millennium Development Goals by 2015. They are:

- to eradicate extreme poverty and hunger;
- to achieve universal primary education;
- to promote gender equality and empowering women;
- to reduce child mortality rates;
- to improve maternal health;
- to combat HIV/AIDS, malaria, and other diseases;
- to ensure environmental sustainability; and
- to develop a global partnership for development.

The importance of the Millennium Development Goals is that funders have increasingly asked grantees to chart their results against these desired outcomes.

Calls for evidence of such results has led to more investment in evaluation and monitoring. For example, a leader in developing an evidence base is the International Initiative for Impact Evaluation[3] established in 2008 to fund impact evaluations in development work. The initiative reflects the worldwide focus on the systematic collection of performance data and the assessment of impact to ultimately inform decision-making by both development funders and implementers.

Conclusion

In the United States the audiences for the reporting of results of governmental and nonprofit efforts are more demanding than ever before. Trust in government is low, but expectations for the quality of the evidence provided are high. Advances in information technology have made it easier to collect and analyze vast amounts of data, but the problems that governmental and nonprofit agencies address are more complex and interconnected than ever before.

Looking back, there have been some remarkable changes in thinking about the way in which performance of public and nonprofit agencies should be measured. In the 1960s, reflecting experience with PPBS, the prevalent term was "effective." In the 1980s, "results" and "outcomes" became the terms reflecting efforts undertaken in local governments and popularized by Osborne and Gaebler and the Clinton Administration's NPR. At the beginning of the twenty-first century, the quest for "evidence-based policy" raised expectations for data that could be produced to demonstrate results and impact.

There have been initiatives undertaken by the accounting profession, budgeting professionals, police chiefs, public health professionals, the United Nations, the United Way, foundations, accrediting organizations, and social scientists, all of which are intent on using evidence to improve public policies. These efforts have whetted the public appetite for what information about government and nonprofits should be collected. The efforts and ambitions of the many institutions and individuals described in this chapter have raised public awareness and dialogue about learning how well government works. It is unlikely that demand for high-quality evidence about policy and program results will diminish any time soon, although the willingness to fund the costs of collecting the data is less certain.

However, measuring and reporting on the results of public and nonprofit programs is sometimes quite difficult. The following list provides a list of perhaps the biggest challenges to collecting valid, relevant and reliable outcome measures of public programs:

- *Difficulty of establishing causality:* Attributing desired outcomes to government actions is difficult since there are many other potential causes for observed changes in conditions, or in behaviors of individuals, classes, schools, communities, or larger entities. Changes in the environment, in the units themselves, inadequate, inconsistent or incomplete implementation of the program, or simply faulty methods can make it difficult to make the case for causation.

- *Securing adequate and timely involvement of pertinent stakeholders upfront to envision what and how to measure the outcomes:* Selecting appropriate measures that will be viewed as valid and relevant by the key stakeholders is typically dependent upon getting their input early enough as well as securing consensus among them as to how to measure the desired outcomes.

- *Unclear identification of desired outcomes/objectives of policies and programs due to politics and lack of consensus among key stakeholders on which outcomes to prioritize and measure:* Often laws and regulations are written as a result of political compromise and the stated goals may be conflicting and/or vague, thus rendering measurement difficult. Lack of consensus among key stakeholders occurs often. Differences in preferences among stakeholders or with newly injected stakeholders after measurement has started can also hinder acceptance of measures as valid and legitimate.

- *Complex and recursive relationships among desired outcomes that are affected by different policies, agencies, and/or programs:* Outcomes are typically measured to assess achievement of singular goals set by singular programs, yet many conditions such as health status are affected by many other aspects of the intended beneficiary's life, such as life stressors, housing, access to transportation, access to healthy food options, and access to recreation.

- *Financial and human resources required to measure outcomes for people, neighborhoods, and jurisdictions:* To measure the impact of many interventions or treatments provided by governmental or nonprofit providers takes resources for follow up and may require multiple contacts, or require collection from large groups or from across large areas or multiple communities. This increases the costs to the providers for data collection.

- *The time that is required before some desired outcomes are even measurable:* Some desired outcomes may result only after a longer time period than is available for a required measurement time frame.

- *Inconsistent measurement across jurisdictions:* Differences in definitions of how to measure desired outcomes or in data collection efforts across agencies or jurisdictions or across time hinder collection of reliable measures.

- *Difficulty in measuring outcomes at all in some areas:* There are some highly qualitative outcomes, such as individual "well-being" or democratization of a political regime, for which there are simply no generally accepted or easily operationalizable instruments.

- *Lack of access to pertinent and valid data:* For some outcomes self-reporting may be the only viable option, but that may be too expensive or too intrusive, there may be limits on access to confidential data, or there simply may be no relevant data available at all.

Despite these challenges, efforts will continue to collect data on the impacts that public service providers have on citizens, communities, and institutions, and in combating unwelcome and unanticipated manmade and natural disasters. There is clearly enough political will, societal acceptability, creativity of method-ologists, and consistently advancing technology to give us optimism that progress will be made in measuring what we as a society deem worthy of measuring.

Notes

1 RWJF was the second largest foundation in the United States and it became a leader in calling for performance measurement, especially of outcomes, earlier than most founda-tions.
2 Bogue later was a Professor of Leadership and Policy Studies, University of Tennessee, Knoxville (1991 to 2012), Chancellor at Louisiana State University, Shreveport (1980 to 1991), and the Chief Academic Officer for the Tennessee Higher Education Commission (1974 to 1980).
3 The Institute is a U.S. nonprofit organization with an office in Washington, with pro-grams operating in Delhi and London under the auspices of the Global Development Network and London International Development Centre, respectively, and it is but one of many other organizations seeking answers about what works in fostering develop-ment, such as PAL, IPA, IDEAS, and DIME.

References

Agranoff, Robert. 2007. *Managing within Networks: Adding Value to Public Organizations. Public Management and Change Series*. Washington, DC: Georgetown University Press.

Alexander, Jennifer, Jeffrey L. Brudney, and Kaifeng Yang. 2010. "Introduction to the Symposium: Accountability and Performance Measurement: The Evolving Role of Nonprofits in the Hollow State." *Nonprofit and Voluntary Sector Quarterly* 39(4): 565–570.

Armecin, Graeme, Jere R. Behrman, Paulita Duazo, Sharon Ghuman, Socorro Gultiano, Elizabeth M. King, and Nannette Lee. 2006. *Early Childhood Development through an Integrated Program: Evidence from the Philippines*. World Bank Impact Evaluation Series No. 2 (WPS 3922-IE). Washington, DC: World Bank.

Barnow, Burt S. 2000. "Exploring the Relationship between Performance Management and Program Impact: A Case Study of the Job Training Partnership Act." *Journal of Policy Analysis and Management* 19(1): 118–141.

——, and Jeffrey A. Smith. 2004. "Performance Management of U.S. Job Training Pro-grams." In *Job Training Policy in the United States*, ed. Christopher J. O'Leary, Robert A. Straits, and Stephen A. Wandner, 21–56. Kalamazoo, MI: W.E. Upjohn Institute.

Baruch, Yehuda, and Nelson Ramalho. 2006. "Communalities and Distinctions in the Measurement of Organizational Performance and Effectiveness across For-Profit and Nonprofit Sectors." *Nonprofit and Voluntary Sector Quarterly* 35(1): 39–65.

Behn, Robert D. 2001. *Rethinking Democratic Accountability*. Washington, DC: Brookings Institution Press.

Bernstein, David J. 1999. "Comments on Perrin's 'Effective Use and Misuse of Perfor-mance Measurement.'" *The American Journal of Evaluation* 20(1): 85–93.

Blalock, Ann B. 1999. "Evaluation Research and the Performance Management Movement from Estrangement to Useful Integration?" *Evaluation* 5(2): 117–149.

———, and Burt S. Barnow. 2001. "Is the New Obsession with Performance Management Masking the Truth About Social Programs?" In *Quicker Better Cheaper? Managing Performance in American Government*, ed. Dall W. Forsythe, 485–517. New York: Rockefeller Institute Press.

Brass, Clinton T. 2011. *Obama Administration Agenda for Government Performance: Evolution and Related Issues for Congress*. Washington, DC: Congressional Research Service. www.scribd.com/doc/48106516/CRS-Memo-on-Obama-Performance-Agenda-1-19-11.html (accessed June 9, 2014).

———. 2012. *Changes to the Government Performance and Results Act (GPRA): Overview of the New Framework of Products and Processes*. CRS Report R42379. Washington, DC: Congressional Research Service. www.fas.org/sgp/crs/misc/R42379.pdf (accessed June 9, 2014).

Bratton, William J. 1997. "Crime is Down in New York City: Blame the Police." In *Zero Tolerance: Policing a Free Society*, 2nd ed., ed. Norman Dennis, 29–42. London: IEA.

Breul, Jonathan D., and John M. Kamensky. 2008. "Federal Government Reform: Lessons from Clinton's 'Reinventing Government' and Bush's 'Management Agenda' Initiatives." *Public Administration Review* 68(6): 1009–1026.

Bromberg, Daniel. 2009. "Performance Measurement." *Public Performance & Management Review* 33(2): 214–221.

Charity Navigator. n.d.a. "How Do We Rate Charities' Accountability and Transparency?" www.charitynavigator.org/index.cfm?bay=content.view&cpid=1093#.U5dm AmlOVes (accessed June 10, 2014).

———. n.d.b. "How Do We Plan to Evaluate Results Reporting?" www.charitynavigator.org/index.cfm?bay=content.view&cpid=1507&print=1 (accessed June 10, 2014).

Dahler-Larsen, Peter. 2012. *The Evaluation Society*. Stanford, CA: Stanford University Press.

Das Gupta, Monica, Michele Gragnolati, Oleksiy Ivaschenko, and Michael Lokshin. 2005. *Improving Child Nutrition Outcomes in India: Can the Integrated Child Development Services Program Be More Effective?* Policy Research WPS 3647. Washington, DC: World Bank.

DFID (Department for International Development). 2009. *Building Evidence to Reduce Poverty*. London: DFID. www.gov.uk/government/uploads/system/uploads/attachment_data/file/67729/evaluation-policy.pdf (accessed June 9, 2014).

Dubnick, Melvin J., and H. George Frederickson. 2011a. "Public Accountability: Performance Measurement, the Extended State, and the Search for Trust." National Academy of Public Administration and the Kettering Foundation, June. http://papers.ssrn.com/sol3/papers.cfm?abstract_id=1875024 (accessed June 9, 2014).

———, and ———. 2011b. *Accountable Governance: Problems and Promises*. Armonk, NY: ME Sharpe.

Easterly, William. 2002. *The Elusive Quest for Growth: Economists' Adventures and Misadventures in the Tropics*. Cambridge, MA: MIT Press.

———. 2006. *The White Man's Burden: Why the West's Efforts to Aid the Rest Have Done So Much Ill and So Little Good*. New York: Penguin.

Ebrahim, Alnoor. 2002. "Information Struggles: The Role of Information in the Reproduction of NGO-Funder Relationships." *Nonprofit and Voluntary Sector Quarterly* 31(1): 84–114.

———. 2005. "Accountability Myopia: Losing Sight of Organizational Learning." *Nonprofit and Voluntary Sector Quarterly* 34(1): 56–87.

———. 2010. "The Many Faces of Nonprofit Accountability." Working Paper 10–069, Harvard Business School.

Edwards, Michael, and David Hulme. 1996. *Beyond the Magic Bullet: NGO Performance and Accountability in the Post-Cold War World*. Hartford, CT: Kumarian Press West.

Enthoven, Alain C., and K. Wayne Smith. 1971. *How Much Is Enough? Shaping the Defense Program, 1961–1969*. New York: Harper & Row.

FASB. 1980. *A Statement of Financial Accounting Standards Concept No. 4 on Objectives of Financial Reporting by Nonbusiness Organizations*. www.fasb.org/cs/BlobServer?blobcol= urldata&blobtable=MungoBlobs&blobkey=id&blobwhere=1175820901017&blobhe ader=application%2Fpdf (accessed June 9, 2014).

Feller, Irwin. 2002. "Performance Measurement Redux." *American Journal of Evaluation* 23(4): 435–452.

Fenton, Justin. 2007. "O'Malley Installing StateStat: Statistics-Based Management is Coming to Md. Government." *Baltimore Sun*, February 12. http://articles.baltimor-esun.com/2007-02-12/news/0702120075_1_omalley-relevant-statistics-baltimore (accessed June 9, 2014).

Fillichio, Carl. 2005. "Getting Ahead of the Curve: Baltimore and CitiStat." *Public Manager* 34(2): 51.

Fox, Charles J. 1996. "Reinventing Government as Postmodern Symbolic Politics." *Public Administration Review* 56(3): 256–262.

Frederickson, David G., and H. George Frederickson. 2006. *Measuring the Performance of the Hollow State*. Washington, DC: Georgetown University Press.

García-Moreno, Mauricio, and Jeffrey Tines. 2007. *Primero Aprendo Program in Central America and Dominican Republic*. Calverton, MD: Macro International Inc.

Gates, Bill. 2013. "Annual Letter 2013." www.gatesfoundation.org/Who-We-Are/ Resources-and-Media/Annual-Letters-List/Annual-Letter-2013 (accessed June 10, 2014).

Gore, Albert. 1993. *From Red Tape to Results: Creating a Government that Works Better and Costs Less: Report of the National Performance Review*. Washington, DC: Government Printing Office.

Grant, Gerald. 1979. *On Competence: A Critical Analysis of Competence-Based Reforms in Higher Education*. San Francisco: Jossey-Bass.

Greene, Jennifer C. 1999. "The Inequality of Performance Measurements." *Evaluation* 5(2): 160–172.

Hatry, Harry P. 1999. *Performance Measurement: Getting Results*. Washington, DC: Urban Institute.

———. 2006. *Performance Measurement: Getting Results*, 2nd ed. Washington, DC: Urban Institute.

———. 2008. "Emerging Developments in Performance Measurement: An International Perspective." In *The International Handbook of Practice-Based Performance Management*, ed. P. De Lancer Julnes, F. Stokes Berry, M. Aristigueta, and K. Yang, 3–23. Thousand Oaks, CA: Sage.

———. 2013. "Sorting the Relationships among Performance Measurement, Program Evaluation, and Performance Management." *New Directions for Evaluation* 137: 19–32.

———, and Elizabeth Davies. 2011. *A Guide to Data-Driven Performance Reviews*. Washington, DC: IBM Center for the Business of Government. www.businessofgovernment. org/report/guide-data-driven-performance-reviews (accessed June 8, 2014).

———, Louis H. Blair, Donald M. Fisk, John H. Greiner, John R. Hall Jr., and Philip S. Schaenman. 1977. *How Effective Are Your Community Services? Procedures for Monitoring the Effectiveness of Municipal Services*. Washington, DC: Urban Institute.

———, Joseph J. Wholey, and Kathryn Newcomer. 2010. "Evaluation Challenges, Issues, and Trends." In *Handbook of Practical Program Evaluation*, 3rd ed., ed. J. Wholey, H. Hatry, and K. Newcomer, 668–679. San Francisco, CA: Jossey- Bass.

Heinrich, Carolyn J. 1999. "Do Government Bureaucrats Make Effective Use of Performance Management Information?" *Journal of Public Administration Research and Theory* 9(3): 363–394.

———. 2004a. "Improving Public-Sector Performance Management: One Step Forward, Two Steps Back?" *Public Finance and Management* 4(3): 317–351.

———. 2004b. "Performance Management as Administrative Reform: Is It Improving Government Performance?" *Public Finance and Management* 4(3): 240–246.

———. 2007. "Evidence-Based Policy and Performance Management: Challenges and Prospects in Two Parallel Movements." *The American Review of Public Administration* 37(3): 255–277.

———. 2012. "How Credible Is the Evidence, and Does It Matter? An Analysis of the Program Assessment Rating Tool." *Public Administration Review* 72(1): 123–134.

———, and Gerald Marschke. 2010. "Incentives and their Dynamics in Public Sector Performance Management Systems." *Journal of Policy Analysis and Management* 29(1): 183–208.

———, Laurence E. Lynn, and H. Brinton Milward. 2010. "A State of Agents? Sharpening the Debate and Evidence over the Extent and Impact of the Transformation of Governance." *Journal of Public Administration Research and Theory* 20(s1): i3–i19.

Hendricks, Michael, Margaret C. Plantz, and Kathleen J. Pritchard. 2008. "Measuring Outcomes of United Way-Funded Programs: Expectations and Reality." *New Directions for Evaluation* 119: 13–35.

Hossain, S.M. Moazzem, Arabella Duffield, and Anna Taylor. 2005. "An Evaluation of the Impact of a US $60 Million Nutrition Programme in Bangladesh." *Health Policy and Planning* 20(1): 35–40.

Imas, Linda G. Morra, and Ray C. Rist. 2009. *The Road to Results: Designing and Conducting Effective Development Evaluations*. Washington, DC: The World Bank

Jacobs, Rowena, and Maria Goddard. 2007. "How Do Performance Indicators Add Up? An Examination of Composite Indicators in Public Services." *Public Money and Management* 27(2): 103–110.

Kelling, George L., and William J. Bratton. 1998. "Declining Crime Rates: Insiders' Views of the New York City Story." *The Journal of Criminal Law and Criminology* 88(4): 1217–1232.

Kettl, Donald F. 2005. *The Global Public Management Revolution*. Washington, DC: Brookings Institution Press.

Khagram, Sanjeev, Craig Thomas, Catrina Lucero, and Subarna Mathes. 2009. "Evidence for Development Effectiveness." *Journal of Development Effectiveness* 1(3): 247–270.

Knutsen, Wenjue Lu, and Ralph S. Brower. 2010. "Managing Expressive and Instrumental Accountabilities in Nonprofit and Voluntary Organizations: A Qualitative Investigation." *Nonprofit and Voluntary Sector Quarterly* 39(4): 588–610.

Kusek, Jody Zall, and Ray C. Rist. 2001. "Building a Performance-Based Monitoring and Evaluation System: The Challenges Facing Developing Countries." *Evaluation Journal of Australasia* 1(2): 14–23.

Lewis, Michael. 2003. *Moneyball: The Art of Winning an Unfair Game*. New York: W.W. Norton.

Light, Paul C. 1997. *The Tides of Reform: Making Government Work, 1945–1995*. New Haven: Yale University Press.

———. 2005. *The Four Pillars of High Performance: How Robust Organizations Achieve Extraordinary Results*. New York: McGraw-Hill.

———. 2008. *A Government Ill Executed: The Decline of the Federal Service and How to Reverse It*. Cambridge, MA: Harvard University Press.

Lomax, A. 2007. *Creating Stronger Linkages between Community Indicator Projects and Government Performance Measurement Efforts. A Research Report*. Washington, DC: The Alfred P. Sloan Foundation.

Manning, R. 2007. "Policies and Efforts of Bilateral Donors." *OECD Journal on Development* 8(1): 67.

Martin, Lawrence L., and Peter M. Kettner. 2010. *Measuring the Performance of Human Service Programs*, 2nd ed. Thousand Oaks, CA: Sage

Metzenbaum, Shelley H. 2006. *Performance Accountability: The Five Building Blocks and Six Essential Practices*. Washington, DC: IBM Center for the Business of Government.

———. 2011. "Saving Taxpayer Dollars with Moneyball." *U.S. Office of Management and Budget*, September 28. www.whitehouse.gov/blog/2011/09/28/saving-taxpayer-dollars-moneyball (accessed June 9, 2014).

Moynihan, Donald P. 2008. *The Dynamics of Performance Management: Constructing Information and Reform*. Washington, DC: Georgetown University Press.

———, and Stéphane Lavertu. 2012. "Does Involvement in Performance Management Routines Encourage Performance Information Use? Evaluating GPRA and PART." *Public Administration Review* 72(4): 592 602.

———, and Sanjay K. Pandey. 2010. "The Big Question for Performance Management: Why Do Managers Use Performance Information?" *Journal of Public Administration Research and Theory* 20(4): 849–866.

Moyo, Dambisa. 2010. *Dead Aid*. New York: Douglas and McIntyre.

Mumssen, Yogita, Lars Johannes, and Geeta Kumar. 2010. *Output-Based Aid: Lessons Learned and Best Practices*. Washington, DC: World Bank.

Muskin, Selma, Harry Hatry, et al. 1969. *Implementing PPB in State, City and County: A Report on the 5–5–5 Project*. Washington, DC: The George Washington University.

Newcomer, Kathryn. 1997. "Using Performance Measurement to Improve Public and Nonprofit Programs." *New Directions in Program Evaluation* 75: 5–14.

———. 2008. "Assessing Program Performance in Nonprofit Agencies." In *The International Handbook of Practice-Based Performance Management*, ed. P. De Lancer Julnes, F. Stokes Berry, M. Aristigueta, and K. Yang, 25–44. Thousand Oaks, CA: Sage.

———, and C.T. Brass. 2013. "Reconceiving 'Performance Management': Situating Performance Measurement within Program Evaluation, and Program Evaluation as a Mission-Support Function." Paper presented at the American Society for Public Administration 2013 Annual Conference, March 15–19, New Orleans.

———, and Sharon Caudle. 2011. "Public Performance Management Systems: Embedding Practices for Improved Success." *Public Performance and Management Review* 35(1): 108–132.

———, Laila El Baradei, and Sandra Garcia. 2013. "Expectations and Capacity of Performance Measurement in NGOs in the Development Context." *Public Administration and Development* 33(1): 62–79.

Nielsen, Steffen Bohni, and Nicolaj Ejler. 2008. "Improving Performance? Exploring the Complementarities between Evaluation and Performance Management." *Evaluation* 14(2): 171–192.

———, and David E.K. Hunter. 2013. "Challenges to and Forms of Complementarity between Performance Management and Evaluation." *New Directions for Evaluation* 137: 115–123.

Nutley, Sandra M., Isabel Walter, and Huw T.O. Davies. 2007. *Using Evidence: How Research Can Inform Public Services*. Bristol: Policy Press.

Olsson, Tina M. 2007. "Reconstructing Evidence-Based Practice: An Investigation of Three Conceptualisations of EBP." *Evidence & Policy: A Journal of Research, Debate and Practice* 3(2): 271–285.

Osborne, David, and Ted Gaebler. 1992. *Reinventing Government: How the Entrepreneurial Spirit is Transforming the Public Sector*. Reading, MA: Addison-Wesley.

Packard, Thomas. 2010. "Staff Perceptions of Variables Affecting Performance in Human Service Organizations." *Nonprofit and Voluntary Sector Quarterly* 39(6): 971–990.

Patton, Michael Quinn. 2011. *Developmental Evaluation: Applying Complexity Concepts to Enhance Innovation and Use*. New York: The Guilford Press.

Paxson, Christina H., and Norbert Rüdiger Schady. 2007. *Does Money Matter? The Effects of Cash Transfers on Child Health and Development in Rural Ecuador*. World Bank Impact Evaluation Series No. 15, WPS 4226. Washington, DC: World Bank.

Perrin, Burt. 1998. "Effective Use and Misuse of Performance Measurement." *American Journal of Evaluation* 19(3): 367–379.

———. 1999. "Performance Measurement: Does the Reality Match the Rhetoric? A Rejoinder to Bernstein and Winston." *American Journal of Evaluation* 20(1): 101–111.

———. 2006. *Moving from Outputs to Outcomes: Practical Advice from Governments around the World*. Washington, DC: IBM Center for the Business of Government.

Pollitt, Christopher, and Geert Bouckaert. 2000. *Public Management Reform: A Comparative Analysis*. New York: Oxford University Press.

Power, Michael. 1997. *The Audit Society: Rituals of Verification*. New York: Oxford University Press.

Radin, Beryl. 2006. *Challenging the Performance Movement: Accountability, Complexity, and Democratic Values*. Washington, DC: Georgetown University Press.

———. 2009. "What Can We Expect from Performance Measurement Activities?" *Journal of Policy Analysis and Management* 28(3): 505–512.

Ridley, Clarence Eugene, and Herbert A. Simon. 1938. *Measuring Municipal Activities: A Survey of Suggested Criteria and Reporting Forms for Appraising Administration*. Chicago: International City Managers' Association.

Savedoff, William D., Ruth Levine, and Nancy Birdsall. 2005. *When Will We Ever Learn? Recommendations to Improve Social Development through Enhanced Impact Evaluation*. Washington, DC: Center for Global Development

Schady, Norbert Rüdiger, and Maria Araujo. 2006. *Cash Transfers, Conditions, School Enrollment, and Child Work: Evidence from a Randomized Experiment in Ecuador*. World Bank Impact Evaluation Series No. 3, WPS 3930-IE. Washington, DC: World Bank.

Schainblatt, Alfred H. 1977. *Monitoring the Outcomes of State Mental Health Treatment Programs: Some Initial Suggestions*. Washington, DC: The Urban Institute.

Schalock, Robert L., and Gordon S. Bonham. 2003. "Measuring Outcomes and Managing for Results." *Evaluation and Program Planning* 26(3): 229–235.

Schneider, Rose, Fabio Luelmo, and Diana Roses. 2008. *TB Child Survival and Health Grants Program Evaluation*. Washington, DC: U.S. Agency for International Development, April. http://pdf.usaid.gov/pdf_docs/PDACM042.pdf (accessed June 9, 2014).

Shadish, William R., Thomas D. Cook, and Laura C. Leviton. 1991. *Foundations of Program Evaluation: Theories of Practice*. Newbury Park, CA: Sage.

Shane, Jon M. 2007. *What Every Chief Executive Should Know: Using Data to Measure Police Performance*. Flushing, NY: Looseleaf Law Publications.

Soeung, Sann Chan, John Grundy, Cheng Morn, and Chham Samnang. 2008. "Evaluation of Immunization Knowledge, Practices, and Service-Delivery in the Private Sector in Cambodia." *Journal of Health, Population, and Nutrition* 26(1): 95.

Sowa, Jessica E., Sally Coleman Selden, and Jodi R. Sandfort. 2004. "No Longer Unmeasurable? A Multidimensional Integrated Model of Nonprofit Organizational Effectiveness." *Nonprofit and Voluntary Sector Quarterly* 33(4): 711–728.

Stone, Melissa M., and Susan Cutcher-Gershefeld. 2001. "Challenges of Measuring Performance in Nonprofit Organizations." In *Measuring the Impact of the Nonprofit Sector,* ed. Patrice Flynn and Virginia Hodgkinson, 33–57. New York: Kluwer Academic/Plenum Publishers.

Talbot, Colin. 2010. *Theories of Performance: Organizational and Service Improvement in the Public Domain.* Oxford: Oxford University Press.

United Nations. n.d. "Millennium Development Goals and Beyond 2015." www.un.org/millenniumgoals/ (accessed June 10, 2014).

USAID. 2011. *Evaluation: Learning from Experience; USAID Evaluation Policy.* Washington, DC: USAID.

U.S. Department of Health, Education, and Welfare. 1969. *Toward a Social Report.* Washington, DC: U.S. Government Printing Office.

U.S. Executive Office of the President. n.d. *High Priority Performance Goals.* www.whitehouse.gov/sites/default/files/omb/performance/high-priority-performance-goals.pdf (accessed July 15, 2014).

U.S. GAO. 2004. *Informing our Nation: Improving How to Understand and Assess the USA's Position and Progress.* Report GAO-05–1. Washington, DC: U.S. GAO, November. www.gao.gov/new.items/d051.pdf (accessed June 9, 2014).

———. 2008a. *Government Performance: Lessons Learned for the Next Administration on Using Performance Information to Improve Results.* Report GAO-08–1026T. Washington, DC: U.S. GAO, July 24. www.gao.gov/assets/130/120846.pdf (accessed June 9, 2014)

———. 2008b. *Government Performance: 2007 Federal Managers Survey on Performance and Management Issues.* Report GAO-08–1036SP. Washington, DC: U.S. GAO, July. www.gao.gov/special.pubs/gao-08-1036sp/ (accessed June 9, 2014).

———. 2010. *Employment and Training Administration: Increased Authority and Accountability Could Improve Research Program.* Report GAO-10–243. Washington, DC: U.S. GAO, January. www.gao.gov/new.items/d10243.pdf (accessed June 9, 2014).

———. 2011. *Key Indicator Systems: Experiences of Other National and Subnational Systems Offer Insights for the United States.* Report GAO-11–396. Washington, DC: U.S. GAO, March. www.gao.gov/new.items/d11396.pdf (accessed June 9, 2014).

———. 2012. *Designing Evaluations: 2012 Revision.* Report GAO-12–208G. Washington, DC: U.S. GAO, January. www.gao.gov/assets/590/588146.pdf (accessed June 9, 2014).

———. 2013. *Managing for Results: Data-Driven Performance Reviews Show Promise But Agencies Should Explore How to Involve Other Relevant Agencies.* Report GAO-13–228. Washington, DC: U.S. GAO, February. www.gao.gov/assets/660/652426.pdf (accessed June 9, 2014).

U.S. OMB. 2010. "Evaluating Programs for Efficacy and Cost-Efficiency." Memorandum M-10–32, July 29. www.whitehouse.gov/sites/default/files/omb/memoranda/2010/m10-32.pdf (accessed June 9, 2014).

———. 2011. *Circular No. A-11: Preparation, Submission, and Execution of the Budget.* Washington, DC: OMB, August. www.whitehouse.gov/sites/default/files/omb/assets/a11_current_year/a_11_2011.pdf (accessed June 9, 2014).

——. 2012a. *Circular No. A-11: Preparation, Submission, and Execution of the Budget.* Washington, DC: OMB. www.whitehouse.gov/omb/circulars_a11_current_year_a11_toc (accessed June 9, 2014).

——. 2012b. "Use of Evidence and Evaluation in the 2014 Budget." Memorandum M-12–14, May 18. www.whitehouse.gov/sites/default/files/omb/memoranda/2012/m-12-14_1.pdf (accessed June 9, 2014).

——. 2013. "Memorandum for the Heads of Departments and Agencies." Memorandum M-13–14, May 29. www.whitehouse.gov/sites/default/files/omb/memoranda/2013/m-13-14.pdf (accessed June 9, 2014).

Van Dooren, Wouter, Geert Bouckaert, and John Halligan. 2010. *Performance Management in the Public Sector.* New York: Routledge.

Vio, Ferrucio. 2005. *Midterm Evaluation of Health Alliance International's Central Mozambique (Manica and Sofala Provinces) Child Survival and Maternal Care Project.* Seattle: Health Alliance International.

Waiswa, Peter, Margaret Kemigisa, Juliet Kiguli, Sarah Naikoba, George W. Pariyo, and Stefan Peterson. 2008. "Acceptability of Evidence-Based Neonatal Care Practices in Rural Uganda—Implications for Programming." *BMC Pregnancy and Childbirth* 8(1): 21.

Weisburd, David, Stephen D. Mastrofski, Ann McNally, Rosann Greenspan, and James J. Willis. 2003. "Reforming to Preserve: Compstat and Strategic Problem Solving in American Policing." *Criminology & Public Policy* 2(3): 421–456.

Williams, Bob, and Richard Hummelbrunner. 2011. *Systems Concepts in Action: A Practitioner's Toolkit.* Stanford, CA: Stanford University Press.

Winston, Jerome A. 1999. "Performance Indicators—Promises Unmet: A Response to Perrin." *The American Journal of Evaluation* 20(1): 95–99.

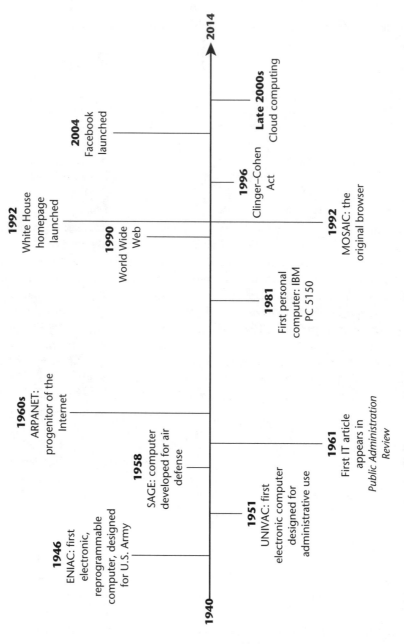

FIGURE 8.1 From Paper to Cloud: Benchmarks across Time

8

FROM PAPER TO CLOUD

Jooho Lee and B.J. Reed

> The printing press made possible the production of a larger number of manuscript copies, in a more consistent form, and at a far lower cost than possible by professional copyists . . . Gutenberg's invention increased dramatically the potential for the diffusion of knowledge and information . . . the printing press increased the rate at which knowledge was created.
>
> *(Giles 1996, 613)*

> In science, cloud computing is a synonym for distributed computing over a network, and means the ability to run a program or application on many connected computers at the same time.
>
> *(Wikipedia 2014a)*

We live in the digital era. Although written documents are still produced by the printing press and distributed by publishing companies, more documents are now electronically written, printed in PDF format, distributed through networked computers via the Internet, and stored on various computer-related devices such as laptops, smartphones, and the "cloud." Most articles in journals, newsletters, and magazines are now electronically accessible and students can purchase and read most textbooks electronically. Many reports from the Government Accountability Office are available online at www.gao.gov. In fact, government officials use information technology (IT) on a daily basis. It is hard to imagine how government could work without it. In addition to conventional tools, such as paper, face-to-face interaction, and telephone, officials use websites, email, Twitter, and Facebook to distribute information and to communicate with co-workers, lawmakers, citizens, and other stakeholders.

Since the mid-1860s, the Government Printing Office (GPO) has published and disseminated the paper-based documents of all three branches of government. But now printing hardcopies at the GPO has decreased as it steadily moves to online publishing. For instance, the GPO was accustomed to printing approximately 25,000 copies of the *Congressional Record* every morning in the 1980s, but that had decreased to 2,800 copies by 2012 (Rein 2012). More taxpayers are now e-filing their returns and the number of state e-filings grew from approximately 52.9 million in 2003 to 119.6 million in 2012, while paper filings decreased from approximately 78.6 million in 2003 to 28.3 million in 2012 (Wallack 2013). This comes with a substantial cost savings. The Internal Revenue Service estimates that it costs 15 cents to process an e-filing, compared with $3.50 for each paper filing (Wallack 2013).

Technological inventions exploded at the turn of the twentieth century with the creation of the automobile (1908), the airplane (1903), the motion picture (1910), and radio tuners (1916). Up until the latter 1900s, much of our use of data and communication technology remained largely the purview of manual typewriters, which first appeared in the 1800s, followed by mass production of the electric typewriter in the 1940s. Information was stored on paper and in file cabinets. It was not until the transition from typewriters to word processors in the 1970s and 1980s that we began to see the true shift from paper to electronic storage. This discussion of the shift from paper to cloud starts in the 1940s and 1950s with the birth of the "electronic computer" (Cowan 1997, 294).

Public administration and IT go hand-in-hand. Before we explore the timeline for this inter-relationship, it is important to acknowledge the context of IT in a public management environment. We believe James Q. Wilson (1989) best described this when he said that public bureaucracies are constraint-driven and obsessed with contextual goals, leaving innovation and the application of technology on the sidelines. By this he meant that what we define as the factors of production—labor and capital—are often controlled by those outside the agency in the form of courts and legislative bodies, just as are decisions about types and levels of revenue. In addition, goals are often determined by these same outside forces. For example, except for some enterprise-fund activities, in public budgeting the relationship between where the revenue derives and where expenditures are directed is artificially created through the political process. There is no direct relationship between the factors of production and the revenue generated through that production. As a result, political mechanisms are put into place to establish that relationship. Similarly, because so many of the goals associated with public organizations are set externally, are vague or conflicting, and lack clear measurement, agencies and managers focus on the front end, meaning procedures and processes.

Why is this important to understanding the progression of IT in public organizations? First, it means that IT development in public environments is often not tied directly to achieving specific goals. Instead, it is used to help improve processes and procedures. Second, IT may be seen as an end unto itself and agencies will latch on to the technology without clear linkages back to the outcomes. Third, the processes of acquiring IT may become wrapped in procedural due process and "input" specifications rather than "production" outputs or outcomes. However, there are exceptions to these characteristics. In times of war, for example, research and development as well as production can be highly efficient and effectively implemented. The use of drones is an example. But more often than not, IT becomes a manifestation of processes and procedures in search of a purpose. Much of IT innovation for both public and private uses has come from either defense initiatives or where government has a clear, compelling vision or goal. The race to the moon by the National Aeronautics and Space Administration provides an example. But for every "success" there are multiple examples of IT failures. IT is a tool, and as we describe its complicated history in government it is important to understand how important context is, and how that has led to its many successes and also its many failures.

A Brief History of IT Diffusion in the Public Sector

Our focus for this chapter is on IT as it has impacted the field since the 1940s. Obviously, IT goes back as far as BC 3000 with the first written language, and the first numerical systems were developed around 100 CE. The creation of moveable type, slide rules, and other computation tools segued to leaps in the 1800s with the telegraph and Morse code, followed by the telephone. That was followed by electromagnetic computers and punch card systems, followed by desktop computing and floppy disks, and now there is cloud computing.

Much of what we think of today as the emergence of IT forms around World War II. As one author noted:

> Techniques . . . [that] scientists and engineers developed during the war, the techniques for managing large research and development projects, were the most revolutionary wartime technological changes of all because they had such a profound impact on the postwar years.
>
> *(Cowan 1997, 258)*

Many of the precursors to contemporary IT had their birth during this period, including the ENIAC in the early 1940s and UNIVAC in 1951, which was the first high-speed general purpose computer. Figure 8.2 shows the rapidity with which computer use became a staple in the federal government for the period 1950–1979. The federal government had only two computers in 1950; the numbers increased to 12,190 by 1979.

The federal government was not unique in its widespread adoption of computers. Cross-sectional statistics allow for a snapshot of computer adoption by state and local governments. As of 1960, it was estimated that state and local

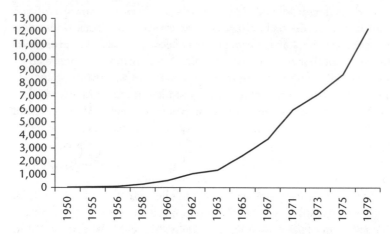

FIGURE 8.2 Number of Computers in the Federal Government, Selected Years, 1950–1979

Source: Adapted from Cortada 2008, 188, Table 6.1. Used by permission of Oxford University Press, USA.

governments used a total of 250 computers: 163 computers in state governments and 87 computers in local governments, including cities, counties, and school districts (Fite 1965). Table 8.1 shows that a total of 243 computers were used by states in 1963. By then, 40 of 43 reporting states were using at least one computer but three states—Arizona, Rhode Island, and Wyoming—had no computers. Five states used more than ten computers.

How did governments use computers in this early stage? Then, as now, much of government's work was information-intensive. A benefit of using computers in an information-rich environment is to increase the efficiency of internal and day-to-day operations by minimizing human errors, generating accurate information, and processing information in a timely manner. An early study on computer use in state government provides a list of functional areas and typical applications. Table 8.2 shows that in 1963, many state governments used computers in the areas of accounting and maintaining tax, human resources, vehicle registration, and licensing records.

At the local level, computers were widely and quickly adopted by government in the 1980s and early 1990s. Figure 8.3 demonstrates the diffusion of computing in local government by size. According to International City/County Management Association (ICMA) survey data collected in 1975, 1985, and 1993 (Norris and Kraemer 1996), only 51 percent of municipalities (1,170) had adopted computers in 1975. The adoption rate increased to 97 percent by 1985. At the early stage of adoption, in 1975, smaller municipalities lagged behind (for example, 42 percent of municipalities with a population of under 50,000,

TABLE 8.1 Number of Computer Systems in State Governments in 1963

Reporting state	Small	Medium	Large	Total
Alabama	6			6
Alaska	3			3
Arkansas	4			4
California	24	3	3	30
Colorado	4		1	5
Connecticut	6	3		9
Delaware	3			3
Florida	4	1		5
Georgia	9	1		10
Hawaii	3			3
Idaho	1			1
Indiana	4	1		5
Iowa	5	1		6
Louisiana	5	2		7
Maine	1			1
Massachusetts	10			10
Michigan	7	3		10
Minnesota	3	1		4
Mississippi	1			1
Missouri	7	2		9
Montana	4			4
Nevada	2			2
New Hampshire	2			2
New Jersey	7			7
New Mexico	4			4
New York	18	2	4	24
North Carolina	1	1		2
North Dakota	3			3
Ohio	6	1	1	8
Oklahoma	4			4
Oregon	4	2		6
Pennsylvania	3	2		5
South Carolina	6			6
South Dakota	2			2
Tennessee	2			2
Texas	7		2	9
Utah	7			7
Vermont	1			1
Virginia	6			6
Wisconsin	5	2		7
Total	204	28	11	243

Source: Price and Mulvihill 1965, 144. Reprinted with permission.

92 percent of municipalities with a population of over 50,000, and 98 percent of municipalities with a population of over 100,000), but their rate of adoption matched that of larger municipalities in 1985 and 1993. As discussed later, the primary computing technologies in municipalities were what was then called microcomputers because, unlike large mainframes that consumed an entire room,

TABLE 8.2 Computer Applications in State Governments in 1963

Application area	Typical applications	Number of states
Public works	Highway computation and accounting	38
Revenue	Corporation tax, income tax, sales tax	26
Finance	Expenditure and encumbrance accounting, payroll	26
Employment	Benefits, employer contributions	20
Motor vehicle	Licensing, registrations	18
Welfare	Grant computation, check-writing	16
Employee retirement	Contribution, pensions	15
Health and mental hygiene	Vital statistics, patient billing	13
Insurance	Workmen's compensation	13
Education	Scholarship, state aid	12
Civil service	Exams, eligible lists	12
Purchasing	Inventory, purchase order writing	11
Law enforcement	Arrest record	10
Conservation	Hunting, fishing and motorboat licenses	10
Agriculture	Milk control, disease control	7
Equalization	Equalization computation, per capita aid	5
Liquor control	Inventory licensing	5

Source: Price and Mulvihill 1965, 145. Reprinted with permission.

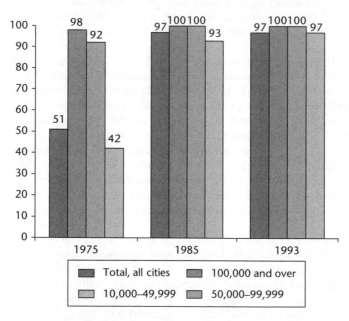

FIGURE 8.3 Diffusion of Computing in Municipalities by Size

Source: Adapted from Norris and Kraemer 1996.

Note: In 1975, there were 2,294 responses; in 1985, 754; in 1993, 2,465.

they could fit on a worker's desk. One of the driving forces in adoption was cost. Computing technologies have dropped in cost since the first microcomputer, IBM PC 5150, was released in August 1981 (Cortada 2008). As computer prices dropped, jurisdictions readily adopted inexpensive business-oriented computing platforms.

Another key technological invention that became the precursor to the modern Internet was developed in 1958 by the U.S. Defense Department and it was called SAGE (Semi-Automatic Ground Environment) (Akera and Nebeker 2002; Garson 2010). This referred to a computerized system to detect enemy missiles by networked computing. This capacity expanded in the 1960s as other innovations were occurring, such as the transistor that would replace bulky and unreliable vacuum tubes.

Most innovation in networked technology was developed by the federal government or by universities in the 1950s and 1960s. Commercial application of networked solutions began with airline reservation systems as well as stock transactions at a national and international level. The real shift, however, occurred with the creation of ARPANET and the Internet in the 1960s (Cowan 1997, 124). Once again it was the Defense Department that created an experimental computer network in 1969 that made significant strides in networking diverse computer centers and systems. This innovation enabled computer systems to interact with each other and created terms we are all familiar with today, including Internet Protocol and Transport Control Protocol. The growth continued in the 1970s and 1980s when Internet applications moved beyond closed defense networks to academic, commercial, and broader government applications. This culminated in the early 1990s when commercial usage became available. While this transformation from stand-alone computer capacity to networked systems and the Internet may have happened under any circumstances, it was government investment, research, and development that led to its rapid expansion from the 1990s to today.

Table 8.3 shows that approximately 50 percent of 2,367 cities used Local Area Network technology according to the 1993 ICMA Survey of Computing in Local Governments (Norris and Kraemer 1996). Sixty-one percent of those 2,367 cities adopted one mainframe/minicomputer and 92 percent of those cities each used an average of thirty-four microcomputers. The survey also reveals that larger cities adopted more mainframe/minicomputers and microcomputers than smaller cities.

A natural outgrowth of the Internet was the creation of the World Wide Web in 1990 and the creation of a MOSAIC web browser in 1992 (Garson 2010). The resulting explosion of web applications has continued unabated since that time. In 1993 it was unheard of to think of the web as a ubiquitous tool, but by the end of the century it was everywhere (Cowan 1997, 131). In 1992, the first White House homepage was launched on the web (Garson 2010). Since then, the U.S. government has actively adopted web technologies to provide information

TABLE 8.3 Types of Computers in Municipalities in 1993

City classification	Number of reporting cities	Mainframe/Minicomputer		Microcomputer	
		Percent of reporting cities (%)	Average number of computers	Percent of reporting cities (%)	Average number of computers
Total, all cities	2,367	61	1	92	34
Population group					
250,000 and over	28	96	3	100	655
25,000–249,999	461	92	2	94	96
Under 25,000	1,878	54	1	91	11

Source: Norris and Kraemer 1996, 570. Reprinted with permission.

and transaction services, which is often referred to as electronic government (e-government). At the federal level, the Postal Service has provided e-government services, especially financial transaction services in the form of stamps, since 1998 (Garson 2010). The official U.S. government portal, FirstGov.gov, was launched in 2000 and its name was changed to USA.gov in 2007.

State government has also adopted e-government services. At the initial stage of development, making government information available at government websites—mainly as a form of text—was the dominant e-government service. Thanks both to advanced technologies and to the vertical and horizontal integration of applications, e-government has evolved to the point where it provides not only text-based information, but also audio and video clips, downloadable forms, email, as well as online tax filing, vehicle registration, and parking ticket payment, among other services. Figure 8.4 shows that by 2002 more than 90 percent of federal and state governments were providing various online information services such as government publications and contact information in the form of phone numbers and addresses. The number of multimedia e-government services in the form of audio and video clips has increased, on average, from about 5 percent in 2000 to more than 40 percent in 2008.

Moreover, since 2000, both federal and state governments have provided an increasing number of "complete" e-government services, such as online purchasing of state park memberships (West 2008). Figure 8.5 shows that 78 percent of federal and state governments provided no complete e-government transaction services in 2000 and that percentage had decreased to 11 percent by 2008. Meanwhile, only 2 percent of federal and state governments provided three or more "complete" e-government services in 2000 and that percentage had increased to almost 70 percent by 2008.

At the local level, municipalities have widely adopted e-government since early 2000. In Table 8.4, an early study on the adoption of local e-government shows that municipal e-government had an adoption rate of 83.6 percent in 2000, 87.7 percent in 2002, and 96.2 percent in 2004 (Coursey and Norris 2008).

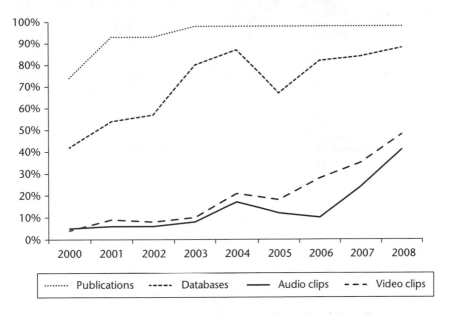

FIGURE 8.4 Diffusion of E-Government Services in Federal and State Government, 2000–2008

Source: Adapted from West 2008, 2.

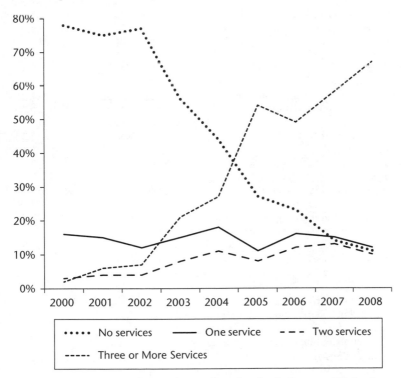

FIGURE 8.5 Frequency of Complete Online Service in State and Federal Government, 2000–2008

Source: Adapted from West 2008, 2.

TABLE 8.4 Municipal Government Website Adoption in 2000, 2002, and 2004

	2000		2002		2004	
	Percent	N	Percent	N	Percent	N
Adoption	83.6	1,571	87.7	1866	96.2	1,791
Nonadoption	16.4	308	12.3	262	3.8	71

Source: Adapted from Coursey and Norris 2008, 527. Reprinted with permission.

TABLE 8.5 Municipal E-Government Services in 2004 and 2011

	2004		2011	
	Number	Percent	Number	Percent
Information and communication				
Council agenda/minutes	1,483	86.6	1,169	93.5
Codes/ordinances	1,303	77.4	1,124	90.9
Forms that can be downloaded from manual completion (e.g., voter registration, etc.)	1,199	71.2	1,097	88.6
Employment information/applications	1,303	77.1	1,096	88.0
Online communication with individual elected and appointed officials	1,215	73.6	843	68.7
Geographical information systems (GIS) mapping/data	639	38.9	784	64.8
E-newsletters sent to residents/businesses	531	32.6	754	64.1
E-alters	N/A	N/A	739	60.3
Streaming video	221	13.9	632	50.7
Video on demand	N/A	N/A	557	45.4
Mobile apps (iPhone or Droid)	N/A	N/A	199	17.0
Customer relationship management (CRM)/311	N/A	N/A	195	17.2
Interactive voice response (IVR)	N/A	N/A	189	16.7
Podcasts	N/A	N/A	133	11.6
Moderated discussions	N/A	N/A	84	7.3
Instant messaging (IM)	N/A	N/A	83	7.1
Chat rooms	N/A	N/A	32	2.8
Transaction–based services				
Online requests for services, such as pothole repair	586	34.8	700	57.9
Online payments of utility bills	224	13.6	613	53.4
Online requests for local government records	522	31.1	597	49.7
Online registration for use of recreational facilities/activities, such as classes and picnic areas	370	22.4	571	47.9
Online payments of fines/fees	183	11.0	474	40.5
Online delivery of local government records to the requestor	363	22.0	433	36.7
Online payment of taxes	218	13.2	417	35.9
Online completion and submission of permit applications	215	12.8	398	33.7
Online completion and submission of business license applications/renewals	133	8.1	256	22.1
Online property registration, such as animal, bicycle registration	61	3.9	142	12.5
Online voter registration	50	3.2	101	9.0

Source: Norris and Reddick 2013, 169. Reprinted with permission.

A later municipal e-government study (Norris and Reddick 2013) compared services available in 2004 and 2011 and reported that municipal government had increased the number of e-government services during this time period. Table 8.5 illustrates, for example, that the percentage of streaming video services at municipal e-governments increased from 13.9 percent in 2004 to 50.7 percent in 2011. Also, online payments of utility bills were available at only 13.6 percent of municipal e-governments in 2004 but they had become widely available at 53.4 percent of municipal e-governments by 2011.

Since social networking site Facebook was launched in 2004 (Wikipedia 2014b), the use of social media platforms such as Twitter and YouTube, among a host of others, has grown among private and nonprofit organizations as well as citizens (Mossberger, Wu, and Crawford 2013). Accordingly, governments have adopted social media as a means of communicating with the public more effectively. At the federal level, for instance, "as of May 2012, . . . the Department of Defense alone has created 2,468 Facebook pages, 653 Twitter accounts, 448 YouTube channels, and 427 Flickr accounts" (Mergel 2012, 282). Most state governments have also provided social media services to the public. According to a 2010 survey of social media use in state government (NASCIO 2010), most states have engaged with citizens through three major social media channels: Facebook (thirty-seven states), Twitter (thirty-six states), and YouTube (thirty-three states). At the local level, a recent study explored social media use by seventy-five of the largest cities and found that social media technologies have been rapidly and widely adopted. Figure 8.6 shows that only 13.3 percent of large

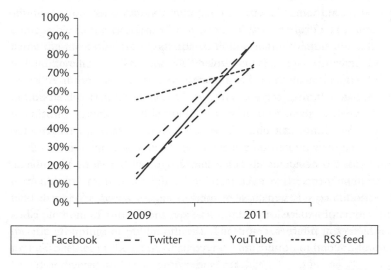

FIGURE 8.6 Social Media use by Large Cities in the United States, 2009 and 2011

Source: Adapted from Mossberger, Wu, and Crawford 2013, 353.

cities used Facebook in 2009, but that number dramatically increased to 86.7 percent in 2011. Similarly, the use of Twitter in the cities increased from 25.3 percent in 2009 to 86.7 percent in 2011. In other words, it took only two years for cities to dramatically increase social media technologies.

More recently, government has adopted cloud computing—defined as "a model of computing in which computer processing, storage, software, and other services are provided as a pool of virtualized resources over a network" (Laudon and Laudon 2014, 183)—as a means to effectively share government resources and to achieve coherence and economy of scale. Although cloud computing is characterized as having a number of positive attributes such as on-demand self-service (Mell and Grance 2011), it has some drawbacks in that government may face greater security risks and become dependent on the cloud computing vendor (Laudon and Laudon 2014). In spite of these debates, governments are increasing their reliance on cloud computing. For example, the state of Wyoming became the first state government to fully adopt Google cloud for apps (for example, gmail) in 2011. A recent survey (CDW 2013) demonstrated that 42 percent of 150 federal government respondents had implemented cloud computing services in 2012, up from 29 percent in 2011. The survey further revealed that 23 percent of state and local government respondents had adopted cloud computing services in 2011, and in 2012 that had increased to 27 percent.

One distinctive feature of e-government services—especially government-to-citizens/government-to-business—is that the end-users are not government or government officials, but citizens or business firms. The full benefits of e-government service provision are not realized unless those end-users actually use it. Thus, the focus is now shifting to the accessibility of e-government services to nongovernmental end-users. According to surveys conducted by the Pew Internet and American Life Project in 2001, 2003, and 2009 (Rainie and Larsen 2002; Horrigan 2004; Smith 2010), more American citizens have used transaction-based e-government services—such as online driver's license renewal or online payment for a fishing license or a parking ticket—while fewer citizens have utilized information-based e-government services for downloadable forms and information about a public policy, except for information about, or applying for, government benefits. Table 8.6 shows that only 12 percent of survey respondents reported that they renewed their driver's license using e-government applications in 2001 while 33 percent of respondents answered that they used it in 2009. Meanwhile, 77 percent of respondents in 2001 gained recreational or tourist information from agency websites, but only 30 percent of respondents in 2009 used the same service. Perhaps this reduction reflects the degree to which web businesses have increased their presence on the Internet. Just as jurisdictions are relying more heavily on social media, so are citizens. Smith (2010) reported that respondents used Twitter in government (7 percent, $n = 307$), the blog of a government agency or official (13 percent, $n = 1,613$), and followed or became a fan of an agency or official through their page on a social networking site (9 percent, $n = 849$).

TABLE 8.6 Use of E-Government by Citizens

E-government service	2001 (n = 815)	2003 (n = 2,925)	2009 (n = 2,258)
Renewed a driver's license or auto registration	12%	N/A	33%
Applied for a fishing, hunting, or other recreational license	4%	N/A	11%
Paid a fine, such as a parking ticket	2%	N/A	15%
Looked for information about a public policy or issue of interest to you	62%	N/A	48%
Downloaded government forms	63%	N/A	41%
Looked up what services a government agency provides	63%	N/A	46%
Got advice or information from a government agency about a health or safety issue	49%	28%	25%
Got recreational or tourist information from a government agency	77%	34%	30%
Researched official government documents or statistics	70%	41%	35%
Got information about or applied for government benefits	20%	23%	23%
Got information about how to apply for a government job	24%	N/A	19%

Source: Rainie and Larsen 2002; Horrigan 2004; Smith 2010.

Note: Compiled by authors using e-government survey data collected in 2001, 2003, and 2009

Assessing the Diffusion and Adoption of IT in Public Administration

As discussed earlier, recent decades have witnessed, and continue to witness, the adoption of an ever-expanding number of IT applications by jurisdictions, agencies, and citizens: personal computing, communication via the Internet and websites, social media, and cloud computing. One lesson we have learned is that the degree of IT adoption as well as the speed of its adoption is uneven. Some government organizations or individuals adopt an IT application at a certain time while others do not.

How can we systematically understand the differential adoption rate? IT is an innovative tool that is often perceived to be new (Rogers 1995). Scholars have long attempted to address questions of diffusion and adoption by using various theoretical frameworks (Brown and Garson 2013; Fountain 2001; Kraemer, Dutton, and Northrop 1981; Norris and Moon 2005). For example, theories of diffusion of innovation mainly focus on the patterns of innovation penetration across time (for example, the classic S-shaped curve) and how innovation spreads through communication processes. These models have found economic variables, such as price, to be one of the driving forces behind innovation diffusion yet adoption models are more focused on the decision-making process (Bretschneider and Mergel 2011). These models have identified environmental and organizational factors as triggers of adoption. Drawing on models of reinforcement politics (Kraemer, Dutton, and Northrop 1981), technology enactment (Fountain 2001), technology acceptance (Davis 1989), and diffusion and adoption of innovation (Rogers 1995), we now describe three factors that affect the adoption of IT at the organizational and individual levels: environmental, organizational/institutional, and individual factors.

Environmental Factors

The resource environment surrounding governments plays a crucial role in shaping decisions and actions toward new IT adoption. There is ample evidence at the local government level that adoption is facilitated when there are (1) available and competent local IT vendors (Perry and Danziger 1980; Rocheleau 1994); (2) external funding or slack resources provided by an outside funding agency (Perry and Danziger 1980); (3) larger community size (Brudney 1988; Brudney and Selden 1995; Norris 1984); (4) greater number of public service needs (Brudney and Selden 1995); and (5) public policies in support of IT (Kraemer, Gurbaxani, and King 1992; Kraemer and Perry 1979).

Local governments tend to adopt innovative IT when their level of visibility is higher, which allows jurisdictions to gain attention from external stakeholders (Perry and Danziger 1980). Because government usually purchases IT packages from vendors or outsources the implementation and customization of IT products to private vendors, who act as suppliers and collaborators, vendors have played a crucial role in adoption. For example, one study reports that decision-making participants in police departments in Illinois selected police software when they positively assessed both the vendor's experience and the presentations, training, and marketing that vendors provided (Rocheleau 1994). Early studies in the 1970s (Kraemer and Perry 1979) emphasized the crucial role of federal policies in the diffusion of computer technologies in local governments. Later studies found that the investment in computer technologies in Asia-Pacific countries had been facilitated by broader fiscal and trade policies as opposed to computing policies, such as computer-related education or public awareness (Kraemer, Gurbaxani, and King 1992).

More recent studies on e-government adoption reveal similar patterns. For example, county governments in California adopt municipal websites when citizens' socioeconomic status and their political interests (that is, voter registration levels) are higher (Weare, Musso, and Hale 1999). Another study shows that the adoption of municipal e-government is driven by complexity in that communities that have greater diversity tend to adopt it more readily (Jun and Weare 2011).

Organizational and Institutional Factors

Government's adoption of IT has been influenced by various organizational factors such as size, professionalism, and agency structure. Size has consistently been identified as a key factor affecting IT adoption in the public sector (see, for example, Holden, Norris, and Fletcher 2003; Norris 1984). Larger agencies tend to adopt IT innovations earlier than smaller ones because they face greater internal and external needs, and have appropriate budgets and necessary IT skills (Cortada 2008). For example, county governments tend to establish websites earlier when they have a greater number of functions as well as IT employees (Manoharan 2013).

Another factor is professionalism, such as the presence of a city manager and a council-manager form of government as compared to a mayor-council system (Brudney 1988; Brudney and Selden 1995; Norris 1984). More recent e-government research also confirms that the council-manager form of government has enabled municipalities to adopt e-government (Jun and Weare 2011; Moon 2002).

Organizational structure in general, and IT governance structure in particular, has also been known to be a key factor. One of the distinctive structural characteristics in public organizations is the slowness of administrative decision making. In spite of scholarly efforts to identify the relationship between excessive administrative delay and IT innovation, research shows mixed findings. That is, such delays have both negative (Yu and Bretschneider 1998) and positive (Moon and Bretschneider 2002) effects on county managers' interest in adopting new IT. A centralized IT governance structure is also known as an innovation facilitator. For example, Norris and Kraemer (1996) analyzed a 1993 ICMA survey and found that a central IT department in local government was associated with the adoption of advanced technologies, which, at the time, meant portable computers.

Institutional and management capacity has also played a crucial role in affecting the adoption of IT. For example, Brown and Brudney (1998) reported that local governments with greater management capacity (that is, project management, strategic planning, and teamwork) successfully implement Geographic Information Systems (GIS) while working in concert with IT contractors. Since the Clinger–Cohen Act of 1996 mandated a Chief Information Officer (CIO) at each federal agency and top management involvement in IT strategic planning (Garson 2010), scholars have paid attention to the role of institutional design in the adoption of innovative IT applications. In their study on e-government diffusion, for instance, Tolbert, Mossberger, and McNeal (2008) compared the development of e-government in 2000 and 2004 and found that state governments have successfully sustained innovations when they are equipped with institutional capacities such as the presence of a state IT board, e-procurement systems, a CIO in the state's executive body, a professionalized legislature, and the existence of an IT committee in their legislatures. A recent IT project failure in the California Department of Motor Vehicles (Wood 2013) is consistent with the lessons from studies in the 1980s and 1990s (for example, see Perry and Danziger 1980; Rocheleau 1994), which emphasized that government's capacity to manage key external stakeholders, such as private IT contractors, plays a significant role in shaping the successful implementation of IT innovation.

Individual Factors

Lastly, it is known that the adoption of IT innovation in the public sector is affected by its perceived benefits and costs by chief executives and other key decision makers. Especially, it has been believed that the chief executive's support plays a crucial role in the adoption of innovative applications (Perry and Danziger 1980). In fact, studies as early as the 1970s attempted to understand the sources of chief executives' support and found that it stems from the perceived benefits of computer technologies to government operations (Dutton and Kraemer 1978). In terms of the role of the executive in the adoption of computers, however, there are mixed findings. Perry and Kraemer (1980) found that the chief executive's support did not lead to the adoption of computer applications by large local governments. In a similar vein, although the involvement of top management in the adoption of strategic IT planning has been highlighted in business and management information systems literature, some researchers (Holley, Dufner, and Reed 2002) found that a county government tends to adopt strategic information system planning when that entity gains support from career managers, such as the county's CIO—as opposed to political leaders—because they participate in county-wide IT decision making processes.

Now, let us shift attention to IT diffusion and adoption inside organizations. Although most IT and e-government studies have mainly studied adoption at the organizational level, several researchers (Berry 1997; Berry, Berry, and Foster 1998; Bugler and Bretschneider 1993; Lee 2008; Rocheleau 1994) have examined factors affecting adoption on the part of individual users. Although new IT may be adopted by jurisdictions, this does not mean that all individuals will use it. In fact, there is often variation in terms of adoption by individual users. Several models have been offered for a theoretical lens through which we can better understand this. These include, but are not limited to, the technology acceptance model (TAM) (Davis 1989), the information systems success model (DeLone and McLean 1992), and the task-technology-fit model (Goodhue and Thompson 1995). Of these, the TAM has been widely applied. The essence of TAM is that end-users tend to adopt new IT systems when the new systems both benefit them and are easy to use (Davis 1989).

The perceived benefits to lower level employees and their participation in decision-making processes have increased the likelihood that they will use it. For example, Rocheleau (1994) conducted an exploratory study on computer software adoption by a municipal police department in Illinois and found that adoption is affected by the perceived benefits and costs of software in terms of its performance, reporting capacity, access to neighboring departmental and state/federal records, and ease of use. Nedovic-Budic and Godschalk (1996) found that government employees in four county agencies in North Carolina—the transportation, mapping, community assistance, and planning departments—used GIS applications when they perceived its relative advantages, had computer experience, and were exposed to the technology. Another study found that supervisors in the Department of Motor Vehicle and Highway Safety in the state of Florida accepted Supervisor Assistant Systems (SAS) when they perceived greater benefits to their decision making and they confirmed that it was easier to use it than to not use it (Berry 1997).

Berry, Berry, and Foster (1998) show that characteristics of the work environment, such as perceived pressure from top management and the user's involvement in developing new information systems, have positively affected SAS adoption by middle managers. Another study (Lee 2008) demonstrates that government officials in South Korea view the adoption of electronic approval systems (EAS) positively because the innovative technologies present an opportunity to gain organizational power. In terms of the role of administrative rank and position, middle-level managers (as opposed to top-level managers) in program agencies (as opposed to the IT department) were more interested in, and served as champions for, the adoption of new IT innovations (Bugler and Bretschneider 1993), strategic information systems planning in local government (Holley, Dufner, and Reed 2002), and IT strategies in federal government (Caudle 1990). But, Lee (2008) reported that program staff in central agencies and IT staff in local governments in South Korea tend to adopt the EAS earlier. Lastly, training has been identified as a key factor in helping users overcome technological and managerial limitations of new IT (Northrop et al. 1994).

As discussed earlier, most federal and state governments have provided various e-government services to the public even though citizens do not use many of these services. For example, almost 90 percent of state and large municipal governments provide major social media services. But only about 10 percent of citizens use those services. That is, many e-government services remain underutilized although some have exceeded projections. Online vehicle registration and driver's license renewal are examples. Recently, scholars have been attempting to understand the factors that affect citizens' adoption of e-government services (Belanger and Carter 2008; Carter and Belanger 2005; Lee and Kim 2014). Because of the wide array of e-government services, however, there is still too little known about why citizens use or do not use various electronic participation services, and social media, or how government can best promote their use of e-government services.

Assessing the Impact of IT over Time in the Public Sector

Another lesson gained from a brief history of adoption in government is that the effects of IT on public administration are complicated and diverse. Why? Early studies mainly focused on offering a normative approach to understanding the conditions under which IT adoption produces better benefits to government and government officials. For example, Harry Fite, who published the first IT-related article that appeared in *Public Administration Review* (1961), advocated a decentralized design for automated data processing in state government. More recent scholars (Bretschneider and Mergel 2011; Brown and Garson 2013) have offered four different frameworks—technological determinism, reinforcement theory, system theory, and socio-technical theory—as the means to understand how IT has changed organizational outputs and outcomes. In their research, Brown and Garson (2013) applied those frameworks to the relationship between IT use in government and its effects on public organizations and behaviors. They found that the effects of IT on organizational structure, behavior, and organizational change are mixed. Others have analyzed prior research to trace the effects of IT in government over the past decades. For instance, Andersen and his colleagues (2010) reviewed scholarly articles published from 2003 to 2009 to better understand the positive, negative, or mixed effects of e-government on four broader domains: capabilities, interactions, orientations, and value distribution. The effect of e-government on capabilities, for example, assesses "whether [information communication technology] has an effect on the manner in which a unit deals with its environment in an attempt to control the environmental effects on its behavior and to extract values from the environment" (p. 566). The domain of capabilities includes specific categories including data access, data quality, productivity gain, staff reduction/substitution, improved control, time-saving measures, improved decision processes, and improved planning. In their assessment, they conclude that overall, the effects of e-government on those four domains are positive.

Taking a similar research method, a more recent study (Moon, Lee, and Roh 2014) examined articles published in six major public administration journals from their first volumes through 2010. This study used Rosenbloom's three competing approaches to public administration as a theoretical framework for analyzing IT and e-government studies. The authors find that IT and e-government research has mainly focused on the managerial impact of IT and the effect of e-government on organizational structure (centralized vs. decentralized), red tape, strategic management, and improvement of public services. But they also find that there has been increased research on the effects of IT/e-government on political values such as the representation of political interests, the promotion of political accountability to political authority, and the promotion of bureaucratic accountability to citizens.

As prior research has well documented the diverse impacts of IT, we look at the impact of information over time through the lens of public administration scholars who have written extensively on the topic over the last forty years. Kenneth Kraemer may be the most recognized of such scholars and his work since the 1970s reflects the eclectic nature of how IT has woven itself into public management. Computer modeling, technology innovation and diffusion, impacts on communications, computer ethics, municipal information systems, and technological information systems are all topics he has touched upon (Elliott and Kraemer 2008; Kraemer 1974, 1987; Kraemer and Dedrick 1997; Kraemer and Dutton 1985).

IT and Managerial Value

IT has reshaped how public organizations manage (Baschab and Piot 2007; Dahlin and Ekman 2011). In the beginning of the modern information age, in the 1950s and 1960s, data and information were largely centralized and controlled through a central portal with limited access. With the advent of distributive computing in the 1980s and 1990s, more and more operational use of data by end-users dramatically shifted both the control and operation of data information systems. It is hard to comprehend how far we have come in such a short period of time.

So, what are the managerial implications of this widespread adoption? First, roles have shifted downward. Work that was centralized in the 1980s and 1990s (for example, human resources, financial management) has shifted from being managed from the top of most organizations to being increasingly managed at the unit level. Approvals for decisions often occur in a "post-audit" phase rather than a "pre-approval" stage. As a result, clerical work that was once done by staff employees, such as secretaries, has shifted to line employees. And support personnel have become technology "workers" managing data entry and data management in everything from personnel to finance. These workers manipulate databases to create reports for decision support purposes. Technology skills that were never imagined at the unit level are now routinely required. Additionally, a new subcategory of employee, often referred to as "business analysts," is being created in increasing numbers to provide decision support for the end-user with little direct oversight at the central level.

Second, tools associated with technology have exploded while the management capacity to utilize and manage these tools often lags. There are several examples of how rapidly these have proliferated. The most ubiquitous of these are word processing, spreadsheets, and database management software. While word processing, beginning with the advent of the typewriter, has always been a technology tool that operates throughout any organization, the use of spreadsheets, database management, and statistical software moved rapidly to end-users with the advent of the microcomputer. This "democratization" of IT revolutionized how work was done in organizations and fundamentally shifted how decision support occurred. New analytic tools were developed and often they were applied without the knowledge and skills to use them effectively or as intended. This is the classic case of tools driving decisions rather than decisions driving tools. Also, as database management systems grew in capacity and sophistication they also moved from centralized "command and control" structures to structures that could be accessed and manipulated at the lowest levels of the organization. New challenges emerged evolving around access and security that were compounded by growth in computer networks that reached beyond the organization. One such challenge is the threat of a security breach. The ability of individuals inside and outside the organization to legally or illegally access database management systems that store large sets of personal, confidential, or privileged information has expanded exponentially.

Another area that has had considerable focus is the impact of IT on human resource (HR) management. The common view is that IT improves productivity, decision support, and organizational effectiveness. This is certainly true when discussion occurs about human resources and yet there is no empirical evidence to show an association between IT and HR effectiveness. Still, Haines III and Lafleuer (2008) find that the database management capacity to handle large analyses frees HR professionals to think more strategically about organizational effectiveness and efficiency. As with other trends affected by technology, work has shifted down the hierarchy. Paper systems in the 1980s and 1990s have been replaced with electronic systems that require offices closer to the street level to reallocate and expand staff effort in order to manage documents associated with recruitment, performance appraisal, payroll and benefits, and compliance. Similarly, software systems have been acquired to manage hiring, background checks, performance reviews, personnel compliance with training, pay and benefit calculations and other HR functions, bringing an increased workload to the office level. Organizational benefits derive from the ability to organize, manage, and manipulate data for decision support but costs have increased not only for staffing but also for training and support for these new systems.

Some would argue that the advent of technology-driven HR processes has exacerbated the impersonal nature of governmental organizations and actually lessened the human aspect of human relations (Bovens and Zouridis 2002; Milward and Snyder 1996). The uses of electronic applications, correspondence by email, and software driven performance systems all create a disconnect between the human interactions that existed before technology became ubiquitous. Others would argue that the use of technology has increased the ability of individuals to connect in ways that would have been too cumbersome or time-consuming to have occurred without these tools. Still, line administrators have learned to adapt to using these tools to recruit, assess, and manage their organizations to achieve their goals.

A final area of managerial impact that we focus on is communication. This is often referred to as information communication technologies. Zorn, Flanagin, and Shoham (2011) noted that budgets and organizational size of nonprofits are closely associated with adoption of information communication technologies. This is very similar to findings of governmental organizations. Adoption of communication technologies is also linked to drives for efficiency and effectiveness and the desire to be perceived externally as responsive to calls for accountability (Zorn, Flanagin, and Shoham 2011, 5). Not surprisingly, these authors found that leaders in organizations who were scanning how their peer organizations use technology were more likely to use IT as part of their own communication systems.

Public organizations are often searching for ways to bring large groups of individuals together to address complex administrative problems. To this end, IT provides a way to meet the communication and collaboration needs of public entities. For example, networking strategies, collaborative practices, and decision support systems can be taught in labs that take advantage of technology. See, for example, the collaboration science project implemented at the University of Nebraska Omaha (http://collaboration.unomaha.edu/). It brings various organizational stakeholders together to improve collaboration and communication. This tool uses technology to establish "parallel groups" to create larger numbers of teams to address problems more efficiently (de Vreede, Briggs, and Reiter-Palmon 2010). This is but one new tool that did not exist until recently and has enhanced decision support in a significant way. Another area of rapid transition is accounting information system development, which has transformed the way accounting data have become integral to the rise of quality improvement programs, such as balanced scorecards, and to manage complex financial reporting systems (Mancini, Vaassen, and Dameri 2013).

IT and Democratic Value

There is no doubt that the explosion of technology tools has increased democratic access for citizens around the world. Tools such as the Internet and social media have become a way to "democratize" access to information in a way that could not have happened before the advent of these communication mechanisms (Haque and Loader 1999). Twitter, Facebook, Instagram, and other communication systems have shifted power away from centralized control, such that entities such as Wikileaks and low-level data-entry workers such as Edward Snowden can change what we know about policies and actions that heretofore were hidden from public view. The Arab Spring of 2011 was facilitated by Twitter and other mass communication tools. While the National Security Agency's reach of surveillance may be an abuse of government power, the ability to use technology to spur transparency brings with it a dynamism never before encountered by the state.

Similarly, much is written about the use of technology to support non-democratic regimes and movements (Khatib 2006). Khatib notes that the use of websites and hyperlinks by various affiliated groups has helped Hezbollah spread its message both locally and globally (Khatib 2006, 169). Those who planned the September 11, 2001 attacks relied heavily on e-mail and Internet chat rooms.

Since then, efforts to close down websites or limit use of chat rooms that spread the messages of extremist groups have been thwarted by the fluid nature of the Internet itself. This reflects the truism that as public agencies look to grow e-government or e-commerce, IT has a double-edged blade, enabling those opposed to government policies to challenge and undermine operations.

Polling data for the last several years shows an erosion of trust and confidence in government in the United States, in some cases at alarming rates (Gallup 2014). Questions arise as to whether IT has accelerated this decline. Research shows conflicting conclusions, in that some studies find that e-government has increased trust (Kim and Lee 2012) while other findings indicate little, if any, connection between citizens' use of technology and their trust in government (Horsburgh, Goldfinch, and Gauld 2011; Morgeson III, Van Amburg, and Mithas 2011). For example, West (2004) reports no significant relationship between citizens' use of e-government and trust in federal government, while Welch and his colleagues (2005) demonstrate that citizens' use of e-government is positively associated with satisfaction and trust in government. Tolbert and Mossberger (2006) deliver mixed results in that citizens' use of e-government is associated with trust in government, but only at the local level, not at the state and federal levels.

More recently, the glitch-plagued Healthcare.gov websites resulted in a botched rollout of the Affordable Care Act in 2013. This very public display of ineptitude shows that poor oversight of the IT contractor, CGI Federal, deteriorated citizens' trust in government as well as cost-effectiveness. According to the 2013 American Consumer Satisfaction Index (ACSI) survey conducted between October and December 2013 (ACSI 2014), citizen satisfaction with federal e-government services dropped from 69.5 percent in 2012 to 66.1 percent in 2013. Similarly, citizen trust in specific federal agencies decreased from 71 percent in 2012 to 67 percent in 2013 and for overall federal government, trust decreased from 43 percent in 2012 to 35 percent in 2013. All these decreases are thought to be associated with the problematic rollout of Healthcare.gov, in which the website crashed and consumers spent hours rather than minutes accessing health insurance packages (ACSI 2014).

In sum, the failure of government to protect information, as was the case with Edward Snowden's revelations in 2013, or the fear that government has used technology to greatly reduce individual privacy as reflected in the National Security Agency's collection of personal information on citizens, significantly impacts trust in government. Rule (2007) notes that there is not an explicit "right to privacy" in the Constitution. However, both the Fourth Amendment and the Bill of Rights implicitly seek to protect an array of privacy interests (Rule 2007). Still, he notes that national security issues have changed the course of privacy rights versus security protection. Notwithstanding, the Privacy Act of 1974 still provides protections even after passage of the Patriot Act in 2001 (Rule 2007). What has changed is the capability of government to access records through the use of technology and the massive shift from paper- to cloud-based repositories of records and information.

While technology has the capability to protect data through encryption, it also has increased the capacity of public and private entities to access individual and organizational information at an unprecedented rate. As Rule notes, "technology problems of protecting personal data are child's play compared to the sophisticated measures devoted to creating, collecting, transmitting, and using personal data mobilized by surveillance interests" (Rule 2007, 191).

Digital divide issues, both in terms of access to technology and in terms of the skills necessary to utilize the technology available, have been a primary focus at all governmental levels since the dawn of the Internet age. Research has consistently found disparities based on age, race/ethnicity, income and education (Belanger and Carter 2009). A number of initiatives and efforts have been undertaken to address this gap (Servon 2002). Access divides have narrowed with the advent of more affordable, user-friendly devices, along with increased public access to the World Wide Web. However access is not sufficient to increase utilization of technology for personal or organizational benefit. Programs specifically for older adults or for children who come from economically disadvantaged backgrounds can be effective. Government is at the center of this effort, be it public schools, governmental and nonprofit agencies, or public dollars allocated to stimulate private efforts. Servon (2002, 226) notes that the Technology Act of 1996 elevated this goal as an important focus of the federal government, but it has yet to be realized. Elimination of the divide may never totally be achieved but success stories exist that show substantial progress is being made.

Conclusion

As noted at the beginning of this chapter, the transition of technology and its impact on government since the 1900s has been staggering. A brief history of IT development in public administration in the United States shows that the rate of IT diffusion keeps accelerating. Where technological innovation at the turn of the last century was measured in years, by 2014 it is being measured in months. In the 1960s we often laughed at science fiction television shows such as Star Trek, with its wireless communicators and universal translation devices. Today we laugh at how clunky those devices seem and marvel at how close we are to real-time language translation. However, as pointed out by Cortada (2008), the major driving forces behind IT adoption and diffusion have not changed much over time. Environmental, institutional/organizational, and individual factors have consistently been the drivers that facilitate the diffusion and adoption of IT in the public sector.

What we did not anticipate were the managerial and policy challenges that the exponential growth in IT created, along with the diverse impacts on public administration. Some studies find that IT has positively contributed to the field in ways ranging from enhanced efficiency of day-to-day operations to improved quality of services and higher levels of trust in government. However, we have also learned that the impacts are not always positive and predictable. And we have seen unexpected results of how IT negatively affects government and citizens. Whether it is cybersecurity or policy decisions around the use of drones, government managers and policy makers must confront life-and-death decisions over how technology should be managed for the public good.

We have learned that, in general, government has improved its management capacity of coping with emerging IT issues (for example, big data). State CIO priorities over the past five years (2009–2014) have demonstrated how states assess emerging IT issues and develop strategies to address them. (See Appendix 8.1 for details.) As to future research on IT in the public sector, we call your attention to the following questions:

- What impact will there be in terms of how public organizations are staffed and the expectations for IT literacy up and down the organization?
- In terms of the anticipated growth of probability analysis and big data analytics and its impact on citizen and democracy, will it serve as a way to anticipate and meet citizens' expectations about government? Will it allow a new kind of democratization of government or will it lead to new ways to manage and control citizens' access to government?
- Will new "tools" such as database management, business analytics, big data, and predictive modeling add value to government effectiveness and efficiency or will these overwhelm public capacity to manage such technology effectively?
- Will IT continue to raise significant privacy and security issues and how well invested and prepared are government agencies to address the threats to sensitive information?
- Can government invest and reinvest quickly enough to address expectations of the public, not only in areas of transactional e-governance but also in expectations concerning transparency and access to government?

Answers to these questions are a work in progress. One thing we can say is that technology will continue its exponential impact on public organizations. Challenges abound and it will be the role of government executives and managers to continue to harness technology in a way that serves the public interest. If typewriters and telegraphs were the biggest information innovations of the 1800s, just think what is coming in the twenty-first century.

References

ACSI. 2014. "ACSI Federal Government Report 2013." News release, January 28. www.theacsi.org/news-and-resources/customer-satisfaction-reports/customer-satisfaction-reports-2013/acsi-federal-government-report-2013 (accessed June 10, 2014).

Akera, Atsushi, and Frederick Nebeker. 2002. *From 0 to 1: An Authoritative History of Modern Computing.* New York: Oxford University Press.

Andersen, Kim, Helle Henriksen, Rony Medaglia, James Danziger, Moyfrid Sannarnes, and Mette Enemarke. 2010. "Fads and Facts of E-Government: A Review of Impacts of E-Government (2003–2009)." *International Journal of Public Administration* 33: 564–579.

Baschab, John, and Jon Piot. 2007. *The Executive's Guide to Information Technology.* Hoboken, NJ: John Wiley and Sons.

Belanger, France, and Lemuria Carter. 2008. "Trust and Risk in E-Government Adoption." *Strategic Information Systems* 17: 165–176.

——, and ——. 2009. "The Impact of the Digital Divide on E-Government Use." *Communications of the Association for Computing Machinery* 52(4): 132–135.

Berry, Frances. 1997. "Explaining Managerial Acceptance of Expert Systems." *Public Performance and Management Review* 20(3): 323–335.

——, William Berry, and Stephen Foster. 1998. "The Determinants of Success in Implementing an Expert System in State Government." *Public Administration Review* 58(4): 293–305.

Bovens, Mark, and Stavros Zouridis. 2002. "From Street-Level to System-Level Bureaucracies: How Information and Communication Technology Is Transforming Administrative Discretion and Constitutional Control." *Public Administration Review* 62(2): 174–184.

Bretschneider, Stuart, and Ines Mergel. 2011. "Technology and Public Management Information Systems: Where We Have Been and Where We Are Going." In *The State of Public Administration: Issues, Challenges, and Opportunities,* ed. Donald Menzel and Harvey White, 187–203. Armonk, NY: M.E. Sharpe.

Brown, Mary, and Jeffrey Brudney. 1998. "A 'Smart, Better, Faster, and Cheaper' Government: Contracting and Geographic Information Systems." *Public Administration Review* 58(4): 335–345.

——, and G. David Garson. 2013. *Public Information Management and E-Government: Policy and Issues.* Hershey, PA: IGI Global.

Brudney, Jeffrey. 1988. "Computers and Smaller Local Government." *Public Performance and Management Review* 12(2): 179–192.

——, and Sally Selden. 1995. "The Adoption of Innovation by Smaller Local Governments: The Case of Computer Technology." *American Review of Public Administration* 25(1): 71–86.

Bugler, Daniel, and Stuart Bretschneider. 1993. "Technology Push or Program Pull: Interest in New Information Technologies within Public Organizations." In *Public Management: The State of the Art,* ed. Barry Bozeman, 275–293. San Francisco: Jossey-Bass.

Carter, Lemuria, and Frances Belanger. 2005. "The Utilization of E-Government Services: Citizen Trust, Innovation and Acceptance Factors." *Information Systems Journal* 15: 5–25.

Caudle, Sharon. 1990. "Managing Information Resources in State Government." *Public Administration Review* 50(5): 515–524.

CDW. 2013. *2013 State of the Cloud Report.* Vernon Hills, IL: CDW. www.cdwnewsroom.com/2013-state-of-the-cloud-report/ (accessed January 15, 2014).

Commonwealth of Massachusetts. 2013. "NASCIO State CIO Priorities." https://wiki.state.ma.us/confluence/display/itstrategicplan/NASCIO+State+CIO+Priorities (accessed June 10, 2014).

Cortada, James. 2008. *The Digital Hand, Vol. III: How Computers Changed the Work of American Public Sector Industries.* New York: Oxford University Press.

Coursey, David, and Donald Norris. 2008. "Models of E-Government: Are They Correct? An Empirical Assessment." *Public Administration Review* 68(3): 523–536.

Cowan, Schwartz. 1997. *A Social History of American History.* New York: Oxford University Press.

Dahlin, Peter, and Peter Ekman. 2011. *Management and Information Technology: Challenges for the Modern Organization.* New York: Routledge.

Davis, Fred. 1989. "Perceived Usefulness, Perceived Ease of Use, and User Acceptance of Information Technology." *MIS Quarterly* 13(3): 319–340.

DeLone, William, and Ephraim McLean. 1992. "Information Systems Success: The Quest for the Dependent Variable." *Information Systems Research* 3(1): 60–95.

de Vreede, Gert-Jan, Robert Briggs, and Roni Reiter-Palmon. 2010. "Exploring Asynchronous Brainstorming in Larger Groups: A Field Comparison of Serial and Parallel Subgroups." *The Journal of Human Factors and Ergonomics Society* 52(2): 189–202.

Dutton, William and Kenneth Kraemer. 1978. "Determinants of Support for Computerized Information Systems: The Attitudes of Local Government Chief Executives." *American Review of Public Administration* 12(1): 19–40.

Elliott, Margaret, and Kenneth Kraemer. 2008. *Computerization Movements and Technology Diffusion: From Mainframes to Ubiquitous Computing.* Medford, NJ: Information Today.

Fite, Harry. 1961. "Administrative Evolution in ADP in State Government," *Public Administration Review* 21(1): 1–7.

——. 1965. *The Computer Challenge to Urban Planners and State Administrators.* Washington, DC: Spartan Books.

Fountain. Jane. 2001. *Building the Virtual State: Information Technology and Institutional Change.* Washington, DC: Brookings Institution Press.

Gallup. 2014. "Trust in Government." www.gallup.com/poll/5392/trust-government. aspx (accessed June 10, 2014).

Garson, G. David. 2010. "Public Information Technology and E-Government: A Historical Timeline." In *Handbook of Public Information Systems*, ed. Christopher Shea and G. David Garson, 7–28. New York: CRC Press.

Giles, Michael. 1996. "From Gutenberg to Gigabytes: Scholarly Communication in the Age of Cyberspace." *The Journal of Politics* 58(3): 613–626.

Goodhue, Dale, and Ronald Thompson. 1995. "Task-Technology Fit and Individual Performance." *MIS Quarterly* 19(2): 213–236.

Haines, Victor III, and Genevieve Lafleur. 2008. "Information Technology Usage and Human Resource Roles and Effectiveness." *Human Resource Management* 47(3): 525–540.

Haque, Barry, and Brian Loader. 1999. *Digital Democracy: Discourse and Decision Making in the Information Age.* New York: Routledge.

Holden, Stephen, Donald Norris, and Patricia Fletcher. 2003. "Electronic Government at the Local Level." *Public Performance and Management Review* 26(4): 325–344.

Holley, Lyn, Donna Dufner, and B.J. Reed. 2002. "Got SISP: Strategic Information Systems Planning in U.S. State Governments." *Public Performance and Management Review* 25(4): 398–412.

Horrigan, John. 2004. "How Americans Get in Touch with Government." *Pew Research Internet Project*, May 24. www.pewinternet.org/2004/05/24/how-americans-get-in-touch-with-government/ (accessed June 16, 2014).

Horsburgh, Simon, Shaun Goldfinch, and Robin Gauld. 2011. "Is Public Trust in Government Associated with Trust in E-Government?" *Social Science Computer Review* 29(2): 232–241.

Jun, Kyu-Nahm, and Christopher Weare. 2011. "Institutional Motivations in the Adoption of Innovations: The Case of E-Government." *Journal of Public Administration Research and Theory* 21: 495–519.

Khatib, Lina. 2006. "Communicating Islamic Fundamentalism as Global Citizenship." In *Reformatting Politics: Information Technology and Global Civil Society*, ed. Jon Anderson, Dean Jodi, and Geert Lovink, 69–84. New York: Routledge.

Kim, Soonhee, and Jooho Lee. 2012. "E-Participation, Transparency, and Trust in Local Government." *Public Administration Review* 72: 819–828.

Kraemer, Kenneth. 1974. *Integrated Municipal Information Systems: The Use of the Computer in Local Government*. New York: Praeger.

———. 1987. *Datawars: The Politics of Modeling in Federal Policymaking*. New York: Columbia University Press.

———, and Jason Dedrick. 1997. "Computing and Public Organizations." *Journal of Public Administration Research and Theory* 7(1): 89–112.

———, and William Dutton. 1985. *Modeling as Negotiation: The Political Dynamics of Computer Models in the Policy Process*. Norwood, NJ: Ablex Publishing Corporation.

———, and James Perry. 1979. "The Federal Push to Bring Computer Applications to Local Governments." *Public Administration Review* 39(3): 260–270.

———, William Dutton, and Alana Northrop. 1981. *The Management of Information Systems*. New York: Columbia University Press.

———, Vijay Gurbaxani, and John King. 1992. "Economic Development, Government Policy, and the Diffusion of Computing in Asia-Pacific Countries." *Public Administration Review* 52(2): 146–156.

Laudon, Kenneth, and Jane Laudon. 2014. *Management Information Systems: Managing the Digital Firm*. New York: Prentice Hall.

Lee, Jooho. 2008. "Determinants of Government Bureaucrats' New PMIS Adoption: The Role of Organizational Power, IT Capability, Administrative Role, and Attitude." *American Review of Public Administration* 38(2): 180–202.

———, and Soonhee Kim. 2014. "Active Citizen E-Participation in Local Governance: Do Individual Social Capital and E-Participation Management Matter?" In *Proceedings of the Forty-Seventh Hawaii International Conference on System Science (HICSS 2014)*, January 6–9, Waikoloa, Hawaii.

Mancini, Daniela, Eddy Vaassen, and Renata Dameri. 2013. *Accounting Information Systems for Decision Making*. Heidelberg: Springer.

Manoharan, Aroon. 2013. "A Three Dimensional Assessment of U.S. County E-Government." *State and Local Government Review* 45(3): 153–162.

Mell, Peter, and Timothy Grance. 2011. *The NIST Definition of Cloud Computing*. NIST Special Publication 800–145. Gaithersburg, MD: National Institute of Standards and Technology, U.S. Department of Commerce, September.

Mergel, Ines. 2012. "The Social Media Innovation Challenge in the Public Sector." *Information Policy* 17: 281–292.

Milward, Brinton, and L. Snyder. 1996. "Electronic Government: Linking Citizens to Public Organizations through Technology." *Journal of Public Administration Research and Theory* 6(2): 261–276.

Moon, M. Jae. 2002. "The Evolution of E-Government among Municipalities: Rhetoric or Reality?" *Public Administration Review* 62(4): 424–433.

———, and Stuart Bretschneider. 2002. "Does the Perception of Red Tape Constrain IT Innovativeness in Organizations? Unexpected Results from a Simultaneous Equation Model and Implications." *Journal of Public Administration Research and Theory* 12(2): 273–292.

——, Jooho Lee, and Cheol Yong Roh. 2014. "The Evolution of Internal IT Applications and E-Government Studies in the Public Administration Discipline: Research Themes and Methods." *Administration & Society* 46(1): 3–36.

Morgeson, Forrest III, David van Amburg, and Sunil Mithas. 2011. "Misplaced Trust? Exploring the Structure of the E-Government-Citizen Trust Relationship." *Journal of Public Administration Research and Theory* 21: 257–283.

Mossberger, Karren, Younghong Wu, and Jared Crawford. 2013. "Connecting Citizens and Local Governments? Social Media and Interactivity in Major U.S. Cities." *Government Information Quarterly* 30: 351–358.

NASCIO (National Association of State Chief Information Officers). 2010. *A National Survey of Social Media Use in State Government: Friends, Followers, and Feeds.* Washington DC: NASCIO.

Nedovic-Budic, Zorica, and David R. Godschalk. 1996. "Human Factors in Adoption of Geographic Information Systems: A Local Government Case Study." *Public Administration Review* 56(6): 554–567.

Norris, Donald. 1984. "Computers and Small Local Governments: Uses and Users." *Public Administration Review* 44(1): 70–78.

——, and Kenneth Kraemer. 1996. "Mainframe and PC Computing in American Cities: Myths and Realities." *Public Administration Review* 56(6): 568–576.

——, and M. Jae Moon. 2005. "Advancing E-Government at the Grassroots: Tortoise or Hare." *Public Administration Review* 65(1): 64–75.

——, and Christopher Reddick. 2013. "Local E-Government in the United States: Transformation or Incremental Change?" *Public Administration Review* 73(1): 165–175.

Northrop, Alana, Kenneth Kraemer, Debora Dunkle, and John King. 1994. "Management and Policy for Greater Computing Benefits: The Versatility of Training." *Social Science Computer Review* 12(3): 383–404.

Perry, James, and James Danziger. 1980. "The Adoptability of Innovations: An Empirical Assessment of Computer Applications in Local Government." *Administration & Society* 11(4): 461–492.

——, and Kenneth Kraemer. 1980. "Chief Executive Support and Innovation Adoption." *Administration & Society* 12(2): 158–177.

Price, Dennis, and Dennis Mulvihill. 1965. "The Present and Future Use of Computers in State Government." *Public Administration Review* 25(2): 142–150.

Rainie, Lee, and Elena Larsen. 2002. "The Rise of the E-Citizen: How People Use Government Agencies' Websites." *Pew Research Internet Project*, April 3. www.pewinternet.org/2002/04/03/the-rise-of-the-e-citizen-how-people-use-government-agencies-web-sites/ (accessed June 16, 2014).

Rein, Lisa. 2012. "U.S. Printing Office Shrinks with Round of Buyouts." *Washington Post*, January 25. www.washingtonpost.com/politics/printing-office-shrinks-with-round-of-buyouts/2012/01/25/gIQAkIefRQ_story.html (accessed June 10, 2014).

Rocheleau, Bruce. 1994. "The Software Selection Process in Local Governments." *American Review of Public Administration* 24(3): 317–330.

Rogers, Everett. 1995. *Diffusion of Innovations.* New York: The Free Press.

Rule, James. 2007. *Privacy in Peril: How We Are Sacrificing a Fundamental Right in Exchange for Security and Convenience.* New York: Oxford University Press.

Servon, Lisa. 2002. *Bridging the Digital Divide: Technology, Community and Public Policy.* Malden, MA: Blackwell.

Smith, Aaron. 2010. "Government Online." *Pew Research Internet Project*, April 27. www.pewinternet.org/2010/04/27/government-online/ (accessed June 16, 2014).

Tolbert, Caroline, and Karren Mossberger. 2006. "The Effects of E-Government on Trust and Confidence in Government." *Public Administration Review* 66: 354–369.

——, ——, and Ramona McNeal. 2008. "Institutions, Policy Innovation and E-Government in the American States." *Public Administration Review* 68(3): 549–563.

USA.gov. 2007. "FirstGov.gov Is Now USA.gov." www.usa.gov/About/New-Name.shtml (accessed June 10, 2014).

Wallack, Todd. 2013. "Mass. Seeks to Get All Taxpayers to File Returns Online." *The Boston Globe*, March 12. www.bostonglobe.com/business/2013/03/11/massachusetts-tax payers-please-file-taxes-online/O9wEN1rS5JxBsk6aLjjIIL/story.html (accessed June 10, 2014).

Weare, Christopher, Juliet Musso, and Matthew Hale. 1999. "Electronic Democracy and the Diffusion of Municipal Web Pages in California." *Administration & Society* 31(1): 3–21.

Welch, Erick, Chris Hinnant, and M. Jae Moon. 2005. "Linking Citizen Satisfaction with E-Government and Trust in Government." *Journal of Public Administration Research and Theory* 15: 371–391.

West, Darrel. 2004. "E-Government and the Transformation of Service Delivery and Citizen Attitudes." *Public Administration Review* 64(1): 15–27.

——. 2008. *State and Federal Electronic Government in the United States.* Washington, DC: Brookings Institution.

Wikipedia. 2014a. "Cloud Computing." http://en.wikipedia.org/wiki/Cloud_comput ing (accessed June 10, 2014).

——. 2014b. "Facebook." http://en.wikipedia.org/wiki/Facebook (accessed June 15, 2014).

Wilson, James. 1989 *Bureaucracy: What Government Agencies Do and Why They Do It.* New York: Basic Books.

Wood, Colin. 2013. "California DMV Cancels IT Modernization Project Contract." *Government Technology*, February 14. www.govtech.com/e-government/DMV-IT-Modernization-Project.html (accessed January 15, 2014).

Yu, Pyong Jun, and Stuart Bretschneider. 1998. "Executive Perceptions of Innovativeness in Information Management." *Korean Review of Public Administration* 3: 179–213.

Zorn, Theodore, Andrew Flanagin, and Mirit Shoham. 2011. "Institutional and Non-Institutional Influences of Information and Communication Technology Adoption and Use among Nonprofit Organizations." *Human Communication Research* 37: 1–33.

Appendix

TABLE 8A.1 Priority Strategies, Management Processes, and Solutions

Priorities	2009	2010	2011	2012	2013	2014
1	Consolidation	Budget and cost control	Consolidation/optimization	Consolidation/optimization	Consolidation/optimization	Security
2	Shared services	Consolidation	Budget and cost control	Budget and cost control	Cloud services	Consolidation/optimization
3	Budget and cost control	Shared services	Health care	Governance	Security	Cloud services
4	Security	Broadband and connectivity	Cloud computing	Health care	Mobile services/mobility	Project and portfolio management
5	Electronic records management/digital preservation/e-discovery	American Recovery and Reinvestment Act	Shared services	Cloud computing	Budget and cost control	Strategic IT planning
6	Enterprise Resource Planning (ERP) strategy	Security	Governance	Security	Shared services	Budget and cost control
7	Green IT	Transparency	Security	Broadband and connectivity	Health care	Mobile services/mobility
8	Transparency	Infrastructure	Broadband and connectivity	Shared services	Legacy modernization	Shared services
9	Health information technology	Health information	Legacy modernization	Portal	Interoperable Nationwide Public Safety Broadband Network (FirstNet)	Interoperable Nationwide Public Safety Broadband Network (FirstNet)
10	Governance	Governance	Data and information management	Mobile services/mobility	Disaster recovery/business continuity	Health care

TABLE 8A.2 Priority Technologies, Applications, and Tools

Priorities	2009	2010	2011	2012	2013	2014
1	Virtualization	Virtualization	Virtualization	Virtualization	Cloud computing	Cloud computing
2	Document/content/email management	Networking, voice and data communications, unified communications	Cloud computing	Legacy application modernization/renovation	Mobile workforce technologies	Security enhancement tools
3	Legacy application modernization and upgrade	Document/content/records/email management	Networking	Cloud computing	Virtualization	Mobile workforce
4	Networking, voice and data communications, unified communications	Cloud computing, software as a service	Legacy application modernization/renovation	Mobile workforce technologies	Legacy application modernization/renovation	Enterprise Resource Planning (ERP)
5	Web 2.0	Security enhancement tools	Identity and access management	Networking	Identity and access management	Virtualization
6	Green IT technologies and solutions	Enterprise Resource Planning (ERP)/legacy application modernization-renovation	Document/content/records/email management	Enterprise Resource Planning (ERP)	Enterprise Resource Planning (ERP)	Legacy application modernization/renovation
7	Identity and access management	Geospatial analysis and Geographical Information Systems	Security enhancement tools	Identity and access management	Security enhancement tools	Business Intelligence (BI) and Business Analytics (BA)

(continued)

TABLE 8A.2 *(continued)*

Priorities	2009	2010	2011	2012	2013	2014
8	Geospatial analysis and Geographical Information Systems	Business Intelligence (BI) and Business Analytics (BA) applications	Business Intelligence (BI) and Business Analytics (BA) applications	Business Intelligence (BI) and Business Analytics (BA) applications	Networking	Disaster recovery/ business continuity
9	Business Intelligence (BI) and analytics applications	Identity and access management	Enterprise Resource Planning (ERP)	Document/content/ records/email management	Business Intelligence (BI) and Business Analytics (BA) applications, Big Data	Identity and access management
10	Mobile workforce enablement	Social media and networking	Social media and networking	Public Safety Radio Network	Document/content/ records/email management	Networking

Source: Commonwealth of Massachusetts 2013.

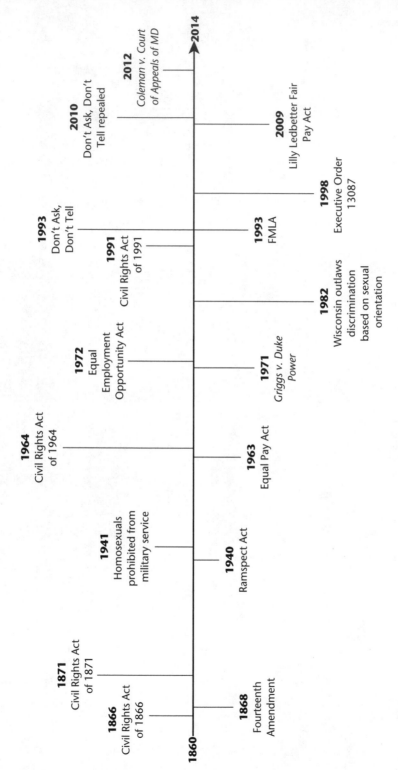

FIGURE 9.1 From Sameness to Differentness: Benchmarks across Time

9

FROM SAMENESS TO DIFFERENTNESS

Norma M. Riccucci

In June 2013, the U.S. Supreme Court issued several rulings that affected social equality measures in different ways for different groups. The *United States v. Windsor* (2013) decision opens the door for marriage equality and, as a corollary, the extension of federal benefits to same-sex marriages (for example, social security; military leave; tax advantages). In *Fisher v. University of Texas* (2013), the Court effectively placed affirmative action on the back burner by asking the Fifth Circuit Court of Appeals to review its decision upholding affirmative action in university admissions. In *Shelby County v. Holder* (2013), the High Court dealt a blow to people of color by striking down Section 4 of the Voting Rights Act, which will permit states predominantly in the South to develop measures that could severely limit their constitutional right to vote. In short, the Supreme Court surprisingly showed some beneficence to gays and lesbians, showed indifference to race-based admissions policies, and completely subverted African Americans and Latinos in terms of their voting rights.

These decisions in a way reflect the manner in which "differentness" has evolved in the field of public administration as well as how different groups have been and are treated by public employers. In many cases the treatment follows statutory, constitutional, or case law, but in other realms it follows pattern or practice. And, as with the 2013 Court rulings noted above, it has been a give-and-take process or, as Mary Guy (1993) aptly characterized, the progress women have made in the federal service: "Three Steps Forward, Two Steps Backward."

This chapter begins with a short summary of how differentness evolved and how it has replaced expectations of sameness. The primary focus of the chapter is on looking ahead vis-à-vis differentness—where progress is lacking and areas to target for change. As will be seen, some of the prescriptions for change are not new and progress has been slow. For example, despite calls for greater diversity in the upper reaches of government at every level, sameness perdures. The field is also beginning to advance our knowledge into other realms of differentness, such as the employment of lesbians, gays, bisexuals, transgendered and questioning (LGBTQs). This issue will also be addressed. So, too, will be the issue of family responsibilities discrimination (FRD), or caregiver discrimination, which abrogates the rights of both women and men who are the primary caregivers for children, aging parents, or sick spouses or partners. Differentness is not simply a matter of change to the social composition of the workplace. Its importance also manifests in organizational cultures that support differences in choice, such as the ability of workers to make choices about parenting and caregiving.

Background

Historically, the U.S. government workplace at every level has been predominately male, white, and Eurocentric. The same can be said for the private sector. Discrimination on the basis of gender, race, ethnicity, color, religion, nationality, disability, age, and, more recently, sexual or gender identity, prevailed even after laws proscribing discrimination were passed. For example, after passage of the Equal Employment Opportunity Act of 1972, which extended Title VII of the Civil Rights Act of 1964 to the public sector, municipal police and fire departments set up covert barriers to the hiring of women and people of color. The most common were height and weight requirements. In addition, some police and fire departments attempted to set gender as a bona fide occupational qualification to prevent women from being hired (see *Manley v. Mobile County, Ala.* 1977).

Slowly and incrementally the public sector moved toward differentness particularly in terms of gender, race, and ethnicity in large part due to court-ordered affirmative action programs (Kellough 2006; Riccucci 2002; Naff 2001). While these programs or policies helped to reshape the social landscape of public employment, white males often sought to derail the efforts with claims of "reverse discrimination," a most inexact, inauspicious term that further obfuscated and impeded diversity efforts. Courts sometimes rebuffed those challenges, but even judicial intervention has been mercurial, resulting in gains at times followed by setbacks. For example, the landmark High Court ruling in *Griggs v. Duke Power Co.* (1971) made it less complicated for alleged victims of employment discrimination to prove their Title VII case. If alleged victims could demonstrate that the employment practice in question had a harsh or adverse impact on them, the burden of proof would shift to the employer to demonstrate "business necessity" (for example, that the employment tool was job related). The standards of law created by *Griggs* were completely eviscerated by the U.S. Supreme Court's 1989 decision in *Wards Cove v. Antonio* (1989). In *Wards Cove*, the Court stated that after a showing of adverse impact, the burden of proof remains with the alleged victims, who must demonstrate that the employment tools were intentionally used for illegal purposes; in other words that the employer intentionally discriminated against them, which is extremely difficult to prove. In effect, Title VII was gutted by the Court. The *Griggs* ruling was essentially restored with passage of the Civil Rights Act of 1991.

More recently, the U.S. Supreme Court's 5–4 ruling in *Ledbetter v. Goodyear Tire & Rubber Company* (2007) effectively made it more difficult for public and private sector employees to file pay-discrimination complaints against their employers. When Lilly Ledbetter, a supervisor at the Goodyear's tire assembly department in Gadsden, Alabama, became aware—some ten years later—that she was making less money than her male counterparts, she filed suit. The Court ruled that she was time-barred from filing suit because she failed to file the lawsuit within the first 180 days of receiving the first unequal pay check, notwithstanding the fact that she had no knowledge the checks were unequal. Recognizing the absurdity of the ruling, Congress passed the Lilly Ledbetter Fair Pay Act in 2009, which states that the 180-day statute of limitations for filing a lawsuit resets with each new pay check affected by the discriminatory treatment.

In short, efforts to promote diversity or differentness particularly in the areas of race, ethnicity, and gender can be characterized by fits and starts. Government employers and courts steered the movement toward differentness. Sometimes Congress would step in to rectify regressive rulings by the courts. As can be seen in the following section, some progress, in effect, has been made. Unfortunately, data showing composition of the workforce are not available prior to passage of the Civil Rights Act, for it was not until then that employers were required to report the demographics of their workers. Another way to think about this is that, not until the mid-1960s was it deemed important enough to monitor access to jobs for all citizens.

Progress in Promoting Differentness

Certainly, in the aggregate, public sector workforces are much more diverse today than, say, fifty years ago. A number of studies have charted the progress, illustrating the inroads women and people of color made in state, local, and federal workforces (see, for example, Guy 1993; Guy and Fenley 2014; Naff 2001; Riccucci 2002, 2009). Figures 9.2 and 9.3 summarize the changes.[1] For example, Figure 9.2 illustrates changes in the demographic characteristics of the federal government from 1964 to 2013. Not surprisingly, white employees have enjoyed the greatest share of federal jobs during these time periods. Racial and ethnic minorities have held the fewest jobs. It can also been seen that all groups suffered from losses and gains in various time intervals (e.g., from 1980 to 2000, with whites experiencing more dramatic cuts during this period). All groups made gains between 2000 and 2010, with a slight dip going into 2013.

Figure 9.3 shows demographic employment data at the state and local levels of government. As with the federal workforce, whites have the highest levels of

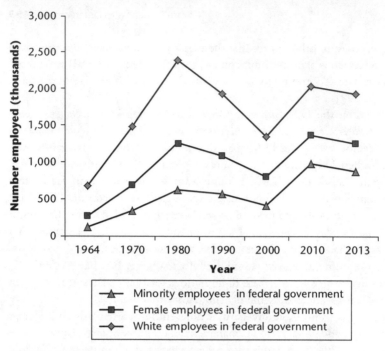

FIGURE 9.2 Employees in Federal Government

Source: Calculated from King et al. 2010.

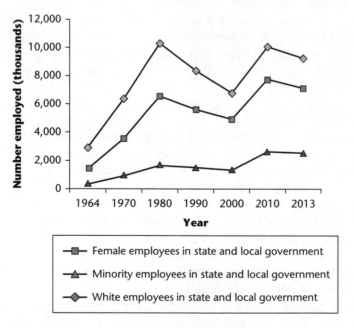

FIGURE 9.3 Employees in State and Local Government

Source: Calculated from King et al. 2010.

employment, while persons of color have the lowest. And the difference here is quite stark. For example, even when job levels peaked for all workers in 1980, people of color represented not even 10 percent of state and local government jobs, while whites held over 56 percent and women 35 percent.[2] By 2010, people of color represented 13 percent of those jobs, with whites holding close to 50 percent and women holding about 37 percent.

Thus, there has been some progress in the social landscape of all governments in terms of women and people of color, at least in terms of overall employment levels. Yet, as the figures illustrate, the levels of employment for people of color are much "flatter" than for those of women and whites. Also, as the research has consistently illustrated, progress in terms of pay and promotion to upper levels of employment has been lacking (see, for example, Guy and McCandless 2012; Guy and Fenley 2014; Riccucci 2009; Naff 2001). This will be addressed in the next section.

It should also be noted that the research on representative bureaucracy demonstrates the significance of differentness in bureaucracies (see Bradbury and Kellough 2011; Meier and Nicholson-Crotty 2006; Wilkins 2007). The theory of representative bureaucracy holds that government workforces will perform better and more democratically if their demographic makeup reflects the population they serve. In the passive sense, representative bureaucracy asks if the workplace mirrors the social characteristics of the general population. Active representativeness asks whether different groups in the bureaucracy are able to push for the needs and interests of their counterparts in the population.

In short, baby steps have been taken forward, but there continues to be a need for progress in promotions and pay, as will be seen shortly. Other areas where progress is lacking include policies that support the rights of workers to make choices about caregiving, and policies that promote the employment of LGBTQs. FRD has received very little attention in the public administration literature, but the problem persists. The same can be said for the employment of LGBTQs, where tracking accurate data continues to be challenging.

Taking "Steps Forward"

There are several areas of public employment where greater progress is needed. Addressed in this chapter are (1) pay and promotion; (2) FRD; and (3) the employment of LGBTQs.

Pay and Promotion

As it has been repeatedly demonstrated, the upper levels of government employment are still dominated by white men (see, for example, Guy and Fenley 2014). Although some progress has been made, women and people of color continue to lag. As Table 9.1 indicates, women increased their overall representation in Senior Executive Service (SES) posts. However, overall they constitute only 33.5

percent of these jobs compared to 66.5 percent for men. African-American men had the smallest gain as SESers (8.3 percent), and American-Indian or Alaskan-Native men experienced a decrease (−10 percent). White men also experienced a small decrease (−4.1 percent), but they continue to hold the largest share of SES positions (55.1 percent). Also, while the numbers are extremely low, men of unspecified or more than one race experienced an overwhelmingly large gain in SES jobs.

TABLE 9.1 SES Employment by Race, Ethnicity, and Gender, 2007 and 2012

	Number (Percent) 2007	Number (Percent) 2012	Percent change
Total SES	7,473	8,004	7.1
Women	2,141	2,678	25.1
	(30.0)	(33.5)	
Men	5,332	5,326	−0.1
	(70.0)	(66.5)	
African-American			
Women	251	383	52.6
	(3.4)	(4.8)	
Men	342	446	30.4
	(4.6)	(5.6)	
Latino			
Women	72	105	45.8
	(1.0)	(1.3)	
Men	206	223	8.3
	(2.8)	(2.8)	
Asian or Pacific Islander			
Women	67	105	56.7
	(0.9)	(1.3)	
Men	111	158	42.3
	(1.5)	(2.0)	
American-Indian or Alaskan Native			
Women	30	37	23.3
	(0.4)	(0.5)	
Men	60	54	−10.0
	(0.8)	(0.7)	
White			
Women	1,713	2,037	18.9
	(23.0)	(25.4)	
Men	4,597	4,407	−4.1
	(62.0)	(55.1)	
Unspecified or more than one race			
Women	8	11.0	37.5
	(0.1)	(0.1)	
Men	16	38.0	137.5
	(0.2)	(0.5)	

Source: Calculated from data provided by the U.S. Office of Personnel Management (OPM).

Note: Totals may not equal 100 due to rounding errors.

TABLE 9.2 Federal Civilian Employment by Senior Pay, Race, Ethnicity, and Gender, 2004 and 2010

	Senior pay level* (in %)		Percent change
	2004	2010	
Total Executive Branch	18,991	29,171	53.6
Women	25.8	31.1	20.5
Men	74.2	68.9	−7.1
African-American			
Women	2.7	2.9	7.4
Men	3.8	3.5	−7.9
Latino			
Women	1.0	1.3	30.0
Men	2.5	2.8	12.0
Asian or Pacific Islander			
Women	0.9	3.7	311.1
Men	2.3	6.1	165.2
American-Indian or Alaskan Native			
Women	0.2	0.4	100.0
Men	0.6	0.7	16.7
White			
Women	21.0	22.8	8.6
Men	65.0	55.9	−14.0

Sources: Calculated from U.S. OPM n.d.; for 2010 data, U.S. OPM 2011

Notes: Totals may not equal 100 due to rounding errors; *Senior pay levels include, for example, the following pay plans: SES, Executive Level, Senior Foreign Service, Administrative Law Judges, Board of Contract Appeals, and Foreign Service Chiefs of Mission, and Scientific and Professional. The Senior-level pay indicator was created in 1991. Senior pay ranges from about $100,000 upwards to approximately $200,000.

Table 9.2 provides data on employment at the senior pay levels by race, gender, and ethnicity. Interestingly, between 2004 and 2010, there were very small changes for women with the exception of Asian or Pacific Islanders, whose share of senior jobs rose from 0.9 percent in 2004 to 3.7 percent in 2010. For men, the picture is quite different. As seen in Table 9.2, the African-American and white share of senior-level jobs decreased, with the latter experiencing the largest drop, from 65 percent in 2004 to 55.9 percent in 2010. Asian men experienced the largest increase in positions at the senior pay level. In 2004 they held 2.3 percent of these jobs; that rose to 6.1 percent in 2010. Latino men experienced a relatively small rise during these time periods.

Differentness in the overall employment of women and people of color is important, but so too is differentness in pay and employment levels. Higher level jobs come with greater power and authority as well as salary. This continues to be an area where progress has stagnated.

FRD

Elements of differentness are also reflected in FRD, which affects both women and men. As noted earlier, it is important that organizational cultures support differences as they are manifested in choices. Choice begets difference; women who choose to have a child or men who choose to care for an ill elderly parent must be able to exercise those choices without fear of reprisal. Unfortunately, the culture of organizations allows for the punishment of employees who exercise those choices or who take responsibility for parenting or caregiving.

In terms of FRD, given that women are largely responsible for caregiving, working mothers represent the majority of FRD claimants.[3] As Swiss and Walker (1993) have argued, women in the workplace hit a "maternal wall"; that is, there are barriers that hinder their ability to balance family and work life.

There is no federal law that expressly prohibits discrimination based on family responsibilities. Rather, the claims are brought under Title VII of the Civil Rights Act as amended,[4] the Family Medical Leave Act, or state or local laws.[5] Insofar as discrimination occurs as a result of caring for disabled children or relatives, the Americans with Disabilities Act also protects workers from FRD (Williams and Bornstein 2006, 2008). In 2007, after hearings on the matter, the U.S. Equal Employment Opportunity Commission (EEOC) issued guidelines on the treatment of workers with caregiving responsibilities. Participants at the hearing provided testimony on the way in which stereotypes lead to FRD:

> Female employees tend to be less committed to work once they have children. Female employees will want a reduced schedule or less responsibility once they have children. Fathers are not the primary caretakers of young children, women are. Fathers don't need to take as much time off to care for their children.
>
> *(Scott 2007)*

The EEOC guidelines clearly state that a new protected class category is not being created. Rather the guidelines are intended to demonstrate that discrimination against caregivers might constitute unlawful disparate treatment. The guidelines (U.S. EEOC, 2007a) offer the following as relevant evidence for FRD claims:

- Whether the respondent asked female applicants, but not male applicants, whether they were married or had young children, or about their childcare and other caregiving responsibilities;
- Whether decision makers or other officials made stereotypical or derogatory comments about pregnant workers or about working mothers or other female caregivers;

- Whether the respondent began subjecting the charging party or other women to less favorable treatment soon after it became aware that they were pregnant;
- Whether, despite the absence of a decline in work performance, the respondent began subjecting the charging party or other women to less favorable treatment after they assumed caregiving responsibilities;
- Whether female workers without children or other caregiving responsibilities received more favorable treatment than female caregivers based upon stereotypes of mothers or other female caregivers;
- Whether the respondent steered or assigned women with caregiving responsibilities to less prestigious or lower-paid positions;
- Whether male workers with caregiving responsibilities received more favorable treatment than female workers;
- Whether statistical evidence shows disparate treatment against pregnant workers or female caregivers;
- Whether respondent deviated from workplace policy when it took the challenged action;
- Whether the respondent's asserted reason for the challenged action is credible.

In 2010, the Center for WorkLife Law conducted a study which examined over 2,100 cases involving FRD (Calvert 2010). The Center reports that lawsuits filed by workers with family caregiving responsibilities have increased by about 400 percent in the past decade. Based on the Center's analysis, it reported the following three themes in case law: (1) new supervisors or managers change or eradicate work shifts, and/or flexible scheduling and impose onerous productivity requirements; (2) FRD is more likely when a woman is on her second pregnancy, which is taken as an indication that her commitment to the organization will subside; and (3) a growing number of FRD cases involving workers providing care for their aging parents.

FRD claims tend to be litigated as disparate treatment cases, where one employee is treated differently than another based on a protected-class characteristic. One significant factor regarding these FRD cases is that stereotyping evidence can be offered in a disparate treatment cause of action. Traditionally, proving disparate treatment involves the use of a similarly-situated comparator to illustrate that the alleged victim of FRD is being treated worse (see Williams and Bornstein 2006). In *Back v. Hastings on the Hudson Union Free School District* (2004), the U.S. Court of Appeals for the Second Circuit held that disparate treatment under Title VII, in the absence of a comparator, can be proven with evidence of gender stereotyping. The case involved Elana Back who was hired as a school psychologist on a three-year tenure-track line. Back was denied tenure after three years on the grounds, according to the school district, that she lacked interpersonal and organizational skills. Back argued that the termination was based on gender stereotyping: that as a young mother, she would be unable to demonstrate a commitment to her job.

In her first year, Back had received "superior" and "outstanding" job evaluations from her supervisors. In her second year, she took about three months of maternity leave. Shortly after her return, she continued to receive high performance ratings. However, Back stated that her supervisors began to make discriminatory comments; they "(a) inquired about how she was 'planning on spacing [her] offspring,' (b) said '[p]lease do not get pregnant until [you] retire,' and (c) suggested that [she] 'wait until [her son] was in kindergarten to have another child'" (*Back v. Hastings* 2004, 115). The court found that stereotyped remarks can serve as evidence that gender played a part in an adverse employment decision. It stated:

> On the facts alleged, [supervisors] stereotyped the plaintiff as a woman and mother of young children, and thus treated her differently than they would have treated a man and father of young children. . . . such differential treatment was unlawful.
>
> *(Back v. Hastings 2004, 129)*

In another case, *Lust v. Sealy* (2004), the Seventh Circuit Court of Appeals found that a successful salesperson was not promoted because her supervisor assumed she would not relocate on the basis of her family status. In fact, as the court pointed out, Tracey Lust's supervisor

> admitted that he didn't consider recommending Lust for the [promotion] because she had children and he didn't think she'd want to relocate her family, though she hadn't told him that. On the contrary, she had told him again and again how much she wanted to be promoted, even though there was no indication that a . . . [management] position would open up any time soon [locally]. . . . antidiscrimination laws entitle individuals to be evaluated as individuals rather than as members of groups having certain. . . . characteristics.
>
> *(Lust v. Sealy 2004, 583)*

In the end, the court allowed Lust to introduce gender-based stereotypes of mothers as evidence of FRD and ruled in her favor.

The EEOC guidelines (EEOC 2007b) discussed earlier point to a number of "best practices" to encourage organizations to change their culture to support workers with caregiving responsibilities. These include, for example:

- Be aware of, and train managers about, the legal obligations that may impact decisions about treatment of workers with caregiving responsibilities;

- Develop, disseminate, and enforce a strong EEO policy that clearly addresses the types of conduct that might constitute unlawful discrimination against caregivers based on characteristics protected by federal anti-discrimination laws;
- Ensure that managers at all levels are aware of, and comply with, the organization's work–life policies;
- Respond to complaints of caregiver discrimination efficiently and effectively;
- Protect against retaliation;
- Implement recruitment practices that target individuals with caregiving responsibilities;
- Identify and remove barriers to re-entry.

When employers fail to prevent FRD, they not only create a culture of fear, but they also shortchange themselves to the extent that they potentially lose talented, loyal employees over illogical myths and stereotypes. Moreover, FRD not only impedes productivity through morale problems, it can also affect the career advancement of women in particular, ensuring that they are unable to reach higher-paying, upper-level jobs (Bock Mullins 2012).

The employment of LGBTQs

As noted at the beginning of this chapter, the U.S. Supreme Court ruled in *United States v. Windsor* (2013) that it is unconstitutional to define marriage as it was in the 1996 federal law, Defense of Marriage Act, as a "legal union between one man and one woman." While this case does not engage employment matters, it may serve as a bellwether for the treatment of LGBTQs in this nation.[6] For example, as a result of this decision, a number of states across the country began to allow same-sex marriages.[7] Moreover, it has personnel implications in that it opens the doors for the extension of benefits to same-sex marriages (for example, social security; health insurance; tax advantages). Also, the Ninth Circuit Court of Appeals issued a ruling that gays and lesbians may not be excluded from juries based on sexual orientation.[8] In addition, in November 2013, the U.S. Senate voted to consider for the first time since 1996, the enactment of the Employment Nondiscrimination Act, which would outlaw employment discrimination based on sexual orientation and gender identity. In short, a cultural shift in the manner in which this nation treats LGBTQs may be in the offing.[9]

While there is no federal protection for LGBTQ employees, a number of states have enacted laws to protect them in the workplace, as seen in Table 9.3. In addition, over 137 cities and counties have passed laws or developed policies to prohibit discrimination on the basis of gay, lesbian, bisexual, or gender identity for both public and private employees. While most of these localities are in states that prohibit gender identity discrimination, some are not

TABLE 9.3 Antidiscrimination Laws for LGBTs (lesbian, gay, bisexual, transgendered)

Public and private sectors	Public sector only	Gender identity
California	Delaware	California
Colorado	Indiana	Colorado
Connecticut	Michigan	Connecticut
District of Columbia	Montana	District of Columbia
Hawaii	Pennsylvania	Hawaii
Illinois		Illinois
Iowa		Iowa
Maine		Massachusetts
Maryland		Maine
Massachusetts		Minnesota
Minnesota		New Jersey
Nevada		New Mexico
New Hampshire		Nevada
New Jersey		Oregon
New Mexico		Rhode Island
New York		Vermont
Oregon		Washington State
Rhode Island		
Vermont		
Washington State		
Wisconsin		

Sources: FindLaw n.d.; Human Rights Campaign 2013.

Note: Gender identity refers to self-identification, apart from biological sex or gender.

(for example, Miami Beach and Tampa, Florida; Tucson, Arizona; Boise, Idaho; Louisville, Kentucky; Charleston, South Carolina; Austin, Dallas; and El Paso, Texas).

Research on LGBTQs is certainly impeded by the lack of reliable data (Norman-Major and Becker 2013; Borrego and Johnson III 2013). Notwithstanding, scholars such as Greg Lewis, Charles Gossett, and Rod Colvin have made extraordinary progress in advancing our knowledge about the employment status of LGBTQs.[10] Lewis in particular has been a pioneer here, addressing this issue from a variety of perspectives. In an early piece, when the subject was not in vogue, Lewis (1997) offered an excellent examination of the federal government's policies toward gays and lesbians. He finds that to the extent to which the employment rights of gays and lesbians was politicized, progress was subverted. As he points out, for example:

> When the Republicans attacked the Democrats for being soft on Communism in the 1950s, homosexuals became an easy target for both parties because "sex perverts" were so widely despised that not even the American Civil Liberties Union would stand up for them. The politicians strengthened laws and pushed the bureaucracy to enforce them, and the

bureaucratic structure—especially the Civil Service Commission and the FBI—continued to enforce the exclusion of gay employees long after the political issue had died down.

(Lewis 1997, 394)

The politicization of gays in the military later led to the infamous "Don't Ask, Don't Tell" policy on gays serving in the military.

In a more recent study, Lewis et al. (2011) examine the employment status of lesbians, gays, and bisexuals (LGBs) in federal, state, and local government workforces. Based on a 5 percent sample of the 2000 Census, they find, for example, that

[p]artnered lesbians are at least as likely as heterosexually partnered women to hold government jobs, and partnered gay men are as likely as other partnered men to work for state governments. Partnered LGBs' share of management jobs in SLGs [state and local governments] is higher than their share of either SLG or private sector employment.

(Lewis et al. 2011, 173–175)

They also make the important point that without reliable data, other critical questions, such as whether passive representation of LGBs leads to active representation, cannot be answered.

Interestingly, the U.S. Supreme Court has ruled that same-sex sexual harassment is actionable under Title VII, opining that the gender of the harasser is not the issue, rather it is the *action* of harassment, or the act of sex (see *Oncale v. Sundowner Offshore Services* 1998). Yet, LGBTQ employees filing sexual harassment claims under Title VII for gender non-conformity have been struck down (see *Dawson v. Bumble & Bumble* 2005). Here, plaintiffs argue that they are the subject of sexual harassment for not conforming to traditional gender stereotypes.[11] Ultimately, as Guy and Fenley (2014) point out, "LGBTQ individuals are left with little protection against sexual harassment because orientation is an unprotected status and legitimate charges of sex harassment may be trumped by claims that discrimination stemmed from sexual orientation, not sex."

As cultures of organizations change, and individuals feel safe to express who they are, levels of differentness will certainly increase in the workplace. This, in turn, will allow for the collection of more reliable data on LGBTQ employees in public and private sector workforces. Without this shift, research on this issue and tracking the progress that LGBTQs are making in the workplace will be greatly deterred.

Conclusion

Citizens of this nation are becoming increasingly different. In effect, the definition of differentness continues to expand. Indeed, moving into the next fifty years or so, it will become more difficult to "categorize" people by gender, race, ethnicity, nationality, and sexuality. Government employers are thus challenged to ensure differentness in their workforces, as a key mission of government is to provide services to *all* individuals. While progress has been made in some realms (for example, overall employment of women and people of color), much more is needed in, as presented here, such areas as promotions, pay, FRD (and accompanying family-leave policies), and the employment and equal treatment of LGBTQs. While proaction by the executive branch is critical, so too will be progressive actions by Congress and the U.S. Supreme Court.

Notes

1 These figures do not illustrate the lack of progress women and people of color have made in certain local jobs such as in firefighting and police. In particular, women represent only 3.6 percent of the nation's firefighters, and while people of color have made some progress, they continue to lag in terms of promotions to upper-level posts in the uniformed services (see, for example, Riccucci and Saldivar 2014).
2 The data could not be broken down by race/ethnicity and gender.
3 Calvert (2010) points out that 88 percent of the plaintiffs in FRD cases are women.
4 The Pregnancy Discrimination Act of 1978 amended Title VII to prohibit discrimination against employees on the basis of pregnancy and childbirth.
5 Four states—Alaska, Connecticut, New Jersey, and Oregon—and the District of Columbia enacted laws expressly prohibiting FRD. In addition, at least sixty-seven localities in twenty-two different states have local laws that prohibit FRD (see Williams et al. 2012).
6 However, it should be noted that in January 2014, the High Court issued an order halting same-sex marriages in Utah while the state appeals a district court decision that ruled the state's ban on gay marriage violated the constitutional rights of gays.
7 As of the time of writing there are seventeen states that permit such marriages.
8 *Smithkline Beecham Corporation v. Abbott Laboratories* (2014).
9 As of the time of writing, however, thirty-two states have state laws or constitutional amendments limiting marriage to a woman and a man.
10 See, for example, Lewis 1997, 2001, 2010; Gossett 2012; Colvin 2007, 2012; and Lewis et al. 2011.
11 But see the U.S. EEOC's rulings in *Veretto v. Donahoe* (2011) and *Macy v. Holder* (2012). In *Veretto*, the EEOC ruled that sex stereotyping can result when an assumption is made that men can only marry women. Thus, a male U.S. Postal worker who was harassed when he announced he was marrying his male partner could claim discrimination and harassment under Title VII. In *Macy*, the EEOC found for an employee who was discriminated against based on being transgendered.

References

Back v. Hastings on the Hudson Union Free School District. 2004. 365 F.3d 107 (2nd Cir.).

Bock Mullins, Lauren. 2012. "Balancing Work and Family: How Does Family Responsibilities Discrimination Affect Career Advancement?" Unpublished conference paper. Northeast Conference on Public Administration, Boston, November 2–3.

Borrego, Espiridion A., and Richard Greggory Johnson III. 2013. "Has Public Administration Grown Up? A Case for Sexual Orientation/Gender Identity and the Intersection of Public Administration in the 21st Century." *Journal of Public Management and Social Policy* 19(1): 1–4.

Bradbury, Mark, and J. Edward Kellough. 2011. "Representative Bureaucracy: Assessing the Evidence on Active Representation." *American Review of Public Administration* 41: 157–167.

Calvert, Cynthia Thomas. 2010. *Family Responsibilities Discrimination: Litigation Update 2010.* San Francisco: Center for WorkLife Law. www.worklifelaw.org/pubs/FRDupdate.pdf (accessed January 8, 2014).

Colvin, Roddrick A. 2007. "The Rise of Transgender-Inclusive Laws: How Well Are Municipalities Implementing Supportive Nondiscrimination Public Employment Policies?" *Review of Public Personnel Administration* 27(4): 336–360.

———. 2012. *Gay and Lesbian Cops: Diversity and Effective Policing.* Boulder, CO: Lynne Rienner.

Dawson v. Bumble & Bumble. 2005. 398 F.3d 211 (2d Cir.).

FindLaw. N.d. "Sexual Orientation Discrimination in the Workplace." http://employment.findlaw.com/employment-discrimination/sexual-orientation-discrimination-in-the-workplace.html (accessed January 14, 2014).

Fisher v. University of Texas. 2013. 133 S. Ct. 2411.

Gossett, Charles W. 2012. "Lesbian, Gay, Bisexual and Transgendered Employees in the Public Sector Workforce." In *Public Personnel Management: Current Concerns, Future Challenges,* 5th ed., ed. Norma M. Riccucci, 60–76. New York: Longman Press.

Griggs v. Duke Power Co. 1971. 401 U.S. 424.

Guy, Mary E. 1993. "Three Steps Forward, Two Steps Backward: The Status of Women's Integration into Public Management." *Public Administration Review* 53(4): 285–292.

———, and Vanessa M. Fenley. 2014. "Inch by Inch: Gender Equity since the Civil Rights Act of 1964." *Review of Public Personnel Administration* 34(1): 40–58.

———, and Sean McCandless. 2012. "Social Equity: Its Legacy, Its Promise." *Public Administration Review* 72(s1): 5–13.

Human Rights Campaign. 2013. "State Employment Laws and Policies." http://hrc-assets.s3-website-us-east-1.amazonaws.com//files/assets/resources/statewide_employment_5-2014.pdf (updated; accessed January 14, 2014).

Kellough, J. Edward. 2006. *Understanding Affirmative Action: Politics, Discrimination, and the Search for Justice.* Washington, DC: Georgetown University Press.

King, Miriam, Steven Ruggles, J. Trent Alexander, Sarah Flood, Katie Genadek, Matthew B. Schroeder, Brandon Trampe, and Rebecca Vick. 2010. *Integrated Public Use Microdata Series, Current Population Survey: Version 3.0.* Machine-readable database. Minneapolis: University of Minnesota. https://cps.ipums.org/cps/index.shtml (accessed December 1, 2013).

Ledbetter v. Goodyear Tire & Rubber Company. 2007. 550 U.S. 618.

Lewis, Gregory B. 1997. "Lifting the Ban on Gays in the Civil Service: Federal Policy toward Gay and Lesbian Employees since the Cold War." *Public Administration Review* 57(5): 387–395.

———. 2001. "Barriers to Security Clearances for Gay Men and Lesbians: Fear of Blackmail or Fear of Homosexuals?" *Journal of Public Administration Research and Theory* 11(4): 539–557.

———. 2010. "Modeling Nonprofit Employment: Why Do So Many Lesbians and Gay Men Work for Nonprofit Organizations?" *Administration & Society* 42(6): 720–748.

―――― et al. 2011. "Representation of Lesbians and Gay Men in Federal, State, and Local Bureaucracies." *Journal of Public Administration Research and Theory* 21(1): 159–180.

Lust v. Sealy. 2004. 383 F.3d 580 (7th Cir.).

Macy v. Holder. 2012. 2012 WL 1435995.

Manley v. Mobile County, Ala. 1977. 441 F.Supp. 1351 (S.D.Ala.).

Meier, Kenneth J., and Jill Nicholson-Crotty. 2006. "Gender, Representative Bureaucracy, and Law Enforcement: The Case of Sexual Assault." *Public Administration Review* 66: 850–860.

Naff, Katherine C. 2001. *To Look Like America: Dismantling Barriers for Women and Minorities in Government.* Boulder, CO: Westview Press.

Norman-Major, Kristen, and Carol Becker. 2013. "Walking the Talk: Have the Infrastructure Necessary to Implement and Enforce LGBT and Gender Identity Rights?" *Journal of Public Management and Social Policy* 19(1): 31–49.

Oncale v. Sundowner Offshore Services. 1998. 523 U.S. 75.

Riccucci, Norma M. 2002. *Managing Diversity in Public Sector Workforces.* Boulder, CO: Westview Press.

―――. 2009. "The Pursuit of Social Equity in the Federal Government: A Road Less Traveled?" *Public Administration Review* 69(3): 373–382.

―――, and Karina Saldivar. 2014. "The Status of Employment Discrimination Suits in Police and Fire Departments across the U.S." *Review of Public Personnel Administration* 34(3): 263–288.

Scott, Amy M. 2007. "Family Responsibility Discrimination: Regulatory Update." *Employee Benefit Plan Review* (August). www.klgates.com/files/tempFiles/b84b6bee-b677-439c-91ae-faecdb7d2b3c/Article_Scott_Responsibility_Discrimination.pdf (accessed January 7, 2014).

Shelby County v. Holder. 2013. 133 S. Ct. 2612.

Smithkline Beecham Corporation v. Abbott Laboratories. 2014. www.gpo.gov/fdsys/pkg/USCOURTS-ca9-11-17357/pdf/USCOURTS-ca9-11-17357-0.pdf (accessed January 27, 2014).

Swiss, Deborah J., and Judith P. Walker. 1993. *Women and the Work/Family Dilemma: How Today's Professional Women Are Confronting the Maternal Wall.* New York: John Wiley & Sons.

United States v. Windsor. 570 U.S. ___ (2013) (Docket No. 12-307).

U.S. EEOC. 2007a. "Enforcement Guidance: Unlawful Disparate Treatment of Workers with Caregiving Responsibilities." www.eeoc.gov/policy/docs/caregiving.html (accessed January 7, 2014).

―――. 2007b. "Employer Best Practices for Workers with Caregiving Responsibilities." www.eeoc.gov/policy/docs/caregiver-best-practices.html (accessed January 8, 2014).

U.S. OPM. N.d. "Demographic Profile of the Federal Workforce: 2004 Data." www.opm.gov/feddata/demograp/demograp.asp#RNOData (accessed March 12, 2008).

―――. 2011. *Federal Civilian Workforce Statistics: Demographic Profile of the Federal Workforce as of September 2010.* Washington, DC: OPM, 2011. www.opm.gov/policy-data-oversight/data-analysis-documentation//federal-employment-reports/demographics/2010-demographic-profile/ (accessed January 6, 2014).

Veretto v. Donahoe. 2011. 2011 WL 2663401.

Wards Cove Packing Co. v. Antonio. 1989. 490 U.S. 642.

Wilkins, Vicky M. 2007. "Exploring the Causal Story: Gender, Active Representation, and Bureaucratic Priorities." *Journal of Public Administration Research and Theory* 17(1): 77–94.

Williams, Joan C., and Stephanie Bornstein. 2006. "Caregivers in the Courtroom: The Growing Trend of Family Responsibilities Discrimination." *University of San Francisco Law Review* 41: 171–190.

——, and ——. 2008. "The Evolution of 'FRED': Family Responsibility Discrimination and Developments in the Law of Stereotyping and Implicit Bias." *Hastings Law Journal* 59: 1311–1358.

——, Robin Devaux, Patricija Petrac, and Lynn Feinberg. 2012. "Protecting Family Caregivers from Employment Discrimination." Fact sheet 264, August. Washington, DC: AARP Public Policy Institute. www.aarp.org/content/dam/aarp/research/public_policy_institute/health/protecting-caregivers-employment-discrimination-fs-AARP-ppi-ltc.pdf (accessed January 7, 2014).

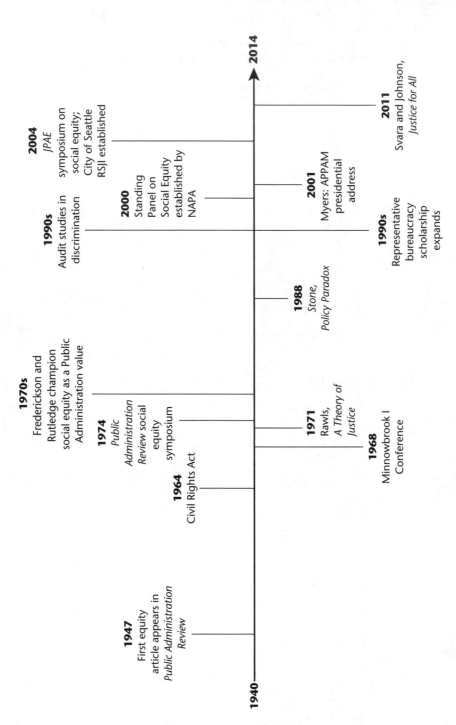

FIGURE 10.1 From Equality to Social Equity: Benchmarks across Time

10

FROM EQUALITY TO SOCIAL EQUITY

Susan T. Gooden

The bumpy road from equality to social equity in public administration has been largely shaped by the enduring challenge of reconciling stark differences between the democratic principle of equality and the implementation of social equity. While the terms are often used interchangeably, they are, in fact, quite different. Equality pertains to the principle that the same rights apply to all. Social equity is linked to the notion of justice and implies fair treatment of all. While the value of equality has been widely accepted in the United States, the implementation of equity has been far slower and much more unevenly received.

This chapter looks at the evolution from equality to social equity in the United States within the context of five complex, enduring questions, with their analysis corresponding roughly to decades:

1. What is the context for equality? (Pre–1960s)
2. Who is "we"? (1960s–1970s)
3. How much inequity exists? (1980s–1990s)
4. Why does social inequity persist? (2000s–2010s)
5. How is accountability for social equity achieved? (2010s and beyond)

What Is the Context for Equality?

The context for equality in the United States is formal and deeply entrenched. Both the Declaration of Independence and the U.S. Constitution concretely affirm a commitment to equality in the United States. Adopted July 4, 1776 by the thirteen former colonies, these new United States of America proclaimed in their Declaration of Independence: "We hold these truths to be self-evident, that all men are created equal, that they are endowed by their Creator with certain unalienable Rights, that among these are life, liberty, and the pursuit of happiness." While this sentence represents a fundamental ideal, the exclusion of women, the enslavement of blacks, and the gross mistreatment of the first Americans—American Indians—left a huge gulf in the implementation of this democratic principle.

The opening words of the supreme law of the land, the U.S. Constitution, are "We the people . . . " But, the extension of the term "we" to include African-Americans via the Thirteenth, Fourteenth, and Fifteenth Amendments, and the enfranchisement of women via the Nineteenth Amendment occurs nearly 100 years, or over 100 years, later, respectively. And, the extension of equal rights to women is still not contained in the U.S. Constitution. The Pledge of Allegiance, a legally adopted United States expression of loyalty, first penned in 1892 by Frances Bellamy contains the ending phrase, "with liberty and justice for all." Yet again, the implementation of this ideal of justice falls woefully short, particularly considering official U.S. American Indian removal policies beginning with the Trail of Tears in 1813, and the unjust treatment of African Americans with Jim Crow policies that were legal until the Civil Rights Act of 1964.

These pronounced shortcomings of American democratic ideals have been acknowledged by public leaders and scholars alike almost since the beginning of our history as a nation. The most egregious example is in the area of slavery. In writing on the deliberation and subsequent passage of the Declaration of Independence, Thomas Jefferson offered the following critique on June 7, 1776:

> The clause too, reprobating the enslaving the inhabitants of Africa, was struck out in complaisance to South Carolina and Georgia, who had never attempted to restrain the importation of slaves, and who, on the contrary, still wished to continue it. Our northern brethren also, I believe, felt a little tender under those censures; for though their people had very few slaves themselves, yet they had been pretty considerable carriers of them to others . . . As the sentiments of men are known not only by what they receive, but what they reject also. . . . "
>
> *(Jefferson 1944, 21)*

As Jefferson, himself a slaveowner, notes, excluding slaves from the concept of equality was not merely a thoughtless omission by our Founding Fathers, but rather a conscious rejection of the principle of democratic inclusion.

In his famous July 3, 1852 speech, "What, to the Slave, is the Fourth of July?" Frederick Douglass states,

> that precisely what I have now denounced is, in fact, guaranteed and sanctioned by the Constitution of the United States, that the right to hold and to hunt slaves is a part of that Constitution, framed by the illustrious Fathers of this Republic.
>
> *(Cited in Daley 2006, 31)*

Similarly, W.E.B. DuBois in his "color line speech" delivered in 1900 captures the magnitude of the unfulfilled democratic principle of equality:

> The problem of the twentieth century is the problem of the color line, the question as to how far differences of race—which show themselves chiefly in the color of the skin and the texture of the hair—will hereafter be made the basis of denying to over half the world the right of sharing to their utmost ability the opportunities and privileges of modern civilization.
>
> *(Cited in Daley 2006, 85)*

While equality is a fundamental "self-evident" principle of American democracy, the implementation of this proclaimed principle has been much more problematic. Although a key premise of the "American Dream" is an equal opportunity to participate and a reasonable anticipation of success, as Hochschild (1995, 26) explains:

> The first tenet, that everyone can participate equally and can always start over, is troubling to the degree that it is not true . . . For most of American history, women of any race and men who were Native American, Asian, black or poor were barred from all but a narrow range of electable futures.

Social equity recognizes the historical, political, social, and economic influences that structurally influence the prospects for access, opportunity, and outcomes. In public administration, social equity further recognizes the importance of public servants and public sector organizations in fulfilling the democratic principle of fairness:

> Despite the long-standing commitment to fairness as an administrative principle, administrators must be humbled by the realizations that they contributed to the discrepancy and in many places helped to institute inequality in the past by enforcing discriminatory laws and using their broad discretion to advance exclusionary social mores.
>
> *(Smith 2002, 14)*

One of the earliest analyses of public administration's role in promoting equity is offered by Frances Harriet Williams in her 1947 *Public Administration Review* article, "Minority Groups and OPA." In reflecting on the activities of the Office of Price Administration (OPA) to ration a range of goods following World War II, Williams (1947, 123) writes:

> One-tenth of these citizens are American Negroes. There are also Spanish-speaking Americans, Chinese-Americans, Japanese-Americans, and American Indians. These groups and certain low-income groups made

> up of various European and Oriental People are all subjected to some
> discrimination at various times and places in the administration of our
> laws . . . To what degree were these programs impartially administered?

Williams's article is the genesis of a developed analytical focus of equity in public
administration and calls attention to the critical responsibility of our profession to
advance its realization.

Who Is "We"?

Held every twenty years since 1968 and widely recognized as the "cicadas of
public administration," Syracuse University's Minnowbrook conferences "are
intended as an opportunity to take stock of where the field is, where the field is
going, and where the field needs to go" (Kim et al. 2010, 1). Against the background of social justice and civil rights, Minnowbrook I participant H. George
Frederickson took the lead in identifying social equity as an important focus for
the future of public administration. In a critique of American democracy, Frederickson (1971, 311) asserted that "the procedures of representative democracy
presently operate in a way that either fails or only very gradually attempts to
reverse systematic discrimination against disadvantaged minorities." In reflecting
on his 1971 essay, Frederickson later noted,

> Although the word "equity" appears in the original Woodrow Wilson
> ([1887] 1941) essay and in other public administration classics, this essay
> is the first relatively full elaboration of the concept of social equity and its
> application to public administration. And, it is the first to claim that social
> equity should form part of the normative base of public administration.
>
> *(Frederickson 2010, 3)*

The concept of social equity in public administration is inextricably linked to
John Rawls's *A Theory of Justice*. Rawls developed a principle of justice as "fairness" in which "each person is to have an equal right to the most extensive basic
liberty compatible with a similar liberty for all" (1971, 250). As Rawls argues, a
modern theory of government equalizes the distribution of social and economic
advantages. He challenges us to put ourselves behind a "veil of ignorance" and
to use our innate sense of justice to derive principles of equity without the bias
of knowing our own situation. For Rawls, equity includes social primary goods,
such as power, opportunity, civil rights, and wealth (Stone 1997, 54).

Within the national 1960s context focused on civil rights, racial inequality,
and injustice, the young Minnows noted: "A government built on a Constitution claiming the equal protection of the laws had failed in that promise. Public
administrators, who daily operate the government, were not without responsibility" (Frederickson 1990, 228). Reflecting in 2005, Frederickson recalled:

"It was during the 1960s that it became increasingly evident that the results of governmental policy and the work of public administrators implementing those policies were much better for some citizens than for others" (Frederickson 2005).

A fundamental legacy of the Minnowbrook I Conference was the foundational basis of New Public Administration, which rejected the idea that administrators are value neutral. Rather, it recognized a constellation of five normative core values that, although legitimate, can often be conflictual. These values include responsiveness, worker and citizen participation in decision-making, social equity, citizen choice, and administrative responsibility (Frederickson 1980). As Frederickson wrote: "A primary managerial means to achieve social equity includes a managerial commitment to the principle that majority rule does not overturn minority rights to equal public services" (1980, 47). In fact, the link between New Public Administration and social equity is so strong that Shafritz and Russell (2002, 466) define it as "[a]n academic advocacy movement for social equity in the performance and delivery of public service; it called for a proactive administrator with a burning desire for social equity to replace the traditional impersonal and neutral gun-for-hire bureaucrat."

As Frederickson later explains:

> It is time for public administrators of all kinds to ask the so-called second question. The first question is whether an existing public program or proposed program is effective or good. The second question is more important. For whom is this program effective or good?
>
> *(Frederickson 2005, 35)*

While Frederickson was theorizing and conceptualizing social equity and its linkage to public administration, another giant in the field, the late Philip Rutledge, was fervently working to advance social equity's applied dimension. Much of his lifelong legacy involved holding our field's professional associations accountable to social equity. As Frederickson explains:

> Although we were having a conversation about social equity, conversations were never enough for Phil. He was the social equity entrepreneur. During his ASPA presidency, he asked Dwight Waldo to include a symposium on social equity in the *Public Administration Review* (January/February 1974). During this period, ASPA was rewriting its code of ethics and Phil encouraged the drafting committee to include a social equity standard. He was the force behind the continuing environmental justice project panels at the National Academy of Public Administration (NAPA). Phil also was the driving force behind what is now the Standing Panel on Social Equity in Governance of NAPA and the series of annual NAPA social equity conferences.
>
> *(Frederickson 2010, 126)*

George Frederickson and Philip Rutledge forced the field of public administration to critically examine an important question: Who is "we"? Frederickson poses this question to the field conceptually and theoretically. He advances the case that public administrators must examine the "we" served by public sector policies and programs. Diversity, another closely related area to social equity, started to expand its examination of the concept of representative bureaucracy. Connected largely to human resource management, public administration scholars began to examine the composition of the public sector workforce and how closely it mirrors the demographics of the population it serves (see Gooden and Portillo 2011).

Rutledge also poses this same question as that posed by Frederickson but directs its examination in a different manner. He advances performance accountability for the "we" by forcing direct examination within the profession. For Rutledge, the "we" includes the public administration associations we convene, the codes we implement, and the journals that offer visibility to our scholarship. What emerges from Frederickson and Rutledge is the present-day notion of the "we" of public administration as all-inclusive—it is public administration scholars, practitioners, and students. Performance assessment should be inclusive of all of those we serve—citizens, residents, and communities—spanning all races/ethnicities, genders, income levels, sexual orientations, and ability levels.

How Much Inequity Exists?

During the 1980s and 1990s the advancement of the concept and measurement of equity was influenced considerably by political science, public policy, and economics, with public administration research focusing primarily on questions related to representative bureaucracy. Social equity, as a public administration research focus, was not yet a part of the field's "mainstream" topics. (This point is covered in more detail in the next section of this chapter.)

With the concept of social equity broadly defined, the next task was to measure it. But, as political scientist Deborah Stone illustrated in her seminal work, *Policy Paradox: The Art of Political Decision Making* (1997), determining the appropriate standard for equity is complex. By posing the challenge of how to equitably distribute a chocolate cake, Stone demonstrates that the simple idea of one slice per person is inherently problematic because it does not permit the consideration of important contextual factors, such as hunger, allergies, preferences, economics, hierarchy, and democratic decision making. As Stone (1997, 42) states:

> Here is the paradox of distributive problems: Equality may in fact mean inequality; equal treatment may require unequal treatment; and the same distribution may be seen as equal or unequal, depending upon one's point of view. I have used the word "equality" to denote sameness and to signify

the part of a distribution that contains uniformity—uniformity of slices, or of meals, or of voting power, for example. I have used "equity" to denote distributions regarded as fair, even though they contain both equalities and inequalities.

Many public administration scholars aggressively analyzed a variety of groups and their representation in the public sector relative to employment, wages, or position. For example, some of the topics relating to gender included occupational segregation and gender discrimination (Lewis 1994; Miller, Kerr, and Reid 1999), and glass ceiling and advancement (Vertz 1985; Bremer and Howe 1988; Kelly et al. 1991; Bullard and Wright 1993; Naff 1994; Newman 1994; Mani 1999).

Greg Lewis's research on representational equity in the federal workforce spanned multiple dimensions of equity including gender, race/ethnicity, sexual orientation, and disability status (see, for example, Kim and Lewis 1994; Lewis 1988, 1994, 1997a, 1997b; Lewis and Allee 1992). In offering a rich analysis of multiple populations, these analyses contribute to the field's comparative and nuanced understanding of equity among groups. For example, Kim and Lewis (1994) discuss the important disparity between level of education and position among Asian Americans:

> In the federal service, Asian Americans resemble white non-Hispanics in education, salary, grade, and supervisory authority more than they resemble other minority groups. Nonetheless, they continue to earn lower salaries, attain lower grades, and wield less supervisory authority than comparably educated and experienced whites.
>
> *(Kim and Lewis 1994, 289)*

In addition to the empirical examination of representational equity in public sector bureaucracies, equity in public policies and programs also came to the fore. Researchers trained in public policy and economics began to measure equity largely by attempting to isolate discrimination in the provision of public services through the use of audit studies or paired-testing. For example, in 1998, the U.S. Department of Housing and Urban Development sponsored an Urban Institute conference "focusing on the use of new methodologies for creating a national report card on the state of racial discrimination in America" (Fix and Turner 1999, xi).

These methodologies were largely intended as an improvement over more commonly used statistical methods, such as regression analysis, to better isolate the presence of discrimination by matching individuals on all relevant characteristics except the factor that is expected to lead to discrimination. For example, these methodologies allowed researchers to better assess to what extent fair housing is actually fair (see, for instance, Fix, Galster, and Struyk 1993; Galster 1993;

Schwemm 1990; Turner 1992; Turner, Struyk, and Yinger 1991; Yinger 1986, 1991). One paired testing study concerning the availability of information on housing found that

> black home buyers learn about 23.7 percent fewer houses than do their white teammates, black renters learn about 24.5 percent fewer apartments, Hispanics learn about 25.6 percent fewer houses and Hispanic renters learn about 10.9 percent fewer apartments. All of these net differences are statistically significant.
>
> *(Yinger 1998, 32)*

Examining methodological techniques to detect discrimination continued to receive attention at the turn of the twenty-first century. For example, the Committee on National Statistics[1] convened the Panel on Methods of Assessing Discrimination in 2001 "to define racial discrimination; review and critique existing methods used to measure such discrimination and identify new approaches, and make recommendations regarding the best of these methods" (National Research Council 2004, xi). After evaluating four major methods to measure racial discrimination (laboratory experiments, field experiments, analysis of observational data and natural experiments, and survey and administrative records) the National Research Council concluded that "each method has strengths and weaknesses, particularly for drawing a causal inference that an adverse outcome is the result of race-based discriminatory behavior" (2004, 5).

Regardless of the specific methodological techniques employed, the findings are that significant inequities exist by race/ethnicity, gender, and income. To reduce social inequities, public administrators and policymakers cannot solely invest in more and more sophisticated measures of equity, but rather they must aggressively treat the inequities that are well documented. Gooden (2010, 56) articulates the need to move beyond this "ready, aim . . . study more" sequence:

> Researchers who analyze social equity find themselves in a disconcerting cycle. A fixed response to social equity analysis (by policymakers, agencies, and other academic researchers) is not to accept the research results because a higher standard of proof is needed. The burden of proof for "finding" social inequities becomes unattainable. It becomes a repetitive chase. The de facto "more evidence needed" response facilitates the avoidance of advancing public policy solutions.

While measuring the magnitude of social inequities remained important, toward the end of the twentieth century the field of public administration began to turn toward more non-quantitative analysis to examine why social inequities endure.

Why Does Social Inequity Persist?

In considering this question, public administration began to draw upon scholarship that analyzes the role of organizational culture, leadership, and structure to understand the complexity of social equity. Building upon much earlier work,[2] public administration scholars at the turn of the twenty-first century heightened their examination of these factors by providing a more explicit focus on social equity. As Rice (2004, 144) wrote: "The connection between social equity and diversity takes into account the fact that public organizations and public administrators, managers, and public service delivery personnel can profoundly affect how well they manage and deliver services to all groups of society."

Under the leadership of Phil Rutledge, the work of the National Academy of Public Administration (NAPA)'s Standing Panel on Social Equity in Governance was instrumental in both developing a working definition of social equity and in incorporating a direct focus on social equity into NAPA's strategic plan. These actions were important in repositioning social equity research into the "mainstream" of the field. The panel's definition of social equity became a cornerstone in solidifying a shared understanding of the term within the field:

> The fair, just, and equitable management of all institutions serving the public directly or by contract, and the fair, just and equitable distribution of public services, and implementation of public policy, and the commitment to promote fairness, justice, and equity in the formation of public policy
> *(NAPA 2014)*

Additionally, NAPA's Board of Directors formally adopted social equity as the fourth pillar of public administration. As Wooldridge and Gooden explain:

> More recently, the case for social equity has been strengthened by the establishment of the Standing Panel on Social Equity in the year 2000 by the National Academy of Public Administration (the Academy) and by the Academy's 2005 strategic plan. Goal 2 of this plan states:
> The Academy's Board of Directors adopted social equity as the fourth pillar of public administration, along with economy, efficiency and effectiveness. To pursue social equity with the same success as it has pursued the other pillars, the Academy will:
>
> - Increase recognition of the Academy as a leader in social equity governance. The Academy will become a leader in defining social equity benchmarks, barriers and best practices.
> - Increase the diversity of Fellows and staff. The Academy will continue to diversify its Fellowship and Academy staff, and provide opportunities for minority and female professionals to serve as associates on panels, work groups and other initiatives.

- Improve the Academy's capacity to address social equity issues. To meaningfully pursue social equity with external audiences, the Academy will continue to build social and intellectual capital among Fellows, staff and clients.
- Pursue social equity concerns in studies and programs. The Academy will pursue social equity issues in its studies and programs. It will develop a series of papers and tools that outline operational and implementation approaches to do so.

(Wooldridge and Gooden 2009, 225)

This same panel developed four criteria for measuring social equity including quantitative and qualitative dimensions: procedural fairness, access, quality, and outcomes. These criteria were important in facilitating analysis beyond how much social inequity exists to considering *why* such inequity patterns remain entrenched:

Procedural fairness involves the examination of problems or issues of procedural rights (due process), treatment in a procedural sense (equal protection), and the application of eligibility criteria (equal rights) for existing policies and programs . . . Practices such as failure to provide due process before relocating low-income families as part of an urban renewal project, using racial profiling to identify suspects, or unfairly denying benefits to a person who meets eligibility criteria all raise obvious equity issues.

Access—distributional equity—involves a review of current policies, services, and practices to determine the level of access to services/benefits and analysis of reasons for unequal access . . . Equity can be examined empirically—do all persons receive the same service and the same quality of service . . . or normatively—should there be a policy commitment to providing the same level of service to all?

Quality—process equity—involves a review of the level of consistency in the quality of existing services delivered to groups and individuals . . . For example, is garbage pickup the same in quality, extent of spillage or missed cans, in all neighborhoods? Do children in inner-city schools have teachers with the same qualifications as those in suburban schools?

Outcomes involve an examination of whether policies and programs have the same impact for all groups and individuals served . . . Equal results equity might conceivably require that resources be allocated until the *same results* are achieved . . . a critical issue in consideration of equity at this level is how much inequality is acceptable and to what extent government can and should intervene to reduce the inequality in results.

(Johnson and Svara 2011, 20–22)

Following NAPA's adoption of social equity as the fourth pillar of public administration, social equity scholarship gained increasing momentum within the field. In his 2001 presidential address at the Association of Public Policy Analysis and Management (APPAM), Samuel L. Myers, Jr. cited concern for the paucity of curriculum and training in race and ethnicity analysis at public affairs schools. One important factor that may contribute to the persistence of social inequity is lack of social equity education and training provided by graduate programs in public affairs education (Myers 2002). To assess this factor, Gooden and Myers co-edited a symposium of the *Journal of Public Affairs Education* (*JPAE*) to examine what students know of social equity and what they should know (2004, 91). The articles suggested that the performance of public affairs education warranted improvement. For example, in examining introductory courses in public administration, Svara and Brunet (2004, 104) found "[s]tudents are not likely to find the phrase 'social equity' in introductory public administration books."

How Is Accountability for Social Equity Achieved?

Promoting social equity assessment and accountability of public agencies is an important challenge for public administration. Although the "E" of equity represents a pillar of public administration, it is largely absent in terms of agency accountability. Ideally, accountability in government offers the promise of democracy, justice, ethical behavior, and performance (Dubnick 2005). Johnson and Svara (2011) contend that much work remains in expanding the scope and commitment to advance social equity. To this end, they identify seven specific ways to improve performance and accountability. First, they suggest that public administrators speak out "by clearly identifying the aspects of social equity problems that are attributable to policy commissions or omissions" (p. 275). As they further explain, "public administrators should promote equal distribution, compensatory redistribution, and efforts to correct past discrimination, depending upon the nature of the problem being addressed" (p. 276). Second, the need for public administrators to employ "imaginative and targeted outreach that makes affirmative efforts to reach underserved or high need groups is imperative" (pp. 276–277). Third, "public administrators have the authority and the obligation to promote process equity—equal access and opportunity, equal treatment and protection, and due process" (p. 277). Fourth, "public administrators can give issues of fairness the same creativity and attention they give to measuring performance and improving productivity . . . Attention to equity can be added to assessment of programs that may be contracted out and monitor service delivery" (p. 278). Fifth, "public administrators need to measure social equity and track progress in alleviating disparities" (p. 278). This follows the concept that "what gets measured gets done." Sixth, "public administrators must take proactive and creative action to ensure that all people, regardless of resources or individual characteristics, have a place at the table when needs are identified, policy options discussed, and programs and services assessed" (p. 278). Finally, "public administrators must build partnerships with other organizations and the community to address equity issues" (p. 278).

Emblematic of this guidance, a leading pioneer in promoting accountability in social equity is the City of Seattle. As prominently stated on the City of Seattle's website:

> The Seattle Race and Social Justice Initiative (RSJI) is a citywide effort to end institutionalized racism and race-based disparities in City government. RSJI builds on the work of the civil rights movement and the ongoing efforts of individuals and groups in Seattle to confront racism. The Initiative's long term goal is to change the underlying system that creates race-based disparities in our community and to achieve racial equity.
>
> *(Seattle.gov n.d.)*

There are at least three important aspects of the Seattle RSJI. First, it is an initiative designed by local government to eliminate institutional racism in the provision of local government services. The City of Seattle is acknowledging that institutional racism exists in the services they provide and that the city is committed to its elimination. Second, the RSJI has been actively sustained since its inception in 2004, despite leadership changes at the highest levels of local government. Third, the RSJI is having a significant impact, with specific performance improvements both within the City of Seattle and among local governments throughout the United States. Some examples of accomplishments in Seattle RSJI are shown in the list below. Additionally, the City of Seattle hosts an annual Governing for Racial Equity conference designed to promote equity and accountability by local governments.

- Boiler inspectors from the Department of Planning and Development carry translation cards to help them conduct boiler inspections with business owners who speak little or no English.
- The Department of Information Technology surveyed Seattle residents' use of the internet, cell phones, and other technology, and analyzed the information by race and ethnicity. Tracked over time, the City will use these measures to improve customer services, shape the City's information technology systems, and increase communities of color's access to new technologies.
- The Seattle Office for Civil Rights released the results of fair housing testing in 2011 that revealed widespread racial discrimination in housing application procedures. Six property managers were charged with illegal discrimination based on the test results.
- The City Attorney's Office now seeks sentences of 364 days (rather than 365 days) for gross misdemeanors, thereby avoiding a potential deportation trigger

under federal law for any non-citizen. The Washington State Legislature followed Seattle's example and instituted the same policy across the state. The City Attorney's Office also assessed and made changes to laws having a disproportionate impact on communities of color. For example, the City Attorney discontinued prosecuting simple possession of marijuana, driving while license suspended, and third degree for non-payment, and drafted a new wage theft law adopted by the City Council and Mayor.

- The Office provides continuing legal education anti-racism training to lawyers throughout the community.
- The Office of Housing helped save the John C. Cannon House in the Central Area from foreclosure and maintained community-based ownership. Cannon House provides assisted living for Medicaid recipients, many of whom are African Americans.
- The Seattle Department of Transportation used a race and social justice lens to develop its Pedestrian Master Plan.
- The City of Seattle has more than tripled the use of women- and minority-owned business enterprises in non-construction goods and services since the Initiative began, from $11 million to $34 million.
- The City's Personnel Department wrote new rules to create more equitable out-of-class work opportunities for City employees. The City's Workforce Equity Committee developed best practices for filling out-of-class positions and trained supervisors to use best practices to achieve racial equity.
- The Seattle Fire and Police Departments are making concerted efforts to ensure communities of color are aware of recruiting, testing, and hiring opportunities.
- The City has reduced the number of unnecessary criminal background checks conducted as part of hiring processes. Background checks now occur only if they directly relate to the position being filed. The change was made to increase employment opportunities for people of color, who are disproportionately represented in the criminal justice system.
- Seattle Public Utilities has reduced the requirement for a college education in positions where a college degree is not actually necessary.
- The Seattle Fire Department and the Seattle Department of Transportation consider equity when giving overtime assignments. The Fire Department has rewritten its hiring and promotional interview questions to ensure that applicants recognize the diversity of the community.
- Seattle City Light has incorporated the RSJI in its succession planning to reduce racial disparities among management, professional, and line staff.
- Over 8,000 City employees have participated in RSJI training, including training in inclusive outreach and public engagement. Most departments have trained all their employees.
- In an RSJI Employee Survey in October 2010, 83 percent of the 5,200 respondents said they believe it is valuable to examine the impact of race, and

over 3,000 employees stated they are actively involved in promoting RSJI changes in their workplace.

- All City departments have Change Teams that support implementation of departments' annual work plans. A Core Team works across departments on citywide issues.
- The Office of Arts and Cultural Affairs' smART ventures and neighborhood/community arts funding programs create cultural bridges with communities of color—65 percent of the funding goes to underserved communities. The Office of Arts and Cultural Affairs also works with partnering agencies to sponsor community outreach.
- The Department of Planning and Development partners with communities of color to review the department's website. User groups review, test, and give input to determine final website design.
- Policies first introduced in 2007 require all City departments to provide free language interpretation to customers on request, and to develop translations of key service information in the six most common languages spoken by Seattle residents.
- The Department of Neighborhoods uses Public Outreach Liaisons to engage underrepresented communities in civic processes. Bilingual and bicultural advocates work directly with immigrant and refugee communities and other under-represented groups to increase access to information about community events and provide language interpretation at the events themselves.
- Translated documents about City services extend to the City's website, which offers program and service information in thirty languages. The Seattle Channel web site offers videos in Spanish, Cantonese, Mandarin, and Vietnamese on residential recycling, food and yard waste, and how to recycle electronic equipment.

(Data derived from Seattle Office for Civil Rights, RSJI n.d.)

On the federal level, in February 2014, the Obama Administration announced the "My Brother's Keeper Initiative" focused on young men of color. Citing data that substantiate the magnitude of social inequities crossing education, economic, and criminal justice spheres, the Obama Administration explained:

> For decades, opportunity has disproportionately lagged behind for boys and young men of color—particularly in our African American and Latino communities. As recently as 2013, only 14 percent of black boys and 18 percent of Hispanic boys scored proficient or above on the 4th grade reading component of the National Assessment of Educational Progress compared to 42 percent of white boys and 21 percent of black and Hispanic girls. Youth who cannot read "proficiently" by third grade are four times less likely to graduate high school by 19. By the time students have reached 9th grade, 42 percent of black male students have been suspended or

expelled during their school years, compared to 14 percent of white male students. While black youth account for 16 percent of the youth population, they represent 28 percent of juvenile arrests, and 37 percent of the detained population. While just over 6 percent of the overall population, black males of all ages accounted for 43 percent of murder victims in 2011.

(Jarrett and Johnson 2014)

This interagency effort will work across executive departments and agencies to examine federal policies and programs of particular relevance to men of color, disseminate information through an online portal on promising programs and practices, and offer recommendations for sustainability.

These examples across levels of government suggest an increasing emphasis on performance accountability relative to social equity in public administration. These approaches also recognize that social inequities are structural; that is, they are heavily influenced by the cumulative impact of inter-institutional dynamics, institutional resource inequities, and historical legacies (Grant-Thomas and Powell 2006). They also recognize that social inequities do not operate in public policy silos. This means that the pattern of equity distribution is mutually compounding across multiple aspects of public policies. Environmental inequities affect health inequities, which affect educational inequities, which affect criminal justice inequities, and so forth. These inequities compound in predictable patterns and are maintained from generation to generation (Gooden 2014).

Additionally, equity is commonly framed as a compromiser of efficiency. As Myers (2002, 170) notes: "What is evident in our discipline, however, is the tension between the equity and efficiency criteria and the inherent trade-offs between the two." Similarly, Patton and Sawicki (1993, 204) contend: "In many instances programs that prove to be very efficient also prove to be very inequitable. The two criteria are seldom both maximized in the same program." More recently, return on investment studies suggest there are significant economic costs of social inequity to society (Norman-Major and Wooldridge 2011). For example, Anton and Temple (2007) performed a social return on investment study of youth intervention programs in Minnesota. A primary finding was that intervention programs aimed at "at-risk" youth can produce returns of up to fourteen dollars for every state dollar invested, realizing reduced costs in court costs, school dropout rates, adult crime prosecution, and expenditures on public assistance.

As Gooden and Portillo (2011, 169) explain:

> With few recent exceptions,[3] most social equity research in public administration focuses on a particular identity category, e.g., race/ethnicity and gender. . . . However, identities are often more complicated than this, encompassing characteristics such as sexual orientation, age, ability and education, and the ways in which these characteristics uniquely intersect for individuals.

Accountability for social equity is an important global concern as well. Human rights violations involving women, minorities, and children are far too common. "The constant technological advancements that shrink physical distance also transcend physical boundaries and will force an equity orientation that is by default regional and global, rather than jurisdictional or national" (Gooden and Portillo 2011, i72). Examining social equity issues in a comparative context will help to foster the identification of innovative approaches that can be shared across global public administration communities.

Conclusion

The quest to shorten the distance between the principle of equality and the performance of social equity is a continuous one. More than seventy-five years ago, the value of equality was largely rhetorical, with both formal policies and empirical practices based firmly in inequality. During the 1960s, there was a strong legal shift to equality, although empirical administrative practice lagged behind. During the 1980s, the emphasis on audit studies and discrimination testing were major steps forward in terms of providing statistical measures of inequity; however, the net impact in terms of sustained consequences was sporadic and uneven. The 2000s brought significant steps forward with equity being adopted as a core pillar of public administration, accompanied by an increased emphasis on equity in the public administration profession, particularly in NAPA. Most recently (2010 and beyond), there is an emerging emphasis on performance measurement and accountability relative to social equity.

As Frederickson insightfully writes, "[s]ocial equity seldom stands still long enough to allow for conclusions" (2010, 133). The specific social equity challenges of public administrators today will differ from the challenges of tomorrow as progress continues, new areas of inequity gain traction, and outcomes are assessed:

> Central to the field, social equity is several things: It is a habit of mind for the decision maker, and it is an administrative goal that can be measured. It is also a lens through which needs are identified and processes are grounded. Before it dangles the promise of a fair and just society.
>
> *(Guy and McCandless 2012, 59)*

The sails of social equity in public administration are directed by a set of complex winds comprised of historical, political, economic, legal, and moral motivators that shape public policy formulation and administrative behavior. In each instance, the democratic principle of equality is the common, steadfast anchor that strengthens our social equity work.

Notes

1 A committee of the Division of Behavioral and Social Sciences and Education of the National Research Council of the National Academies.
2 See, for example, Blau (1970, 1974) and Schein's (1985) examination of the importance of culture and norms in organizations, as well as Lipsky's (1980) examination of the importance of administrative discretion exercised by the street-level bureaucrat in determining a client's "life chances" particularly for low-income individuals.
3 See, for example, Bearfield 2009.

References

Anton, P.A., and J. Temple. 2007. *Analyzing the Social Return on Investment in Youth Mentoring Progress: A Framework for Minnesota.* St. Paul, MN: Wilder Research, March.

Bearfield, Dominic A. 2009. "Equity at the Intersection: Public Administration and the Study of Gender." *Public Administration Review* 69(3): 383–386.

Blau, Peter. 1970. "A Formal Theory of Differentiation in Organizations." *American Sociological Review* 35(2): 201–218.

———. 1974. *On the Nature of Organizations.* New York: John Wiley.

Bremer, Kamala, and Deborah A. Howe. 1988. "Strategies Used to Advance Women's Careers in the Public Service: Examples from Oregon." *Public Administration Review* 48(6): 957–961.

Bullard, Angela M., and Deil S. Wright. 1993. "Circumventing the Glass Ceiling: Women Executives in American State Governments." *Public Administration Review* 53(3): 189–202.

Daley, James, ed. 2006. *Great Speeches by African Americans.* New York: Dover.

Dubnick, Melvin. 2005. "Accountability and the Promise of Performance: In Search of the Mechanisms." *Public Performance & Management Review* 28(3): 376–417.

Fix, Michael, and Margery Austin Turner, eds. 1999. *A National Report Card on Discrimination in America: The Role of Testing.* Washington, DC: The Urban Institute.

———, George C. Galster, and Raymond J. Struyk. 1993. "An Overview of Auditing for Discrimination." In *Clear and Convincing Evidence: Measurement of Discrimination in America,* ed. M. Fix and R.J. Struyk, 1–49. Washington, DC: Urban Institute Press.

Frederickson, H. George. 1971. "Toward a new public administration." In *Toward a New Public Administration: The Minnowbrook Perspective,* ed. Frank Marini, 309–331. Scranton, PA: Chandler.

———. 1980. *New Public Administration.* Tuscaloosa, AL: University of Alabama Press.

———. 1990. "Public Administration and Social Equity." *Public Administration Review* 50: 228–237.

———. 2005. "The State of Social Equity in American Public Administration." *National Civic Review* 94(4): 31–38.

———. 2010. *Social Equity and Public Administration.* Armonk, NY: M.E. Sharpe.

Galster, George C. 1993. "Use of Testers in Investigating Discrimination in Mortgage Lending and Insurance." In *Clear and Convincing Evidence: Measurement of Discrimination in America,* ed. M. Fix and R. J. Struyk, 287–334. Washington, DC: Urban Institute Press.

Gooden, Susan T. 2010. "Social Equity in Public Administration: The Need for Fire" in *The Future of Public Administration around the World,* ed. Rosemary O'Leary, David M. VanSlyke, and Soonhee Kim, 53–57. Washington, DC: Georgetown University Press.

———. 2014. *Race and Social Equity: A Nervous Area of Government.* Armonk, NY: M.E. Sharpe.

———, and Samuel Myers, Jr. 2004. "Social Equity in Public Affairs Education." *JPAE* 10(2): 91–97.

———, and Shannon Portillo. 2011. "Advancing Social Equity in the Minnowbrook Tradition." *Journal of Public Administration Research and Theory* 21: 61–76.

Grant-Thomas, Andrew, and John A. Powell. 2006. "Toward a Structural Racism Framework." *Poverty & Race* (November/December). www.prrac.org/full_text.php?text_id=1095&item_id=10188&newsletter_id=90&header=Symposium:%20Structural%20Racism (accessed June 8, 2014).

Guy, Mary E., and Sean McCandless. 2012. "Social Equity: Its Legacy, Its Promise." *Public Administration Review* 72(Special Issue): 5–13.

Hochschild, Jennifer L. 1995. *Facing Up to the American Dream: Race, Class and the Soul of the Nation.* Princeton, NJ: Princeton University Press.

Jarrett, Valerie, and Broderick Johnson. 2014. "My Brother's Keeper: A New White House Initiative to Empower Boys and Young Men of Color." *The White House Blog*, February 27. www.whitehouse.gov/blog/2014/02/27/my-brother-s-keeper-new-white-house-initiative-empower-boys-and-young-men-color (accessed July 16, 2014).

Jefferson, Thomas. 1944. "Autobiography." In *The Life and Selected Writings of Thomas Jefferson*, ed. Adrienne Koch and William Peden, 3–114. New York: Random House.

Johnson, Norman J., and James H. Svara, eds. 2011. *Justice for All: Promoting Social Equity in Public Administration.* Armonk, NY: M.E. Sharpe.

Kelly, Rita Mae, Mary E. Guy, Jane Bayes, Georgia Duerst-Lahti, Lois Duke, Mary M. Hale, Cathy Johnson, Amal Kawar, and Jeanie Stanley. 1991. "Public Managers in the States: A Comparison of Career Advancement by Sex." *Public Administration Review* 51(5): 402–412.

Kim, Pan Suk, and Gregory Lewis. 1994. "Asian Americans in the Public Service: Success, Diversity, and Discrimination." *Public Administration Review* 54(3): 285–290.

Kim, Soonhee, Rosemary O'Leary, David M. Van Slyke, H. George Frederickson, and W. Henry Lambright. 2010. "Introduction: The Legacy of Minnowbrook." In *The Future of Public Administration around the World: The Minnowbrook Perspective*, ed. S. Kim, R. O'Leary, D.M. Van Slyke, H. G. Frederickson, and W. H. Lambright, 1–16. Washington, DC: Georgetown University Press.

Lewis, Gregory B. 1988. "Progress toward Racial and Sexual Equality in the Federal Civil Service." *Public Administration Review* 48(3): 700–707.

———. 1994. "Women, Occupations, and Federal Agencies: Occupational Mix and Interagency Differences in Sexual Inequality in Federal White-Collar Employment." *Public Administration Review* 54(3): 271–276.

———. 1997a. "Lifting the Ban on Gays in the Civil Service: Federal Policy toward Gay and Lesbian Employees since the Cold War." *Public Administration Review* 57(5): 387–395.

———. 1997b. "Race, Sex, and Performance Ratings in the Federal Service." *Public Administration Review* 57(6): 479–489.

———, and Cheryl Lynn Allee. 1992. "The Impact of Disabilities on Federal Career Success." *Public Administration Review* 52(4): 389–397.

Lipsky, Michael. 1980. *Street-Level Bureaucracy: Dilemmas of the Individual in Public Services.* New York: Russell Sage Foundation.

Mani, Bonnie G. 1999. "Challenges and Opportunities for Women to Advance in the Federal Civil Service: Veterans' Preference and Promotions." *Public Administration Review* 59(6): 523–534.

Miller, Will, Brinck Kerr, and Margaret Reid. 1999. "A National Study of Gender-Based Occupational Segregation in Municipal Bureaucracies: Persistence of Glass Walls?" *Public Administration Review* 59(3): 218–230.

Myers, Samuel L. Jr. 2002. "Analysis of Race as Policy Analysis." *Journal of Policy Analysis and Management* 21(2): 169–190.

Naff, Katherine C. 1994. "Through the Glass Ceiling: Prospects for the Advancement of Women in the Federal Civil Service." *Public Administration Review* 54(6): 507–514.

NAPA. 2014. "Social Equity in Governance." Accessed at www.napawash.org/fellows/standing-panels/social-equity-in-governance.html (accessed November 24, 2014).

National Research Council. 2004. *Measuring Racial Discrimination.* Washington, DC: The National Academies Press.

Newman, Meredith Ann. 1994. "Gender and Lowi's Thesis: Implications for Career Advancement." *Public Administration Review* 54(3): 277–284.

Norman-Major, Kristen, and Blue Wooldridge. 2011. "Using Framing Theory to Make the Economic Case for Social Equity: The Role of Policy Entrepreneurs in Reframing the Debate." In *Justice for All: Promoting Social Equity in Public Administration,* ed. Norman J. Johnson and James H. Svara, 209–227. Armonk, NY: M.E. Sharpe.

Patton, Carl V., and David S. Sawicki. 1993. *Basic Methods of Policy Analysis and Planning.* Upper Saddle River, NJ: Prentice Hall

Rawls, J. 1971. *A Theory of Justice.* Cambridge, MA: Harvard University Press.

Rice, Mitchell F. 2004. "Organizational Culture, Social Equity, and Diversity: Teaching Public Administration Education in the Postmodern Era." *JPAE* 10(2): 143–154.

Schein, Edgar. 1985. *Organizational Culture and Leadership.* San Francisco: Jossey Bass.

Schwemm, Robert G. 1990. *Housing Discrimination: Law and Litigation.* Deerfield, IL: Clark Boardman Callaghan.

Seattle Office for Civil Rights, RSJI. N.d. *Accomplishments 2009–2011.* Seattle, WA: Seattle. www.seattle.gov/documents/departments/rsji/rsjiaccomplishments2009-2011.pdf (accessed July 16, 2014).

Seattle.gov. N.d. "About RSJI." www.seattle.gov/rsji/about (accessed July 16, 2014).

Shafritz, J.M., and E.W. Russell. 2002. *Introducing Public Administration,* 3rd ed. Boston: Addison Wesley Longman.

Smith, J. Douglas. 2002. *Managing White Supremacy: Race, Politics, and Citizenship in Jim Crow Virginia.* Chapel Hill, NC: University of North Carolina Press.

Stone, Deborah. 1997. *Policy Paradox: The Art of Political Decision Making.* New York: W.W. Norton.

Svara, James, and James Brunet. 2004. "Filling in the Skeletal Pillar: Addressing Social Equity in Introductory Courses in Public Administration." *JPAE* 10(2): 99–109.

Turner, Margery Austin. 1992. "Discrimination in Urban Housing Markets: Lessons from Fair Housing Audits." *Housing Policy Debate* 3(2): 185–215.

——, Raymond J. Struyk, and John Yinger. 1991. *Housing Discrimination Study: Synthesis.* Washington, DC: U.S. Department of Housing and Urban Development.

Vertz, Laura L. 1985. "Women, Occupational Advancement, and Mentoring: An Analysis of One Public Organization." *Public Administration Review* 45(3): 415–423.

Williams, Frances Harriet. 1947. "Minority Groups and OPA." *Public Administration Review* 7(2): 123–128.

Wooldridge, Blue, and Susan Gooden. 2009. "The Epic of Social Equity: Evolution, Essence, and Emergence." *Administrative Theory and Praxis* 31(2): 225–237.

Yinger, John. 1986. "Measuring Discrimination with Fair Housing Audits: Caught in the Act." *American Economic Review* 76(December): 881–893.

———. 1991. "Acts of Discrimination: Evidence for the 1989 Housing Discrimination Study." *Journal of Housing Economics* 1(December): 318–346.

———. 1998. "Evidence on Discrimination in Consumer Markets." *Journal of Economic Perspectives* 12(2): 23–40.

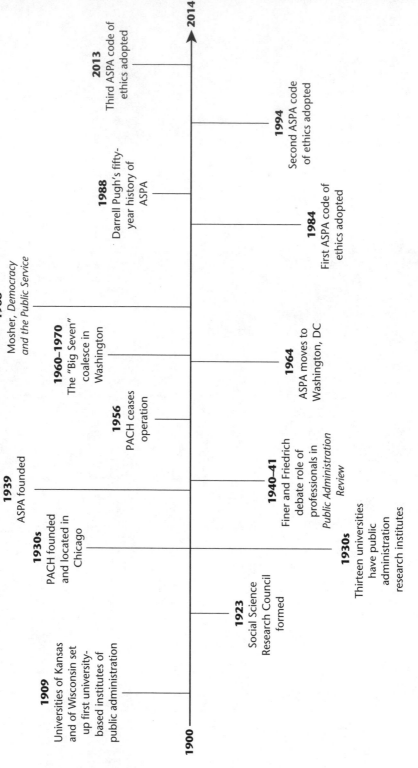

FIGURE 11.1 Seventy-Five Years of Professionalization: Benchmarks across Time

11

SEVENTY-FIVE YEARS OF PROFESSIONALIZATION

Jeremy F. Plant

In December 1939, as soldiers of the British, French, and German armies settled into winter quarters for the so-called "Phony War" in Europe, a select group of academicians, public officials, and association executives met at the Wardman Park Hotel in Washington, DC, to put in motion the final steps necessary to create the American Society for Public Administration (ASPA). This would be the first organization designed to bring together under one inclusive umbrella the various audiences concerned with professional public administration. Despite the menacing international situation, the mood was one of optimism. Public administration was seemingly poised to become recognized as a professional field comparable to the established professions of law, medicine, and accountancy, to name the most obvious counterparts. Public administration was still understood to be different, as will be discussed below, but the years preceding the formation of ASPA at the cusp of the new decade had seen changes that made the sense of optimism also realistic: new academic graduate programs that had already begun populating agencies at all levels of government; growth in the role of government under the leadership of progressive presidents from Theodore Roosevelt to the incumbent, Franklin D. Roosevelt; constructive dialogue between public administration and its cognate fields and disciplines in the social sciences, in particular its "mother discipline" political science; the growing literature in the field that spoke across sectors to both its academic and practitioner audiences; and a plethora of associations representing the professional interests and needs of specific groupings of public officials. The time was right, it seemed, to pull the strands together in the name of an over-arching vision of public administration as a field of diverse study and professional practice.

Seventy-five years later, ASPA perseveres, albeit in a vastly altered context. The centrifugal tendencies that ASPA hoped to counteract in 1939 have changed, but the dynamic is similar: the more concentrated attractions of one's specific affiliation often trump the call of the broader but more distant general identification with public service professionalism. In the academic world, the desire for more sophisticated research clashes with the needs of practitioners for timely and grounded research for immediate application. Growth in the roles of government continues, but often by utilizing indirect measures of administration through contracting, public–private partnerships, and other forms of collaboration that have altered the role of public managers. Associations representing public officials have proliferated, moving away from a strictly professional development orientation to one that provides services to individual members on the one hand or lobbies for public policies on the other.

Professionalism has been a concept that has proven difficult over time for Public Administration (PA) to accept and absorb. PA has always assumed it is a professional field—but is it? Should PA follow the lead of Dwight Waldo, who in 1968 advised it to "act as if it is a profession" even if it lacked many of the attributes of more established professions such as law, medicine, and the ministry? Should it emulate those professional fields and work to develop clear standards for educating, testing, certifying, and disciplining its members, or accept a more loosely coupled sense of professional identity? Is public administration too general or too diverse a field of action to form the basis of a single professional identity, and, if so, should it recognize the pluralism of its professionalism and embrace the range of professions found in public service careers and organizations? Does it really matter to public service professionals or to stakeholders and society at large how these questions are addressed and resolved?

Writing in 2009, James Svara offered this view of professionalism in governance:

> Public professionalism is the overarching knowledge, values, and standards of practice that apply to serving society and advancing the public interest and to securing sound, democratic governance. The knowledge, values, and standards are shaped by and apply to the professionals of governance and are relevant to the other professionals in government who are less likely to see the big public picture from their more specialized organizational vantage point.
>
> *(p. 1037)*

Although the context of governance has changed profoundly in the past seventy-five years, the founders of ASPA defined public professionalism in an analogous manner. William Mosher, a key figure in the formation of ASPA, noted a similar set of factors: a foundation of shared knowledge, techniques, and skills; a sense of community and pride in belonging; an ethical code; and a set of values that puts the interest of the public above self-interest (Mosher 1938, 333). Knowledge, values, and standards of practice—these have remained the bases of professionalism since the inception of public administration as a self-aware field of study and practice.

This chapter reviews the role that professionalism and public official associations have played in governance since 1939, with particular emphasis on ASPA. ASPA is central to the discussion because it represents one model of professional identification for public administration, a challenging and risky one: an inclusive, membership-based association bringing together in one place academicians, students, and practitioners of a field lacking the strict licensing requirements of more established professions. From the outset, this model has been challenged by three competing visions: an academy of the elite, self-selected and chartered to speak for the profession; a dispersed grouping of specialized associations organized around specific job categories or occupational training; or a collaborative grouping of associations concerned primarily with advancing the policy preferences of units or levels of government, with membership on an institutional rather than individual basis.

Before moving forward it is important to identify the state of the field of public administration in 1939, in particular the associations that had been formed to advance the field in the years before the formation of ASPA and the sense of professionalism that provided common ground for their activities and aspirations.

Public Official Associations and Professionalism in Public Administration at ASPA's Founding

It is no exaggeration to say that from its earliest beginnings, recognition as a profession, with the status and influence that inheres in such identification, was a goal of the emergent field of public administration. How to develop a shared sense of the competencies, attitudes, values, and relationships necessary for professional identity became a major question for those advancing the art and science of public administration. As Chester Newland notes, the attraction of science and the scientific method was seen as part of a broader social awakening to the needs of society:

> Expert practitioners and academicians were nourished by discipline—and almost from the beginnings their expertise as associated with a strong though too-simple belief in positive science as the vehicle to ride the one best way. But in those early days disciplined expertise was rarely a cause of or excuse for alienation from political and civic leaders of reform. Expertise was associated with positive science; professionalism was associated with civic duty and public service; and both were deemed essential to political reform and associated changes in government and business.
>
> *(Newland 1994, 1x)*

Universities were critical not just for educating individuals for professional careers, but also as institutions that could provide the funding and support for a range of professional activities and enterprises. Three sorts of support for professional public administration grew out of this reform period. First, several public universities set up university-based research institutes, beginning with the Universities of Kansas and Wisconsin in 1909. By 1931 thirteen university-based bureaus or institutes focusing on public administration were in operation (Arnold and Plant 1994, 56). Second, universities gradually developed curricula in public administration. The Master of Public Administration (MPA) degree was the generalist degree that originated in this era, but more specialized curricula in fields such as planning, public health, public works, and public finance were also spawned prior to our target year of 1939. Third, universities offered space and other forms of institutional support for public official associations, and often provided a means by which such groups could receive financial support from foundations and benefactors. The most important of these university–association partnerships was the support of the University of Chicago for the Public Administration Clearing House (PACH), a grouping of public official associations representing a variety of state and local officials, which is discussed in more detail later in the chapter.

Good-government groups—sometimes caricatured by their opponents as "Goo Goos"—played a vital role in the development of professional public administration. Four major types came into existence in the reform era: city good-government groups in large cities such as Cleveland, Baltimore, and Boston; national membership organizations devoted to reform causes such as the National Civil Service League and National Municipal League; research bureaus such as the New York Bureau of Municipal Research that applied basic research methods to address public problems and issues; and individually or institutionally membered public official associations. Only the last of these was still a major factor in public administration by the time that ASPA was founded.

Although they have received only occasional attention in the literature of public administration (Arnold and Plant 1994; Bowen 1973; Farkas 1971; Haider 1974), public official associations represented the logical development of good-government groups and research bureaus, and they grew in numbers and professional activities in the first four decades of the twentieth century. Three leading figures in the maturation of public official associations were Louis Brownlow, Charles Merriam, and Luther Gulick. Brownlow, as an early convert to the profession of city management, worked to make the International City/County Management Association (ICMA) an exemplary public official association. Merriam was chair of the Political Science department at the University of Chicago and a leading figure not just in his home discipline but also in the full array of social sciences, which he helped coordinate through the formation of the Social Science Research Council in 1923. Gulick was Executive Director of the Institute of Public Administration, the successor to the New York Bureau of Municipal Research. In 1930, when plans were underway to coordinate the numerous public official associations under a common secretariat and support system, Gulick was chair of the Public Administration Committee of the Social Science Research Council. Together, and with funding from the Spelman Fund, Merriam, Gulick, and Brownlow came up with a plan to move those associations showing interest in coordination to the campus of the University of Chicago with the PACH providing central support. The goal was to advance the overall professionalization of the field by bringing what Barry Dean Karl called the existing "chaos of specifics" of reform together (Karl 1963, 9).

The Clearing House was a success, in part because it was able to funnel financing from the Spelman Fund to both the individual associations and to support PACH itself, and in large measure due to the leadership of Brownlow, who assumed the role of director of PACH. Throughout the 1930s, the Clearing House at 1313 East 60th Street in Chicago was the epicenter of efforts to create a professional focus for public administration, one heavily weighted toward the levels of government most affected by the reform movement: states and local government.

The Formation of ASPA

Why, then, was there a perceived need for the sort of central membership organization that became ASPA? Why not continue with the umbrella approach of PACH? One factor was location. Chicago was an ideal central location for associations of state and local officials, and it enjoyed propinquity with a great and supportive university. But the New Deal had led to a dramatic expansion of the role of the federal government, and many of the graduates of the new MPA programs were assuming roles in Washington and not as city managers or state budget officers. The growing prospects of involvement in the war possibly added to the sense that a national as well as state and local focus for public administration was necessary. A second factor was the inherent limitations of the umbrella approach. The Clearing House worked in large part because Brownlow knew not to step on the toes of the constituent groups. In his words:

> They [the association directors] worked together in such bodies as the Board of Directors of the Public Administration Service. They worked together well in smaller groups when matters came up of common interest. But I was always careful, extremely careful, not to attempt to bind them together in any way as a corporate body, and I was meticulous in observing their utter independence.
>
> (Brownlow 1958, 290)

At this point, two other key leaders stepped up to push for a new approach to a professional association of public administrators. Charles Beard of Columbia University was perhaps the best-known political scientist of the era, and over the course of many years had been sympathetic to and supportive of the growth of public administration as a profession and field of study. William Mosher, Dean of the Maxwell School at Syracuse University, was arguably the most respected academic leader in public administration and an advocate of a single, central association that could do for the field what he saw as essential for any discipline: hold annual conferences, support an academic journal, and foster a sense of common identity, values and ethics of the sort that characterized the more established professions. Mosher, who apparently was disappointed at being neglected by the Roosevelt administration as it developed close ties with other leading figures in public administration, may also have seen it as an opportunity to leave his mark on developments dominated up to then by Columbia and especially the University of Chicago. Also, many of the top graduates of Maxwell were filling professional positions in the federal government as the New Deal sought graduates of the new MPA programs.

Brownlow, representing the associations clustered around the PACH in Chicago, was greatly concerned about the sort of organization envisioned by Mosher (Pugh 1988, 19–20). As related by Darrell Pugh, much of Brownlow's opposition was based on what he saw as the professionalization of the field that would be fostered by ASPA: its establishment of professional standards, academic credentials (Brownlow himself was an autodidact without scholarly credentials), and other artifacts of professional groups. Although he softened to the idea as it became evident that ASPA would come into being, he did not embrace it the way he embraced the clearing house approach to public official representation. Nonetheless, he accepted the presidency of the association in 1943 and as Herbert Emmerich noted after Brownlow's passing in 1963 "to his last breath he remained its critical but devoted friend" (Emmerich 1963, 265).

From the outset, ASPA initiated activities designed to advance the professional character of the field. One thing that public administration lacked up to that time was a distinguished journal that would relate administrative theory to practice and serve to establish public administration as a serious academic and professional practice field. Up to then scholarship in the field was found in cognate discipline journals in political science and business administration, or in specialized journals associated with 1313 organizations. This need was answered with the creation of the *Public Administration Review* with a distinguished scholar/practitioner, University of Chicago professor and Civil Service Commissioner Leonard D. White, as the first editor-in-chief.

Along with the formation of a journal, the fledgling association agreed on two other basic activities: an annual conference and creation of local chapters. As a membership-based organization, its activities would be open only to those who chose to belong and pay dues to support the organization, distinct from public official associations whose membership was institutional in nature, as was the case with many of the 1313 associations.

Thus was laid the groundwork for the advancement of professionalism in the still loosely defined field of public administration. While the formation of ASPA was a success in the view of all concerned at the time, it also put in motion forces over time that would prove challenging as the context of higher education and governance changed. The assumption that ASPA could meet the needs both of practicing public officials and academicians did not foresee the changes in the social sciences that made the connection of theory and practice so problematic in the post-World War II decades. The idea that public service provided a common ground for individuals in a plethora of public sector occupations ran counter to the increasingly specialized nature of work in the expanding administrative state. The focus on professional managers and management did not fit with the increasing interest in public policy and intergovernmental relations in the postwar years. The assumption of common values uniting public officials discounted the turbulence as under-represented groups challenged the status quo. These centripetal forces, played out both in the context of public administration and within ASPA as an association, would prove eventful as ASPA and the field of PA evolved over the next seventy-five years.

Professionalism in Post-World War II Public Administration: Generalists, Specialists, and the Changing Context of Governance

Writing in 1949, Albert Lepawsky opined that "to establish more securely the educational, scientific, and professional status first of public administration and finally of administration generally is the main task now facing the study of administration" (Lepawsky 1949, 668). The task would not be easy, though. Lepawsky (p. 669) concludes his assessment of the "main risk" of professionalization of public administration in this way: "Their very professional perfection may intensify the atomism and specialism of modern life. On the other hand, by subscribing to humanitarian principles and sound values, they can become one of the most cohesive forces of modern civilization."

Lepawsky represented the thinking of a generation of younger scholars in the field who came of age in the 1930s and whose thinking on administration was forged in the crucible of total war. World War II drove changes that were profound and lasting, altering the context in which public administration operated and forcing changes in administrative practice that were nothing short of transformational. Looking back over the period from 1939 to 1949, Charles S. Ascher, president of ASPA in 1950, concluded:

> Certainly the war presented urgencies of size, complexity and speed that forced changes in administrative practice. The urgencies led to some unhappy improvisations, but they showed us, too, that some of our

> long-established mechanisms were not only inadequate but unnecessary. The prime fact is that we devised practices that helped win a war. But one may be permitted in reviewing trends to view these turbulences as eddies in a stream of evolving practices. Clearly, when the war was over public administration did not revert to 1939 . . . we confront a new configuration of administration.
>
> *(Ascher 1950, 249)*

The "new configuration" Ascher outlined included a number of inter-related developments that altered the field in the period he called "'From Brownlow Commission to Hoover Commission,' or 'From Reorganization Act of 1939 to Reorganization Act of 1949'" (Ascher 1950, 250). These changes included:

- greater importance of program planning and performance budgeting;
- recognition of the role that fiscal policy plays in budget preparations and overall policy direction;
- devolution of authority to line supervisors and movement of management more to lower levels of the hierarchy;
- introduction of operations research and the promotion of administrative management as a set of skills and competencies;
- attention to administration as a social process;
- broader social involvement and seeking of advice from the public in public policy and administration;
- wider use of the social sciences in governance;
- "manful efforts" to improve legislative–executive relationship at all levels of the federal system;
- growth in scope and importance of intergovernmental relations;
- integration of administrative structure while at the same time proliferation of programs and responsibilities;
- humanization of management, moving from formal to informal approaches;
- coordination as the key problem in the complex world of postwar domestic and international affairs.

Ascher's description of changes between 1939 and 1949 highlight in detail the basic question facing public administration at mid-century: would the field of administration be dominated by generalists with a broad view of the role of government in society and general administrative responsibility, the sort of new professionals produced by MPA programs and given far-reaching discretionary authority during the war; or would it represent the specialized professional landscape wrought by the proliferation of new programs, the rise of the social sciences and their tendency toward specialized knowledge and disciplinary siloes. Lepawsky's concluding question echoed this theme: professionalization was inevitable in the postwar context; would it lead to a general profession of public administration or to a collection of separate, specialized professions needed to run the increasingly complex administrative state? On a personal level, would the professionals in public administration see themselves as broadly interested in and protective of the general public interest or see the world largely through the specifics of their varied backgrounds and programmatic responsibilities?

Public official associations were a critical factor in determining the direction professionalization would take in this new context. In particular, ASPA in the postwar years continued to support the ideal of public administration as a single field with a shared vision of professionalism. At a time when choices between careers in government or academia had not yet hardened, its leadership was drawn from professionals who often had experience in both sectors (Pugh 1988). But no matter how eminent these individuals were, some fundamental problems were evident almost from the outset of ASPA's operations and continued to plague the organization throughout the 1940s and 1950s. These included most prominently the role of local chapters vis-à-vis the national organization; financing; attracting and retaining members; and whether ASPA should be neutral or silent on policy issues or take positions on major issues of the day. Its broad and diverse base of membership, in particular its efforts to bridge theory and practice by appealing to practitioners and academics, led to Frederick Mosher's cogent assessment of its basic problem:

> [ASPA] has its feet planted firmly in both meadows—to a greater extent in the operative area than almost any other academic professional organization, and to a greater extent in the academic field than almost any of the associations of professional practitioners.
>
> *(Mosher 1956, 178)*

This problem, unique to ASPA among the associations promoting public administration and policy, would increasingly separate ASPA from the direction in which other public official associations were moving, toward policy advocacy and closer ties to federal agencies concerned with intergovernmental programs and issues.

From Professionalism to Policy: Changing Directions of Public Official Associations

In 1956, amid declining funding from its principal funding source, the Spelman Fund, the PACH was terminated. The constituent associations survived and began to assume more autonomy as their existence required them to assume separate staffs and functions. The executive directors of the associations assumed more importance with the passing of Brownlow's leadership through the Clearing House.

In the 1950s and 1960s, the split between specialized professional associations and those representing political and administrative generalists became pronounced, in large part a reflection of changes in the approach to governance that characterized policy in this period. The growth of federally funded intergovernmental programs skyrocketed, and with them the importance of program managers with specialized education and mindsets. The officials represented by the state, city, and county generalist organizations—mayors, city managers, governors, county executives, state legislators—felt that power was moving from central leadership institutions to alliances of specialists arrayed in specific program areas. To counter this centrifugal pull, the generalist associations hit upon a three-pronged strategy. First, develop strategic alliances with federal agencies sharing their generalist orientation, such as the Bureau of the Budget (later Office of Management and Budget) and the newly formed Advisory Commission on Intergovernmental Relations, set up in 1959 to help rationalize the plethora of intergovernmental programs set up in the postwar era. Second, create a coalition among the major generalist groups to push for policies strengthening the roles of mayors, city managers, governors, state legislators, and county executives in intergovernmental programming and policy. Third, relocate to Washington to be close to the action and act as lobby groups for policies favorable to the generalist perspective.

Now free from the clearing house idea of cooperation, the alliance of the major generalist associations was forged in the early 1960s by the executive directors of the so-called "Big Six" associations: the Council of State Governments, National Governors Association, National League of Cities, United States Conference of Mayors, ICMA, and National Association of County Officials. A seventh group, the National Conference of State Legislators, later joined the group, known then as the "Big Seven." Although it was also headquartered in Washington by 1964 and was clearly a generalist association, ASPA was not invited to join the grouping, presumably because it was more professionally than policy-oriented in its mission. Close communication between ASPA and the other associations, however, was facilitated by ASPA executive directors known and respected by the directors of the Big Seven.

The approach differed fundamentally from the clearing house approach to collaboration. The associations maintained total independence regarding leadership, staffing, strategy, and policy decisions. The alliance was strictly voluntary and informal. The term "network" was not used to describe such arrangements at the time, but the generalist coalition was very much a network of the sort without a central staff or budget or physical location. The glue for the coalition was a theory of the public interest shared by generalist officials at all levels of the system. As described by David Arnold and Jeremy Plant:

> The instruments of coalition building were the associations. The agents were the staff directors. The goal around which the unity was forged was policy designed to advance the interests of generalist officials systemwide: policy that would provide freedom and discretion for levels of government to make critical decisions on allocation of benefits, and that would be

designed in such a way that program officials would have to be accountable to elected officials and generalist executives. To keep the coalition unified, policies that would appeal to generalists at all levels of the system were sought, and those that favored one level over another were avoided.

(Arnold and Plant 1994, 98–99)

The best example of such a unifying policy was handed to the coalition by the Nixon administration: general revenue sharing, which was part of the Republican and Democratic party platforms in 1968 and which Nixon embraced as part of his strategy of overall executive control over agencies and programs, over the perceived dominance of specialized bureaucracies in program development and implementation.

The upshot of these developments, as noted by Donald Haider in 1974, was the almost complete transformation of the associations from groups promoting greater professionalism in government to lobby groups pushing for policies favoring generalist interests. The exception was ICMA, which unlike the other Big Six/Seven was membership-driven and more professional in its orientation. Its presence in the alliance was useful to the other groups to avoid any perception of a split in perspective among the municipal groups and to maintain some ties to the academic community.

The context of the 1960s and 1970s was conducive to maintaining the informal network of generalist groups. Ideological differences were less intense than in earlier or later periods of time, and elected and executive officials at all levels of the federal system felt under attack from the rise of specialized professionals in new program areas. The associations did not have to deal with the divisive issues that continued to plague ASPA: differences between and among the local chapters, and between chapters and the national association, on policy questions; financing based on a membership base that was volatile due to its diverse nature and competition with more specialized professional membership groups; and ASPA's leadership approach, which favored elected leaders over staff directors. Given these fundamental differences, ASPA was not perceived as a relevant partner in the Big Six/Seven coalition effort. ICMA instead became the facilitator of interactions between the Big Seven groups and ASPA, the Network of Schools of Public Policy, Affairs, and Administration (NASPAA), and the National Academy of Public Administration (NAPA) in the 1970s and 1980s.

One result was the growing distance between the generalist groups and academic public administration that was almost inevitable once the connection to higher education through the Clearing House/University of Chicago ties was severed. A second result was a distancing of ASPA from groups that appeared to function primarily as lobbyists for policy goals. ASPA's unease with taking strong policy positions, and the lack of evidence that an organization with such a dispersed and diverse membership would have much clout, made it unlikely to be a strong player in the national policy arena. In the late 1960s, another profound difference emerged as ASPA was rocked by demands to be more democratic in its internal operations and more committed to goals of social equity and diversity, dynamics characteristic of a membership organization with leadership and decision-making protocols unlike those of the institutionally-based associations.

Professionalism Revisited: Mosher and the Professional State

As Waldo was pondering the issue of public administration as a profession, his friend and Berkeley colleague Frederick Mosher was putting the finishing touches on the first edition of his seminal 1968 book, *Democracy and the Public Service*. In this brief volume, Mosher presented a picture of professionalism somewhat at odds with the prevailing notion of professionalism in PA that dated back to the earlier period of the field's development. In that view, professionalism was guided by the small cadre of managers trained in MPA programs and employed largely as generalist line managers or the professional group within central staff support functions such as budgeting, planning, human resource management, and evaluation. Rather than seeing public administration as a bifurcation between professional managers and non-professional workers, Mosher described a much more nuanced and complex set of relationships within an increasingly professionalized federal service. No longer was the core group of MPA-educated administrators seen as the only professionals bringing wisdom and light to the less educated. Instead, Mosher drew a picture of federal service becoming dominated by those with a variety of professional degrees, often associated with the core work of a particular agency or program, with dynamic and often problematic relationships between line professions, staff professions, professions such as the military or the diplomatic corps wholly within government, and professions such as law, economics, and accounting found both in government service and in the private sector.

Mosher's book introduced the concept of public sector professionalism and it (in both its 1968 first edition and the second edition in 1982) remains today the gold standard of works on the topic. However, Mosher's analysis was also focused, at least explicitly, on the federal government. This limited the view of public professions by excluding an entire class of public service professions, those in at-will or market-based job categories such as city- and county-appointed managers, budget and human resource managers, school superintendents, chiefs of police and fire services, and others who owe their positions to professional qualifications but who are outside the tenured civil service system. Such jobs are, with only a few exceptions, not found in federal service, and hence were not part of Mosher's analysis.

Adding the at-will professions to the categories established by Mosher provides a first cut at categorizing professionals in government service into four distinct professional groups:

1. General PA professionals. This category includes those utilizing the traditional knowledge, skills, and values associated with MPA programs, in jobs that involve general management, budgeting, program planning and evaluation, human resource management, and other generalist job categories involving internal management concerns.
2. Public sector professionals. This grouping includes professionals with technical expertise in policy and program areas found only or predominantly in the public sector, including the military, public health, diplomacy, public safety and corrections, K–12 education, and other job categories that reflect the role of government in society.
3. Publicly employed professionals. These professionals work for and in public sector organizations but are members of professions that span the public and private sectors, such as government attorneys, accountants, physicians, scientists, and engineers. Given trends in third-party governance and contracting out, vast numbers are now employed in private, for-profit, and non-profit organizations that perform government work.
4. At-will professionals. As described above, individuals who owe their non-tenured appointment to professional expertise and not political or partisan biases, and who are not expected to be agents of elected officials in pursuing their agenda. Most are employed in county and municipal government. While similar in many respects to the other groupings, these individuals do not generally enjoy tenure in their positions and enjoy the benefits and costs of the more fluid nature of their pay and employment.

In addition to these government-based professionals, the field has embraced the non-profit sector in the years since the publication of *Democracy and the Public Service*. Professional non-profit and association managers are in many ways analogous to the at-will professionals found in local government, but larger non-profit organizations mirror the range of professions noted above in government service. Thus, these individuals may be seen as fitting into subcategories of the first and second groupings rather than constituting a completely distinct grouping. Applying these categories suggests that the earlier idea of a bifurcation of public professionals between generalists and specialists oversimplifies the realities of professionalism in public service occupations.

Adding to the complexity of professionalism confronting ASPA has been the growing importance of academicians in the membership and leadership of the organization. The earlier career model of spending time in both the world of practice and of academia shifted, with most academics finding it impossible to develop the record of research and publication necessary to survive in the university setting without making a full-time and permanent choice. As fewer academicians combined practice and scholarship, ASPA found itself increasingly divided between the benefits academicians saw in membership—conference presentations, academic journals supported by the association, elected leadership positions of prominence—and those favored by practitioners. This continues to be a challenge for ASPA. Many of the academicians active in ASPA see the benefits of strong practitioner involvement in conference panels, publications, and elected leadership positions in the Society. More research needs to be done to test whether the forces of cohesion among its diverse membership on which ASPA was predicated are still strong.

The Normative Challenge: Ethics, Diversity, and Social Equity

Sometimes pictures convey meaning more compellingly than words. Darrell Pugh's 1988 monograph *Looking Back, Moving Forward* provides a two-page spread of the first thirty-two presidents of ASPA. There is not a woman or person of color among them. What diversity exists consists of the institutional position held at the time of their presidency: eighteen hold positions in higher education, nine are practitioners, and five are working in private research institutes. But even this breakdown should be qualified, as many of the individuals had held positions in both government and higher education at some time in their careers, and many of the academicians held university administrative positions, including three university presidents. Many of the practitioners were contributors at some point to the literature of the field. They represented the great generalist tradition of U.S. public administration (notably, such distinguished émigrés as Fritz Morstein-Marx and Carl Friedrich were not among the ASPA leaders).

The group also represented two distinct generations of public administration professionals. A group of distinguished professionals represented the first generation of professionals who began careers in the first third of the century, including such luminaries as William Mosher, Harold Smith, Louis Brownlow, Luther Gulick, Charles Ascher, Leonard White, John Gaus, and Donald Stone. The majority of those were educated in the 1930s and 1940s and joined the professional field in the heady years of the New Deal, World War II, and the growth of government after the war. They shared a core belief in the value of government's role in society, in a general education in the field to assume gradually more responsible positions in public organizations, and identification with a profession of public administration that required a continuous dialogue between academia and the world of practice.

This bi-generational consensus was about to fracture in the late 1960s. Several factors converged to push ASPA into collision with social and intellectual drivers of change. Pugh (1988) provides an in-depth account of the turmoil within ASPA in the late 1960s and early 1970s. Much of it was driven by a new definition of professionalism characterized as New Public Administration:

> Whereas post World War II scholars of public administration had criticized
> the "orthodoxy" of the 1920s and 1930s, the young scholars of the New

Public Administration movement denounced the field's "over-emphasis" on positivism and scientism during the 1950s and 1960s. Furthermore, they advocated turning away from traditional issues such as planning, budgeting, and personnel, as well as techniques such as operations research. Instead, these New Public Administration scholars posited that public administration should be more relevant, client-focused, and anti-bureaucratic: that the study of public administration should center on issues of personal growth, interpersonal relations, group dynamics, morals, ethics, and values.

(Pugh 1988, 67)

Specific goals of the New Public Administration group within ASPA included two primary objectives: democratization of the nomination and elections process to select members of the National Council and the presidency; and inclusion of topics of contemporary relevance in the annual conference. Beginning with successful challenges to the slate of nominees for the National Council in 1969 and the holding of a "counter-conference" alongside the official annual conference in Philadelphia in 1970, the demands for a new vision of public professionalism coincided with demands in society for greater inclusiveness for under-represented groups. ASPA began to change, electing its first African-American president, Philip Rutledge, for the 1974–1975 term of office, and its first woman, Nesta Gallas, two years later. Between 1977 and 1988 two additional women and one other African-American man were elected to ASPA's top spot.

The more normative, internalized view of professionalism that was gaining momentum at this time also stimulated interest in ethics. Ethics and broader concerns for normative aspects of administrative life were seen by a growing number of public administrationists as fundamental to professional stature. Specifically, those advocating a greater role for ethics in public administration focused on three objectives: first, development of a code of ethics of general applicability to the field, and institutionalized in its general-membership organization, ASPA; second, greater attention to the subject of ethics in professional education and the literature of the field; and third, the creation of a section on ethics within ASPA to draw together those in the academic and practitioner communities concerned with spreading knowledge and practical wisdom on ethics.

It is not too much of an overstatement to say that these trends have led to a transformation not just of ASPA but also of the meaning of public service professionalism. Although the old order was forced to give way on all the aforementioned objectives, the victories exposed significant differences among those arguing for new approaches to the field. While risking oversimplification of a complex reality, it is possible to identify three distinct groups that emerged from the breakup of post-World War II orthodoxy: a group calling itself the ethics community, composed of scholars and practitioners focused on advancing the literature of public administration dealing with ethical issues and bringing ethical knowledge to bear on education of professionals and the application of ethical principles in the practice of public administration; the legatees of the New Public Administration movement, concerned less with ethics per se than the advancement of social equity and gains for under-represented and marginalized groups in society; and those interested in critical and post-modern theories whose main interest is in presenting a vision of public administration that is driven not by top-down technocratic processes but one that is guided by dialogue between professionals and citizens. Each of these groupings has found an institutional home within the profession. For the ethicists, it is the Ethics Section of ASPA. For those identified with social equity, it is the Standing Panel on Social Equity of the NAPA. For the critical theorists, it is the Public Administration Theory Network.

Taken together, these normative tectonic forces have redefined the field of public administration and the meaning of public professionalism. ASPA introduced its first code of ethics in 1984, followed by a fundamental revision in 1994 (Van Wart 1996). These efforts to codify ethical behavior focus on broad sources of ethics in public professionalism: putting public interest ahead of private gain; law and formal rules; personal integrity; organizational dynamics; and professionalism. What the ASPA code lacked was an element of enforcement, which many saw as necessary to a true sense of professionalism, and which one public sector leader, the ICMA, had long institutionalized.

A concern that the 1994 code no longer met the needs of ASPA members led to a third iteration of the code adopted in 2013, which is described in more detail in Chapter 12. Efforts were made successfully to involve not just a group of experts but ASPA members as a whole in the exercise. During the discussion of the code, a basic issue was raised: was the exercise designed to identify and support ethical conduct for ASPA members primarily, or was it a way of defining what it means to work ethically in public service occupations more generally? While not answered explicitly, the goal seemed to most to span both the needs of ASPA and to serve as a way of defining the ethical foundations of all public service work.

With the value of hindsight, it is clear that the ethics thrust was hindered by a lack of attention to the complexity of professionalism and professional identity in public administration. As in the early years of the twentieth century there was an implicit assumption of professional identity based more on government employment than the shared body of knowledge, values, and organizational infrastructure that characterizes fully developed and self-conscious professions. The burden of promoting ethical standards and conduct fell most heavily on MPA-trained generalists who would become agents of a more ethical and equitable approach, as in the New Public Administration model, or who would inject programs of ethical awareness and individual ethical competence and training into the work of public management, as in the field's more traditional ethicists espoused.

In short, what these changes collectively have meant is that to be a professional in a public service setting is to understand normative as well as technical demands of the job; to have a sense of ethical competency in dealing with situations that bring both technical and ethical challenges to bear; and to expect professional peers to have similar ethical education and competence. Earlier generations of public professionals felt less need to codify what they saw as public service values and ethical competence. In today's more complex milieu what was assumed and implicit now requires education, training, and the conscious application of ethical standards of conduct.

A Crowded Marketplace for Public Service Professionals

As the 1980s began, ASPA's membership peaked at slightly over 18,000 paid members. Since 1982, a steady decline has led to a loss of over half of that peak number, with ASPA's current membership holding steady at around 8,000. While each decision to join, leave, or rejoin the Society is individual in nature, both external and internal factors were at work driving these choices. Perhaps most significant was the crowded marketplace for public service professional associations. Both professional public administrators and academicians now have many choices before them beyond ASPA. As documented by Svara and Terry (2009, 1054), ASPA is now much smaller in membership than many other associations with public service professional membership, such as the American Public Works Association, the National Association of Social Workers, the International Public Management Association-Human Resources, and the International Association of Chiefs of Police. Perhaps more telling is the difference in membership between ASPA and the Federal Managers Association, which has more than double the membership of ASPA while competing directly for generalist federal managers. The dilemma faced by ASPA goes to the heart of what it means to be a generalist association serving public professionals, as the authors note:

> Is the function of the society to build trust, professional standards, and a commitment to governance within the confines of public administration scholarship and practice as an expressive association, or is the development of social capital and the achievement of objectives that bridge the instrumental organization to the broader community a priority? How does ASPA compete with specialized professional public official associations and with purely academic associations?
>
> *(Svara and Terry 2009, 1057)*

To compete in the crowded marketplace of associations, it is necessary to identify what added value membership provides to individuals and how best to attract and retain members. In short, it requires a strategic approach that sees threats and opportunities in the Society's environment and develops a plan to maximize opportunities. To its credit, ASPA recognized the need to address the future through a coordinated set of changes since 1990. It has simplified its leadership structure, strengthened the roles of elected executives and staff directors, provided more direct services to members, and engaged in strategic planning exercises designed to identify where the association needs to be to compete and collaborate with peer organizations. However, it still faces the reality that competing models pose attractive alternatives to its historic identity as a broad-based membership association bridging theory and practice. The notion of an elite organization self-selecting only the top professionals is filled by NAPA. Academicians in the field can choose between ASPA and the Association for Public Policy Analysis and Management or the Public Management Research Association, as well as associations in cognate disciplines. Many also participate in the NASPAA, which is not an individual-membership-based organization but which provides individuals with opportunities for conference presentations and involvement in professional accreditation and education in the field.

ASPA has addressed the generalist/specialist issue through the addition of sections, making it in a sense an umbrella organization that attracts individuals not just through a generalized interest in public service but one that also provides many of the attributes of specialized associations through section sponsorship of journals, newsletters, conference panels, and awards. ASPA currently sponsors twenty-eight sections of varying size and history. Most draw members from specialized interests in the field, both well-established professional areas such as budget and finance and human resource management and emerging areas of interest such as complexity studies and LGBT advocacy. Three of the sections promote diversity—the Conference of Minority Public Administrators; the Section on Women in Public Administration; and the LGBT Advocacy Alliance Section—and three represent international regions, Korea, China, and the Middle East.

Although the growth of sections has allowed ASPA to provide some services of an umbrella organization, section development has been largely left to members advocating new sections rather than a strategic or holistic approach to creating a true umbrella approach. Sections vary in terms of what they offer members and what they charge in dues. Perhaps the greatest challenge sections face is recruiting and retaining members whose interest is largely in the specialized section and not in the generalist approach of ASPA per se. With few exceptions, sections have been losing members in the past decade despite efforts to provide value through journal subscriptions, conference events, and section awards. Many based on occupational categories find strong competition from other associations geared entirely to membership of specialists, who may find it unnecessary to invest also in ASPA membership.

ASPA's generalist orientation lives on through geographically-based chapters. Here, as in the case of sections, the decline in participation has affected local chapters. Only five states—California, Florida, New York, North Carolina, and Texas—have more than two chapters, while another five have two apiece. Of the fifty states, thirty-two have active chapters as does the District of Columbia. There is also an International chapter, and the three aforementioned regionally-based sections pursue general governance issues. ASPA also provides the highly respected magazine *The Public Manager* to members to provide a generalist publication that relates to the needs of practitioner members who find the *Public Administration Review* largely devoted to academic research.

As interest in sections and chapters dwindles, ASPA has focused on individualized benefits of membership and up-to-date ways of communicating with members. In keeping with the range of value-added products and services provided by other associations, ASPA provides job listings, webinars, an electronic newsletter, email alerts, and credit card and insurance programs. While the annual conference and sponsored publications such as *Public Administration Review* and *PA Times* remain the most common ways members connect with the Society, it strives to find ways to provide value in keeping with changes in the field.

ASPA leadership has also embraced the need for collaboration with other associations, both in the United States and internationally. Both elected leaders and executive directors have developed links to groups with shared interests, even if such organizations are in other respects competitors in the association marketplace. For example, in recent years ASPA's executive director has been an active member of a grouping of discipline-based associations concerned with public service education (Plant 2009, 1047–1048). Largely through the efforts of ASPA, elected executives' connections have been made with non-U.S.-based associations that share public service values and interests. Such efforts and the growing body of research and writing shared between U.S. and international scholars and practitioners are indications that public service professionalism in the future will be defined in large measure by understanding of not just domestic policies and programs but also those that are international or global in character.

Conclusion: ASPA and the Ideal of Public Service

What makes public service a profession? What are its defining characteristics and shared identity? Is it best seen as a single profession with specialties, such as law or medicine, or a collection of separate professional fields loosely joined around concepts of public service and the public interest? Is it possible for an association such as ASPA to find enough common ground to link the diverse elements of professionalism in governance?

Professionalism wherever found requires a community of peers to flourish and function. This explains the desire to associate in generalist organizations such as ASPA that serve to advance a broad vision of public professionalism. But the desire for involvement in specific occupational areas within public service runs counter to this, giving rise to more and more specialized professional groupings and associations to bind them together. In this regard public administration seen as a general profession has been less able to establish and institutionalize itself than other more established professional fields such as law, medicine, and engineering. The quandary that professional associations create for public administration is the sheer number, variety, and nature of associations representing public professionals. In this regard the plethora of associations and the inability of any single association such as ASPA to speak for and define professionalism in public service reflect the changing nature of governance.

The history of public professionalism in the past three-quarters of a century suggests that these dilemmas will never be resolved. This may be of great benefit to the field of public administration and those that labor in its vineyards. The essence of all professional life is the constant challenge of employing knowledge, ethical norms, and standards of practice to unique situations, usually with great consequences for those affected by such action. Professionalism requires responsible action, as Carl Friedrich noted in 1940, and nothing since then has altered this basic truth.

Public official associations began as a way of connecting the pioneer professionals in the field, often the first or only individuals educated in the early MPA programs or schooled in the reform movement to see public service as a field of professional endeavor. They have evolved over time to advocate public policy positions, certify professional or ethical competence, and share research findings. The challenge they face is to remain relevant to professionals as they wrestle with serving the public in a globalized, networked, and often distrustful governance setting. The issues change, but the need for professionalism in service to the public remains steady.

References

Arnold, David S. and Jeremy F. Plant. 1994. *Public Official Associations and State and Local Government: A Bridge across One Hundred Years.* Fairfax, VA: George Mason University Press.

Ascher, Charles S. 1950. "Trends of a Decade in Administrative Practice." *Public Administration Review* 10(4): 249–255.

Bowen, Don L., ed. 1973. *Public Service Professional Associations in the Public Interest.* Philadelphia: American Academy of Political and Social Science.

Brownlow, Louis A. 1958. *A Passion for Anonymity.* Chicago: University of Chicago Press.

Emmerich, Herbert. 1963. "Louis Brownlow and the American Society for Public Administration." *Public Administration Review* 23(4): 265–267.

Farkas, Suzanne. 1971. *Urban Lobbying: Mayors in the Federal Arena.* New York: New York University Press.

Friedrich, Carl J. 1940. "Public Policy and the Nature of Administrative Responsibility." *Public Policy* 1: 1–20.

Haider, Donald. 1974. *When Governments Come to Washington: Governors, Mayors, and Intergovernmental Lobbying.* New York: Free Press.

Karl, Barry Dean. 1963. *Executive Reorganization and Reform in the New Deal.* Cambridge, MA: Harvard University Press.

Lepawsky, Albert. 1949. *Administration: The Art and Science of Organization and Management.* New York: Alfred A. Knopf.

Mosher, Frederick C. 1956. "Research in Public Administration: Some Notes and Suggestions." *Public Administration Review* 16(Summer): 169–178.

——. 1968. *Democracy and the Public Service*. New York: Oxford University Press.

Mosher, William E. 1938. "Public Administration: The Profession of Public Service." *The American Political Science Review* 32(2): 332–342.

Newland, Chester A. 1994. "Foreword." In *Public Official Associations and State and Local Government: A Bridge across One Hundred Years*, ed. David S. Arnold and Jeremy F. Plant, vii–xiii. Fairfax, VA: George Mason University Press.

Plant, Jeremy F. 2009. "Good Work, Honestly Done: ASPA at 70." *Public Administration Review* 69(6): 1040–1049.

Pugh, Darrell L. 1988. *Looking Back, Moving Forward: A Half-Century Celebration of Public Administration and ASPA*. Washington, DC: American Society for Public Administration.

Svara, James H. 2009. "Introduction to the Symposium: The Nature of Public Professionalism and the Future of ASPA." *Public Administration Review* 69(6): 1037–1039.

——, and Larry D. Terry II. 2009. "The Present Challenges to ASPA as an Association That Promotes Public Professionalism." *Public Administration Review* 69(6): 1050–1059.

Van Wart, Montgomery. 1996. "The Sources of Ethical Decision Making for Individuals in the Public Sector." *Public Administration Review* 56(6): 525–533.

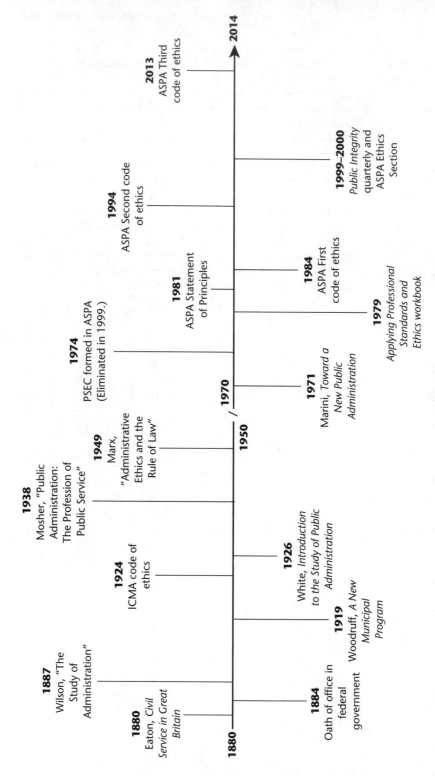

FIGURE 12.1 From Ethical Expectations to Professional Standards: Benchmarks across Time

12

FROM ETHICAL EXPECTATIONS
TO PROFESSIONAL STANDARDS[1]

James H. Svara

It is entirely appropriate to view ethics in public administration in terms of its continuity. However, there are commonly expressed views that counter this perspective—the perspective that ethics was ignored in traditional public administration, which stressed a narrow, bureaucratic perspective that omitted shared and individual responsibilities (Dvorin and Simmons 1972). As Henry (1975, 33) summarized this view, until recently "public administrators needed morality no more than a hotel clerk carrying out his daily duties." On the contrary, the expectation that administrators will uphold values and norms has always accompanied the consideration of how organized administrative activity contributes to, and impacts, society. Ethics for administrators has been grounded in personal integrity but has also stressed social and political responsibilities.

In the United States and in the American Society for Public Administration (ASPA), continuity in ethics has been accompanied by considerable change, but those changes have not been about "whether" there is and should be ethics in public administration but rather "what" the principles and standards should be and "how" they should be expressed and advanced. This chapter reviews the expression of ethical values in public administration from the nineteenth century through the 1960s and then focuses on the promotion of standards for the field as a whole in ASPA through a code of ethics. The discussion of the development of the ASPA codes illustrates the challenges and accomplishments of converting widely held ethical expectations into a coherent set of ethical standards for all professionals who serve the public. The chapter concludes with a call to be open to further change. Public administrators should be constantly vigilant to ensure that their norms express the highest ethical standards and that their standards are actively supported and upheld. Continuity does not mean stasis.

Values and Standards in Traditional Public Administration

Those who crafted the Constitution expected administrators to be "public spirited" (Bowman and West 2011, 33), and President Washington, who stressed the importance of "virtue and moral excellence" among public administrators, was an exemplar in stressing the importance of preparation for public service (Cook and Klay 2014, 47). These same values were explicitly advanced by reformers in the late nineteenth century (Richardson and Nigro 1987, 368). It is noteworthy that President Hayes in support for civil service reform in 1877 called for "a return to the principles and practices of the founders of the Government" (Curtis in Eaton 1880, viii). The Congress in 1884, after passage of the Pendleton Civil Service Reform Act in 1883, adopted the oath to be taken by executive branch employees that is still used today (5 U.S.C. §3331) (U.S. OPM n.d.). Administrators in the federal government are not swearing their allegiance to the government. They are committing themselves to uphold the Constitution and advance its purposes as well as to "faithfully discharge the duties" of their office. The oath of office "provides for bureaucrats the basis of a moral community" (Rohr 1989, 69–70).

To identify prevailing normative standards at the beginning of modern public administration in the United States, it is useful to examine two works that provide the foundation for professional public administration: Dorman Eaton's 1880 study of implications of British civil service reform for the United States and Woodrow Wilson's essay of 1887 that examined how administration can be differentiated from politics while interacting with it. Eaton and Wilson offer an outline of ethical expectations regarding how administration and administrators should and should not act.

Eaton (1880) contrasts the values of the "old system" of patronage-dominated government with the "new system" enabled by reform. Eaton asserts that in the United Kingdom, "you do not find servile officers . . . but men of self-reliance, who have succeeded, through public competitions, in which they have established the highest capacity and character" (p. 322). "Official life is a place of duty and responsibility" composed of officials with "pure" character who "stand manfully for principles and fear not to expose abuses; condemn all intrigue and manipulation for deceiving or coercing the people" (p. 323). Eaton asserts that public office is a solemn trust and officials should affirm that a "fidelity to principles and to public interests" takes precedence over "all the selfish claims of individuals and parties" (p. 324). He advocated changes that would make the "vast machinery of government" in the United States "a mighty force in the interest of education, justice, and public virtue" (p. 325).

Wilson (1887) sets forth the conditions that must be met for administrators to be trusted. He offers a fairly comprehensive array of standards for administrators:

- Public administrators should treat office as a "public trust" and be "unpartisan" (p. 210). The administrator should "not be a mere passive instrument" (p. 212).
- Administrators should be "thoroughly trained" and demonstrate "good behavior" (p. 216).
- Public administrators must be worthy of trust and act in a responsible, accountable way.[2]
- Administrators should be accountable for achieving "open and honest success" (p. 213).
- The public officer should "serve, not his superior alone but the community also, with the best efforts of his talents and the soberest service of his conscience" (p. 221).
- "Administration in the United States must be at all points sensitive to public opinion" (p. 216).
- Administration should avoid the conditions that produce "bureaucracy" or "domineering, illiberal officialism" (p. 216).
- Administrators must not preempt the policy making role of elected officials (pp. 216–217).
- Administration/administrators cannot "be removed from the common life of the people" (p. 217).
- Leaders should stress the "true public spirit" in order to prevent "arrogant and perfunctory bureaux" and promote "public-spirited instruments of just government" (p. 217).

Wilson concluded that

> the ideal for us is a civil service cultured and self-sufficient enough to act with sense and vigor, and yet so intimately connected with the popular thought, by means of elections and constant public counsel, as to find arbitrariness or class spirit quite out of the question.
>
> *(1887, 217)*

Eaton and Wilson do not use the word "ethics" in these works, but they clearly convey standards of behavior that reflect ethical commitments to public service, democracy, independence, and adherence to professional standards.

These views would be advanced by many other early scholars who called for active administrators who would be expected to maintain high standards of behavior. Goodnow (1900, 85) recognized that "much must be left to official discretion, since what is demanded of the officers is not the doing of a concrete thing, but the exercise of judgment." In "semi-scientific, quasi-judicial, and quasi-business," what is expected of administrators is "the exercise of foresight and discretion" and "the pursuit of truth" as well as gathering information, maintaining impartiality, and promoting efficiency. White (1926, 32) observed that "the influence of the administration has been at times very great in the formulation of legislative policy," and he valued administrators who were leaders: "the highest types of official will be in the advance guard of public opinion, and will concern himself to educate opinion to the standards which he knows should be applied" (p. 419).

In the 1930s, Gulick (1933, 66) recognized that every act of government has always been a "seamless web of discretion and action." In addition, he asserted that the executive side of government involves public administrators who are acting as planners and policy formulators while legislators act as the reviewers and vetoers of plans. The policy role was accepted by many in the years surrounding ASPA's founding (Haines and Dimock 1935; Gaus, White, and Dimock 1936; Herring 1936; Hyneman 1939; and the International City/County Managers Association (ICMA) as discussed later). It was recognized during this period that discretion and policy advice entail ethical responsibilities to balance responsiveness with independent judgment (Lynn 2001, 151).

The public administration community that organized as an association in 1939 had a strong value base and extensive informal professionalism on which to build. The ICMA had developed a code of ethics in 1924 and other specialized professional associations would do so as Plant discusses in Chapter 11. The question was how the values would be articulated and whether they would be codified and enforced for the field as a whole. A summary of prevailing ethical standards in the 1930s is provided by William Mosher (1938), who would become the first president of ASPA in 1939. In his view, ethics is both an individual and shared responsibility. He argued that a code would provide the foundation for a "profession of public service." It should be based on four major themes. First, the "central and dominating theme" of any professional code for civil servants will be the public interest (p. 339). Second, the code should address both relationships with other officials and "official–public relationships" that are paramount "in a going democracy" (p. 339). Third, the code should include provisions to advance "personal integrity." Fourth, there should be a requirement in the code that "public servants must be devoted to the services of the *whole* public, performing their tasks impartially and without fear or favor" (p. 339). Mosher does not present these standards as a radical departure from mainstream thinking in public administration. Indeed, he offers them as shared values in the field.[3]

Just over ten years later, Fritz Morstein Marx (1949) presented a similar set of standards as the basis for a code of ethics. Like Mosher, Marx stressed the linkage between public service and "a long-range concept of the general interest" (p. 1132). Marx argued that "the morals of public management are inseparable from the equalitarian conception of popular government embedded in the American tradition" (p. 1127). Like Wilson and Eaton, he argued that administrators are not "inanimate cogs or mindless robots" but they should not exercise "absolute discretion" in determining the ends they pursue (p. 1127–1128). It is clear that administrators are involved in policy formation because they have the opportunity or formal responsibility "to render advice" on pending measures

(p. 1137).[4] In addition, public administrators must respect the democratic process and avoid compelling actions without "persuasion and explanation" (p. 1140). Despite the calls by Mosher and Marx, there was no serious consideration of adopting a code of ethics in ASPA until the 1970s.

Other scholars, however, stressed the ethical qualities of administrators and the administrative process. Appleby (1952, 55) observed a "special kind of integrity" among public administrators based in part on the "self-selection" of persons searching for an opportunity to serve,[5] although sound judgment was further developed over time. Thus, the hierarchical structure of public organizations was a protector of morality because it assured that decisions would move up levels in the organization to officials with broader perspectives, more experience, and greater political awareness. Bailey (1964) focused on individual moral qualities and individual responsibility. He identified individual virtues as the basis for ethics. The "essential moral qualities of the ethical public servant are: (1) optimism; (2) courage; and (3) fairness tempered by charity" (pp. 235–236). Frederick Mosher (1968) argued that the "professionals of government"—career civil servants—had a greater sense of public responsibility than the "professionals in government" who represented traditionally specialized groups, such as attorneys and engineers, who stressed professional autonomy. A review of the research on approaches to advancing ethics in public administration concluded that the prevailing view was a focus on personal responsibility rather than articulated professional standards (Wakefield 1976).

Artificial Discontinuity: The Policy Role of Administrators

Overlapping these developments was an increasing acknowledgment of the involvement of public administrators in formulating policy. The visibility of this long-standing activity had expanded in the postwar years, but the increased attention to the policy role was accompanied by the distorted view that traditional public administration was characterized by a dichotomy of politics and administration with no administrator involvement in policy. This mischaracterization of the origins of the field led some to argue that a change was needed to replace the amoral, value-free administrators of traditional public administration with ethically aware and committed administrators (Dvorin and Simmons 1972). This view was unfair to early practitioners, ignored earlier scholarship, and had the effect of exaggerating the distinction between politics and administration and making an acceptance of policy responsibilities appear to be a radical departure from the previous practice and theory of public administration.

The demise of the presumed dichotomy challenged the legitimacy of the field, and in Mosher's view (1968, 6) "the finding of a viable substitute may well be the number one problem of public administration today." Presumably some traditionalists from the 1960s through the 1980s had doubts about involvement in policy because of the claims that it departed from the traditional values in the field whereas they could have accepted it if it had been part of their heritage. This dichotomy issue would be a factor in the development of ASPA's first code of ethics.

The idea of greater separation between politics and administration originated with efforts to reduce political interference in the administrative process (Eaton 1880; Wilson 1885). The term "dichotomy" was never used by Wilson or Goodnow and rarely used before the 1940s.[6] Those references made a distinction between the methods and worldviews of politicians and administrators and a rough but not complete division of labor (Vieg 1946, 8; Lepawsky 1949).

The ICMA and originators of the council-manager form of government were unique in the early decades of modern public administration for the explicit support given to policy involvement of administrators. The issue would be a recurring topic of discussion. From its beginning in 1914, the manager was expected to contribute to policy development.[7] The National Municipal League in its endorsement of the council-manager form of government asserted that the city manager was expected to "show himself to be a leader, formulating policies and urging their adoption by the council" (Woodruff 1919, 130). The first code of ethics of the ICMA in 1924 had indicated that it is the council members "who primarily determine public policy." In his field study of city managers, White (1927, 225) cautioned that they should respect the boundaries of their position and not compete with elected officials for public support of their ideas, but he concluded that "the city manager has become the great center of initiating and proposing (but not deciding) public policies."

ICMA adjusted its standards in the 1930s to respond to the political excesses of some early managers who competed with elected officials for public support and to match the mainstream rhetoric of public administration at the time (Roberts 1994). A revised code of ethics in 1938 that included the statement that the manager is "in no sense a political leader" has led to the conclusion that ICMA accepted the political-administrative dichotomy at this point (Stillman 1974, 52), but other provisions in the code[8] and other official publications indicated that ICMA recognized and supported the ethical responsibility of the manager to make policy recommendations (ITMA 1940, 28). After World War II, managers talked openly about their role as "community leaders" (Harrell 1948). Ridley (1958, 18) stated in an ICMA report that managers "are the major source in initiating policy for council-manager cities" and that a "hard-and-fast distinction between policy and administration was never practiced under the council-manager plan and is no longer accepted as valid" (p. 11).

Ironically, in the same year, Wallace Sayre (1958) invented the dichotomy as we have come to understand it and attributed his definition to the origins of public administration (Svara 1999). He argued that the scholars who founded the field accepted the politics–administration dichotomy "as a self-evident truth and as a desirable goal" (Sayre 1958, 102) and viewed administration as a "self-contained world of its own, with its own separate values, rules, and methods."[9]

Furthermore, the responsiveness of administrators to the public was not a concern "because everyone then understood that politics and policy were separate from administration, which was concerned exclusively with the execution of assignments handed down from the realm of politics" (103). Sayre wanted to promote a broad view of public administration as part of the political process in future research, but his simplistic view of the dichotomy as the founding theory of public administration had a strong influence and was increasingly accepted without criticism by other public administration scholars. In the next decade, this view took hold in public administration textbooks (Svara 1999).[10] Reflecting the new perspective, Norton Long (1965, 115) argued that although public administration's intellectual basis was the public–administration dichotomy, "in practice the dogma of the separation of policy and administration has been abandoned." Previously, Henry (1975, 33–34) argued, administrators made decisions on the "comfortable bases of efficiency, economy, and administrative principles"; now decisions would be based "on the more agonizing criteria of moral choices as well." The long-standing ethical implications of the "complementary" relationship of administrators and elected officials were ignored (Svara 2001).

Developments within ASPA

Spurred by Watergate and the attention to social equity raised by the New Public Administration (Marini 1971), ASPA formed the Professional Standards and Ethics Committee (PSEC) in 1974. Reflecting the concerns of ASPA President Nesta Gallas that adopting a code of ethics could be a symbolic act with little impact on behavior (Ink in Mertins 1979), the PSEC decided not to develop a code of ethics. Rather, it developed a workbook that assisted members in conducting self-diagnosis of their ethical values and responsibilities. The workbook *Applying Professional Standards and Ethics* was published in 1979 as "only a first step in a long overdue effort to strengthen professional standards and ethics in the public service" (Ink in Mertins 1979, ii). Mertins (1979, 1) stated in the introduction that "although it is possible to develop a long list of 'thou shalts' and 'thou shalt nots,' as many professions have done, ultimate responsibility for applying standards and ethics still falls on the individual." Thus, the workbook provided a diagnostic approach to help individuals assess their responsibilities and the appropriate response to the challenges they faced.

The topics covered in the workbook were relationships to law, responsibility and accountability, commitment, responsiveness, knowledge and skills, professional development and achievement of potential, citizenship and the political process, conflicts of interest, public disclosure and confidentiality, and professional ethics. Generally, the workbook did not assert value preferences but rather described the topic and explained why it is important. The authors asked questions to clarify the meaning of each area and encouraged readers to decide for themselves what value commitments to affirm. Thus, ASPA continued to rely on a sense of personal ethical responsibility framed through a process of deliberation.

By the time the workbook was published, however, ASPA was already working on the development of ethical standards. In parallel efforts beginning in 1978, a draft code and a statement of principles were developed by members of PSEC.[11] The draft code of ethics was completed in 1981 by a subcommittee chaired by Ralph Clark Chandler. The draft code was a combination of commentary about ethics and specific standards and values. The code (see Chandler 1982) stated a belief in "a public morality" (tenet 1), membership of administrators in a "working community" (tenet 2), and "the sovereignty of the people" (tenet 3).[12] It contained a broad commitment to promote public policies that "enhance freedom, equality, justice, economic well-being, and the celebration of life" (tenet 14). The code contained a commitment to "monitor our membership for compliance with commonly accepted ethical standards and take appropriate action where they have been violated" (tenet 9).

The prevailing view in the PSEC was that adopting a set of guiding principles for public administrators was preferable to adopting the draft code as ASPA's first step in developing ethical standards. At a meeting of the National Council in July 1981, the PSEC submitted the statement of principles.[13] The statement was accepted by the National Council as a draft to be reviewed by the membership, and a final version was approved in December 1981.[14] The principles asserted the importance of "service to the public," the ultimate responsibility of public administrators to the "sovereign" people, and the importance of law. Public administrators should promote "efficient and effective management," support those who "responsibly call attention to wrongdoing," and promote the "merit system, equal opportunity, and affirmative action principles." To safeguard the public trust, "unacceptable" practices such as "subordinat[ing] public positions to private gains" should be opposed, and the "qualities of justice, courage, honesty, equity, competence and compassion" should be actively promoted. The principles concluded with two broad statements that challenged administrators to achieve a high level of ethical commitment. In addition to the other principles, they should be guided by conscience in making choices and avoid instrumental thinking: "good ends never justify immoral means." In addition, "public administrators are not engaged merely in preventing wrong, but in pursuing right through timely and energetic execution of their responsibilities."

The principles provided the foundation for ASPA's first code of ethics approved in 1984.[15] The code based the practice of public administration on integrity and respect for the law. It noted the responsibility to "work to improve" constitutions and other laws "when necessary," and it recognized discretion and obligated administrators to use the public interest as a guide in its use.[16] Administrators are required to serve the public with high standards of quality and responsiveness. They should exemplify integrity and avoid practices that can undermine it. Undue personal gain and conflicts were proscribed. Many of the other tenets focused on aspects of organization and administrative process, but they were broad in scope. Administrators should handle their duties with "a positive attitude and constructively support open communication, creativity, dedication, and compassion"—hardly traditional bureaucratic attitudes. There were commitments to merit and affirmative action and elimination of discrimination, fraud, and mismanagement. Administrators should support colleagues if they are in difficulty because of their efforts to correct organizational abuses. They were expected to seek personal professional excellence and encourage the professional development of others. Thus, although the code used restrained language to describe the roles and responsibilities of administrators, it contained a broad range of responsibilities. The code did not include an enforcement mechanism. In 1985, a set of implementation guidelines that offered commentary on the tenets was adopted by the National Council.

The response to the 1984 code was often critical. Cooper (1987, 327) characterized it as "a conglomeration of prescribed virtues and modes of conduct" which, though useful as individual points, failed to provide "a coherent ethical identity for public administration." To Pugh (1991, 21), it "represents a skein of behavioral guideposts." Some would have preferred a more active and far-reaching code. Denhardt (1989) and Pugh (1991) viewed ASPA's approach to ethics as narrowly administrative and devoid of "political ethos" and democratic ideals.[17] To Denhardt (1989), professional codes were viewed negatively by some practitioners—and the ASPA code was "especially criticized" (p. 192)—"as not being helpful to them in functioning ethically in a political environment that requires an increasingly political role" (p. 189). When professional judgment indicates that an administrator should "actively advocate a particular policy or position, the codes of ethics provide little or no guidance in fulfilling (or limiting) this policy role" (p. 189). Still, the code recognized the responsibility to seek changes "when necessary" and the guidelines called for administrators to recommend changes to superiors or the legislative body "when a law is unenforceable or has become obsolete" (ASPA code 1984, guideline to tenet 8; see note 13).

Pugh follows Chandler in arguing that both the ICMA and ASPA codes demonstrate "an overwhelming concern with the bureaucratic ethos" (1991, 23). The ASPA code (as Chandler had concluded about the principles in 1983) does not draw upon the "criteria of morality such as justice, equity, and the public interest" (Pugh 1991, 23 quoting Chandler 1983, 34) and reflects a narrow "bureaucratic mindset." In fairness, the 1984 code asserted expectations without stating the underlying criteria, but the tenets were not limited to organizational standards.[18] The tenets referred to public service, policy change, integrity, and—although the code did not mention involving the public—citizen participation was included in the guidelines to the code. Ignoring the standards to use the public interest as a guide for exercising discretion and to work to change ineffective laws, Chandler and Pugh concluded that "the politics–administration dichotomy appears to be alive and well" (Pugh 1991, 23, quoting Chandler 1983, 34, who was referring to the 1981 principles) in the code. Reflecting continuing preoccupation with the supposed dichotomy, it appeared that the absence of active commitment to policy advocacy was interpreted by some as the acceptance of a narrow, bureaucratic role despite the broad language contained in the 1984 code and 1981 principles.

Despite the debates surrounding its formation, the code was an important step toward articulating the full scope of administrators' ethical responsibilities. It drew on the ethical values that had long been included in discussions of the characteristics of the ideal administrator and the social purpose of administration. For ASPA, it was an important accomplishment to fill the void in explicit ethics standards that had persisted since its founding in 1939. Cooper (1994, 16), despite describing the code as "a less than excellent document," observed that it had prompted discussion and debate among ASPA members about ethics and "served to institutionalize and legitimize administrative ethics as a significant and useful field of study." He documents the explosion in ethics research that started in the 1980s.

The 1994 code was a major reorientation of the code that addressed the lack of clear logic in the organization of the 1984 code while incorporating as much of the 1984 version as possible.[19] To improve the coherence of the code and to clarify the normative foundations, the content was organized around five major canons or principles derived from what the committee saw as the major sources of ethics in the public sector (Van Wart 1996). The five principles stress the responsibility of administrators to take actions that are consistent with and advance the law, public interest, integrity, and organizational ethics, and that develop excellence in oneself and others. To make the code more useful, the drafters combined the code and separate implementation guidelines into a single statement with five major principles and thirty-four specific tenets that elaborate them.

Specific tenets in the code that expand its scope over the 1984 code include involving and assisting citizens in their dealings with government (tenets I-1 and I-4), encouraging dissent (II-6), taking responsibility for errors (III-5), conducting official acts without partisanship (III-6), promoting ethical behavior in organizations and adopting organizational codes of ethics (IV-3 and IV-7), and strengthening accountability (IV-6). The responsibility to promote change in policy was broadened somewhat: administrators should "work to improve and change laws and policies that are counterproductive or obsolete" (II-2). The new code was well received and widely respected by members of ASPA (Bowman and Williams 1997, 521).

The first step toward linking the code to qualifications for ASPA membership was taken by adding a statement at the end of the code that indicates that it will be enforced in accordance with ASPA bylaws. According to Bowman and Williams (1997, 525), the statement was added late in the approval process and received little attention in the discussion. The bylaws state that "membership shall terminate . . . when in its sole and absolute discretion the Council determines that any member appears to have acted in violation of the Society's Code of Ethics as published from time to time" (Article II, Section 5). Despite this provision, no guidelines have been adopted for a process to exercise this authority, and no members have ever been expelled or censured (Menzel 2010, 122). An action that may have impeded efforts to implement the code was the elimination of the PSEC in 1999 as part of a general streamlining of ASPA. The Ethics Section was created in 2000 to focus on research and teaching of administrative ethics.

A new code was approved by the National Council at the ASPA conference in 2013 following a two-year review by a working group with thirty-one members, which included practitioners, academics, and students.[20] The new code expands the scope of the values and standards and focuses on eight principles (see Appendix 12.1). The code blends perspectives and contains standards based on formal roles, key relationships, and responsibilities to society. It carries forward the five principles of the 1994 code and adds or "elevates" from existing tenets three additional principles dealing with promoting democratic participation (new tenet 3), strengthening social equity (new tenet 4), and fully informing and advising superiors and peers (new tenet 5). It states that administrators should "advance the public interest" (new tenet 1) and seek to "improve laws and policies to promote the public good" (new tenet 2). The new code clearly builds on the previous versions while expanding the scope of ethical standards that it seeks to advance. It uses more aspirational language and, following Chandler's (1983, 34) recommendation, uses active verbs to link the code to actions and behaviors. It returns to the approach taken in 1984 by making the eight principles the code and providing a separate statement to guide the use of the code. It contains specific practices in contrast to the 1985 guidelines that discussed the meaning of the tenets and how they might be used.[21] Having a code along with a separate statement with specific guidelines that link principles to practice is the approach used by the ICMA, the American Institute of Certified Planners (AICP), and the American Psychological Association (APA).[22] As in earlier versions, the code reaches beyond ASPA members in seeking "to increase awareness and commitment to ethical principles and standards among all those who work in public service in all sectors."

Implementation and Prospects for the Future

Once again, ASPA faces the question that Stuart Gilman (in Mertins et al. 1998, 6), chair of the PSEC, posed years ago: "Now that we have a revised Code of Ethics, is it to be hortatory, symbolic, or enforced?" The debate about enforcement has been both pragmatic and substantive. There is a legitimate concern about legal liability (Menzel 2010, 122) and, thus, disciplinary action would need to be based on a fair review process. Winn advocates moving beyond the position that "individual administrators should assume personal ethical responsibility for their behavior" guided by the aspirations in the code to using the code as a statement of "shared ethics values that can be enforced" (in Menzel 2010, 123 and 124). Based on an assessment by Gilman (2005) of the characteristics associated with successful codes of ethics across countries and sectors, it is useful to think broadly about how codes are implemented rather than simply enforced—a term that implies an exclusive focus on reviewing and potentially taking disciplinary action in response to complaints. In Gilman's view, effective codes require an implementation process that involves interpreting the code and providing education and training, as well as enforcing the code.

The process of upholding the code through this broad range of actions is underway in ASPA. The former PSEC will be re-established as the standing Ethics and Professional Standards Committee based on a vote of members to change the ASPA bylaws in November 2014.[23] It will concentrate on professional development and training of all ASPA members thus contributing to what has been labeled the "ethical competence" of practitioners (Cooper and Menzel 2013). Continuing the tradition of workbooks in ASPA, development activities should be encouraged with special emphasis on individual and organizational assessment. The new committee will interpret the code and respond to requests for ethics guidance by ASPA members, and it will examine claims from ASPA members when they feel they have been penalized by their organization for actions that uphold the code of ethics, and the proposed committee will support them if the claim is substantiated.[24] Finally, the committee will seek to resolve complaints about unethical behavior using a process that protects the due process rights of members and will advise the National Council regarding what action to take if a complaint about a serious ethical violation is upheld. The code, supported by expanded implementation activities, can offer guidance to administrators as they make ethical commitments and grapple with ethical dilemmas.

ASPA has the opportunity to play a leadership role in defining public service ethics and working with other specialized associations. ASPA is a uniquely "pan-generalist" organization that includes a wider range of member types and substantive interests than other associations of public professionals (Svara and Terry 2009). The broadened ASPA code can complement the more focused codes of other specialized associations of public officials. Approaching an ethical decision using both codes can help administrators understand the full scope of responsibilities they have as public servants as well as their specific responsibilities as city managers, policy analysts, social workers, police and security officials, or other categories of public service professionals.

It will also be important to develop resources that elaborate the code of ethics for use in universities. Modules can be developed for public administration courses. In addition, materials should be developed that provide guidance to programs in public affairs in organizing the public service values in their curriculum in order to meet standards of the Network of Schools of Public Policy, Affairs, and Administration (NASPAA).[25] The ASPA code attempts to provide a comprehensive array of shared standards that can be used as a reference point in defining the values that are foundational to Master's programs in public affairs.

The long-standing ethical values in public administration have been codified and amplified by the ASPA ethics process. In its seventy-fifth year, ASPA is amplifying its status as a professional association that upholds and advances ethical standards in the public service. Professionals must still be responsible for upholding ethical values, but they can be challenged to re-examine their own value commitments and behavior by seeing examples of conduct that are judged to be deficient, or celebrated as meritorious, by their professional peers. Furthermore, the profession can deepen its understanding of ethical expectations by applying its standards to concrete cases of individual behavior or organizational action.

Conclusion: The Continuing Need for Change

Responsible public administration has always been based on the foundation of ethical standards. As we have seen, there was an extended period in modern public administration when ethics were assumed to be present if supporting practices were in place to ensure that capable public-spirited persons were chosen to fill administrative positions. Administrators were encouraged to identify and carry out their responsibilities as public servants. Specialized professional associations defined standards explicitly for their members, and ASPA began articulating standards for the field in 1984. The scope of these ethical standards has expanded over time. Just as important, the meaning of the standards has broadened and deepened, as chapters in this book document. A commitment to equality is an enduring premise in public administration and was included in the 1984 and 1994 ASPA codes, but we apply it to a wider range of personal characteristics now than we did twenty or thirty years ago as seen in Chapter 9. The concept of social equity has been incorporated increasingly in the way we think about the values of the field, as discussed in Chapter 10, but it was not included in the earlier ASPA codes. It is a principle in the 2013 code. Each major principle of administrative ethics should be examined on an ongoing basis to determine how it has evolved and the current challenges that administrators confront when upholding it.

Ethical commitments in public administration are elevated by active exchange of ideas and perspectives among members of the professional community. The full range of communications related to practice, teaching, and research contribute to a fuller understanding of the nature of ethics. The weakest area in the field of public affairs has been consideration of ethical issues in practice, not only in public service but also in the process of teaching and conduct of research. Enhancing professional discourse on a continuing basis is a central feature of the new code's implementation process, along with raising awareness about ethics and providing training and assessment tools. As members seek guidance in handling difficult choices, seek support when sanctioned for adhering to high standards of behavior, identify examples of exemplary behavior, or examine how to reconcile their behavior with the expectations in the code of ethics, the field expands its shared understanding of "who we think we are" and forms "images of what professional administrators believe we should live up to" (Chandler 1989, 617). "Ethical discourse," Chandler observes, "brings order, direction, and idealism to public service" (p. 617). In addition, the ongoing discussion among peers about ethical choices helps us to broaden and deepen the ways we convert our long-standing aspirational values and principles into action.

Notes

1 Portions of this chapter appear in Svara 2014.

2 Wilson went on to say that "large powers and unhampered discretion seem to be the indispensable conditions of responsibility" (1887, 213).

3 Merriam (1938) supported Mosher's values but doubted that the standards could be applied to the full range of persons in public service positions.

4 Despite his support for strict control of administrators by elected officials, even Finer (1941, 342) conceded that "no one in their right mind would deny the importance of suggestions persuasively presented by the expert."

5 Eaton assumed that the persons drawn to the public service would have positive qualities. Although the exams he emphasized tested only knowledge, he argued that civil service reform would promote character as well as competence among public administrators. Research on the public service motivation of persons in public service would substantiate this tendency (Perry and Wise 1990; Perry 1997).

6 See Svara (1998 and 1999) for an examination of the dichotomy concept.

7 For an expanded discussion of this issue in ICMA, see Nelson and Svara 2014.

8 Tenet 5 included the responsibility of the manager to encourage "positive decisions on policy by the council instead of passive acceptance of his recommendations."

9 To Wilson, "steady, hearty allegiance to the policy of the government they serve will constitute good behavior. That *policy* will have no taint of officialism about it. It will not be the creation of permanent officials, but of statesmen whose responsibility to public opinion will be direct and inevitable" (1887, 216–217).

10 There are other definitions of dichotomy. To Rohr (1986), the essence of the concept is the combination of subordination to politicians and administrative independence without the "naïve view of administration as apolitical" (p. 184). Overeem (2008) stresses the importance of dichotomy because of the extensive influence of administrators in order to make it clear that administrators should not determine policy independently. Chandler (1989) illustrates the ambiguity of the concept by arguing that ethical administrators should both "believe" and "disbelieve the dichotomy."

11 Based on communications with participants in ethics activities in the late 1970s, it appears that members of the PSEC met in early 1978 in Washington, DC, and started developing an initial version of a code of ethics. Late in the year, work began on the statement of principles as a first step to establishing a code, and it continued through the next three years when Harriett Jenkins, Jameson Doig, and Patrick Brannigan chaired the committee. Ralph Clark Chandler was vice chair of PSEC in 1980–1981 (Mertins and Hennigan 1982, 39) and chaired a subcommittee that finalized a draft code, but the PSEC chose to present the statement of principles to the National

Council. The only published accounts of these developments are by Chandler (1982 and 1983). Neither he nor the journals in which his essays appeared identified his personal involvement in the disagreement about whether to choose the draft code or the principles in 1981. Although his involvement was surely known by many ASPA members at the time, subsequent readers would not know from these articles that he promoted the approach that was not accepted in 1981. In Chandler's (1982, 371) view, ASPA had "settled for something considerably less" than a code of ethics. He interpreted the decision as a triumph of a narrow view of the role of public administrators, and the refusal on the part of PSEC and the National Council to display courage, choose active commitment, and use aspirational language. He argued that the decision "affirms the administrator as technician" and "pretends once again that administrators do in fact strictly adhere to value-free decision making" (1983, 34).

12 The draft code prepared by the subcommittee is included in Chandler (1982, 373–374).

13 Chandler (1982, 374) created an inaccurate impression that the statement of principles was a last-minute substitution for the draft code at the National Council meeting in December.

14 The ASPA principles and the 1984 code, 1985 guidelines, and 1994 code are available at ASPA 2013a.

15 Frances Burke was chair of PSEC in 1982–1983 and sought to "provide an action-oriented transition year to the development of the ASPA code." Esther Lawton was chair of PSEC in 1983–1984, and Patrick Brannigan was the chair of the drafting subcommittee. Patricia Florestano who was the president of ASPA in 1983–1984 made the adoption of a code of ethics a major goal, and the code was adopted under the presidency of Bradley Patterson.

16 The guidelines to the code added in 1985 indicated that promotion of new policy was limited in one's official position. Instead, it stated as a guideline for tenet 12 "as a citizen, work for legislation which is in the public interest."

17 Denhardt (1989, 188) observed, however, the administrative values of hierarchy, efficiency, efficacy, expertise, loyalty, and accountability take on a "moral character" by promoting "fairness, justice, avoidance of favoritism, and the consideration of all relevant interests" as well as "a commitment to stewardship of the public's resources through expert management to assure economy, efficiency, and effectiveness."

18 In addition, as noted, the code was meant to build on the principles adopted in 1981. Presumably, ASPA still adheres to the aspirational principles that have not been explicitly restated in the codes.

19 The PSEC was chaired by Mylon Winn at this time, and the subcommittee that revised the code was April Hejka Ekins, Montgomery Van Wart, and Gail Topolinsky. The revision effort was actively supported by ASPA President Christine Gibbs Springer.

20 The co-chairs of the Working Group, James Nordin and James Svara, were appointed by ASPA President Erik Bergrud, and the approval of the draft code was facilitated by his successor, Kuotsai Tom Liou. A summary of the revision process with a list of working group members is available at ASPA 2013a.

21 The 1985 guide is almost 2,200 words in length in addition to the code. The 2013 statement of practices is under 800 words plus the 300-word code. The combined 1994 code with integrated tenets is under 700 words.

22 ICMA has tenets and guidelines—sometimes presented separately and sometimes as a combined document. AICP has principles and twenty-five enforceable "Rules of Conduct." APA has ten standards with eighty-nine specific standards. The National

Association of Social Workers has statements of values and principles followed by sixteen pages of standards.

23 Steve Condrey, ASPA President in 2013–2014, oversaw the development of the new ethics committee.

24 The Committee on Professional Ethics, Rights, and Freedoms of the American Political Science Association considers both complaints about the violation of the ethics standards as well as grievances from members who claim that they have been mistreated. For ASPA, the results of the review of an action that led to sanctions could be a letter of support for a member who, for example, was fired for whistleblowing or providing information that elected officials did not want to receive.

25 "Public service values are important and enduring beliefs, ideals and principles shared by members of a community about what is good and desirable and what is not." For accreditation standards, see NASPAA 2009.

References

Appleby, Paul H. 1952. *Morality and Administration in Democratic Government*. Baton Rouge, LA: Louisiana State University Press.

ASPA. 2013a. "ASPA Code of Ethics." March. www.aspanet.org/public/ASPA/ Resources/Code_of_Ethics/ASPA/Resources/Code_of_Ethics/Code_of_Ethics1. aspx (accessed July 17, 2014).

———. 2013b. "Practices to Promote the ASPA Code of Ethics." March 16. www.aspanet. org/public/ASPADocs/ASPA%20Code%20of%20Ethics-2013%20with%20Practices. pdf (accessed July 17, 2014).

Bailey, Stephen K. 1964. "Ethics and the Public Service." *Public Administration Review* 24: 234–243.

Bowman, James S., and Jonathan P. West. 2011. "The Profession of Public Administration: Promise, Problems and Prospects." In *The State of Public Administration: Issues, Challenges, Opportunities*, ed. Donald C. Menzel and Harvey L. White, 25–35. Armonk, NY: M.E. Sharpe.

———, and Russell L. Williams. 1997. "Ethics in Government: From a Winter of Despair to a Spring of Hope." *Public Administration Review* 57(6): 517–526.

Chandler, Ralph Clark. 1982. "The Problem of Moral Illiteracy in Professional Discourse: The Case of the Statement of Principles of the American Society for Public Administration." *American Review of Public Administration* 16: 369–386.

———. 1983. "The Problem of Moral Reasoning in American Public Administration: The Case for a Code of Ethics." *Public Administration Review* 43(1): 32–39.

———. 1989. "A Guide to Ethics for Public Administrators." In *Handbook of Public Administration*, ed. James L. Perry, 602–618. San Francisco: Jossey-Bass.

Cook, Scott A., and William Earl Klay. 2014. "George Washington and Enlightenment Ideas on Educating Future Citizens and Public Servants." *Journal of Public Administration Education* 20: 46–55.

Cooper, Terry L. 1987. "Hierarchy, Virtue, and the Practice of Public Administration: A Perspective for Normative Ethics." *Public Administration Review* 47: 320–328.

———. 1994. "The Emergence of Administrative Ethics as a Field of Study in the United States." *In Handbook of Administrative Ethics*, ed. Terry L. Cooper, 3–30. New York: Marcel Dekker.

———, and Donald Menzel, eds. 2013. *Achieving Ethical Competence for Public Service Leadership*. Armonk, NY: M.E. Sharpe.

Denhardt, Kathryn G. 1989. "The Management of Ideals: A Political Perspective on Ethics." *Public Administration Review* 49(2): 187–193.

Dvorin, Eugene P., and Robert H. Simmons. 1972. *From Amoral to Human Bureaucracy.* San Francisco: Canfield Press.

Eaton, Dorman B. 1880. *Civil Service in Great Britain: A History of Abuses and Reforms and Their Bearing upon American Politics.* New York: Harper & Brothers.

Finer, Herman. 1941. "Administrative Responsibility in Democratic Government." *Public Administration Review* 1(4): 335–350.

Gaus, John M., Leonard D. White, and Marshall E. Dimock. 1936. *The Frontiers of Public Administration.* Chicago: University of Chicago Press.

Gilman, Stuart. 2005. *Ethics Codes and Codes of Conduct as Tools for Promoting an Ethical and Professional Public Service: Comparative Success and Lessons.* Washington, DC: World Bank.

Goodnow, Frank J. 1900. *Politics and Administration.* New York: MacMillan.

Gulick, Luther. 1933. "Politics, Administration, and the 'New Deal.'" *The Annals* 169: 55–66.

Haines, C.G., and Marshall E. Dimock, eds. 1935. *Essays on the Law and Practice of Governmental Administration.* Baltimore: Johns Hopkins Press.

Harrell, C.A. 1948. "The City Manager as a Community Leader." *Public Management* 30(October): 290–294.

Henry, Nicholas L. 1975. *Public Administration and Public Affairs.* New York: Prentice Hall.

Herring, Edward Pendleton. 1936. *Public Administration and the Public Interest.* New York: McGraw-Hill.

Hyneman, C. 1939. "Administrative Reorganization: An Adventure into Science and Theology." *The Journal of Politics* 1: 62–75.

ITMA (Institute for Training in Municipal Administration). 1940. *The Technique of Municipal Administration.* Chicago: International City Managers' Association.

Lepawsky, A. 1949. *Administration: The Art and Science of Organization and Management.* New York: Alfred A. Knopf.

Long, Norton E. 1965. "Politicians for Hire—The Dilemma of Education and the Task for Research." *Public Administration Review* 25(2): 115–120.

Lynn, Lawrence E. 2001. "The Myth of the Bureaucratic Paradigm: What Traditional Public Administration Really Stood for?" *Public Administration Review* 61(2): 144–160.

Marini, Frank, ed. 1971. *Toward a New Public Administration: The Minnowbrook Perspective.* San Francisco: Chandler Publishing.

Marx, Fritz Morstein. 1949. "Administrative Ethics and the Rule of Law." *American Political Science Review* 43(6): 1119–1144.

Menzel, Donald C. 2010. *Ethics Moments in Government: Cases and Controversies.* Boca Raton, FL: CRC Press.

Merriam, Lewis. 1938. "Public Service—Occupation or Industry?" *American Political Science Review* 32(4): 718–723.

Mertins, Herman Jr. 1979. *Professional Standards and Ethics: A Workbook for Public Administrators.* Washington, DC: ASPA.

———, and Patrick J. Hennigan. 1982. *Applying Professional Standards and Ethics in the 1980s: A Workbook Study Guide for Public Administrators.* Washington, DC: ASPA.

———, Frances Burke, Robert W. Kweit, and Gerald M. Pops, eds. 1998. *Applying Professional Standards and Ethics in the 21st Century: A Workbook & Study Guide for Public Administrators.* Washington, DC: ASPA.

Mosher, Frederick C. 1968. *Democracy and the Public Service.* New York: Oxford University Press.

Mosher, William E. 1938. "Public Administration: The Profession of Public Service." *American Political Science Review* 32(2): 332–342.

NASPAA. 2009. "NASPAA Accreditation Standards." October 16. http://naspaaaccreditation.files.wordpress.com/2014/09/naspaa-standards.pdf (accessed November 22, 2014).

Nelson, Kimberly, and James H. Svara. 2014. "The Roles of Local Government Managers in Theory and Practice: A Centennial Perspective." Unpublished paper.

Overeem, Patrick. 2008. "Beyond Heterodoxy: Dwight Waldo and the Politics–Administration Dichotomy." *Public Administration Review* 68: 36–45.

Perry, James L. 1997. "Antecedents of Public Service Motivation." *Journal of Public Administration Research and Theory* 7: 181–197.

———, and Lois R. Wise, 1990. "The Motivational Bases of Public Service." *Public Administration Review* 45: 367–373.

Pugh, Darrell L. 1991. "The Origins of Ethical Frameworks in Public Administration." In *Ethical Frontiers in Public Management*, ed. James S. Bowman, 9–33. San Francisco: Jossey-Bass.

Richardson, William D., and Lloyd J. Nigro. 1987. "Administrative Ethics and Founding Thought: Constitutional Correctives, Honor, and Education." *Public Administration Review* 47: 367–376.

Ridley, Clarence E. 1958. *The Role of the City Manager in Policy Formulation*. Chicago: ICMA.

Roberts, Alasdair S. 1994. "Demonstrating Neutrality: The Rockefeller Philanthropies and the Evolution of Public Administration. 1927–36." *Public Administration Review* 54: 221–228.

Rohr, John A. 1986. *To Run a Constitution: The Legitimacy of the Administrative State*. Lawrence, KS: University Press of Kansas.

———. 1989. *Ethics for Bureaucrats*, 2nd ed. New York: Marcel Dekker.

Sayre, Wallace S. 1958. "Premises of Public Administration: Past and Emerging." *Public Administration Review* 18(2): 102–105.

Stillman, Richard. 1974. *The Rise of the City Manager: A Public Professional in Local Government*. Albuquerque, NM: University of New Mexico Press.

Svara, James H. 1998. "The Politics-Administration Dichotomy Model as Aberration." *Public Administration Review* 58(1): 51–58.

———. 1999. "Complementarity of Politics and Administration as a Legitimate Alternative to the Dichotomy Model." *Administration & Society* 30(6): 676–705.

———. 2001. "The Myth of the Dichotomy: Complementarity of Politics and Administration in the Past and Future of Public Administration." *Public Administration Review* 61: 164–171.

———. 2014. "Who Are the Keepers of the Code? Articulating and Upholding Ethical Standards in the Field of Public Administration." *Public Administration Review* 74(5): 561–569.

———, and Larry D. Terry. 2009. "The Present Challenges to ASPA as an Association that Promotes Public Professionalism." *Public Administration Review* 69: 1050–1059.

U.S. OPM (Office of Personnel Management). N.d. "Oath." Washington, DC: U.S. Office of Personnel Management. http://archive.opm.gov/constitution_initiative/oath.asp (accessed July 17, 2014).

Van Wart, Montgomery. 1996. "The Sources of Ethical Decision Making for Individuals in the Public Sector." *Public Administration Review* 56(6): 525–533.

Vieg, John A. 1946. "The Growth of Public Administration." In *Elements of Public Administration*, ed. Fritz Morstein Marx, 3–26. New York: Prentice-Hall.

Wakefield, Susan. 1976. "Ethics and the Public Service: A Case for Individual Responsibility." *Public Administration Review* 36(6): 661–666.

Wilson, Woodrow. 1885. *Congressional Government*. New York: Houghton Mifflin.

———. 1887. "The Study of Administration." *Political Science Quarterly* 2(June): 197–222.

White, Leonard. 1926. *Introduction to the Study of Public Administration*. New York: The MacMillan Company.

———. 1927. *The City Manager*. Chicago: University of Chicago Press.

Woodruff, Clinton R. 1919. *A New Municipal Program*. New York: D. Appleton and Company.

Appendix 12.1: ASPA Code of Ethics

The American Society for Public Administration (ASPA) advances the science, art, and practice of public administration. The Society affirms its responsibility to develop the spirit of responsible professionalism within its membership and to increase awareness and commitment to ethical principles and standards among all those who work in public service in all sectors. To this end, we, the members of the Society, commit ourselves to uphold the following principles:

1. **Advance the Public Interest.** Promote the interests of the public and put service to the public above service to oneself.
2. **Uphold the Constitution and the Law.** Respect and support government constitutions and laws, while seeking to improve laws and policies to promote the public good.
3. **Promote Democratic Participation.** Inform the public and encourage active engagement in governance. Be open, transparent and responsive, and respect and assist all persons in their dealings with public organizations.
4. **Strengthen Social Equity.** Treat all persons with fairness, justice, and equality and respect individual differences, rights, and freedoms. Promote affirmative action and other initiatives to reduce unfairness, injustice, and inequality in society.
5. **Fully Inform and Advise.** Provide accurate, honest, comprehensive, and timely information and advice to elected and appointed officials and governing board members, and to staff members in your organization.
6. **Demonstrate Personal Integrity.** Adhere to the highest standards of conduct to inspire public confidence and trust in public service.
7. **Promote Ethical Organizations.** Strive to attain the highest standards of ethics, stewardship, and public service in organizations that serve the public.
8. **Advance Professional Excellence.** Strengthen personal capabilities to act competently and ethically and encourage the professional development of others.

(Approved by the ASPA National Council 3/16/13)

Note: A separate document contains practices that serve as a guide to behavior for members of ASPA in carrying out its principles; see ASPA 2013b.

13

LOOKING BACK, MOVING FORWARD[1]

Mary E. Guy and Marilyn M. Rubin

Public administration is both normative and empirical, values-laden and evidence-based, theoretical and operational. Its boundaries are but hazy shadows, for it touches all aspects of the public service environment and borrows from several disciplines. Despite—and perhaps because of—the breadth of its reach, the most important questions lie at its doorstep: How best to know and execute the public interest? How best to advance the public will?

The stories that this book tells begin in the early twentieth century at the cusp of what Newland refers to as the "Golden Era" of public administration. It was then that the reform movement helped to build trust in government's ability to address and bring to bear the resources of a nation to address huge problems. It was then that the first initiatives were put in place to systematically train government workers. It was also then that several nonprofit associations were established that would underpin the creation of the first organization to promote the professionalization of public administration. This occurred in 1939 when a critical mass of forward-thinking practitioners and scholars convened at the annual meeting of the American Political Science Association to form the American Society for Public Administration (ASPA) and shortly thereafter to establish a new journal, *Public Administration Review*, which remains the journal of record for the field. With its newfound confidence and an identity separate from political science, ASPA began to influence, and be influenced by, the field and profession of public administration.

As the years passed and the field matured, subgroups began splintering off from ASPA, forming entities bounded by the interests that unified a subset of its members. Both Plant's and Yang's chapters speak to this dynamic. Those interested in education for public service careers are active in, and identify with, the Network of Schools of Public Policy, Affairs and Administration. Senior practitioners and scholars held in high regard by their peers are elected to, and identify with, the National Academy of Public Administration. Those who are primarily interested in policy and its implementation identify with the Association of Public Policy and Management. Those who wish to belong to an association of scholars interested in empirical work in administration and management join the Public Management Research Association. Those interested in theory join the Public Administration Theory Network. Those who focus on sub-areas within the field join one of the many sections of the ASPA. For example, members who have an interest in budget and finance join the Association for Budgeting and Financial Management. All these acorns from the ASPA tree are a sign of the vitality and breadth of the enterprise. A proliferation of scholarly journals has accompanied the maturation of the field, providing many more outlets for research than existed in its adolescence.

There have been many twists and turns along the public administration road since the 1930s, beyond the establishment of professional associations, outlets for research, and academic programs to educate public service workers. Changes have extended to how we think about public administration. For this reason, each of the experts who contributed to this volume traces the evolution of one dimension of the field, describing what has endured and what has changed over the course of the past seventy-five years. Each perspective should be looked upon as a work in progress, enhancing our capacity to visualize the future.

The "From–To" format differs from what is usually found in a book such as this. Chapters do not focus on defining public administration nor do they hew to its classic subspecialties: budgeting, human resource management, organization theory, public finance, ethics, planning, and leadership. Instead, to capture overarching trends and reflect the tenor of the times, the dimensions slice the field differently. Stillman poses the question in the Foreword as to whether this format rewrites the logic model of the field. This is an interesting question and one best answered by contemporary philosophy as it tells us that skeptical postmodernism has given way to inclusive metamodernism (Vermeulen and van den Akker 2010). This transition has been punctuated by the 9/11 attacks, global financial crises, terrorism, climate change, the proliferation of identity politics, and advances in information technology. It is not that the logic model has changed so much. It is, instead, that the larger frame of reference within which public administrators act is changing, flattening, interconnecting, globalizing.

Increasingly, globalized societies exist in a worldwide archipelago with fewer centers. Conflicts, especially emanating from the Middle East, are asymmetric and dissociated from nation states. Cities that can no longer afford to provide all of the services demanded by their citizens are forming regional taxing and service districts that embrace multiple jurisdictions. Cash-strapped states are forming regional cooperative pacts to take advantage of economies of scale. Hierarchy is morphing into heterarchy as both O'Leary and Kettl explain.

Current times can no longer be characterized from the universal purview of the white, western male as Gooden discusses, nor by a postmodern pastiche of distinct bounds of race, gender, class, or locale, as Riccucci describes. Rather, these traditional lenses are being replaced by globalized perceptions and shifting sands of power. So, yes, the approach of this book is different than if it had been written in earlier years because the times are different.

Yet there are the continuities and imperatives that Rosenbloom traces. The constitutional forces and tensions that mold the institutions within which public administration happens are persistent and enduring despite the alterations made as the courts inch interpretations of the Constitution forward. Though one need not go far to find examples of discontinuities, they are more often five-degree rather than ninety-degree turns. In fact, they are, as Lindblom observed more than fifty years ago, incremental changes that can only be appreciated when viewed retrospectively (Lindblom 1959). And, yes, the ghosts of Wilson, Appleby, Brownlow, Waldo, and so many other luminaries from the past emerge in these pages. It is their writings that created the skeleton around which today's authors continue to build the field and contribute to its evolution.

In the Foreword, Stillman makes the provocative assumption that the chapters portray a field that is disparate, if not disconnected, with little that unifies. On the one hand, Plant's description of the proliferation of professional associations, each with a parochial focus, supports this assumption. On the other hand, O'Leary's discussion of networked alliances, Klingner's emphasis on global interconnections, and Kettl's description of a field without bounds speak to alternative perspectives. Stillman's passionate comparison of public administration today as compared to its study and practice in the mid-twentieth century challenges readers to think harder about the power of effective administration to breathe life and meaning into our democracy.

Can anyone craft a guide that is as certain of how to do public administration as writers in the Golden Era portrayed? Is it still true, as President Kennedy said in 1962, that most of the problems that come to government are administrative problems requiring very sophisticated judgments on questions that are beyond the ken of most people? Based on the substance of these chapters, the answer is resoundingly in the affirmative. It is hard to overstate the importance of public administration and its complexity. A visit with philosophers and their discussion of metamodernism helps to explain how we got to this point and helps to point the way forward.

The metamodern way of thinking contrasts with postmodernism in its multiplicity of sharp-edged contradictions and distrust of big narratives. Metamodernism also stands in contrast with modernism's faith in linear progress and unwavering reliance on reason. This is described well by Dutch philosophers Vermeulen and van den Akker (2010) who use an example from the U.S. 2008 presidential campaign to show how contemporary thinking and yearning extends beyond the stasis of postmodernism. They note the degree to which candidate Obama's "Yes we can" mantra—a speech with a metamodern style—resonated both with the American electorate and globally. The excerpt below from a campaign speech in South Carolina galvanized the crowd and crystallized their support. Note the reference to a future that moves beyond demographic splits, pairs pragmatism with idealism, asserts that change is within reach, and offers hope for a new era on the horizon:

> This election is about . . . whether we settle for the same divisions and distractions and drama that passes for politics today or whether we reach for a politics of common sense and innovation, a politics of shared sacrifice and shared prosperity. . . . When I hear the cynical talk that blacks and whites and Latinos can't join together and work together, I'm reminded of the Latino brothers and sisters I organized with and stood with and fought with side by side for jobs and justice on the streets of Chicago. So don't tell us change can't happen. . . . Yes, we can. Yes, we can change. . . . Yes, we can seize our future. And as we leave this great state with a new wind at our backs, and we take this journey across this great country, a country we love, with the message we've carried from the plains of Iowa to the hills of New Hampshire, from the Nevada desert to the South Carolina coast, the same message we had when we were up and when we were down, that out of many we are one, that while we breathe we will hope, and where we are met with cynicism and doubt and fear and those who tell us that we can't, we will respond with that timeless creed that sums up the spirit of the American people in three simple words: Yes, we can.
>
> *(Obama 2008)*

Metamodernism, in contrast to modernism and postmodernism, "displaces the parameters of the present with those of a future presence that is futureless; and it displaces the boundaries of our place with those of a surreal place that is placeless" (Vermeulen and van den Akker 2010, 12). The "destiny" of the metamodern era is to pursue a horizon that is forever in the distance. The following metaphor captures this distinction well:

> Like a donkey it chases a carrot that it never manages to eat because the carrot is always just beyond its reach. But precisely because it never manages to eat the carrot, it never ends its chase, setting foot in moral realms the modern donkey (having eaten its carrot elsewhere) will never encounter, entering political domains the postmodern donkey (having abandoned the chase) will never come across.
>
> *(Vermeulen and van den Akker 2010, 5)*

It is unusual to borrow from philosophy to speak to the mechanics of public administration but here is the link: the trends that each of these chapters has addressed, and the reality that students of the field will confront for decades to come, will be shaped by the donkey and the carrot.

Megatrends

Juxtaposing the metamodern philosophical framework against global megatrends helps to bring this discussion home, provide perspective, and forecast the work that will be required of public administration. These trends show promise of greater cooperation internationally and, on the domestic scene, greater integration of governments at all levels. And all governments are recognizing the need to develop greater capacity to implement and manage programs and to engage citizens. In the listing below of trends suggested by and adapted from KPMG International (2014), the elements of metamodernism are obvious: boundary-less place, pragmatism paired with idealism, belief that change is within reach, and hope for a new era on the horizon. The list includes seven trends that directly relate to the substance of the chapters in this book:

1. higher life expectancy and falling birth rates increase the proportion of elderly citizens, challenging the solvency of social welfare systems, pensions, and healthcare;
2. the implications of the rise of citizen expectations for government performance;
3. information and communications technology (ICT) has transformed society and connected the globe, testing government's ability to harness the benefits of ICT while providing prudent oversight;
4. the interconnected global economy will see continued increase in international trade and capital flows;
5. the continuing constraint of public debt;
6. global power is rebalancing and this requires that international institutions and national governments have a greater focus on maintaining transparency and inclusiveness; and
7. by 2030, almost two-thirds of the world's population is forecast to live in cities.

Each trend and its impact on the future evolution of public administration is discussed below.

Higher Life Expectancy and Falling Birth Rates

By the middle of the twenty-first century, it is estimated that there will be close to 100 million more people living in the United States than there are today (U.S. Census Bureau 2012). Not only will the population increase in size but it will also be older and will live longer. As birth rates drop to historic lows and the average

age of death rises, the 13 percent of American's population that is currently at least sixty-five years old is forecast to reach about 20 percent by 2050. Newland's discussion of U.S. budget trends shows that, even today, when combined, the percentage of outlays for health, Medicare, income security, and social security, amounts to 65 percent of the federal budget. That does not leave much discretionary space for other expenses in the future.

Baby boomers continue to retire. If, as is expected, birth rates continue to fall, there will be fewer workers in the future to fund pensions, health, and welfare funds, especially if immigration reform slows the influx of new residents. The challenge to the U.S. treasury will be enormous. There will be resistance to putting more money into education, for many seniors will choose to spend or save their money rather than invest it in future generations. This, in turn will challenge local and state budgets and the public education system. There is already significant policy attention focused on American education in terms of student achievement but the funding for it may soon be on the table, as well. Education experts, state and local government finance officers, planners designing space for assisted living and safe, walkable spaces, healthcare access planners, and transportation experts will have their work cut out for them.

The aging of the population and its accompanying problems are not unique to the United States. According to the United Nations:

> Population ageing is . . . without parallel in the history of humanity. Increases in the proportions of older persons . . . are being accompanied by declines in the proportions of the young. . . . By 2050, the number of older persons in the world will exceed the number of young for the first time in history.
>
> *(United Nations 2002, xxviii)*

Even though not all countries, especially those in developing stages, are experiencing this aging phenomenon, observing the implications globally, the United Nations report concludes that it "is evident that unprecedented demographic changes . . . are transforming the world. The profound, pervasive and enduring consequences of population ageing present enormous opportunities as well as enormous challenges for all societies" (xxxi). Given the theme of this book, we can add that there will be enormous challenges for public administrators, as well.

Citizen Expectations of Government

Citizen expectations of government are rising across the globe. This point is illustrated in the findings of a 2012 study of legislative bodies (referred to as parliaments) worldwide. The study found that "politicians are obliged to account publicly for their actions more regularly and routinely" than in the past (United Nations

Development Programme and Inter-Parliamentary Union 2013, 3) and that citizen demand for more accountable government is

> driving the growth of a new breed of parliamentary monitoring organization (PMO) . . . to monitor and often to rate the performance of MPs [members of parliament] inside and outside parliament. More than 191 such organizations exist worldwide, monitoring the activities of over 80 national parliaments.
>
> *(United Nations Development Programme and*
> *Inter-Parliamentary Union 2013, 4)*

A corollary of citizen expectations regarding government performance is their level of trust in government. According to a Fall 2013 Gallup (2014) poll, 51 percent of the U.S. population has a great deal or a fair amount of trust in the Executive Branch, down 22 percentage points since 1972. In regard to Congress, 34 percent have a great deal or fair amount of trust, down 37 percentage points from 1972. By way of comparison, across the same time span, trust in the media went from 68 percent in 1972 to 44 percent in 2013.

Interestingly, trust in government has not diminished across the board. The Gallup survey found that citizens' trust in state governments has remained steady over the decades, while it has increased in local governments. For example, in 2013, the percentage of people with a great deal or fair amount of trust in their state government stood at 62 percent; in 1972 the same polling question yielded 63 percent. At the local level—where government is most personal and closest to the people—71 percent report having a great deal or fair amount of trust, compared to 63 in 1972, indicating that trust at the local level has actually increased.

The issue of citizens' trust in government is not unique to the United States (Manning and Wetzel 2010). According to the Organisation for Economic Co-operation and Development (OECD), just four out of ten residents of its member nations trust their governments. The OECD worries that lack of trust compromises the willingness of citizens and businesses to respond to public policies and contribute to a sustainable economy (OECD 2013).

Newcomer corroborates the low level of trust in government, but also notes that expectations for reliable quality of outcome measures is high, and that the problems facing public service organizations—governmental as well as non-profit—are more complex and interconnected than ever before. Her chapter describes increasing interest in measuring "on the ground" outcomes across government and the nonprofit sectors. Because whatever gets measured is generally most scrutinized, administrators must be judicious as they determine what to measure, how to measure it, and how to use the data that result. This is admittedly a big job, but one that, if successful, may help to restore public confidence in government.

Impact of ICT

Nothing has made the world smaller and more connected than the proliferation of information technologies. The Internet makes it as easy to speak with someone in another country as it is to speak with a colleague at a nearby desk. As Lee and Reed describe, rapidly changing technologies are responsible for profound changes in communication and, therefore, relationships. From issues of how to manage "Big Data," to how to protect citizen privacy, however, there are far more questions than answers. Technology has moved faster than the administrative infrastructure required to manage it.

At all levels of government, the Internet makes it easier for citizens to follow what government officials and employees are doing and e-government makes it possible for local governments to provide services more conveniently accessed by residents and businesses. But many jurisdictions are still pondering how to harness the Internet to engage citizens in planning and decision making. We know that younger citizens eschew neighborhood meetings in favor of engaging in online chats. We also know that older citizens prefer face-to-face community meetings when decisions are to be reached that will impact them. Urban planners are thus left in a quandary as to how to best engage the public in community decision making.

Widespread accessibility of information promotes further flattening of decision making structures that used to be hierarchical. Much has been made of the digital divide that continues to present a challenge to educators and employers. Children who come of age in a home without Internet connections, and adults who lack facility with accessing information via the Internet, are at a significant disadvantage when it comes to job seeking, securing services, and staying up-to-date with information useful to them. Whereas literacy and numeracy have been goals of long standing to prepare job-ready youth, digital literacy is increasingly becoming a sine qua non for most occupations.

The potential of further developments in information technology are staggering, just as are the administrative burdens and benefits it brings to government. ICT is a primary driver of the collaborative and networked services that O'Leary describes. With it, top-down hierarchies and well-defined power centers can flatten and decentralize because communication capacity is present even in the absence of centralized control. Research into collaboration and networks shows that the disabling of hierarchical structures is an uneven process, however, at least partially due to slow adoption of new technology, delays in adopting the necessary infrastructure, and discomfort with change. Nevertheless, it is the wave of the future and information technology is an essential part of the "new normal" facing public administrators.

The Interconnected Global Economy

As hierarchy is morphing into heterarchy, government and nonprofit managers must learn how to function when multiple actors share power: they must become globally competent. Klingner speaks about the importance of global management competencies. Those who are working with immigration or trade programs are already enmeshed in this changed work environment. Many others who perform work seemingly unrelated to a globalizing economy, such as teaching prekindergarten through twelfth grade or working in public health, are also confronted with a mix of cultures and languages. The necessity for multicultural skills thus permeates public services as Riccucci so aptly points out. Public administration is strengthened through an understanding of differentness: different races, genders, sexuality, languages, dress, culture, and customs.

Beyond human service delivery, domestic regulatory regimes have to synchronize with international regulatory regimes and norms. As Rosenbloom reminds us, one of government's key roles is that of regulator. Regulation that is robust and sufficient to anticipate emerging needs and cross-pressures is the ideal. For example, problems related to climate change require communication and strategies that extend across national boundaries. Preservation of natural resources requires pacts with trading partners and geographic neighbors. In other words, as the connections between citizens of all nations increase, so also does the need for regulation and public services that cross jurisdictional lines.

In contrast to postmodernism's parataxis, the interconnections that result from information technology, international travel, and global economies presage development that is quite different from the nation state developments of the past. A rhizomatic rather than linear development is on the horizon. A rhizome has no beginning or end; it is always in the middle, between things, an intermezzo. Rhizomatic means to mimic a rhizome, in other words, to apprehend multiplicities, to acknowledge ceaselessly established connections between, for example, organizations of power, citizen initiatives, trading partners, and social struggles. Interconnections of policies, traditions, history, and culture become a map of attractions and influences with no specific origin or genesis. The Internet has made it so. Research into diffusion hints at the desire to understand this rhizome, as does the attention being paid to collaboration and networks and the growing reality of heterarchy in place of hierarchy.

Paradoxically, as pressures for globalization rise, contrary pressures for localism mount. Internationally, this irony is captured as tribalism versus nationalism. The inward desire for neighborhoods and communities to create their own identity, to determine their own fate, and to self-govern, parallels the outward focus on a global environment. Balancing the tension between parochial interests and global pressures is a high-wire act performed, of course, by public administrators.

ICT is a vehicle for mastering the high-wire act because of its capacity to connect local governments with citizens and governments with governments. By so doing, silos are converted to networks. According to Lee and Reed, government is a slow but steady adopter of ICT. Bidding processes and procurement rules standardize the adoption process and provide transparency but they constrain more rapid acquisition of new technology that would expedite communication and service delivery. The challenge for government is to become a medium-to-fast technology adopter, rather than a slow-to-medium adopter, without sacrificing transparency.

Public Debt

Government's ability to bring debt under control will affect the capacity to respond to major social, economic, and environmental challenges. The problem of government debt that Newland describes is not unique to the United States According to the International Monetary Fund (IMF), although "recent policy moves have helped to broadly stabilize public debt ratios in most advanced economies . . . debt in these countries remains at historic highs" (IMF 2014). KPMG International (2014, 30) estimates that if the status quo is maintained, by the year 2035 net debt will be 133 percent of gross domestic product (GDP) in the Eurozone, 213 percent of GDP in the United States, and 386 percent of GDP in Japan. As if this is not bad enough, in the developing world, rather than infusing economies with additional funds to provide needed public services, the repayment of creditors has become a major priority. According to the World Bank, net public debt flows to developing countries between 1985 and 2010 (that is, the difference between debt inflows and debt payments) stood at $530 billion, which is the equivalent of five Marshall Plans (Millet, Munevar, and Toussaint 2012).

To address pressures of high public debt, governments will have to develop the capacity to control their own finances and live within their means. Although the research is not conclusive as to the impact of public debt on economic growth (other than when it is greater than 100 percent of GDP), the reality is that the need to pay down debt has to be balanced with growing demands for public services—a challenge to public administrators all over the world (Checherita and Rother 2010).

Transparency and Inclusiveness

The rebalancing of global power means that there is an emerging multi-polar world order, a heterarchy, rather than the hegemony that the United States enjoyed in the late twentieth and early twenty-first centuries. A multi-polar world brings interdependence and this means that cross-border solutions are needed to address the risks and reap the benefits of interconnectedness. Contributors to this book have discussed this from several different perspectives. O'Leary describes the flattening of structures and the heterarchy that is replacing hierarchy. Kettl speaks of the networks within which all sectors of the economy everywhere are intersecting and Klingner discusses how interconnections across nations continue to develop and strengthen. Svara and Newcomer write of the imperative for government transparency, with Newcomer making the point that both outputs and outcomes reflect performance. But in a complex environment with numerous points of interest, defining what matters to multinational stakeholders and determining how to measure it is challenging and the decisions vary across space and time. In the United States each presidential administration puts its own stamp on performance and outcomes and ultimately on transparency, which leaves evaluation experts asking how to evaluate amidst complex interconnections.

Across the globe, international institutions seek ways to make their operations more transparent. One example is the Global Transparency Initiative (GTI) that was created to promote openness among international financial institutions, such as the World Bank and the IMF. GTI believes that transparency can help reduce corruption, identify social, environmental, and economic risks and benefits, and can help to avoid damage to communities and sensitive ecosystems (Kocaoglu and Figari n.d.). The irony is that responses to demands for greater transparency actually run the risk of reducing trust. For example, when Edward Snowden exposed the degree to which the U.S. government collects data on citizens and leaders around the globe, America's credibility was seriously damaged. Suffice it to say that there is a need to devise transparency mechanisms that provide accurate information in an accessible fashion without intruding on privacy. It is incumbent on public administrators to ensure that processes, when they meet the light of day, will engender trust, rather than mistrust.

Urbanization

By 2030 the world's population will reach more than eight billion people, two-thirds of whom will reside in urban areas (United Nations Department of Economic and Social Affairs/Population Division 2012). While most urbanization will occur in developed countries, it will also happen in the developing regions of Asia, Latin America, and Africa. Worldwide, population growth and urbanization will have a dramatic effect on the increased demand for jobs, housing, energy, clean water, food, transportation infrastructure, and human services. It will also be a significant factor in magnifying the impacts of global warming.

In the United States, the growth of new suburbs, which began in the 1930s and rapidly accelerated with the baby boom generation, is expected to slow. In its stead is re-urbanization as many central cities become more attractive alternatives, especially for households with few or no children, downsizing baby boomers and ever increasing transportation costs (McIlwain 2010). While arguments can be made for the economies of scale that result from clustering the population in urban centers, there is also a downside. One potential problem is the demand on housing for different demographic and economic groups. Another potential downside is the possibility of increased crime and consequent need for enhanced security. The research is inconclusive as to the impact of urbanization on crime rates. However, instances of people with disparate income levels living in close proximity provide an environment in which frustration and alienation linked to differentials in income, education, housing, and social status can push people, especially the young, into lives of crime.

A third potential problem is the impact on the environment of an increasingly urbanized society. As the population grows more dense, air pollution, water shortages, and environmental hazards are concentrated and the need for remedies increases. Ironically, as Kettl observes, the demands for public services grow stronger at the same time that government is plagued by inadequate budgets.

Fractious Times

The trends already discussed, along with global threats of extreme weather due to climate change and the vulnerabilities it presents—horrific droughts that bring food and water shortages, demands on arable land, and disastrous storms—will bring problems that fall in government's lap. In fact, KPMG International (2014, 43) estimates that the planet will run out of water before it runs out of oil. Stewarding natural resources is already a challenge for all levels of government and it will become more so. Moreover, as climate change continues, storms and other natural disasters will compound the need for government to respond to the consequences of floods, fires, hurricanes, and tornadoes. How much capacity will be required in the aftermath of devastating weather events, to mitigate risk, to ensure sufficient natural resources, and to have resilient systems? What sorts of collaborations will it take? What is the appropriate role for government?

While climate change is a problem to which government must be reactive, budget shortfalls are a problem where government can be proactive. Shortfalls are fixable, though this does not mean that the fix is easy. Fiscal sustainability is a huge challenge and voters have to be convinced that they are all part of the solution. Maintenance of roads and bridges and other infrastructure has been delayed as a hedge against budget shortfalls, risking emergencies to which local governments will have to respond. Parks left unmanaged fall into disrepair and become unsightly and crime-ridden, diminishing property values in surrounding areas. This downward spiral causes reductions in tax coffers, which results in even more cutbacks in services. Underfunded pension systems threaten to bankrupt cities and states while jeopardizing the incomes of retirees. Engaging citizens in an effort to develop acceptable remedies falls on the shoulders of public administrators.

The past seventy-five years saw the increase of consumerism and this has changed the way citizens view their relationship with government. Voters are thinking of themselves as consumers entitled to services rather than citizens with responsibilities and obligations. This means that governments are having a difficult time explaining why they have to raise taxes to provide the benefits to which residents have become accustomed. As if affluence has within it the seeds of its own demise, governments must address citizen expectations and perceptions in the face of budget realities. Alternatively, citizen/consumers must pay for the services they want.

Concurrent with concerns about how to engage citizens in addressing critical issues is the need to design service delivery such that citizens receive the services they need when they most need them and in a form that they can use. At the same time, promoting citizen self-reliance is an important function and, to the degree that it is facilitated, de Tocqueville's (1998) description of America remains true. When he visited the United States in the 1800s to observe how Americans "do" democracy, he noted that citizens feel empowered and when they have an interest in something they form an association with like-minded citizens and move forward on their ideas. This connection results in forward-thinking citizens who are willing to take the initiative to solve their problems and to collaborate to achieve their ends. To the degree that public administrators encourage and advance citizen engagement, the co-production that has made the American democracy succeed has the potential to deal with the fiscal constraints that governments at all levels are facing.

Compounding fiscal issues is the partisan warfare that may be more of a problem now than it was a century ago. Newland explained the fractious give and take between Republican and Democrat office holders at the federal level. At the state level, it currently plays out between Republican and Democrat elected officials as well as between elected leaders and career civil servants. The latter is evidenced by attacks on collective bargaining rights of public employees by Republicans in power in Wisconsin and by Republican inspired changes to public personnel systems that increase the proportion of at-will employees in Florida, Georgia, and Texas. Removal of job protections serves to silence the voices of workers whose partisan leanings differ from those of elected leaders. Paralysis by partisanship endangers a central structure of democracy, which is the ability to make decisions through compromise.

Compounding these problems is the fact that growing income inequality bedevils leaders now and all indications are that it will continue. It riles those who are not reaching what the American dream promises. As inequality increases, impatience with government grows among those who are disadvantaged by the status quo and their demands for more services escalate. The "merit" in the American dream of meritocracy is jeopardized when youth unemployment is high, wages are low, and a growing proportion of the workforce does not have the literacy, numeracy, and technical skills necessary to compete. In fact, the American dream may now be best pursued in Canada, not the United States (Newman 2013). All these challenges, and more, fall on the shoulders of public administrators to address because, as President Kennedy observed more than fifty years ago, the big problems are administrative.

In addition to these realities and the frequent disparity between citizen expectations and what government can afford to provide, there is also the issue of the impact of increasing diversity. The workforce is different now and mirrors a population more diverse than when the first textbooks on public administration were published almost a century ago. As Riccucci's chapter makes clear, the meaning of diversity has expanded beyond gender, race, ethnicity, and age, to encompass gender identity, and choices about family responsibilities. These changes bring with them tensions in the workplace and the need for employers to re-examine not only their policies but also the organizational culture. It also requires managers with the skills to acknowledge, and know-how to capitalize on, difference, rather than managers who expect sameness.

Moving Forward

As the above discussion illustrates, public service is now operating in the "new normal." And what does the new normal look like? In his discussion of the melding of lines between government, nonprofits, and business, Kettl observes that we have drifted into a system of "blended power" where there is neither a clear rule of law nor a straightforward alternative for accountability. This is an example of the heterarchy that O'Leary describes and applies not only to the United States but also globally. It is changing the face of who public administrators engage with in decision making, service delivery, and the design of accountability measures.

Administrators must therefore grapple with questions of how to organize in multiplex settings, how to share power, and how to ensure accountability when boundaries are hazy, goals are conflicting, and resources are inadequate. Moreover, as interconnections inevitably spread, the challenge will be to identify limits. As Kettl notes, it can be difficult to define where government begins and where it ends. Yet Rosenbloom argues that govern we must and within a constitutional framework.

The challenges are daunting. This book raises more questions than answers and in a metamodern way. But if the optimism within metamodern thinking prevails, we may be on the cusp of a future that is more than the donkey chasing the carrot. Legal, economic, and moral motivators can combine to induce communities and jurisdictions to collaborate and address the most pressing problems—problems too vexing to be handled by just one jurisdiction, one agency, one neighborhood, or one nation.

There are glimmers of answers as one traces the past seventy-five years but some questions will always be on the forefront, never quite settled. And what of the enduring debates: public versus private; politics versus administration; and facts versus values? Both Rosenbloom and Svara speak to the enduring nature of public administration: running a Constitution and doing it with integrity. Newland, O'Leary and Kettl make it clear that the lines between public and private and between politics and administration are becoming more blurred, with "off-book" contractors delivering more public services than employees within the civil service system. And as Herbert Simon (1983) wrote a generation ago, facts without values are as useful as a one-bladed scissor.

What will the future hold for professional associations? Will they continue the progression toward more atomization such that there is too little interest in an umbrella public service organization to sustain it, or will the tide turn back and welcome generalist organizations such as ASPA? If public administration is to be the "get it all together" field as Harlan Cleveland (2002) saw it, what does it mean when its interests continue to disperse, with scholars and practitioners joining narrow associations whose members have unitary interests? That is, they do the same type of work, study the same objects, use the same methodology, talk the same language, and work at similar institutions. Plant, in his discussion of the tapestry of the field, traces the tensions that exist within public administration and the associations that have arisen as a result. It is as if forces analogous to the international versus localism perspectives repeat themselves regarding membership in generalist versus specialty organizations.

Yang, through his query of whether studies of public management and public administration are largely a distinction without a difference, traces the cleavage between public management and public administration but shows that contemporary research is largely similar in both and that the big questions addressed by scholars have significant overlap. Is the field strengthened by this, or not? What will future cleavages look like? Eikenberry (2009) argues that because of the flattened, multisectoral approach to governance, ASPA should hold onto its generalist approach, for that is where the future will be. In other words, as interests continue to differentiate, there will be a need, just as there was in 1939, to have a "get it all together" association of scholars and practitioners.

The upshot of debates about which associations to join gives rise to this question: Does a large, unruly field serve people better than one that is more unitary but narrower, such as that envisioned by Leonard White writing more than seventy-five years ago? The early writers attempted to simplify the complexity of the field by structuring it. However, ours is an increasingly inclusive field and managing across boundaries in a heterarchical environment requires skills very different from those needed in a top-down hierarchy. This is not necessarily a problem. As power is dispersed, there are more opportunities to build creative coalitions and integrate programs. This is the reason that graduate programs in public administration and policy require students to participate in team activities, for the likelihood is that more of their important work will be conducted in teams than by unilateral action.

A theme that traversed the chapters is the notion of justice and the role of government in pursuing social equity. Just as it was at the forefront in 1968 at the first Minnowbrook Conference, it remains center stage, and perhaps even more so now because of the rising level of economic inequality. Gooden discusses the difficulty of operationalizing social equity and putting programs in place at the street level that advance it. At the same time, she questions whether Master of Public Administration programs are doing enough to integrate social equity into graduate curricula. There is little doubt that, like Sisyphus pushing the rock up the hill, this requires continuous attention.

In conclusion, we note that through the alchemy of inspiration and discipline, this volume captures the beginning of professionalized public administration and traces its developments from a number of dimensions. The chapters reflect the complexly fragmented nature of governance. From modernism to metamodernism, the range is reflected as the evolution of the field is described. Having seen the past, glimmers of the future become apparent. Public administration is always seeking its rightful place, a place that does not intrude on individual rights and sovereignty and yet a place that is ready and resilient, prepared to withstand strong headwinds. The big questions remain: What is the purpose of government? How should "public" be defined? What should be government's limits? Who should deliver services that are in the public interest? What barriers exist to increasing public participation? How can technologies—such as online forums, listervs, and social media outlets—influence public participation? How can governments engage citizens to participate to solve problems? The most enduring question is will these be the same issues on the front burner when ASPA commemorates its one-hundredth anniversary?

Note

1 This title is borrowed from Darrell Pugh (1988) who published a history of the ASPA on the occasion of its fiftieth anniversary. The title captured the essence of his book and it seems fitting to appropriate it here as ASPA commemorates its seventy-fifth anniversary.

References

Checherita, Cristina, and Philipp Rother. 2010. "The Impact of High and Growing Government Debt on Economic Growth: An Empirical Investigation for the Euro Area." Working Paper Series, No. 1237. Frankfurt am Main, Germany: European Central Bank, August. www.ecb.europa.eu/pub/pdf/scpwps/ecbwp1237.pdf (accessed June 29, 2014).

Cleveland, Harlan. 2002. *Nobody in Charge: Essays on the Future of Leadership*. San Francisco: Jossey-Bass.

de Tocqueville, Alexis. 1998. *Democracy in America*, abridged ed. London: Wordsworth Editions Ltd.

Eikenberry, Angela M. 2009. "The Present and (Normative) Future of Public Administration and Implications for ASPA." *Public Administration Review* 69(6): 1060–1067.

Gallup. 2014. "Trust in Government." June 29. www.gallup.com/poll/5392/trust-government.aspx (accessed June 29, 2014).

IMF. 2014. *Fiscal Monitor: Public Expenditure Reform—Making Difficult Choices*. Washington, DC: IMF, April. Survey, April. www.imf.org/external/pubs/ft/fm/2014/01/fmindex.htm (accessed June 29, 2014).

Kennedy, John F. 1962. Yale University Commencement Address. June 11. http://millercenter.org/president/speeches/speech-3370 (accessed June 25, 2014).

Kocaoglu, Nurham, and Andrea Figari, eds. n.d. *Using the Right to Information as an Anti-Corruption Tool*. Berlin: Transparency International. http://oas.org/dil/access_to_information_human_Policy_Recommendations_Transparency_International_Right_to_Information_as_an_Anti-Corruption_Tool.pdf (accessed June 29, 2014).

KPMG International. 2014. *Future State 2030: The Global Megatrends Shaping Governments.* Toronto: Mowat Center, November. www.kpmg.com/Global/en/IssuesAndInsights/ ArticlesPublications/future-state-government/documents/future-state-2030-v1.pdf (accessed June 21, 2014).

Lindblom, Charles E. 1959. "The Science of 'Muddling Through.'" *Public Administration Review* 19(2): 79–88.

McIlwain, John. 2010. *Housing in America: The Next Decade.* Washington, DC: Urban Land Institute. http://uli.org/report/housing-in-america-the-next-decade/ (accessed June 29, 2014).

Manning, Nick, and Deborah L. Wetzel. 2010. "Tales of the Unexpected: Rebuilding Trust in Government." In *The Day After Tomorrow: A Handbook on the Future of Economic Policy in the Developing World,* ed. Otaviana Canuto and Marcelo Giugale, 163–179. Washington, DC: The World Bank. http://siteresources.worldbank.org/ EXTPREMNET/Resources/C9TDAT_161-180.pdf (accessed June 29, 2014)

Millet, Damien, Daniel Munevar, and Éric Toussaint. 2012. *2012 World Debt Figures.* Liège: Committee for the Abolition of Third World Debt. http://cadtm.org/IMG/ pdf/2012_worlddebtfigures.pdf (accessed June 30, 2014).

Newman, Rick. 2013. "The American Dream Is Alive and Well—in Canada." *The Exchange,* August 21. http://finance.yahoo.com/blogs/the-exchange/american-dream-alive-well-canada-211401249.html?soc_src=copy (accessed June 30, 2014).

Obama, Barack. 2008. "Barack Obama's South Carolina Primary Speech." *New York Times,* January 26. www.nytimes.com/2008/01/26/us/politics/26text-obama.html? pagewanted=all (accessed June 21, 2014).

OECD. 2013. "Trust in Government." www.oecd.org/gov/trust-in-government.htm (accessed June 29, 2014).

Pugh, Darrell L. 1988. *Looking Back, Moving Forward: A Half-Century Celebration of Public Administration and ASPA.* Washington, DC: ASPA.

Simon, Herbert. 1983. *Reason in Human Affairs.* Berkeley, CA: Stanford University Press.

United Nations. 2002. *World Population Ageing 1950–2050.* New York: United Nations. www.un.org/esa/population/publications/worldageing19502050/pdf/62executive summary_english.pdf (accessed June 29, 2014).

United Nations Department of Economic and Social Affairs/Population Division. 2012. *World Urbanization Prospects: The 2011 Revision: Highlights.* New York: United Nations. www.preventionweb.net/english/professional/publications/v.php?id=26141 (accessed November 22, 2014).

United Nations Development Programme and Inter-Parliamentary Union. 2013. *Global Parliamentary Report.* Geneva: United Nations Development Programme. www.ipu. org/pdf/publications/gpr2012-es-e.pdf (accessed June 29, 2014).

U.S. Census Bureau. 2012. "Table 1. Projections of the Population and Components of Change for the United States: 2015 to 2060." In *2012 National Population Projections: Summary Tables.* Washington, DC: Government Printing Office. www.census.gov/ population/projections/data/national/2012/summarytables.html (accessed June 29, 2014).

Vermeulen, Timotheus, and Robin van den Akker. 2010. "Notes on Metamodernism." *Journal of Aesthetics & Culture* 2: 1–14.

ABOUT THE EDITORS AND CONTRIBUTORS

Susan T. Gooden is a professor of public administration and policy in the L. Douglas Wilder School of Government and Public Affairs and Executive Director of the Grace E. Harris Leadership Institute at Virginia Commonwealth University. She is a fellow of the National Academy of Public Administration and Vice President of the American Society for Public Administration (ASPA). She is a Fulbright Specialist Award recipient. A native of Martinsville, Virginia, she received her PhD from the Maxwell School of Citizenship and Public Affairs at Syracuse University.

Mary E. Guy is a professor of public administration in the School of Public Affairs at the University of Colorado Denver. She is a past president of the ASPA and a fellow of the National Academy of Public Administration (NAPA). Her research focuses on the human processes involved in public service delivery as well as public administration in general. She has written widely on the subject of the difference that gender makes and on the subject of emotionally intense jobs in public service. Her work on emotional labor has earned a number of awards for her work, including five Best Book Awards for *Emotional Labor: Putting the Service in Public Service* (2008) and *Emotional Labor and Crisis Response: Working on the Razor's Edge* (2012) (both co-authored with Sharon Mastracci and Meredith Newman).

Donald F. Kettl is Dean of the University of Maryland School of Public Policy and a nonresident senior fellow at the Brookings Institution. He is the author or editor of many books, including *The Politics of the Administrative Process*, 6th ed. (2015), *System under Stress* (2014), *The Next Government of the United States* (2008), and *The Global Public Management Revolution* (2005). He has twice won the Louis Brownlow Book Award of NAPA for the best book published in public administration. In 2008, Kettl won the American

Political Science Association's John Gaus Award for a lifetime of exemplary scholarship in political science and public administration. He holds a PhD in political science from Yale University and has held appointments at University of Pennsylvania, Columbia University, the University of Virginia, Vanderbilt University, and the University of Wisconsin-Madison. He is a fellow of NAPA.

Donald E. Klingner is a distinguished professor in the School of Public Affairs at the University of Colorado, Colorado Springs. He is an elected fellow (2007) of NAPA and was President (2008–2009) of ASPA. He is the co-author of *Public Personnel Management*, 6th ed. (2010), which was also published in Spanish and Chinese. He has been a Fulbright Senior Scholar (Central America 1994), a visiting professor at National Autonomous University of Mexico, Mexico (1999–2003), and a consultant to the United Nations, the World Bank, and the Inter-American Development Bank on public management capacity building. He was a faculty member at Indiana University–Purdue University Indianapolis (1974–1980) and Florida International University (1980–2001). Prior to earning a PhD in public administration from the University of Southern California in 1974, he worked for the U.S. government's central personnel agency (U.S. Civil Service Commission, 1968–1973).

Jooho Lee is an assistant professor in the School of Public Administration at the University of Nebraska, Omaha (UNO). Before joining UNO, he was an assistant professor at the Department of Political Science, University of Idaho. His research interests include public management, the antecedents and consequences of public sector innovations (e.g., information technologies, e-participation) and inter/intraorganizational networks. His research has appeared in public administration and information technology journals such as *Public Administration Review, American Review of Public Administration, Administration and Society, Government Information Quarterly*, and *International Journal of Electronic Government Research*. He earned his PhD in public administration from the Maxwell School of Citizenship and Public Affairs at Syracuse University.

Kathryn E. Newcomer is Director of the Trachtenberg School of Public Policy and Public Administration at the George Washington University. She teaches public and nonprofit, program evaluation, research design, and applied statistics. She routinely conducts program evaluations for U.S. federal government agencies and nonprofit organizations, and conducts training on program evaluation in the United States and internationally. Dr. Newcomer has published five books including *The Handbook of Practical Program Evaluation*, 3rd ed. (2010) and *Transforming Public and Nonprofit Organizations: Stewardship for Leading Change* (2008), as well as numerous articles in journals including the *American Journal of Evaluation* and *Public Administration Review*. She is an elected fellow of NAPA. She served as President of the National Association of Schools of Public Affairs and Administration (NASPAA) for 2006–2007. She received her BS and MA at the University of Kansas and her PhD in political science at the University of Iowa.

Chester A. (Chet) Newland is Emeritus Duggan Distinguished Professor of Public Administration, University of Southern California. He is a past national president of the ASPA. He was editor-in-chief of the *Public Administration Review* from 1984 to 1990. He has been a fellow of NAPA since 1975. He has been an honorary member of the International City/County Management Association since 1980. He was the initial director of the Lyndon Baines Johnson Presidential Library, and he served twice as the director of the Federal Executive Institute. In 2007, he received the Dwight Waldo Award for lifetime practice, teaching, and scholarship. In 2011, he received the Los Angeles ASPA Earl Warren Award for Public Service. Fundamental themes of Chet Newland's work have been the disciplined values and practices of constitutional democracy: searches for human dignity and reasonableness via the rule of law.

Rosemary O'Leary is the Edwin O. Stene Distinguished Professor of Public Administration at the University of Kansas. Previously she was on the faculties of the Maxwell School of Syracuse University and the School of Public and Environmental Affairs at Indiana University-Bloomington. Dr. O'Leary is the author or editor of eleven books and more than 100 articles and book chapters on public management. She has won ten national research awards and nine teaching awards. She is the only person to win three NASPAA awards for Best Dissertation (1989), Excellence in Teaching (1996), and Distinguished Research (2004). Dr. O'Leary is an elected member of NAPA. Her areas of expertise are public management, collaboration, conflict resolution, environmental and natural resources management, and public law. Dr. O'Leary received her PhD from the Maxwell School of Syracuse University.

Jeremy F. Plant is a professor of public policy and administration in the School of Public Affairs at Penn State Harrisburg, where he has taught since 1988. Prior to joining Penn State he served on the faculty of George Mason University and the University at Albany. Plant's research focuses on the areas of administrative ethics, homeland security, and transportation policy and administration. Dr. Plant has written/edited two books and numerous articles that have appeared in such academic journals as *Public Administration Review*, *American Review of Public Administration*, *Review of Policy Research*, *Public Integrity*, *Journal of Urban Affairs*, *International Journal of Public Administration*, *Public Works Management & Policy*, and several other journals. He received an AB in political science from Colgate University and MA and PhD degrees in government from the University of Virginia.

B.J. Reed is Vice Chancellor at the University of Nebraska Omaha, where he has been on the faculty since 1982. He has published in numerous leading public administration journals, several of which focus on the emergence of technology in online education and state and local performance in technology. He is also the author of several books on diverse topics including economic development, strategic planning, financial administration, and intergovernmental management.

Norma M. Riccucci is Distinguished Professor of Public Administration at the School of Public Affairs and Administration, Rutgers University-Newark. Professor Riccucci has published extensively in the areas of public management, affirmative action, and human resource management. Her publications include *Public Administration: Traditions of Inquiry and Philosophies of Knowledge* (2010; received the 2012 Best Book Award from the Research Section of the ASPA), and *How Management Matters: Street Level Bureaucrats and Welfare Reform* (2005; received the 2009 Best Book Award from the Public Administration Section of the APSA). Professor Riccucci is the recipient of several national awards including the ASPA Charles H. Levine Award for excellence in teaching, research, and service to the community. In 2005 she was inducted into NAPA.

David H. Rosenbloom is Distinguished Professor of Public Administration at American University in Washington, DC. He holds a PhD in political science from the University of Chicago. A major contributor to the field of public administration and a fellow in NAPA, he has received numerous awards, including the Gaus Award for exemplary scholarship in political science and public administration, the Waldo Award for outstanding contributions to the literature and leadership of public administration, the Levine Award for excellence in public administration, and the Brownlow Award for his book, *Building a Legislative-Centered Public Administration* (2000). He edited *Public Administration Review*, co-edited the *Policy Studies Journal*, and now serves on the editorial boards of about twenty academic journals. In 1992, Dr. Rosenbloom served on the Clinton–Gore Presidential Transition Team for the U.S. Office of Personnel Management.

Marilyn M. Rubin is a professor of public administration at John Jay College of the City University of New York where she is also Director of the MPA Program. Dr. Rubin has published articles in several professional journals including the *Public Administration Review* and *Public Budgeting and Finance* and has authored chapters in a number of books. She is co-editor of the recently released book, *Sustaining the States: The Fiscal Viability of American State Government* (2014). Dr. Rubin is a former chairperson of the Association for Budgeting and Financial Management of ASPA and a member of the editorial board of *Public Budgeting and Finance*. She is a fellow in NAPA and has lectured in universities and/or provided technical assistance to the governments of several countries outside of the United States including China, Korea, Thailand, Colombia, Brazil, Ecuador, Azerbaijan, and Georgia.

Richard Stillman is a professor of public administration at the University of Colorado Denver and from 2006 through 2011 served as editor-in-chief of *Public Administration Review*. His text, *Public Administration: Concepts and Cases*, 9th ed. (2010), is adopted for teaching at over 400 universities and colleges and his book, *Preface to Public Administration* (1991), was recently ranked as the third most influential book in the field published since 1990.

James H. Svara is Visiting Professor, School of Government, University of North Carolina Chapel Hill, and Emeritus Professor, School of Public Affairs, Arizona State University. He served as the co-chair (with James Nordin) of the Working Group to Revise the ASPA Code of Ethics (2011–2013) and the chair of the Ad Hoc Committee on Implementation of the ASPA Code (2013–2014). Support for these activities was provided by the Lincoln Center for Applied Ethics, Arizona State University. Research assistance was provided by Chin-Chang Tsai, doctoral student in public administration at Arizona State University. His current research focuses on social equity as a dimension in local government sustainability programs.

Kaifeng Yang is a professor of public administration in the Askew School of Public Administration and Policy, Florida State University and the School of Public Administration and Policy, Renmin University of China. His research interests include public and performance management, citizen participation, governance, and organizational theory. He has widely published in leading journals and is the managing editor of *Public Performance & Management Review*. He is also a fellow of NAPA.

AUTHOR INDEX

SUBJECT INDEX

A

Abu Ghraib xi, xix
academicians 103, 249–50; ASPA 233,
  235, 239, 245–6
Academy of Management 109–10
accountability 20, 32, 67, 71, 125, 138,
  140, 143, 179, 288; administrative 28,
  269; as scholarly topic 111; ASPA codes
  261, 264; blended power 33; charities
  142; citizen demands 34, 176, 281;
  democratic-constitutional value 14,
  243, 257; freedom of information 6;
  government managers 118; improving
  136; intelligence experts xi; interactions
  across sectors 67; performance 127–8;
  separating policy and administration 30;
  social equity 211, 215, 221–2, 225–6;
  western democracies 127
accounting 133–4, 147, 162, 164, 244;
  information systems 179
Adarand Constructors v. Pena 9
Administration & Society 110
advanced methodologies xii
Advisory Commission on
  Intergovernmental Relations 242
affirmative action 7, 262–3; ASPA code
  of ethics 274; court rulings 193–4;
  laws 75; sex 9; tokenism 51; university
  admissions 193
Affordable Care Act xi, 18, 51; rollout
  31–3, 180

Afghanistan 49, 67, 71–2
Africa 58, 69, 212, 285
African Americans 10, 224; ASPA 247;
  enfranchisement 212; Medicaid 223;
  population 68; socio-economic status
  198–9; treatment 212; voting rights 193
agencies: accountability xi, 221; aid,
  146; agency boundaries 11, 88, 148;
  assessments of 133; budget 134;
  competencies 6; community indicator
  projects 145; complicance with law
  117, 135; core missions and purposes
  6, 13–14, 135, 244; county 175;
  factors of production 160; federal 3,
  5–6, 11, 13, 24, 41–2, 52–53, 130,
  133–6, 139–40, 173, 180, 225, 241–3;
  freedom of information 6–7; funding
  172; graduate programs 233; hiring
  25, 233; information technology 161,
  173; independent 12; interconnections
  among 34, 85, 87, 90–1, 94, 137,
  224–5; international development 72;
  management of 133; multi-agency
  efforts 5; nonacquiescence 3; nonprofit
  129, 141–44, 147, 181; performance
  7, 129, 135, 138, 148, 160; politicizing
  52; program 175; public 2, 10, 69,
  71, 77, 116, 125–6, 129, 180, 221,
  288; regulatory 44, 105; rulemaking
  4–5; security 60, 182; social equity
  analysis 218; strategic planning 31;
  staff 136–7; studying 106; structure 19,